Lecture Notes in Computer Science   8964

Commenced Publication in 1973
Founding and Former Series Editors:
Gerhard Goos, Juris Hartmanis, and Jan van Leeuwen

More information about this series at http://www.springer.com/series/7409

Sai Ravela · Adrian Sandu (Eds.)

Dynamic Data-Driven Environmental Systems Science

First International Conference, DyDESS 2014
Cambridge, MA, USA, November 5–7, 2014
Revised Selected Papers

 Springer

Editors
Sai Ravela
Massachusetts Institute of Technology
Cambridge, MA
USA

Adrian Sandu
VA Polytechnic Institute
and State University
Blacksburg, VA
USA

ISSN 0302-9743   ISSN 1611-3349   (electronic)
Lecture Notes in Computer Science
ISBN 978-3-319-25137-0   ISBN 978-3-319-25138-7   (eBook)
DOI 10.1007/978-3-319-25138-7

Library of Congress Control Number: 2015950441

LNCS Sublibrary: SL3 – Information Systems and Applications, incl. Internet/Web, and HCI

Springer International Publishing AG Switzerland is part of Springer Science+Business Media
(www.springer.com)

Preface

Addressing the challenges in environmental sustainability requires an effective integration of sensing, observation, and inference with physical, chemical, biological, and social models. The necessary integration of data and science is multifaceted and symbiotic with applications from model-based sensing to data-driven modeling. While the attendant issues of predictability, uncertainty, and risk reduction are of great interest in multiple areas of science, engineering, and mathematics, a rigorous forum to present collective advances has been missing.

The Dynamic Data-Driven Environmental Systems Science (DyDESS) Conference coalesces the environment with computation, systems science, and machine intelligence. It provides a forum for scientists and engineers in the emerging environmental systems research issues, an opportunity for young researchers to meet leading scientists, and brings together those interested in the dynamic data-driven application systems framework for environmental applications. It provides an interdisciplinary forum to help methodology meet application, and to showcase results and new, promising methodologies.

Original papers in coupling of data and models for environmental applications are presented in this volume including methodology and experiments. As a single-track conference, DyDESS included papers are in the following areas:

(a) Sensing, imaging and retrieval for the oceans, atmosphere, space, land, earth and planets that is informed by the environmental context
(b) Algorithms for modeling and simulation, downscaling, model reduction, data assimilation, uncertainty quantification and statistical learning; methods that tackle nonlinear and high-dimensional problems
(c) Methodologies for planning and control, sampling and adaptive observation, and efficient coupling of these algorithms into information-gathering and observing system designs
(d) Applications of methodology to environmental estimation, analysis and prediction including climate, natural hazards, oceans, cryosphere, atmosphere, land, space, earth and planets

On behalf of the Program Committee, we are grateful to Prof. R. van der Hilst, Earth, Atmospheric and Planetary Sciences at MIT, for being a strong sponsor of this event. We are grateful to the General Co-Chairs, whose support significantly enhanced participation. We plan to continue the conference to bridge computational intelligence, systems engineering, and the environment, broadly inclusive of all topics in Earth, Atmospheric and Planetary Science.

December 2014

Sai Ravela
Adrian Sandu

Organization

DyDESS 2014 was organized by the Department of Earth Atmospheric and Planetary Sciences, Massachusetts Institute of Technology, with support from the Aeronautics and Astronautics Department (MIT)

Program Co-chairs

Sai Ravela (*Chair*)	MIT, USA
Dennis Bernstein	University of Michigan, USA
Adrian Sandu	Virginia Tech, USA

General Co-chairs

Jonathan How	MIT, USA
John Marshall	MIT, USA

Program Committee

Jeffery Anderson	NCAR, USA
Mark Berliner	OSU, USA
Jesse Belden	NUWC, USA
William Blackwell	MIT, USA
Han-Lim Choi	KAIST, Korea
Dacian Daescu	PSU, USA
Dara Entekhabi	MIT, USA
Patrick Heimbach	MIT, USA
Pierre Lermusiaux	MIT, USA
John Leonard	MIT, USA
Abani Patra	University at Buffalo, USA
Hanu Singh	WHOI, USA

Session Chairs

John Leonard	MIT, USA
Pierre Lermusiaux	MIT, USA
Youssef Marzouk	MIT, USA
Kamran Mohesni	UFL, USA
Abani Patra	University at Buffalo, USA
Sai Ravela	MIT, USA
Adrian Sandu	MIT, USA
Puneet Singla	University at Buffalo, USA

Local Arrangements

Kurt Sternlof   MIT, USA
Julie Marquardt   MIT, USA

Panel and Keynotes

1. Carl Wunsch (MIT/Harvard), Perspectives from Ocean State Estimation
2. Maarten De Hoop (Purdue), Imaging Earth's Interior with Active and Passive Source Seismic Data
3. George Haller (University of Michigan), Objective Detection of Lagrangian Vortices in Unsteady Velocity Data
4. Dennis Bernstein (University of Michigan), Adaptive Control and Model Refinement
5. Frederica Darema (AFOSR) and Todd Leen (NSF), Research Directions and infrastructures for Dynamic Data Systems Environments
6. P.J. van Leeuwen (Reading), P.F.J. Lermusiaux (MIT), K. Mohseni (UFL), and P. Singla (Buffalo), The DyDESS Challenge

Contents

Sensing

Small Satellite Constellations for Data Driven Atmospheric
Remote Sensing 3
    W. Blackwell and K. Cahoy

A Novel Approach to Atmospheric Measurements Using Gliding UASs 10
    Ru-Shan Gao, James W. Elkins, Gregory J. Frost,
    Allison C. McComiskey, Fred L. Moore, Daniel M. Murphy,
    John A. Ogren, Irina Petropavlovskikh, and Karen H. Rosenlof

In Situ Sampling of Volcanic Emissions with a UAV Sensorweb:
Progress and Plans 16
    David Pieri and Jorge Andres Diaz

Advances in Light Field Imaging for Measurement of Fluid
Mechanical Systems 28
    Jesse Belden, Jonathon Pendlebury, Alexander Jafek, and Tadd Truscott

Environmental Applications

Multiscale Method for Hazard Map Construction 41
    E. Ramona Stefanescu, Abani Patra, E. Bruce Pitman, Marcus Bursik,
    Puneet Singla, and Tarunraj Singh

Coupled Dynamic Data-Driven Framework for Forest Fire
Spread Prediction 54
    Carlos Brun, Ana Cortés, and Tomàs Margalef

iSPUW: A Vision for Integrated Sensing and Prediction of Urban Water
for Sustainable Cities 68
    Dong-Jun Seo, Branko Kerkez, Michael Zink, Nick Fang, Jean Gao,
    and Xinbao Yu

Local-Scale Assessment of Tropical Cyclone Induced Storm Surge
Inundation over the Coastal Zones of India in Probabilistic
Climate Risk Scenario 79
    A.D. Rao, Jismy Poulose, Puja Upadhyay, and Sachiko Mohanty

A Data Driven Scientific Approach to Environmental Probes 89
    Craig C. Douglas, Tainara Mendes de Andrade Soares,
    and Maurício Vieira Kritz

Towards Intelligent Closed-Loop Workflows for Ecological Research   100
JD Knapp, Matias Elo, James Shaeffer, and Paul G. Flikkema

Reduced Representations and Features

Objective Detection of Lagrangian Vortices in Unsteady Velocity Data   115
George Haller

Statistical Inference for Coherent Fluids.   121
Sai Ravela

Reduced Order Probabilistic Prediction of Rogue Waves
in One-Dimensional Envelope Equations   134
Will Cousins and Themistoklis P. Sapsis

Analytical Approximation of the Heavy-Tail Structure for Intermittently
Unstable Complex Modes   144
Mustafa A. Mohamad and Themistoklis P. Sapsis

Multiscale Stochastic Representation in High-Dimensional Data
Using Gaussian Processes with Implicit Diffusion Metrics   157
*Charanraj Thimmisetty, Arman Khodabakhshnejad, Nima Jabbari,
Fred Aminzadeh, Roger Ghanem, Kelly Rose, Jennifer Bauer,
and Corinne Disenhof*

Recent Advances in Scaling Up Gaussian Process Predictive Models
for Large Spatiotemporal Data   167
*Kian Hsiang Low, Jie Chen, Trong Nghia Hoang, Nuo Xu,
and Patrick Jaillet*

A Gaussian Process-Enabled MCMC Approach for Contaminant Source
Characterization in a Sensor-Rich Multi-Story Building   182
Joon-Hong Seok, Su-Jin Lee, and Han-Lim Choi

An Empirical Reduced Modeling Approach for Mobile, Distributed
Sensor Platform Networks   195
Isaac J. Sledge, Liqian Peng, and Kamran Mohseni

Data Assimilation and Uncertainty Quantification

A One-Step-Ahead Smoothing-Based Joint Ensemble Kalman Filter
for State-Parameter Estimation of Hydrological Models   207
Mohamad E. Gharamti, Boujemaa Ait-El-Fquih, and Ibrahim Hoteit

A Sampling Approach for Four Dimensional Data Assimilation   215
Ahmed Attia, Vishwas Rao, and Adrian Sandu

Ensemble Learning in Non-Gaussian Data Assimilation 227
  Hansjörg Seybold, Sai Ravela, and Piyush Tagade

Variational Data Assimilation Based on Derivative-Free Optimization 239
  Elias D. Nino and Adrian Sandu

Aspects of Particle Filtering in High-Dimensional Spaces. 251
  Peter Jan van Leeuwen

A Hybrid Particle-Ensemble Kalman Filter for High Dimensional
Lagrangian Data Assimilation 263
  Laura Slivinski, Elaine Spiller, and Amit Apte

Specification of the Ionosphere-Thermosphere Using the Ensemble
Kalman Filter 274
  Humberto C. Godinez, Earl Lawrence, David Higdon, Aaron Ridley,
  Josef Koller, and Alexei Klimenko

Ensemble Adjustment Kalman Filter Data Assimilation for a Global
Atmospheric Model 284
  Tarkeshwar Singh, Rashmi Mittal, and H.C. Upadhyaya

Planning and Adaptive Observation

A Greedy Approach for Placement of Subsurface Aquifer Wells
in an Ensemble Filtering Framework 301
  Mohamad E. Gharamti, Youssef M. Marzouk, Xun Huan,
  and Ibrahim Hoteit

Parameter Estimation of Atmospheric Release Incidents Using Maximal
Information Collection 310
  Reza Madankan, Puneet Singla, and Tarunraj Singh

Centralized Ensemble-Based Trajectory Planning of Cooperating Sensors
for Estimating Atmospheric Dispersion Processes 322
  Juliane Euler, Tobias Ritter, Stefan Ulbrich, and Oskar von Stryk

Active Singularities for Multivehicle Motion Planning
in an N-Vortex System 334
  Francis D. Lagor and Derek A. Paley

A Stochastic Optimization Method for Energy-Based Path Planning 347
  Deepak N. Subramani, Tapovan Lolla, Patrick J. Haley Jr.,
  and Pierre F.J. Lermusiaux

Author Index 359

Sensing

Small Satellite Constellations for Data Driven Atmospheric Remote Sensing

W. Blackwell[1]($\boxtimes$) and K. Cahoy[2]

[1] MIT Lincoln Laboratory, Lexington, MA 02420, USA
wjb@ll.mit.edu
[2] Space Systems Laboratory, Department of Aeronautics and Astonautics,
Massachusetts Institute of Technolology, Cambridge, MA 02139, USA
kcahoy@mit.edu

Abstract. Nanosatellite missions flying microwave radiometers for high-resolution microwave sounding are quickly proliferating, as microwave instrumentation is particularly well suited for implementation on a very small satellite, as the sensor requirements for power, pointing, and spatial resolution (aperture size) can be accommodated by a nanosatellite platform. The first mission, the Microsized Microwave Atmospheric Satellite (MicroMAS), will demonstrate temperature sounding in nine channels near 118 GHz. MicroMAS is currently onboard the International Space Station awaiting deployment for a 100-day mission. The Microwave Radiometer Technology Acceleration (MiRaTA) cubesat will demonstrate multi-band atmospheric sounding and co-located GPS radio occultation. MiRaTA will launch in early 2016, and will fly a tri-band sounder (60, 183, and 206 GHz) and a GPS radio occultation (GPS-RO) sensor. We present recent work to develop and demonstrate nanosatellite technologies for earth atmospheric remote sensing using microwave radiometry, and describe approaches for transitioning these new technologies into new research constellation missions to provide unprecedented measurement capabilities. Of particular interest is the potential of the constellation to provide data-driven sensing capabilities.

Keywords: Cubesat · Nanosatellite · Constellation · MicroMAS · MiRaTA · Atmospheric sounding · Temperature · Moisture · Forecasting · Hurricane

1 Introduction

The need for low-cost, mission-flexible, and rapidly deployable spaceborne sensors that meet stringent performance requirements pervades the NASA Earth Science measurement programs, including especially the recommended NRC Decadal Survey missions. The challenge of data continuity further complicates mission planning and development and has historically been exacerbated by uncertain and sometimes substantial shifts in national priorities and budget

© Springer International Publishing Switzerland 2015
S. Ravela and A. Sandu (Eds.): DyDESS 2014, LNCS 8964, pp. 3–9, 2015.
DOI: 10.1007/978-3-319-25138-7_1

availability that have degraded and delayed critical Earth Science measurement capabilities. Furthermore, the recently published Midterm Assessment of NASA's Implementation of the Decadal Survey finds that:

The nations Earth observing system is beginning a rapid decline in capability as long-running missions end and key new missions are delayed, lost, or canceled. The projected loss of observing capability could have significant adverse consequences for science and society. The loss of observations of key Earth system components and processes will weaken the ability to understand and forecast changes arising from interactions and feedbacks within the Earth system and limit the data and information available to users and decision makers. Consequences are likely to include slowing or even reversal of the steady gains in weather forecast accuracy over many years and degradation of the ability to assess and respond to natural hazards and to measure and understand changes in Earth's climate and life support systems.

To address these challenges, we have initiated a number of technology development and demonstration efforts to enable high-resolution atmospheric sensing from very small satellite platforms that are relatively inexpensive to build, launch, and operate. These efforts have included microwave receiver technology, intermediate frequency processing, calibration, and advanced attitude determination and control. These efforts have been funded in part by the NASA Earth Science Technology Office and NOAA. The MicroMAS and MiRaTA missions will be the first demonstrations of single-band and multi-band (respectively) cubesat radiometers.

1.1   Overview of Observables

Cross-track-scanning passive microwave radiometers measure upwelling thermal emission near atmospheric absorption bands, typically due to oxygen and water vapor. Measurements along these lines at multiple frequencies permit the retrieval of vertical profiles (function of altitude). Observations near oxygen lines are used to retrieve temperature profiles, and measurements near water vapor lines are used to retrieve moisture profiles. The typical vertical resolution of these products ranges from approximately three to five kilometers with uncertainties of approximately 2 K (RMS) for temperature and 25 % (RMS, as a percentage of mean mass mixing ratio), respectively. Measurements of precipitation based on scattering signatures from ice cloud tops are also possible. Observations of temperature, moisture, and precipitation are critically important for the characterization of the hydrologic cycle and associated climate studies. Global observations updated continuously at approximately 30-min intervals are needed to improve understanding and forecasting of tropical cyclones, convective thunderstorms, and other dynamic meteorological events. This capability currently does not exist, as current low-earth-orbiting systems only comprise a few satellites. Therefore, a constellation of approximately 20 nanosatellites could provide unprecedented rapid-revisit observations. This current unmet need is a key driver for the work discussed here.

2 MicroMAS

The Micro-sized Microwave Atmospheric Satellite (MicroMAS) is a 3U CubeSat ($30 \times 10 \times 10$ cm, $\sim$4 kg) hosting a passive cross-track-scanning microwave spectrometer operating near the 118.75-GHz oxygen absorption line. MicroMAS aims to address the need for low-cost, mission-flexible, and rapidly deployable spaceborne sensors. The focus of the current MicroMAS mission is to observe convective thunderstorms, tropical cyclones, and hurricanes from a near-equatorial orbit. As a low cost platform, MicroMAS is a core element of a new observing system comprising multiple satellites in a constellation that can provide near-continuous views of severe weather. The existing architecture of few, high-cost platforms, infrequently view the same earth area thus potentially missing rapid changes in the strength and direction of evolving storms leading to degraded forecast accuracy. MicroMAS is a scalable CubeSat-based system that will pave the path towards improved revisit rates over critical earth regions, and achieve state-of-the-art performance relative to current systems with respect to spatial, spectral, and radiometric resolution. The MicroMAS radiometer is housed in a 1U ($10 \times 10 \times 10$ cm) payload section of the 3U ($10 \times 10 \times 30$ cm) CubeSat. The payload is scanned about the spacecraft's velocity vector as the spacecraft orbits the earth, creating crosstrack scans across the earth's surface. The first portion of the radiometer comprises a horn-fed reflector antenna, with a full-width at half-maximum (FWHM) beamwidth of 2.4°. Hence, the scanned beam has an approximate footprint diameter of 17 km at nadir incidence from a nominal altitude of 400 km. The antenna system is designed for a minimum 95 % beam efficiency. The next stage of the radiometer consists of superheterodyne front-end receiver electronics with single sideband (SSB) operation. The front-end electronics includes an RF preamplifier module, a mixer module, and a local oscillator (LO). The RF preamplifier module contains a low noise RF amplifier and a weakly coupled noise diode for radiometric calibration. The mixer module comprises a HEMT diode mixer and an IF preamplifier MMIC. The LO is obtained using a 30-GHz dielectric resonant oscillator (DRO) and a resistive diode tripler to obtain a 90-GHz LO frequency.

3 MiRaTA

The MiRaTA CubeSat will carry out mission objectives over a 100-day mission, including the on-orbit checkout and validation period. MiRaTA is a 3U (30 cm $\times$10 cm $\times$10 cm) CubeSat comprising V- and G-band radiometers (52–58 GHz, 175–191 GHz, and 203.8–206.8 GHz), the Compact TEC/Atmosphere GPS Sensor (CTAGS) with three-element patch antenna array, and relatively standard CubeSat spacecraft subsystems for attitude determination and

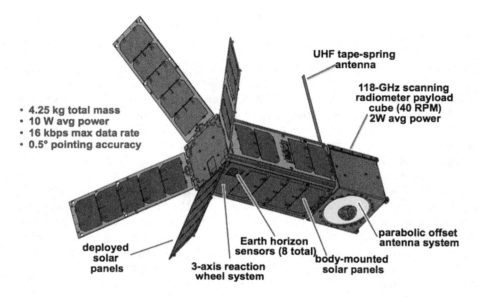

- 4.25 kg total mass
- 10 W avg power
- 16 kbps max data rate
- 0.5° pointing accuracy

UHF tape-spring antenna

118-GHz scanning radiometer payload cube (40 RPM) 2W avg power

parabolic offset antenna system

deployed solar panels

Earth horizon sensors (8 total)

body-mounted solar panels

3-axis reaction wheel system

Fig. 1. The MicroMAS CubeSat.

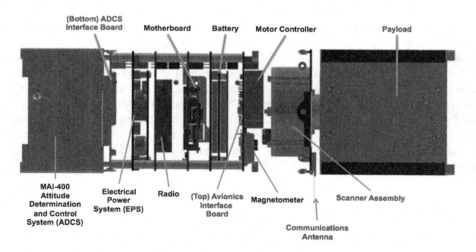

(Bottom) ADCS Interface Board

Motherboard   Battery   Motor Controller   Payload

MAI-400 Attitude Determination and Control System (ADCS)

Electrical Power System (EPS)

Radio

(Top) Avionics Interface Board

Magnetometer

Scanner Assembly

Communications Antenna

Fig. 2. The MicroMAS spacecraft bus. Custom components are shown in blue type, "commercial off-the-shelf (COTS)" parts are shown in black type (Color figure online).

control, communications, power, and thermal control. The spacecraft dimensions
are $10 \times 10 \times 34$ cm, total mass is 4.0 kg, and total average power consumption
is 6 W (Figs. 1 and 2).

3.1   Concept of Operations

The primary MiRaTA mission concept of operations (ConOps) is summarized
in Fig. 3. The MiRaTA spacecraft will perform a slow pitch up/down maneuver
once per orbit to permit the radiometer and GPSRO observations to sound
overlapping volumes of atmosphere through the Earth's limb, where sensitivity,
calibration, and dynamic range are optimal. These observations will be compared
to radiosondes, global high-resolution analysis fields, other satellite observations
(for example, ATMS and the Cross-track Infrared Sounder on the Suomi NPP
satellite) and with each other (GPSRO and radiometer) using radiative transfer
models.

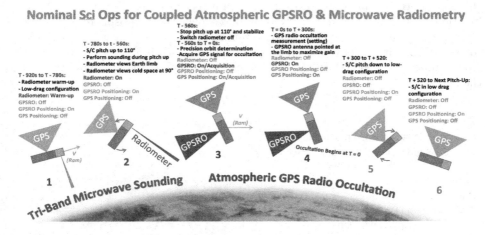

Fig. 3. The MiRaTA primary mission validation concept of operations (ConOps) is
shown above. A slow pitch maneuver ($\sim$0.5°/sec) is used to scan the radiometer field
of view through the Earth's limb and subsequently direct the GPSRO field of view
through the same atmosphere to catch a setting occultation. The entire maneuver
takes about 20 min.

3.2   Spacecraft Overview

The MiRaTA spacecraft is shown in Fig. 4. There are no moving mechanisms and
the only deployable structures (both with flight heritage) are two solar panels and
a simple tape-spring antenna for UHF communications with the NASA Wallops
Flight Facility 18.3-m ground station. The radiometers view the Earth through
the nadir deck of the spacecraft, and in this frame, the GPSRO patch antennas

have a field of view in the zenith direction, which is oriented to the limb during GPSRO sounding via a simple pitch or roll maneuver (see Fig. 3). A separate GPS antenna is used for precision orbit determination during the maneuver. The radiometer and GPSRO fields of view are used to probe the same volume of atmosphere by using the control authority of the reaction wheel assembly to rotate the spacecraft about either the pitch or roll axes approximately once per orbit.

The MiRaTA CubeSat will contain two complete instrument systems, a tri-band atmospheric sounder and CTAGS, which is based on work described in [5]. These two instruments will be operated in a manner to allow cross-comparison and cross-calibration. The tri-band microwave atmospheric sounder provides co-located observations over three frequency bands, 52–58 GHz, 175–191 GHz, and 203.8–206.8 GHz and comprises two radiometer subsystems: (1) V-band (52–58 GHz) front-end receiver with weakly coupled noise diode, low-noise MMIC amplifier, mixer, intermediate frequency (IF) preamplifier, and ultracompact IF spectrometer with highly-scalable LTCC/SIW architecture operating over the 23–29 GHz IF band to provide six channels with temperature weighting functions approximately uniformly distributed over the troposphere and lower stratosphere; and (2) broadband G-band mixer front end operating from 175.31 to 206.8 GHz with a conventional IF spectrometer with lumped element filters. Approximately 1,000 GPSRO + radiometer Earth limb scans are expected over the course of the mission.

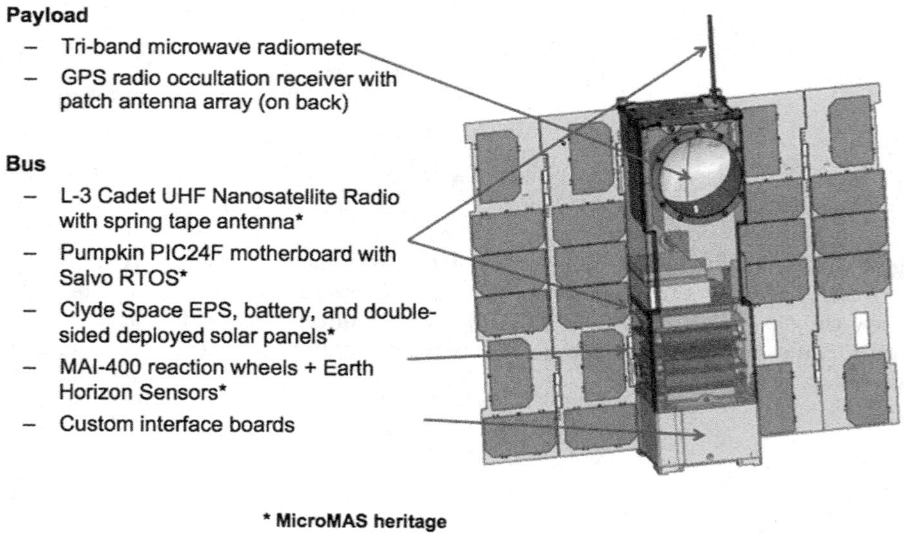

Payload
- Tri-band microwave radiometer
- GPS radio occultation receiver with patch antenna array (on back)

Bus
- L-3 Cadet UHF Nanosatellite Radio with spring tape antenna*
- Pumpkin PIC24F motherboard with Salvo RTOS*
- Clyde Space EPS, battery, and double-sided deployed solar panels*
- MAI-400 reaction wheels + Earth Horizon Sensors*
- Custom interface boards

* **MicroMAS heritage**

Fig. 4. The MiRaTA CubeSat.

4   Toward Data Driven Constellations

We envision a constellation architecture comprising multiple cross-linked Micro-MAS/MiRaTA spacecraft for unprecedented atmospheric measurement fidelity. The cross-linked communication would provide: (1) reduced communications latency to ground, a key performance attribute that is currently lacking in present systems leading to suboptimal utilization of observations of dynamic meteorological events such as tropical cyclones and hurricanes, and (2) data-driven sensing whereby the lead sensor observes dynamic meteorological phenomena and sends a message to the following sensor to temporarily enable a very high resolution sensing mode (a higher sample rate, for example) to better capture the interesting event and preserve spacecraft resources for when they are most needed.

Acknowledgments. This work is sponsored by the National Oceanic and Atmospheric Administration under Air Force Contract FA8721-05-C-0002. Opinions, interpretations, conclusions and recommendations are those of the authors and are not necessarily endorsed by the United States Government.

References

1. Blackwell, W.J., et al.: Nanosatellites for earth environmental monitoring: the MicroMAS project. Proc. 26th Ann. AIAA/USU Conf. Small Sat., SSC12-XI-2, August 2012
2. Blackwell, W.J., et al.: Radiometer calibration using colocated GPS radio occultation measurements. IEEE Trans. Geosci. Remote Sens. **52**(10), 6423–6433 (2014)
3. Ho, S.-P., Goldberg, M., Kuo, Y.-H., Zou, C.-Z., Schreiner, W.: Calibration of temperature in the lower stratosphere from microwave measurements using COSMIC radio occultation data: Preliminary results. Terr. Atmos. Ocean. Sci. **20**, 87–100 (2009)
4. Cucurull, L.: Improvement in the use of an operational constellation of GPS radio occultation receivers in weather forecasting. Wea Forecast. **25**, 749–767 (2010)
5. Bishop, R.L., Hinkley, D.A., Stoffel, D.R., Ping, D.E., Straus, P.R., Brubaker, T.R.: First results from the GPS Compact Total Electron Content Sensor (CTECS) on the PSSC2 Nanosat. Proc. 26th Ann. AIAA/USU Conf. Small Sat., SSC12-XI-2, August 2012

A Novel Approach to Atmospheric Measurements Using Gliding UASs

Ru-Shan Gao[1(✉)], James W. Elkins[2], Gregory J. Frost[1,3],
Allison C. McComiskey[2,3], Fred L. Moore[2,3], Daniel M. Murphy[1],
John A. Ogren[2], Irina Petropavlovskikh[2,3], and Karen H. Rosenlof[1]

[1] Chemical Sciences Division, Earth System Research Laboratory,
National Oceanic and Atmospheric Administration, Boulder, CO 80305, USA
{RuShan.Gao,Gregory.J.Frost,Daniel.M.Murphy,
Karen.H.Rosenlof}@noaa.gov
[2] Global Monitoring Division, Earth System Research Laboratory,
National Oceanic and Atmospheric Administration, Boulder, CO 80305, USA
{James.W.Elkins,Allison.McComiskey,
Fred.Moore,John.A.Ogren,Irina.Petro}@noaa.gov
[3] Cooperative Institute for Research in Environmental Sciences,
University of Colorado, Boulder, CO 80309, USA

Abstract. Atmospheric aerosols and ozone (O_3) have lifetimes of days to weeks and continuously evolve chemically and physically. Frequent and globally spaced vertical profiles of O_3, aerosol optical density, particle size distribution, hygroscopic growth, and light absorption coefficients are highly desired in order to understand their controlling processes and subsequent effects on air quality and climate. High costs and logistical restrictions prohibit frequent profiling on a global scale using current technologies. We propose a new approach using state-of-the-art technologies including 3D printing and an unpowered small Unmanned Aircraft System to make the desired measurements at a fraction of the cost of current conventional methods.

1 Introduction

Atmospheric aerosols play an important role in Earth's climate and are the single largest source of uncertainty in climate model predictions of future climate [1]. Aerosols scatter sunlight, thus directly exerting a negative radiative forcing on climate [2]. A fraction of aerosol particulate mass absorbs sunlight, producing a positive direct radiative forcing [3]. Aerosols also interact with clouds producing either negative or positive forcing depending on the aerosol and cloud properties as well as the atmospheric state.

Aerosols are measured globally using satellites and networks of sun photometers. However, several key properties are not measured regularly due to physical limitations. The most common observations are of column properties such as the aerosol optical depth, giving no vertical profile information. Vertical profiles are key for understanding aerosol sources and cloud interaction; aerosols cannot interact with clouds if they are in a completely different layer of the atmosphere. Vertical information from LiDAR

© Springer International Publishing Switzerland 2015
S. Ravela and A. Sandu (Eds.): DyDESS 2014, LNCS 8964, pp. 10–15, 2015.
DOI: 10.1007/978-3-319-25138-7_2

installations is not sufficiently complete, generally returning only limited information on particle properties such as their size.

Size distributions give key information about how aerosols evolve in time and determine how particle mass impacts climate and air quality. Hygroscopic aerosol particle sizes are affected by ambient relative humidity (RH). These particles grow when ambient RH increases, leading to increased light-scattering. This aerosol hygroscopic effect (AHE) can lead to large changes of the aerosol radiative forcing and visibility following RH changes. Despite its importance, the AHE has not been well characterized observationally due to the continuous evolution of aerosol hygroscopicity throughout aerosol lifetime and the lack of systematic global measurements.

Another parameter that is difficult to determine remotely is the light absorption by particles, which can change the sign of the aerosol climate forcing. Most of the remote observations of aerosol light absorption are from the Aerosol Robotic Network (AERONET), but the uncertainty of these observations is quite high unless the overall aerosol optical depth (AOD) is higher than 0.4 at 440 nm [4, 5]. Since the AOD is above 0.4 only about 10 % of the time, AERONET alone is insufficient for studying light absorption by aerosol.

Ozone (O_3) is a reactive greenhouse gas that can be rapidly produced under poor air quality conditions and warm temperatures in the troposphere. High concentrations of O_3 harm human populations and vegetation. Surface O_3 concentrations are partially controlled by transport [6]. Vertical profiles of O_3 are thus key to accurate forecast of air quality. Currently routine high-resolution O_3 profile measurements are only made in few locations around the globe on a monthly basis. Satellite observations are inadequate for tracking tropospheric O_3 transport due to their low temporal and vertical resolutions.

Both O_3 and aerosol particles in the troposphere have lifetimes of days to weeks in the atmosphere. Understanding their evolution requires extensive observations because ozone and aerosols spread far from their sources yet never become well-mixed enough for a few observations to characterize a global distribution of pollutants. Aerosols continuously change both chemically and physically during their lifetimes. Frequent and globally distributed vertical profiles rather than ground-based measurements alone are highly desired in order to understand the processes that control O_3 and aerosols and their subsequent effects on air quality and climate, and to map aerosol light absorption and its evolution. Conventional profiling using aircraft provides excellent data, but is cost prohibitive on a global scale. Three requirements necessary for a successful global monitoring program are: Low equipment cost, low operation cost, and reliable measurements with well characterized uncertainties.

2   An Innovative Approach

We have devised a new approach that satisfies all three requirements for a successful global observational network (Fig. 1) using instrument packages deployed with a new platform. The platform will consist of a small balloon and a small gliding unmanned aircraft system (gUAS). The gUAS will be released from the balloon at about 5 km altitude, returning a light instrument package to the launch location, and thus allowing for consistent recovery of the payload. Atmospheric profiling can be performed either during ascent or descent (or both) depending on measurement requirements. The new approach, once validated, will be used to form an observation network (Global Ozone and Aerosol profiles and Aerosol Hygroscopic Effect and Absorption optical Depth (GOA^{2}HEAD) network) around the globe.

2.1   New Platform and Instruments

Balloon flights are exempted from U. S. Federal Aviation Administration (FAA) regulations if their payloads are less than 6 lbs. Small weather balloons are fairly inexpensive ($350 per launch) and are essentially the entire disposable operational cost of the GOA^{2}HEAD project since the gUAS and instrument packages are recoverable and reusable. Considering the 6-lbs. FAA limit, the gUAS must be as light as possible. Auto-piloted gliders and small UASs have been evaluated as gUASs. One of the small UASs, 3DRAero by 3DRobotics with a Pixhawk autopilot (https://store.3drobotics. com/products/3DR-Aero), which weighs about 2 lbs. without a motor, propellers, and battery, is currently under consideration for this application in the Global Monitoring Division (GMD) of the NOAA ESRL. Another gUAS, a SkyWisp (Southwest Research Institute, San Antonio, Texas, USA) glider, is also under evaluation. However, parafoils might eventually be more desirable due to their small weight.

Fig. 1. A conceptual sketch. A small weather balloon carries the payload to a desired altitude. Once released from the balloon, the gliding UAS (gUAS) brings the payload back to the launch point. The payload takes data during both ascent and descent.

Sondes that measure relative humidity (RH), pressure (p), and temperature (T) (e.g. iMet-1-RS, InterMet, Grand Rapids, MI, USA) are relatively inexpensive ($\sim$ $230). Electrochemical Concentration Cell ozone sensors (ECC ozonesonde, Droplet Measurement Technologies, Boulder, CO, USA) are available for $\sim$ $800 per unit. However, there are no commercially available aerosol and radiation sondes for small balloons. A few key instruments have been or are being developed in NOAA laboratories that are ideal for balloon applications. The Printed Optical Particle Spectrometer (POPS, 1.8 lbs.) sizes individual aerosol particles between 140 and 3000 nm diameter at ambient RH. This size range is adequate for AOD derivations. The POPS measurements compare well with proven instruments. Dry aerosol particle sizes can be measured with a dryer attachment. The miniature Scanning Aerosol Sun Photometer (miniSASP, 0.7 lbs.) is a 4-wavelength, sun-tracking, azimuth-scanning sunphotometer with a detection limit of 0.02 AOD. Both instruments have been developed at the National Oceanographic and Atmospheric Administration (NOAA) Earth System Research Laboratory (ESRL) in the Chemical Sciences Division using advanced manufacturing techniques such as 3D printing to reduce cost. The NOAA ESRL GMD has developed a filter-based aerosol absorption instrument, the Continuous Light Absorption Photometer (CLAP), which was designed for ground operations, but can easily be miniaturized for this balloon application. The costs for the three instruments and the 3DAero are in the $2 K-$5 K range, quite inexpensive for science-quality instruments, and should satisfy the requirement of low equipment cost mentioned previously. These instruments are not limited to the nighttime operations, thus can be used to track the diurnal changes in aerosol size growth and optical modifications.

Table 1. Measured and derived quantities from the two proposed instrument packages

	Package 1	Package 2
Measured	Aerosol optical depth profile miniSASP	Aerosol absorption coefficient profile (mini-CLAP)
	Dry aerosol number and size distribution profiles (POPS with a dryer)	Ambient RH aerosol number and size distribution profiles (POPS)
	p, T, RH profile (iMet-1-RS)	p, T, RH profile (iMet-1-RS)
	Ozone profile (ECC ozonesonde)	
Derived	RH effect on aerosol size distributions (both packages launched together)	
	Dry AOD	Aerosol absorption optical density (AAOD)
	RH effect on AOD	

2.2 Instrument Packages in Development

Instrument packages must be deployed separately to provide the entire desired measurements due to the 6-lb FAA limit. Two instrument packages are currently under development. The first one consists of an ECC ozonesonde, a POPS with a dryer, a miniSASP, and an iMet-1-RS (for p, T, RH). The second consists of a POPS, an absorption spectrometer (miniaturized Continuous Light Absorption Photometer, or mini-CLAP), and an iMet-1-RS. The POPS computer can serve as a central data system for both instrument packages. Measured and derived quantities from the two instrument packages are listed in Table 1.

Table 2. Comparison between GOA^{2}HEAD and commercial/mature instruments

GOA^{2}HEAD		Commercial/Mature	
Instr.	Performance	Instr.	Performance
ECC O$_3$	Equivalent	ECC O$_3$	Equivalent
POPS	140–3000 nm diam.	DMT PCASP	100-3000 nm diam.
miniSASP	4 wavelengths, 0.02 % precision	CIMEL	8-9 wavelengths < 0.1 % precision
Mini-CLAP	Equivalent	CLAP	Equivalent
iMet-1-RS	Equivalent	iMet-1-RS	Equivalent

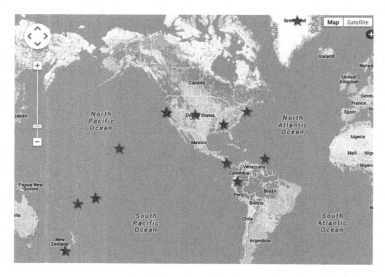

Fig. 2. NOAA O$_3$ sonde stations (Source: http://www.esrl.noaa.gov/gmd/ozwv/network.php)

3 Implementation

We envision a 3-step implementation program. The first step is validating the instruments with other proven in situ instruments in the laboratory and at the NOAA Table Mountain Test Facility (TMTF) via comparison with remote sensing instruments. This initial part of the program will include test launches of the instrument packages at NOAA TMTF, as well as the development of operational and data reduction procedures.

Once the instrument packages are validated and procedures are perfected, the second step of our program would be to deploy at all NOAA ozonesonde stations (Fig. 2). Since these stations use the same type of balloon for ozonesondes, it will be straightforward to launch our packages at these sites. Science quality data are expected from flights at these sites.

The last step would be the full scientific deployment around the world. It is our intention to include as many research institutes as possible. This step is likely several years away, and many details have to be worked out before implementation. Two critical issues are data quality control (including instrument calibration and intercomparison) and data sharing. Careful attention to collaboration with scientific agencies from multiple nations will be necessary to ensure global deployments and maximize scientific return. There are a number of global networks of atmospheric observations stations such as the World Meteorological Organization's Global Atmosphere Watch (GAW) and the GCOS Reference Upper Air Network (GRUAN). These stations could be natural hosts for the GOA^{2}HEAD operations (Table 2).

4 Conclusions

A novel approach for affordable tropospheric O_3 and aerosol profiling has been presented. The approach is based on the use of small weather balloons, a small gliding UAS, and relatively inexpensive state-of-art instrument packages with scientific quality. Measurements currently feasible include profiles of O_3, RH, p, T, aerosol particle size distribution, AOD, and aerosol absorption coefficient.

References

1. Solomon, S., et al. (eds.): Intergovernmental Panel on Climate Change, Climate Change2007: The Physical Science Basis, Contribution of Working Group I to the Fourth Assessment Report of the Intergovernmental Panel on Climate Change, p. 996. Cambridge University Press, Cambridge (2007)
2. Anderson, T.L., Charlson, R.J., Schwartz, S.E., Knutti, R., Boucher, O., Rodhe, H., Heintzenberg, J.: Climate forcing by aerosols - a hazy picture. Science **300**, 1103–1104 (2003)
3. Chung, C.E., Ramanathan, V., Carmichael, G., Kulkarni, S., Tang, Y., Adhikary, B., Leung, L.R., Qian, Y.: Anthropogenic aerosol radiative forcing in asia derived from regional models with atmospheric and aerosol data assimilation. Atmos. Chem. Phys. **10**, 6007–6024 (2010)
4. Ogren, J.: Personal Communication. Scripps-Howard, Cincinnati (2014)
5. Holben, B.N., Eck, T.F., Slutsker, I., Smirnov, A., Sinyukc, A., Schafer, J., Giles, D., Dubovik, O.: AERONET's Version 2.0 quality assurance criteria (2006). http://aeronet.gsfc.nasa.gov/new_web/PDF/AERONETcriteria_final1.pdf
6. Cooper, O., Derwent, R.: Chapter 1 - Conceptual Overview of Hemispheric or Intercontinental Transport of Ozone and Particulate Matter. In: Dentener, F., Keating, T., Akimoto, H. (eds.) Hemispheric Transport of Air Pollution 2010, Part A: Ozone and Particulate Matter, Air Pollution Studies No. 17, New York and Geneva (2011)

In Situ Sampling of Volcanic Emissions with a UAV Sensorweb: Progress and Plans

David Pieri[1] and Jorge Andres Diaz[2]

[1] Jet Propulsion Laboratory, California Institute of Technology,
Pasadena, CA, USA
dave.pieri@jpl.nasa.gov
[2] GasLab of the Center for Investigations in Atomic, Nuclear, and Molecular
Sciences (CICANUM), University of Costa Rica, Sanjose, Costa Rica

Abstract. A consortium of NASA, commercial, and academic partners, we have begun utilize small UAVs and aerostats for in situ sampling of volcanogenic gases and aerosols, using Turrialba Volcano as natural laboratory. Significant progress has been made over the last several years in utilizing single platforms with a number of newly miniaturized instruments appropriate to aircraft with sub-500 gm payloads. For example, we have been mapping the SO_2-water-vapor plume at Turrialba, for comparison with NASA spacecraft-based (e.g., ASTER) data, and are measuring diffuse CO_2 emissions over the volcano's flanks, as well as in and near its eruption column. Future work will include devising strategies, platforms, and instrumentation for deployments of multiple UAV formations ("swarms") as 2D and 3D time-series meshes, to better characterize the mass fluxes and dynamics of emissions. We plan to undertake test flights in the United States, as well as at Turrialba and Poas Volcanoes in Costa Rica. Our most immediate aims are to improve characterizations of local emissions for mitigation of proximal volcanic hazards and for validation of abundance retrievals and transport models based on orbital data. Overall, of course, we strive to better understand how volcanoes work, specifically to better constrain estimates of global SO_2 and CO_2 perennial (diffuse) and event-related (eruptive) emissions—changes in which may foster regional and global climate perturbations.

Keywords: Unmanned aircraft · UAVs · Volcanoes · SO_2 · CO_2 · Diffuse emissions

1 Icelandic Ash and the Rise of the Drones

Our scientific documentation of the products and effects of volcanic eruptions over the past few hundred years of volcanological science has been immeasurably aided by the fact that such manifestations have been accessible on or near the ground. In stark contrast, our knowledge of transient and inaccessible airborne volcanic emissions is regrettably far poorer, since access has only been available from remote observing platforms, or from sparse in situ data acquired during inadvertent, and often heroic, encounters with airborne volcanic ash by manned aircraft [1–4]. As more and larger aircraft more densely populate world-wide air lanes, it has become vitally important to

© Springer International Publishing Switzerland 2015
S. Ravela and A. Sandu (Eds.): DyDESS 2014, LNCS 8964, pp. 16–27, 2015.
DOI: 10.1007/978-3-319-25138-7_3

track the gas and solid aerosol components of volcanic eruptions globally, to more aptly characterize their composition and mass concentrations, and to document and predict drift trajectories in ways that are meaningful to airlines, airframe manufacturers, and national weather agencies (Fig. 1).

Fig. 1. (**A, left**) NASA Global Hawk. for use in high-altitude, long-duration Earth science missions, 13.5 m in length, with a wingspan of 36 m, payloads up to 900 kg and at altitudes of up to 20 km. Its range is greater than 18,500 km and its endurance is greater than 31 h. Dropsondes for nadir deployment into volcanic clouds would be a possibility from Global Hawk—neutral buoyancy heights of most explosive eruption plumes are below the operational ceiling of this aircraft, thus dropsondes or glidesondes could be deployed from this platform, or from Ikhana (**B, right**) NASA Ikhana, named after the Native American Choctaw word for *intelligent, conscious* or *aware*. NASA uses this airborne platform for a variety of long-duration Earth science missions, and to demonstrate and validate electronic sensor technologies. The enlarged fuselage nose accommodates various payloads, including imaging systems, LIDARs and radars. The aircraft is 11 m in length, with a wingspan of 20 m. (Photograph: NASA).

Difficulties in predicting the trajectories, extents, and physical constitutions of drifting ash clouds have on a number of occasions contributed to unplanned aircraft encounters with ash plumes, exposing passengers and crews to high risk. For instance, in December 1989, an ash cloud erupted by of Redoubt Volcano caused the near-fatal all-engine shutdown of a Boeing 747-400 aircraft near Anchorage, Alaska [5]. In another egregious example, in early 2000, an ash plume from Iceland's Hekla volcano (probably masked by ice rinds around ash grains [6, 7]) was encountered over the Atlantic Ocean, several hundred miles northeast of its source. It caused severe engine damage to a Douglas DC-8-72 research aircraft operated by the United States National Aeronautics and Space Administration (NASA) on its way to measure ozone above Scandinavia and Russia [2, 8]). Most generally, both of these surprise transient encounters occurred because of inadequate knowledge of the position and properties (e.g. ash injection altitude, concentration distributions) of the two volcanic clouds, illustrating the inadequate state of our knowledge (then and since) of basic physical extent and plume composition, especially in the context of the use of such parameters as boundary conditions for both mass retrieval and predictive models of cloud trajectories [3, 5, 8] (Fig. 2).

Fig. 2. Medium-sized UAV – NASA SIERRA. SIERRA medium UAV at NASA Ames Research Center, Moffett Field, California. (Photograph: NASA.)

The eruption of Eyjafjallajökull Volcano, beginning in March of 2010 [9], was a watershed moment because it generated a sustained airborne ash hazard that affected prime European airspace and devastated the region's air commerce. It pushed airlines, aviation manufacturers, and researchers to seriously examine the limits of knowledge of aircraft vulnerabilities, as well as to explore all available technical means to characterize ash clouds in detail, including (of special interest here) in situ techniques. Previous to the 2010 Icelandic airborne ash crisis, it was generally accepted that zero ash tolerance (i.e. "zero risk") was the policy most appropriate for aviation. During and after the crisis, however, resulting economic pressures ($5B loss estimated by Oxford Economics [10]) forced aviation interests in the European region to accept some increased risk, with corresponding pressure on researchers for accurate and precise estimates of volcanic ash concentration and variability within airspace transited by commercial and general aviation, as well as by military aircraft [11]. Thus, the near complete lack of in situ validation of constituent concentration and predictive transport models provoked a strong international impetus to find ways to safely penetrate, sample, and otherwise measure ash plumes. In both Europe and America, there was a call for the use of unmanned airborne vehicles (UAVs) to fly into the most problematic and dangerous areas of high ash and gas concentrations, proximal to erupting volcanic vents.

UAVs can indeed address a variety of measurements that are beyond the reach of manned aircraft, mainly for reasons of crew safety, but also because of the endurance required. The direct measurements and sampling that can be achieved by UAVs address serious gaps in knowledge of volcanic processes, and provide important validation data for estimations of volcanogenic ash and gas concentrations gleaned using remote sensing techniques. These data, in turn, constrain key proximal and distal boundary conditions for aerosol and gas transport models [12, 13, and 14], on which are based a number of decisions and evaluations by hazard responders and regulatory agencies. Clearly, a situation in which such estimates and models remain systematically unvalidated is untenable.

Large NASA UAVs, such as the Global Hawk (13.5 m long, 116 ft wingspan, gross takeoff weight of 12,159 kg, ceiling 18.5 km ASL) and the Ikhana (NASA version of the well-known Predator UAV) (11 m long, 20 m wingspan, gross takeoff weight of

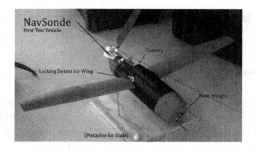

Fig. 3. The steerable NavSonde vehicle by Latitude Engineering, Tucson, AZ. A glidesonde under development within the NASA SBIR Program, it can carry a volcanic ash sampler, camera, or electrochemical gas sensors. It is recoverable, and can be tube-dropped from a standoff vantage point to penetrate volcanic ash plumes—minimum 10:1 glide ratio (Courtesy of Latitude).

4,772 kg, ceiling 7.9 km ASL) are capable, sophisticated and successful in terms of range and payload [15]. For eruption response missions requiring long range and high endurance, they may be suitable. Their complexity, however, demands substantial ground support and incurs high operational expense and extended pre-flight preparation. They represent major capital investment by government and the risk–benefit of operating them in ash contaminated airspace is a serious issue. Thus, it is probably most appropriate to deploy them at the distal margins of dilute volcanogenic ash clouds, for remote sensing and limited in situ sampling, or as launch platforms for small deployable micro-UAV glidesondes (Fig. 3) to acquire atmospheric profile data and to conduct volcanogenic aerosol and gas sampling.

Medium-sized UAVs, such as the Sensor Integrated Environmental Remote Research Aircraft (SIERRA—225 kg empty weight, 45 kg payload) operated by NASA Ames Research Center (ARC) with moderate endurance and payload capabilities, has demonstrated utility for scientific missions in harsh and remote environments (e.g. the 2009 NASA Characterization of Arctic Sea Ice Experiment [CASIE]). SIERRA would be appropriate for eruptions where a relatively quick response is key (less than 1wk, if pre-positioned), and where operations are carried out relatively near the volcano (< 25 km) at altitudes of less than 4 km ASL. Its order-of-magnitude lower operating costs compared to NASA flagship UAVs make it less risk-averse, yet it can still carry substantial payloads (e.g. miniaturized mass spectrometer). If alternatively powered by batteries or fuel cells, as has been discussed, and thus relatively insensitive to ash ingestion, SIERRA will be capable of extending the range of manned observations, both remote sensing and in situ, into the most ash-dense and gas-dense parts of eruption plumes, in all weather, and at night in proximity to hazardous terrain. Its sister UAV, the Viking 400C, as of 2014, is also in the NASA Airborne Science Program inventory, and so multiple aircraft flights are possible, although there is no multi-aircraft medium UAV operational capability at the time of writing. Thus, large and medium-payload UAVs in the NASA inventory do not now offer the possibility of an operational sensor-web. That is, the ability to deploy multiple aircraft simultaneously in response to an evolving volcanic crisis, or to undertake systematic observations at multiple altitudes or from aircraft distributed across an Area of Interest, does not yet exist with this class of NASA UAV.

2   UAV Sensorwebs

The situation for micro-UAVs, such as the Aerovironment Inc. Dragon Eye ($\sim$ 2.7 kg gross takeoff weight; 500 g payload, Fig. 3) or the prospective multi-aircraft Apollo micro-UAV system (comparable to Dragon Eye, J. Elston—personal communication; Fig. 5) is, however, dramatically different. These aircraft are substantially more flexible than large and medium UAVs and can be more easily sacrificed, when necessary. Nevertheless, we have demonstrated [16] they are able to carry out useful scientific missions. Aerostats (e.g. tethered balloons and kites) are also appropriate platforms where measurements are desired over a particular place near a volcano for extended periods of time. To illustrate how the current generation of small UAVs, aerostats and available instruments can be used to investigate relatively low-altitude (3.7 km ASL) plumes from passively emitting volcanoes, we briefly describe near-term plans for our field study at Turrialba Volcano in Costa Rica with multiple Dragon Eye aircraft. Our goal at Turrialba is to undertake a systematic series of in situ measurements of volcanogenic SO_2, CO_2, and other gases, as well as aerosols, in conjunction with over-flights by the NASA Terra Earth orbital platform with the ASTER instrument onboard, and potentially with OMI orbital observations [17, 18] (Fig. 4).

Currently, our plans are to deploy up to a half-dozen Dragon Eye aircraft in the emission plume at Turrialba Volcano in the Central Valley of Costa Rica in March

Fig. 4. NASA Dragon Eye, originally built in 2001 by Aerovironment Inc. This small (0.9 m length, 1.1 m wingspan, 2.7 kg weight) is a rugged and versatile platform for deployment of small sensors ($\leq$ 500 g) into volcanic plumes. It cruises at 65 km/h over a 5–10 km range and flies completely autonomously with automatic ascents and landings. The current NASA ARC Dragon Eye fleet consists of 75 aircraft plus spares, operated by the NASA Airborne Science Program (Photograph: Justin Linick, JPL).

2015. Turrialba is part of a complex volcanic edifice that includes Volcan Irazu, which was a previous center of activity over geologic time. Turrialba is one of the largest volcanic structures in Meso-America and has had ash-flow eruptions within the last several hundred years. It is currently restless, constantly emitting a water vapor and sulfur dioxide gas plume, with occasional small phreato-magmatic bursts up to about 1000 m above its summit crater ($\sim$ 3300 m ASL), which are then entrained into an 3-5 km from the main vent before dissipating. It is this plume that we and colleagues from the University of Costa Rica (UCR) have systematically (twice monthly for almost two years) sampled in single UAV sorties with the NASA Dragon Eye, with the UCR Vector Wing 100 and Vantar UAVs, and with aerostats (Fig. 6A, B).

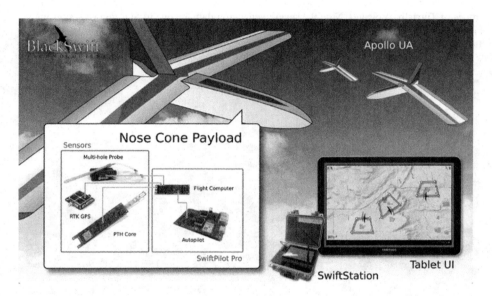

Fig. 5. Illustration of prospective Apollo multi-UAV-based sensorweb showing an intuitive user interface. Currently under development within the NASA SBIR Program (courtesy of J. Elston, BlackSwift Technologies).

Moving to a sensorweb mode next, we plan to create 2D and 3D in situ sampling meshes, using arrays of small UAVs, taking time-series areal and volumetric snapshots of the Turrialba SO_2 plume across its expanse [19]. Knowing the approximate physical dimensions of the plume, along with gas and aerosol concentrations is key to validating species' column abundance estimates from multispectral satellite images, and has only rarely been done to date. It is also important in improving estimates for SO_2 flux from the volcano, changes in which (an increase or decrease) can be precursory to eruptions. Also, in-plume hydrolysis of SO_2 to H_2SO_4 with ultimate precipitation as acid rain has devastated farmlands and forests around the volcano. Better knowledge of the SO_2 flux will help in understanding mechanisms of those processes, and in separating SO_2-related phenomena to similar devastation caused by CO_2 emissions.

Fig. 6. (A) SO$_2$-sonde package ready to be lifted as part of a tethered balloon aerostat on the slopes of Turrialba Volcano. Note the severe vegetation damage due to SO$_2$ and CO$_2$ poisoning, in the background. (**B**) UCR crew pre-flights the Vector Wing 100 UAV on Turrialba (Photo: J. Linick, JPL).

Fig. 7. GPS flight track of a NASA Dragon Eye aircraft over the slopes of Turrialba Volcano, Costa Rica, on 13 March 2013, with an electrochemical SO$_2$ sensor onboard. A relatively thin SO$_2$ plume was present, with intercepted concentrations below 10 ppmv. SO$_2$ concentrations ≥ 30 ppmv have been observed within 3 km of the vent at altitude (Courtesy of CICANUM, UCR)

CO$_2$ emissions at volcanoes can be dichotomous, with strong emissions from the main summit vent(s) of the volcano, and with a more diffuse component whose emission occurs via numerous fractures or faults, often diffusing into the regolith or soil

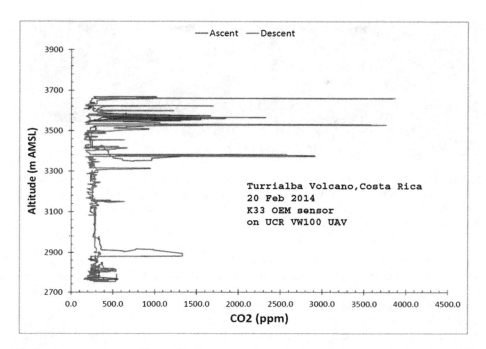

Fig. 8. Concentration profiles obtained with an off-the-shelf commercial CO_2 sensor on board a Vector Wing 100 (Maryland Aerospace; Fig. 6B) operated by the University of Costa Rica in the gas emission plume from Turrialba Volcano, Costa Rica. Values above the active summit crater (3300 mASL) range up to 4000 ppmv. Instrument sensitivity is 10-20 ppmv (Courtesy CICANUM, UCR).

overburden, then into the air. Often, such emissions suffocate root systems of trees, and general die-offs ensue—such a situation is occurring at Turrialba, in addition to acid rain damage.

In addition, changes in the ratio between CO_2 and SO_2 concentrations may be related to pre-eruption dynamics within the volcano's magmatic supply system, and a better understanding of their systematic may improve eruption predictions. Currently, the column abundances of both gases are typically measured vicariously via near-field remote sensing through the plume (e.g., differential optical absorption spectroscopy). Poor knowledge of the dynamic extent of the plume thus induces high errors in the accuracy of flux estimates. Spatial and temporal variability of concentrations across these emission plumes is only poorly known at present. Single UAV measurements along transects are some improvement over point measurements on the ground or near-field remote sensing observations, however, simultaneous multiple UAV-based time-series 2D-3D mesh measurements promise dramatic improvement.

Finally, determining the volcanic flux of CO_2 proves to be particularly difficult, because of rapid dilution of the volcanic contribution by the inherently high (and increasing) background CO_2. Often ubiquitous and diffuse volcanic CO_2 sources (e.g., along fractures and diffusing through regolith and soil overburdens) are difficult to

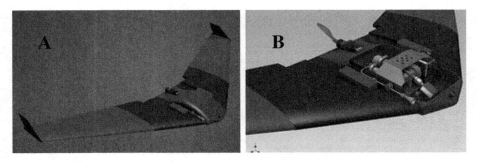

Fig. 9. A (Left) The UCR experimental VectorWing300 design. Figure **9B (Right)** Cutaway illustration of the UCR VectorWing300 with an integrated mini mass spectrometer (3 kg) payload. Wingspan is approximately equivalent to the VectorWing100 aircraft shown in Fig. 6B. (Courtesy of CICANUM, UCR).

differentiate at minimum above-terrain altitudes typical for manned aircraft (300-1000 m AGL or more). Volcanic contributions above background may suffer 10^2 to 10^3 or more dilution factors, even at low altitudes right over volcanic sources. Thus the detection of such small increases requires very high precision, and thus expensive equipment, generally beyond the payload capabilities of small UAVs, although SIERRA has experimentally carried the Picarro gas analyzer (< 1ppmv sensitivity, 35 kg mass).

Small UAVs like Dragon Eye or Apollo, however, can fly very low ($\leq$ 50 m AGL), using commercial-off-the-shelf inexpensive CO_2 detectors (10-20ppmv sensitivity; 100 g), to detect CO_2 emissions right above sources at minimal background dilution (1000-1500ppmv). Of course, within volcanic plumes or over summit vents where gas velocities are high, the CO_2 (and SO_2) signals are very strong (3000-4000ppmv; Figs. 7 and 8). Such devices are easily within the payload and economic range of small UAVs that we fly. In addition, a promising relatively new tunable laser CO_2 detector ($\sim$ 500 g; [20, 21]) can make measurements at the 1ppmv sensitivity level with < 0.3 % lab calibration repeatability and will be deployed this year on Dragon Eye. Finally, sometime in 2015, we are planning to fly the UCR mini mass spectrometer (3 kg, 100 amu range) on the UCR VW300 delta-winged UAV (Fig. 9A and B). We plan to deploy these newer instruments at test sites in the United States, and at both Volcan Turrialba and Volcan Poas in Costa Rica, in support of both the OCO-2 and GOSAT orbital missions, and for fundamental observations of volcanic degassing.

3 Conclusions

The disruption of European and trans-Atlantic airspace in 2010 provoked serious re-examination of aviation procedures with respect to airborne volcanic ash hazards, and increased demands on the scientific and hazard response communities to provide timely, precise, and, above all, accurate data on the presence and character of volcanic emissions that could affect air travel. The estimated resultant economic losses of US

$5B were a particularly strong driver, along with air safety. While orbital platforms and manned aircraft can provide some of the critical boundary condition inputs to ash and gas abundance retrievals and predictive transport models, key proximal zones of high ash and gas concentrations remain beyond their reach, due to crew safety considerations (aircraft) or instrumental limitations (satellites). The future increased use of UAVs was recommended by practitioners in Europe and in America, in their post-mortem analyses [11].

At JPL and UCR, with colleagues at the NASA Ames Research Center, NASA the Wallops Flight Facility of the Goddard Spaceflight Center, and the NASA Glenn Research Center, along with our commercial partners, we have embarked on a program to utilize small UAVs and aerostats to conduct in situ sampling of volcanogenic gases and aerosols, using Turrialba Volcano as our initial natural laboratory. We have made substantial progress in this effort, utilizing single platforms with a number of newly miniaturized instruments appropriate to aircraft with payloads of under 500 g mass. We have mapped the extent and constituent abundances within the SO_2 water-vapor plume at Turrialba, for comparison with NASA spacecraft-based data, and have measured diffuse CO_2 emissions over its flanks and its eruption column, all with single aircraft sorties. Moving forward, we are developing strategies and technologies that will accommodate simultaneous multiple UAV sorties as 2D and 3D mesh time-series sampling areas and volumes to better characterize the mass fluxes and dynamics of volcanic emissions. During the coming year or two, we plan to test and implement this approach at test sites in the United States, as well as at Turrialba and Poas Volcanoes in Costa Rica. Ultimately we hope not only to better characterize local emissions for hazard mitigation and orbital/airborne instrument calibration, but generally, to better constrain estimates of global SO_2 and CO_2 perennial and eruptive emissions from volcanoes— both of which have the potential to perturb regional and global climate [22, 23].

Acknowledgements.   This work was carried out, in part, at the Jet Propulsion Laboratory of the California Institute of Technology under contract to the NASA Earth Surface and Interior Focus Area and the ASTER Project. We also gratefully acknowledge the continued support of Matt Fladeland and his Airborne Science team at NASA ARC (Randy Berthold, Don Herlth, Corey Ippolito, Matt Johnson, Rick Kolyer, Bruce Storms, Mark Sumich), Geoff Bland and Ted Miles at NASA GSFC/WFF, Justin Linick and Vince Realmuto at JPL, Gary Hunter and Paul Greenberg at NASA GRC, Darby Makel (Makel Engineering), Steve Fuerstenau (Radmet LLC), Jack Elston (BlackSwift Engineering), as well as the UCR CICANUM GasLab Team (Alfredo Alan, Oscar Alegria, Sara Azofiefa, Ernesto Corrales, and Yetty Madrigal). We would also like to thank our colleagues Lance Christensen and Florian Schwandner at JPL for helpful technical advice and encouragement.

References

1. Hobbs, P.V., Tuel, J.P., Hegg, D.A., Radke, L.F., Eltgroth, M.W.: Particles and gases in the emissions from the 1980–1981 volcanic eruptions of Mt St. Helens. J. Geophy. Res. **87**, 11062–11086 (1982)

2. Casadevall, T.J., Rose, W.I., et al.: Sulfur dioxide and particles in quiescent volcanic plumes from poas, arenal, and colima volcanoes, costa rica and mexico. J. Geophys. Res. **9**, 9633–9641 (1984)
3. Pieri, D.C., Ma, C., Simpson, J.J., Hufford, G.L., Grove, G., Grindle, T.: Analyses of in situ airborne volcanic ash from the feb 2000 eruption of hekla. Geophys. Res. Lett. **29**, 19-1–19-4 (2002)
4. Carn, S.A., Froyd, K.D., et al.: In situ measurements of tropospheric volcanic plumes in Ecuador and Colombia during TC4. J. Geophy. Res. **116**, D00J24 (2011). http://dx.doi.org/10.1029/2010JD014718
5. Casadevall, T.J.: The 1989–1990 eruption of redoubt volcano, alaska: impacts on aircraft operations. J. Volcanol. Geoth. Res. **62**, 301–316 (1994)
6. Lacasse, C., Karlsdo´ttir, S., Larsen, G., Suusalu, H., Rose, W.I., Ernst, G.G.J.: Weather radar observations of the hekla 2000 eruption cloud, Iceland. Bull. Volc. **66**, 457–473 (2003)
7. Rose, W.I., Gu, Y., et al.: The February–March 2000 eruption of Hekla, Iceland from a satellite perspective. In: Robock, A., Oppenheimer, C. (eds) Volcanism and the Earth's Atmosphere. American Geophysical Union, Geophysical Monograph, vol. **139**, 107–132 (2003)
8. Grindle, T.J., Burcham, F.W.: Nasa/ Tm-2003-212030: Engine Damage To A Nasa Dc- 8-72 Airplane From A High-Altitude Encounter With A Diffuse Volcanic Ash Cloud. NASA, Edwards (2003)
9. Global Volcanism Program : Eyjafjallajokull 03/2010 Fissure eruption and lava flows from E flank on 20 March, Smithsonian Global Volcanism Program. BGVN, 35, 03 (2010). http://www.volcano.si.edu/world/volcano.cfm?vnum=1702-02=&volpage=var#bgvn_3503
10. Oxford Economics.: Volcanic Ash Impact on Air Travel, report for Airbus Industries. Oxford Economics, Oxford (2012). http://www.oxfordeconomics.Com/my-oxford/projects/128815
11. Guffanti, M.: Volcanic-ash hazards to aviation in the post-world: a status report. Presented at TETS 2012. In: Proceedings of the Turbine Engine Technology Symposium 2012, Dayton, 10–13 September. 2012. http://www.meetingdata.utcdayton.com/agenda/
12. Stunder, B.J.B., Heffter, J.L., Draxler, R.R.: Airborne volcanic ash forecast area reliability, weather and forecasting. Weather Forecast. **22**, 1132–1139 (2007). doi:10.1175/WAF1042.1
13. Webley, P.W., Dehn, J., Lovick, J., Dean, K.G., Bailey, J.E., Valcic, L.: Near real time volcanic ash cloud detection: experiences from the alaska volcano observatory. In: Webley, P., Mastin, L. (eds.) Improved Prediction and Tracking of Volcanic Ash Clouds. Journal of Volcanology and Geothermal Research **186**, 79–90 (2009)
14. Webley, P.W., Dean, K.G., Dehn, J., Bailey, J.E., Peterson, R.: Volcanic-ash dispersion modeling of the 2006 eruption of Augustine Volcano using the Puff model. In: Power, J.A., Coombs, M.L., Freymueller, J.T. (eds.) The 2006 Eruption of Augustine Volcano, Alaska. United States Geological Survey, Professional Papers, Ch. 21, vol. **1769**, 507–526 (2010)
15. Springer, P.J.: Military Robots and Drones: A Reference Handbook. ABC-CLIO LLC, Santa Barbara (2013)
16. Pieri, D.C., Diaz, J.A., Bland, G., Fladeland, M., Madrigal, Y., Corrales, E., Alan, A., Alegria, O., Realmuto, V., Miles, T., Abtahi, A.: In Situ Observations and Sampling of Volcanic Emissions with Unmanned Aircraft: A NASA/UCR Case Study at Turrialba Volcano, Costa Rica. In: Remote Sensing of Volcanoes and Volcanic Processes, Geological Society of London Special Publication, SP380: pp. 321–352 (2013)
17. Kreuger, A., Yang, K., Krotkov, N.: Enhanced monitoring of sulfur dioxide sources with hyperspectral UV sensors. In: Picard, R.H., Scha¨fer, K., Comeron, A., Kassianov, E., Mertens, C.J. (eds.) Remote Sensing of Clouds and the Atmosphere XIV. Proceedings of SPIE 7475, SPIE, Bellingham (2009). http://dx.doi.org/10.1117/12.830142

18. Krotkov, N.A., Schoeberl, M.R., Morris, G.A., Carn, S., Yang, K.: Dispersion and lifetime of the SO_2 cloud from the August 2008 Kasatochi eruption. Journal of Geophysical Research **115**, D00L20 (2010). http://dx.doi.org/10.1029/2010JD013984

19. Ippolito, C., Fladeland, M., Yeh, Y.H.: Applications of payload directed flight. In: Proceedings of the Aerospace Conference IEEE, p. 5, Big Sky, MT, IEEE Explore 7–14 March 2009. http://ieeexplore.ieee.org/xpl/freeabs_all.jsp?arnumber=4839612 DOI: 10.1109/AERO.2009.4839612

20. Christensen, L.E., Brunner, B., Truong, K.N., Mielke, R.E., Webster, C.R., Coleman, M.: Measurement of sulfur isotope compositions by tunable laser spectroscopy of SO_2. Anal. Chem. (2007). doi:10.1021/ac071040p

21. Christensen, L.E., Spiers, G.D., Menzies, R.T., Jacob, J.: Tunable Laser Spectroscopy of CO_2 near 2.05 µm: atmosph. retrieval biases due to neglecting line-mixing. J. Quant. Spec Rad. Trans. **110**, 739–748 (2012)

22. Burton, M.R., Sawyer, G.M., Granieri, D.: Deep carbon emissions from volcanoes, 2013. Rev. Mineral. Geochem. **75**, 323–354 (2013)

23. Pedone, M., Aiuppa, A., Giudice, G., Grassa, F., Francofonte, V., Bergsson, B., Ilyinskaya, E.: Tunable diode laser measurements of hydrothermal/volcanic CO2, and implications for the global CO2 budget. Solid Earth Discuss. **6**, 2645–2674 (2014). doi:10.5194/sed-6-2645-2014, www.solid-earthdiscuss.net/6/2645/2014/

Advances in Light Field Imaging
for Measurement of Fluid Mechanical Systems

Jesse Belden[1($\boxtimes$)], Jonathon Pendlebury[2], Alexander Jafek[2],
and Tadd Truscott[2]

[1] Naval Undersea Warfare Center, Newport, RI, USA
jesse.belden@navy.mil
[2] Brigham Young University, Provo, UT, USA

Abstract. Light field imaging is becoming an increasingly useful tool
for measuring fluid mechanical systems. We present advances in light
field imaging for fluids along three directions. The first concerns robust
reconstruction of fluid measurement volumes using synthetic aperture
refocusing followed by deconvolution. Then, we discuss how a flame,
which distorts the refractive index, augments the light field. The error
introduced into particle image velocimetry measurements by this effect
is discussed. Finally, we develop a framework for the application of light
field imaging to the reconstruction of a specular gas-liquid interface.

Keywords: Light field imaging · Experimental fluids · Volume reconstruction · Flames · Specular surfaces

1 Introduction

Modeling of fluid mechanical systems benefits from and often requires high-
fidelity three-dimensional data. This need has pushed experimental fluid dynam-
icists to look to other fields, such as computational imaging, for innovative
measurement methods. Light field (LF) imaging is one (broad) method that has
found traction in experimental fluids, mostly being used for three-dimensional
velocity measurements in laboratory experiments. Levoy [1] provided a review
of LF imaging, which involves sampling the intensity and direction of light rays
intersecting a scene. Knowledge of the direction of individual rays - information
that is not contained in a traditional camera's image - allows for more information to be computed about the scene post-capture.

Of particular interest for fluids measurements is the ability to extract the
depth of objects, which enables three-dimensional velocity measurements via
particle image velocimetry (PIV). Several methods are available for sampling
and post-processing light fields of particle-laden fluid flows. Multiple camera
techniques include Tomographic PIV [2,3], Synthetic Aperture (SA)PIV [4] and

---

© US Government (outside the US) 2015
S. Ravela and A. Sandu (Eds.): DyDESS 2014, LNCS 8964, pp. 28–38, 2015.
DOI: 10.1007/978-3-319-25138-7_4

Defocusing PIV [5]. A single camera technique using a lenslet-based LF camera has also been demonstrated [6]. A lenslet-based LF camera has recently been commercialized (Lytro, Inc.); however the spatial resolution of this off-the-shelf product is too poor for most laboratory fluids experiments. The hardware used to capture the LF sets the spatial and temporal resolution, which has been well explored in the relevant references. The accuracy and speed of algorithms used to reconstruct the 3D volume and extract data of interest are still benefiting from development. In Sect. 2, we discuss a robust 3D deconvolution approach for reconstructing volumes captured using LF cameras and multi-camera SA systems along with ideas for reducing overall computation time.

In the remainder of the paper, we apply LF imaging to the measurement of fluids with variation in refractive index (RI). One topic of interest is the quantification of the 3D shape and velocity fields of reacting flames. For instance, fuel is only burned in a small part of the flame called the flame front. Turbulent flames contain flow structures that can strain the flame front to the point of localized extinctions, allowing fuel to pass through without burning. A more accurate understanding of the turbulent flow field can increase our knowledge of when and where these extinctions might occur and potentially increase fuel efficiency. However, measurements of flames are often inaccurate as the flame temperature gradient causes spatial variation in the RI, which has not been properly accounted for in many published velocimetry studies. In Sect. 3, we use LF imaging to reconstruct the visual hull of a flame. The error that can arise in velocity measurements due to the RI gradient is then assessed. Finally, in Sect. 4 we present a framework for using a LF camera to measure the local orientation and location of a gas-liquid interface. This technique leverages past work on projector-camera systems combined with LF imaging to synthesize a novel method for specular surface geometry measurements.

2 Volume Reconstruction

We focus here on reconstruction of volumes generated using the synthetic aperture (SA) refocusing method, which can be applied to light fields captured using a multi-camera setup [7, 8]. In such a configuration, all cameras view a common measurement volume entirely in focus (i.e., large depth of focus). All cameras are calibrated in a common metric reference frame. In SA refocusing, the images from each camera are reprojected onto a common plane in the measurement volume, and then averaged to produce a synthetic image with a narrow depth-of-focus; this can be expressed mathematically as

$$I_{SA_k} = \frac{1}{N} \sum_{i=1}^{N} I_{FP_{ki}} \tag{1}$$

where I_{SA_k} is the SA image on the kth synthetic focal plane and $I_{FP_{ki}}$ is the image from the ith camera reprojected onto the kth plane. A focal stack can be generated by applying Eq. 1 to several planes spanning the volume; limits on

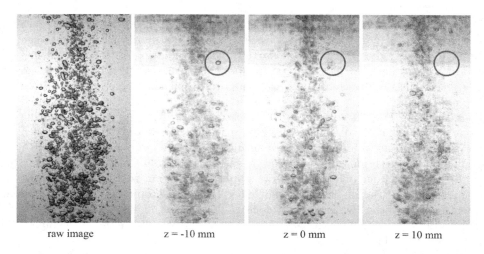

Fig. 1. Raw image from one camera of a nine camera array and slices at three depths from a SA focal stack.

spatial resolution are discussed in [4]. Figure 1 shows slices from a SA focal stack applied to a bubbly flow field as reported in [9]. Generation of a SA focal stack can be considered the "image" resulting from a LF imaging system. Reconstructing the original object requires additional operations on the image to remove artifacts imposed from the SA refocusing. In past experimental fluids studies, objects have been estimated using various focus metrics to remove artifacts of the SA image formation [4,9]. However, a more robust reconstruction method is 3D deconvolution. Consider modeling the SA image formation process as a convolution,

$$v(X, Y, Z) = p(X, Y, Z) \otimes o(X, Y, Z) \qquad (2)$$

where v, o and p describe the intensity distribution of the image, object and the 3D point spread function (psf) of the LF imaging system, respectively. 3D deconvolution is concerned with effectively inverting Eq. 2 to estimate o given v and an estimate of p [10]. For LF images, we opt to perform the deconvolution in the space domain using a constrained iterative algorithm because the psf is often not broadband [11].

SA refocusing involves projecting camera pixels along their lines-of-sight (LOS) and combining these projections across all cameras. The psf for a SA imaging system thus takes on the geometry of the lines of sight. In the work of Levoy et al. [11] using a LF microscope, the psf was accurately assumed to be shift-invariant. However, as demonstrated in Fig. 2, the geometry of the psf will generally be a function of location within the measurement volume due to the different viewing directions of the cameras. A space-domain constrained iterative deconvolution algorithm, such as Richardson-Lucy [10], may still be applied but the psf will be different for each voxel in the volume. When applying the psf

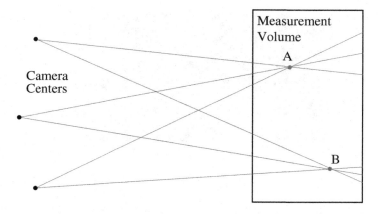

Fig. 2. Schematic of the geometry of the 3D psf associated with an SA imaging system. The psf is dependent on the location of the point within the volume and is thus not shift-invariant.

to the current object estimate, a voxel's intensity must be projected along all camera LOS and interpolated onto the estimated image volume. Thus, an interpolation matrix that determines the contribution of each voxel to all other voxels along the LOS must be stored for each voxel, which requires a large amount of memory. However, if the psf were shift-invariant, then only one interpolation matrix would be required for all voxels, greatly reducing the storage required and the computation time associated with voxel projection.

One scenario for which the psf is shift-invariant is when all camera centers of the array lie on the same plane and the focal planes are fronto-parallel [7]. In this case, after applying an initial homography to each image, each mapping function used to take images to other focal planes are integer pixel shifts of the images. For PIV applications, we can use SA refocused images of individual particles to accurately capture the intensity distribution of the psf. Figure 3(a) shows an X-Z slice of the psf from a simulated SAPIV experiment using nine cameras (for details of simulation see [4]). This psf is used with the Richardson-Lucy (R-L) deconvolution algorithm to reconstruct a particle volume containing 50000 simulated particles that was formed by SA refocusing simulated particle images. The accuracy of reconstruction is first quantified using a reconstruction quality metric, Q, described in [3], which is a normalized correlation coefficient between the reconstructed volume and the true simulated volume; a value of $Q \geq 0.75$ is considered adequate for 3D PIV volumes. Figure 3(b) summarizes Q as a function of number of iterations. In all cases, the reconstruction quality using 3D deconvolution is improved over the thresholding method. Accuracy is also characterized by the number of particles accurately reconstructed in the volume and the number of "ghost" particles (artifacts) that remain in the volume. A particle is considered to be accurately reconstructed if the particle centroid is within 3 voxels (typical particle diameter) of a known particle position. These results are summarized in Fig. 3(c). All reconstruction methods accurately reconstruct greater than 90 % of the true particles. The number of ghost particles - which

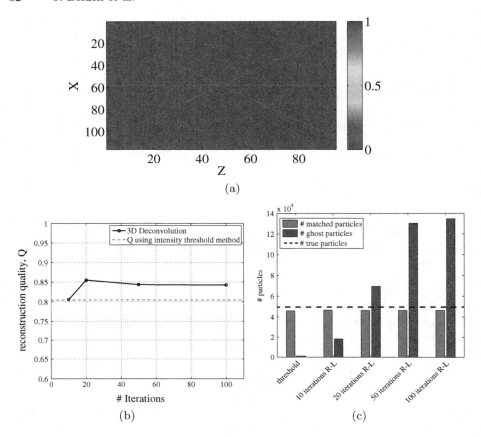

Fig. 3. (a) X-Z slice from a shift-invariant 3D psf for a simulated SA imaging system. (b) Volume reconstruction quality, Q, as a function of number of Richardson-Lucy iterations. (c) Number of accurately reconstructed particles and "ghost" particles for several reconstruction methods.

ultimately reduce accuracy in the PIV velocity measurements - is lowest for the thresholding method and increases with an increasing number of R-L iterations. The performance of the thresholding method is not surprising as the threshold level has been optimized by trial and error for this simulation. In practice, the deconvolution method is far more robust as no trial and error is needed. The thresholding method has already been shown to perform well in actual 3D PIV experiments [4], and thus the proposed 3D deconvolution method is expected to improve results and robustness.

3   Flames

Optical methods are an attractive measurement option for flames because they are non-invasive. LF imaging has the potential to benefit flame measurements by resolving 3D shapes using a process similar to the visual hull method described by Adhikari and Longmire [12], and by resolving 3D PIV giving all three spatial components of velocity through time. PIV, in particular, presents an interesting problem. Reacting flows generate a large amount of heat that can significantly change the RI throughout the measurement volume. This can cause a large error in determining the location of particles in the flame. Interestingly this effect is often ignored by those performing PIV measurements on flames [13–16].

Shape reconstruction of the visual hull of a flame using LF imaging is performed using an array of cameras, all set at different positions and focused on the same volume. Images are processed using the SA refocusing algorithm to produce a focal stack, as shown in Fig. 4. Unlike SAPIV, the focal stack contains images that show the shape of the flame as opposed to particles coming into and out of focus. ISO surfaces are used with a set intensity threshold to recreate the surface of the flame in each image of the focal stack. The surfaces from each image are then stacked onto each other and the resulting volume is a reconstruction of the shape of the flame, an example of which is shown in Fig. 5. The results are shown along with individual images and qualitatively show that the reconstruction captures the shape of the flame.

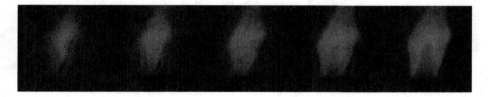

Fig. 4. From left to right; five reconstructed cross sections from the front to the center of a partially premixed Bunsen burner diffusion flame (5 mm depth spacing). These flames are the result of refocusing images from 8 high-speed cameras to form a focal stack.

As discussed before, velocity measurements within a flame are highly sought after, but have been hindered by the inability to compensate for RI gradients. In order to address this problem, we first must understand how the RI gradients affect 2D PIV measurements and 3D SAPIV reconstructions. To assess the former, a grid was placed in the background of an image with a field of view of $\sim$ 70 mm (typical size for PIV). One image was taken with no flow field in front, and another was taken with a flame in front. The difference of the images was found to see how much the lines moved as a result of the refraction field of the flame; the results are shown in Fig. 6. The difference image shown in Fig. 6(c), reveals a maximum shift of two pixels. For 2D PIV, particle motions are typically on the order of 10 pixels and thus the RI gradient introduces quite large error.

When applying SA refocusing to LF images of a flame, the RI gradient introduces an aberration into the formation of 3D particle images. This is depicted in Fig. 7(a); because the cameras are assumed to image in a medium with uniform RI, the LOS don't intersect in a single point. For comparison, Fig. 7(b) shows lines of sight for an experiment in air with no RI gradients. Rather, the refocused particles become larger blobs, with size corresponding to the amount of

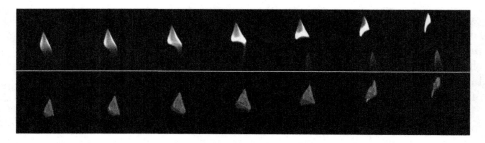

Fig. 5. Images taken in time of a flame (top row) and the corresponding volume reconstruction of the visual hull of the flame (bottom row).

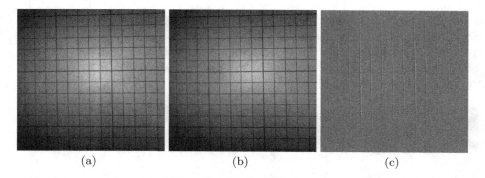

| (a) | (b) | (c) |

Fig. 6. Three images demonstrating the index of refraction shift of a flame. Image 6(a) is an image of a background grid with no flame and 6(b) is a grid background with a flame front. Image 6(c) shows the difference of the two images, highlighting the pixels that have experienced a change.

error introduced by the RI gradient. At best, this effect would introduce error into particle location and at worst it could cause particles to not be reconstructed at all. There has been some recent work on camera calibration through refractive interfaces to suggest the refraction field can be accounted for [17,18] and in a very promising paper Atcheson et al. [19] presented a method for reconstructing the discretized three dimensional index of refraction field of a camp stove flame. The method used an array of cameras arranged in a semi-circle around the flame, each with a noise pattern background. The differences in the images were found using an optical flow method, and combined to find the 3D RI field.

4   Gas-Liquid Interface Measurement

The geometric reconstruction of a diffuse surface can be accomplished with a simple projector-camera system [20]. However, in the case of specular objects - such as a gas-liquid interface (GLI) - these same methods fail to uniquely define surface location and orientation. Several methods have been demonstrated for recovering specular surface geometry including: using multiple cameras with diffuse scene points [21,22], using one camera with images of a calibration target

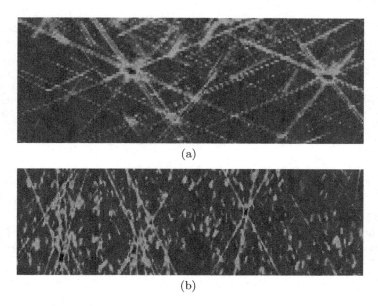

(a)

(b)

Fig. 7. X-Z slices from SA refocused particle-laden volumes (b) in a flame flow in which the RI gradients introduce aberrations into the formation of 3D particle images and (b) in air with no RI gradients.

in two or more locations [23] and resolving the distortion of known geometry imaged by one camera [24,25]. We seek a method that uses one lenslet-based LF camera and one projector to reconstruct a GLI. This setup is attractive for situations that require the hardware to be small to perform measurements in confined spaces.

The geometry of our proposed LF camera-projector system is shown in Fig. 8 for one light ray. The angle ϕ of each ray is assumed to be known, as are the camera extrinsic parameters and location of the laser source relative to the global X-Y-Z coordinate system; the camera fixed coordinate system is x-y-z. The specular surface is locally parameterized by the distance D and the angle β relative to the X axis. The angle that the reflected ray makes with the Y axis is given as

$$\theta = \phi - 2\beta \tag{3}$$

In our system model, all rays are traced exactly until they strike the surface at point (X_s, Y_s). The paraxial approximation is then employed to trace the reflected rays to the main lens of the LF camera (point (X_L, Y_L)). If the camera is angled, then the location and angle at which the ray hits the lens are converted to local camera coordinates,

$$x = (X_L - X_C)\cos\gamma - (Y_L - Y_C)\sin\gamma \tag{4}$$
$$\theta_L = \theta - \gamma \tag{5}$$

where (X_C, Y_C) are the coordinates of the camera center. The angle of the ray inside the camera is computed as

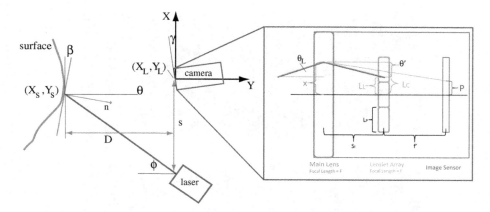

Fig. 8. Schematic of the LF imaging arrangement used to resolve local GLI location and orientation.

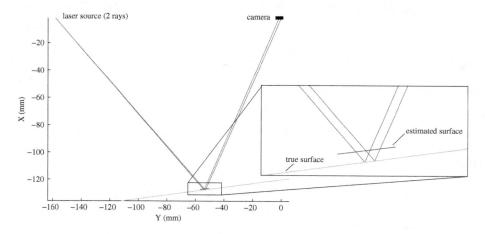

Fig. 9. Simulation showing the ability of the LF camera-projector system to accurately define local surface orientation and location.

$$\theta' = \theta_L - x/F \tag{6}$$

Combined with the distance s_l, this angle determines which lenslet the ray hits. It is then assumed that the lenlsets are focused at infinity and the main lens is at infinity, so the chief ray is traced through the lenlset to determine the pixels the ray strikes, as shown in Fig. 8. In our system, we assume that the image formed on each pixel can be paired with the angle of the light ray that formed it.

When the pixel-lenlset association is known, the angle of the light ray is uniquely defined (with some resolution set by the LF camera). Using Eqs. 3–6, this ray can then be traced backwards through the lenslet, main lens and free-space and the intersection with the source ray can be found. This intersection point fixes the location of the surface and the constraints on angles fixes the orientation of the surface. A Matlab simulation demonstrates the ability of the LF camera-projector system to accurately define local surface orientation and location using this approach. Figure 9 shows two rays hitting an angled specular surface; the estimated surface is the average of the location and orientation found from backward tracing of these two rays; the accuracy on location is < 2 mm and the accuracy on angle is < 1 degree.

5 Conclusions

Advances in light field imaging for fluid flow measurements have been presented. Robust reconstruction of volumes formed through synthetic aperture imaging was demonstrated using a 3D deconvolution technique. Some aspects of light field imaging were then explored for measurements in flames, including visual hull shape reconstruction as well as the error introduced into 2D and 3D PIV due to refractive index gradients. Finally, we developed a framework for resolving specular gas-liquid interface location and orientation using a light field camera-projector system.

Acknowledgments. The authors gratefully acknowledge funding from the Office of Naval Research under task number N0001413WX20545 monitored by program officer Dr. Ronald Joslin (ONR Code 331).

References

1. Levoy, M.: Light fields and computational imaging. IEEE Comput. **39**(8), 46–55 (2006)
2. Scarano, F.: Tomographic piv: principles and practice. Meas. Sci. Technol. **24**(1), 012001 (2013)
3. Elsinga, G.E., Scarano, F., Wieneke, B., van Oudheusden, B.W.: Tomographic particle image velocimetry. Exp. Fluids **41**(6), 933–947 (2006)
4. Belden, J., Truscott, T.T., Axiak, M., Techet, A.H.: Three-dimensional synthetic aperture particle image velocimetry. Meas. Sci. Technol. **21**(12), 125403 (2010)
5. Pereira, F., Gharib, M., Dabiri, D., Modarress, D.: Defocusing digital particle image velocimetry: a 3-component 3-dimensional dpiv measurement technique. application to bubbly flows. Exp. Fluids **29**(1), S078–S084 (2000)
6. Lynch, K., Fahringer, T., Thurow, B.: Three-dimensional particle image velocimetry using a plenoptic camera. In: American Institute of Aeronautics and Astronautics, Reston, VA, Conference Proceedings published by Curran Associates Inc Red Hook, New York, NY pp. 9–12. January 2012
7. Wilburn, B., Joshi, N., Vaish, V., Talvala, E.V., Antunez, E., Barth, A., Adams, A., Horowitz, M., Levoy, M.: High performance imaging using large camera arrays. ACM Trans. Graph. (TOG) **24**, 765–776 (2005)
8. Vaish, V., Garg, G., Talvala, E., Antunez, E., Wilburn, B.,. Horowitz, M., Levoy, M.: Synthetic aperture focusing using a shear-warp factorization of the viewing transform. In: IEEE Computer Society Conference on Computer Vision and Pattern Recognition-Workshops, 2005. CVPR Workshops, pp. 129–129. IEEE (2005)

9. Jesse, B., Sai, R., Truscott, T.T., Techet, A.H.: Three-dimensional bubble field resolution using synthetic aperture imaging: application to a plunging jet. Exp. Fluids **53**(3), 839–861 (2012)
10. Sibarita, J.B.: Deconvolution microscopy. In: Rietdorf, J. (ed.) Microscopy Techniques, Advances in Biochemical Engineering/Biotechnology, vol. 95, pp. 1288–1291. Springer, Heidelberg (2005). doi:10.1007/b102215
11. Levoy, M., Ng, R., Adams, A., Footer, M., Horowitz, M.: Light field microscopy. ACM Trans. Graph. (TOG) **25**(3), 924–934 (2006)
12. Adhikari, D., Longmire, E.K.: Visual hull method for tomographic piv measurement of flow around moving objects. Exp. Fluids **53**(4), 943–964 (2012)
13. Shimura, M., Ueda, T., Choi, G.-M., Tanahashi, M., Miyauchi, T.: Simultaneous dual-plane CH PLIF, single-plane OH PLIF and dual-plane stereoscopic PIV measurements in methane-air turbulent premixed flames. Proc. Combust. Inst. **33**(1), 775–782 (2011)
14. Boxx, I., Sthr, M., Carter, C., Meier, W.: Sustained multi-khz flamefront and 3-component velocity-field measurements for the study of turbulent flames. Appl. Phys. B **95**(1), 23–29 (2009)
15. Filatyev, S., Thariyan, M., Lucht, R., Gore, J.: Simultaneous stereo particle image velocimetry and double-pulsed planar laser-induced fluorescence of turbulent premixed flames. Combust. Flame **150**(3), 201–209 (2007)
16. Tanahashi, M., Murakami, S., Choi, G.-M., Fukuchi, Y., Miyauchi, T.: Simultaneous CH-OH PLIF and stereoscopic PIV measurements of turbulent premixed flames. Proc. Combust. Inst. **30**(1), 1665–1672 (2005)
17. Treibitz, T., Schechner, Y.Y., Kunz, C., Singh, H.: Flat refractive geometry. IEEE Trans. Pattern Anal. Mach. Intell. **34**(1), 51–65 (2012)
18. Belden, J.: Calibration of multi-camera systems with refractive interfaces. Exp. Fluids **54**(2), 1–18 (2013). doi:10.1007/s00348-013-1463-0
19. Atcheson, B., Ihrke, I., Heidrich, W., Tevs, A., Bradley, D., Magnor, M., Seidel, H.P.: Time-resolved 3D capture of non-stationary gas flows. ACM Trans. Graph. (Proc. SIGGRAPH Asia) **27**(5), 132 (2009)
20. Lanman, D., Taubin, G.: Build your own 3d scanner: 3d photography for beginners. In: ACM SIGGRAPH 2009 Courses, p. 8. ACM (2009)
21. Bonfort, T., Sturm, P.: Voxel carving for specular surfaces. In: Proceedings of the Ninth IEEE International Conference on Computer Vision 2003, pp. 591–596. IEEE, (2003)
22. Ding, Y., Li, F., Ji, Y., Yu, J.: Dynamic fluid surface acquisition using a camera array. In: IEEE International Conference on Computer Vision (ICCV) 2011, pp. 2478–2485. IEEE (2011)
23. Bonfort, T., Sturm, P., Gargallo, P.: General Specular Surface Triangulation. In: Narayanan, P.J., Nayar, S.K., Shum, H.-Y. (eds.) ACCV 2006. LNCS, vol. 3852, pp. 872–881. Springer, Heidelberg (2006)
24. Savarese, S., Chen, M., Perona, P.: Local shape from mirror reflections. Int. J. Comput. Vis. **64**(1), 31–67 (2005)
25. Ding, Y., Yu, J., Sturm, P.: Recovering specular surfaces using curved line images. In: IEEE Conference on Computer Vision and Pattern Recognition CVPR 2009, pp. 2326–2333. IEEE (2009)

Environmental Applications

Multiscale Method for Hazard Map Construction

E. Ramona Stefanescu[1], Abani Patra[1]([✉]), E. Bruce Pitman[2], Marcus Bursik[3],
Puneet Singla[1], and Tarunraj Singh[1]

[1] Department of Mechanical and Aerospace Engineering, University at Buffalo,
Buffalo, NY, USA
abani@buffalo.edu
[2] Department of Mathematics, University at Buffalo, Buffalo, NY, USA
[3] Department of Geology, University at Buffalo, Buffalo, NY, USA

Abstract. This work describes a multiscale approach for creating a fast
surrogate of physics based simulators, to improve the speed of applications that require large ensembles like hazard map creation. The novel
framework is applied in determining the probability of the presence airborne ash at a specific height when an explosive volcanic eruption occurs.
The procedure involves representing both the *parameter space* (sample
points at which the numerical model is evaluated) and *physical space*
(ash concentration at a certain height covered well delimited parcel) by
a weighted graph. The combination of graph representation and low rank
approximation gives a good approximation of the original graph (allows
us to identify a well-conditioned basis of the adjacency matrix for its
numerical range) that is less computationally intensive and more accurate when out-of-sample extension is performed at re-sample points as
higher resolution parcels.

Keywords: Hazard map · Multiscale sampling · Low-rank approximation · Out-of-sample extension

1 Introduction

Perhaps the most fundamental product created to characterize the potential for
destruction of a volcano is the hazards map. Often a reasonable hazards map can
be made when the distribution of ash clouds are well-exposed, and easily dated
and mapped. Volcano observatories and volcanic ash advisory centers (VAACs)
predict the likely position of ash clouds generated by explosive volcanic eruptions
using deterministic mathematical models of advection and dispersion, known as
volcanic ash transport and dispersal (VATD) models [1]. These models require
input data on volcanic source conditions as well as the wind field [2]. Probabilistic hazard maps may be generated from using large ensembles of simulations.
However, this strategy fails when simulations are expensive and running of large
ensembles is computationally infeasible especially in a dynamic data environment. In this case, it is common to create "cheap to evaluate" surrogate models

© Springer International Publishing Switzerland 2015
S. Ravela and A. Sandu (Eds.): DyDESS 2014, LNCS 8964, pp. 41–53, 2015.
DOI: 10.1007/978-3-319-25138-7_5

often termed emulators (e.g. Gaussian Process regressions) in the statistics literature. Critical issues then are the cost-efficient creation of these emulators and the fidelity with which they represent the outputs of the underlying simulators.

In this work, we introduce a multiscale scheme for emulator construction. The proposed scheme overcomes a primary limitation of the parameter selection in the Bayesian approaches to emulator construction, which always involve repeated inversion of "correlation matrix", R. The requirement of repeated matrix inversion restricts emulators to small amounts of data mostly because for "large" N, R is also usually poorly conditioned and cost of inverting R using $\mathcal{O}(N^3)$ operations is unaffordable. Geospatial systems like the propagation of volcanic ash require coverage of vast areas in space and several days in time. Model and parametric uncertainty thus lead to a very large system. For ensembles of sufficient size needed to characterize the uncertainty we must deal with large amount of data in the physical space multiplied by the large number of sample points in the parameter space (size of which depends on the sampling techniques that are used). Therefore, a combination of subsampling and out-of-sample extension techniques performed in both spaces (parameter and physical) provides a more suitable representation of the analyzed data at a low computational cost and allows us to form computationally affordable ensembles. The idea of using random projections goes back to the Johnson-Lindenstrauss Lemma [3], which work was continued by [4] who first derived the bound introducing the idea of oversampling beyond the desired rank. Optimally, such a representation would not be affected by the availability of the data or by a sampling method but only rely on the behavior of the observed data and analysis.

Our scheme is based on mutual distances between data points and on a continuous extension of Gaussian functions. It uses a coarse-to-fine hierarchy of the multi-resolution decomposition of a Gaussian kernel. It generates a sequence of approximations at the given function on the data, as well as their extensions to any newly-arrived data point. The subsampling is done by interpolative decomposition of the associated Gaussian kernel matrix in each scale in the hierarchical procedure. In this way a well-conditioned basis is identified and used in the extension/extrapolation process. Use of this strategy for sampling will lead to an accurate and computationally efficient method to create probabilistic hazard maps for ash plume motion, which quantifies the uncertainties present in any model of ash advection and dispersion. Providing such a map will enable public safety officials to make better decisions.

2   The Numerical Model and Hazard Maps

For the purpose of this paper, we will assume that a suitable physical model of geophysical mass transport is the PUFF [5] model of volcanic ash transport. Given an initial ash-laden volume, the PUFF Lagrangian model can be used to populate the volume and then propagate ash parcels in the wind fields. PUFF tracks a finite number of Lagrangian point particles of different sizes, whose location r is propagated from timestep k to timestep $k+1$ via an advection/diffusion equation

$$r_i(t_{k+1}) = r_i(t_k) + W(t_k)\Delta t + Z(t_k)\Delta t + S_i(t_k)\Delta t \qquad (1)$$

Here $r_i(t_k)$ is the position vector of the ith particle at time $k\Delta t$, $W(t_k)$ is the local wind velocity at the location of the ith particle, $Z(t_k)$ is a turbulent diffusion that is modeled as a random walk, and $S_i(t_k)$ is a source term that models the fallout of the ith particle due to gravity. Note therefore that PUFF takes into account dry particle fallout, as well as dispersion and advection.

In developing a complete probabilistic forecast for the ash concentration at a given time and location, we will investigate the effects of aleatoric uncertainty associated with volcanic eruption source parameters. VATD models require input data on volcanic source conditions such as vent radius or vent velocity. The inputs are usually not well constrained, and estimates of the uncertainty in the inputs are needed. Based on our knowledge of the conditions of the source, observations and known constraints, probability distributions are assigned to the eruption source parameters (based on samples of past eruptions which have been collected from the historical record), which are later sampled using both Monte-Carlo and non-Monte Carlo techniques. Note, that as shown in [6] we can solve an inverse problem to refine these assumed distributions. In this contribution, simulation ensembles with different input volcanic source parameters are chosen to predict the average of the output correctly for all the hazard map generation methods as described below. A hazard map is a predictive map for a region which provides a probabilistic measure of a hazard (e.g. ash cloud reaching certain concentration or height that can be considered hazardous/critical). There are numerous ways to create a volcanic hazard map based on ash transport and dispersion modeling. Several approximate techniques are commonly used to approximate the state pdf evolution [7], the most popular being Monte Carlo (MC) methods [8], Gaussian closure [9], and Stochastic Averaging [10,11]. In addition, a Gaussian Process approach to solve nonlinear stochastic differential equations has been proposed in [12]. All of these algorithms except MC methods are similar in several respects, and are suitable only for linear or moderately nonlinear systems, because the effect of higher order terms can lead to significant errors. Simple uncertainty quantification using a Monte Carlo approach for generating such hazard maps will require at least $\mathcal{O}(10^3 - 10^6)$ such simulations. The computational difficulties include managing and accessing select entities from the large data and of processing it using compute intensive operations.

Assessing uncertainty of the spatial phenomenon requires the analysis of the parameters which must be processed by the VATD model. To capture the possibility of a wide range of uncertainty in numerical model response, a large set of geostatistical model realizations needs to be processed. Stochastic spatial simulation can rapidly provide multiple, equally probable realizations [13]. In general, the numerical model is applied to each realization and thereby obtain its repose (e.g., ash height, ash concentration etc.), which may be a single-valued or consist of a time-varying response. If many realizations are processed through the same numerical model, a probability distribution of the response can be constructed and serve as a model of uncertainty.

3   Multiscale Hazard Map

Any simulator/numerical model will naturally require values for input parameters. If the input values for a future event of interest were known exactly, then a hazard map could be generated from a single simulation evaluated at those inputs. Since we lack perfect knowledge of the future, it is necessary to examine flow behavior over a range of inputs. While there are some sampling methods, such as the ones described above, there are far too expensive (resulting in a large number of samples) or to complex to use to create a feasible hazard map. The solution we came up to this problem can be summarized as:

- Running a *relatively* small number of simulations (a few hundred to a few thousand) followed by
- Representing both the sample points and ash concentration at a certain height over a specified parcel as a weighted graph
- Identifying representative points in both parameter and physical space by performing a multiscale sampling (using a randomized projection to obtain a low-rank approximation of the weighted graph adjacency matrix)
- Performing out-of-sample extension at a *relatively* larger number of resample points (a few hundred to a few thousand) in the parameter space which acts as a fast surrogate for the expensive simulator
- Creating *realizations* (interpolation in the physical space) are created at the same or finer resolution
- Generating the hazard map from the fast surrogate.

Although this paper employs the PUFF model, any other numerical model can be used with the appropriately adapted graph representation. The output of the model provides us information of the ash cloud, such as absolute airborne concentration, absolute fallout concentration etc. at every 6 h forecast and every 2000 m pressure levels. In this study we apply our framework for the Eyjafjallajökull eruption from 14–18 April, 2010, being interested in generating a hazard map which will provide information regarding the probability of having ash (absolute airborne concentration > 0) on April 16 12 UTC (36 h forecast) at 2000 m. The framework introduced here provides an approach for developing maps for many hazard scenarios, at a low computational cost. Due to space limitations we review the methods here and refer the interested reader to the dissertation of [14] for details.

3.1   Background

Our methods build on the development of randomized algorithms for numerical linear algebra [15], that provide powerful tools for constructing approximate matrix factorization [16]. The goal is to change the representation of data sets, originally in a form involving a large number of data points (both in the parameter space and physical space), into a low-dimensional description using only a small number data points [17]. The new representation should describe the data in a faithful manner, preserving some quantities of interest such as local mutual distances. These techniques are simple and effective.

We are interested in finding a well-conditioned basis of the given matrix A arising from a graph (at different scales), by applying of a low rank approximation method. We are not interested in the best approximation of specified rank, which is given by the truncated SVD, but rather an approximation that has comparable memory requirements, is efficient to compute and that preserves important structure of the matrix. Most of the graph representing matrices (e.g., kernel matrices and Laplacian matrices) are symmetric positive semi-definite (SPSD) matrices. One common column-sampling-based approach to low-rank approximation of SPSD matrices is the Nyström method. The simplest Nyström-based procedure selects columns from the original data set uniformly at random and then uses those columns to construct a low-rank SPSD approximation [18].

3.2 Multiscale Sampling

We represent both the *parameter space* (sample points at which the numerical model is evaluated) and *physical space* (ash concentration covering a parcel) by a weighted graph $G = (V, E)$ characterized by a set of vertices $V = \{1, \ldots, n\}$ and a set of edges $E = \{e_{ij} | i, j \in V\}$. The n observations (vertices) are considered to be the sample points or the ash concentration at a given location. Let $A = [a_{ij}]$ be the $n \times n$ adjacency matrix, such that $a_{ij} = f(x_i, x_j)$ When the covariance of the data points is unknown, an artificial function has to be chose [19]. A Gaussian covariance is a popular choice in defining the weights of the edges:

$$f(x_i, x_j) = f_\epsilon(x_i, x_j) = exp(-\|x_i - x_j\|^2/\epsilon) \tag{2}$$

where $\| \ldots \|$ constitutes a metric on the space (Euclidean distance in our case). The corresponding covariance (affinities) is

$$(A_\epsilon) = f_\epsilon(x_i, x_j), \; i, j = 1, 2, \ldots, n. \tag{3}$$

The matrix A_ϵ is called the Gaussian kernel over the dataset n. One can think of a kernel function as an implicit map to a higher dimensional space in order to perform certain operations there without paying a high price computationally. It was proven by [20] that using a kernel, the data is now linearly separable in the high-dimensional space, and one can randomly project back down to lower dimensions and preserve this separability. he largest or a few dominant clusters, thus filtering out smaller ones completely.

The combination of graph representation and low rank approximation can give a better approximation of the original graph. A standard low rank computation is likely to only extract information from the largest or a few dominant clusters. [21] used a multiscale approach where a sequence of Gaussian kernel matrices $A_s, s = 0, 1, \ldots,$ have entries defined as:

$$f_\epsilon(x_i, x_j) = \exp(-\|x_i - x_j\|^2/\epsilon_s). \tag{4}$$

ϵ_s is a positive monotonic decreasing function of s, which tends to zero as the scale parameter s tends to infinity (i.e. $\epsilon_s = 2^{-s}$, $s = 0, 1, \ldots$). The kernel approach, used for dimensionality reduction, has been applied with success by [21] for the out-of-sample extension tasks. Kernel methods work under the assumption that the used kernel has a small set of significant eigenvalues that should be considered for the analysis, and the rest are negligible in the sense that they are numerically zero. The above methodology has been also explored in the literature under the Gaussian Process Regression [22–25]. Its main limitation is that memory requirements and computational demands grow as the square and cube respectively, of the number of data points n, effectively limiting a direct implementation to problems with at most a few thousand cases [26–29]. Another concern is declining accuracy of the estimates as the dimension increases, as matrix inversion becomes more unstable with the propagation of errors due to finite machine precision [30, 31]. This problem is more acute if the covariance matrix is nearly rank deficient, which is often the case when the function to be evaluated is considered at nearby points. The above problems necessitate approximation techniques. These schemes rapidly extract information from large datasets often make use of low-rank decompositions of large, sparse data structures such as matrices or tensors. These decompositions usually involve the computation of eigenvectors or singular vectors and fast, scalable approximation to such vectors is important for the underlying scheme to be practical. The benefits of these algorithms is their simple implementation, applicability on large scale problems, and existence of theoretical bounds for the approximation errors [17].

3.3   Stochastic Algorithms for Low Rank Matrix Approximation

In this contribution the relationship between between data points (in the parameter space and physical space) is represented using graphs. Weighted graphs are usually employed to represent a notion of geometry based on the local similarity or interactions between data points. In many situations, each data sample is represented by a collection of numerical attributes, and in this case, the condition for two nodes to be connected is based on the proximity of the corresponding data point in the feature space. Assembling data points according to local similarities

---

Algorithm 1. Random projection algorithm for low-rank approximation

---

Data: $n \times n$ matrix A, the target low-rank k and number of samples
$\quad\quad s = k + p$
Output: $\tilde{A} \in \mathbb{R}^{n \times n}$ which approximately minimizes
$\quad\quad \min_{rank(A') \leq k} \|A - A'\|_F^2$
1. Draw a random test matrix $\Omega_{n \times s}$.
2. Form the product $Y_{n \times s} = A\Omega$
3. Compute an orthonormal basis $Q_{n \times k}$ for the range of Y
4. Return $\tilde{A} = QQ^T A$

---

to obtain reliable scale-dependent global properties, which arise from local similarities implies using algorithms for finding salient, coherent regions that display similar features. An important tool for analysis and interpretation of the data is the low rank approximation of the adjacency matrices or graph Laplacian related to the graphs at hand.

The idea of using random projections to construct approximations of large matrices goes back to Johnson-Lindenstrauss Lemma [3], which work was continued by [4] who first derived the bound introducing the idea of oversampling beyond the desired rank to improve the bounds considerably. This method also arises out of the success of random projection techniques in compressed sensing [32,33]. Most of this literature focuses on the ability to reconstruct a signal from compressive measurements, with theoretical guarantees provided on the accuracy of a point estimate under sparsity assumptions. In contrast, our goal is to accurately approximate the unknown function in a fundamentally different setting. The benefits of using randomized projection algorithms for computing low rank matrix approximations is their simple implementation, applicability on large scale problems, and existence of theoretical bounds for the approximation errors. The randomized algorithm proposed by [16], uses randomness to construct a matrix Y that approximates the dominant subspace of the range of a given matrix A. The error bounds of Algorithm 1 are well defined in [16].

3.4   Out-of-Sample Extension

Let $D = x_1, \ldots, x_n \in \mathbb{R}^d$ be the dataset, where d is the size of the space and let g to be a function that needs to be evaluated at a new data point $x_* \in \mathbb{R} \backslash D$. D can be data points in parameter space or physical space, and $g = [g_1, \ldots, g_n]^T$ can be the ash concentration or ash height. We need need to calculate an extension g_* to x_*. By the application of a randomized projection to A_s, a well-conditioned basis is identified for it numerical range. At each scale g is decomposed into a sum of its projections on this basis and it is extended as $g_*^{(s)}$ (see Algorithm 2). In addition, selection of the proper columns in A_s is equivalent to data sampling of the associated data points. $\tilde{A}^{(s)}$ represents a low rank approximation of A_ϵ is at a scale s.

Algorithm 2. Out-of-sample extension

Data: The sampled data $D_s = \{x_1, \ldots, x_k\}$, $\tilde{A}^{(s)}$, a new data point $x_* \in \mathcal{R}^d$, a function $g = [g_1, \ldots, g_n]^T$ to be extended

Output: $g_*^{(s)}$

1 Calculate the pseudo-inverse $(\tilde{A}^{(s)})^\dagger$ of $\tilde{A}^{(s)}$.;

2 Calculate the coordinates vector of the orthogonal projection of $f^{(s)}$ on the range of $\tilde{A}^{(s)}$ in the basis of $\tilde{A}^{(s)}$'s columns $c = (\tilde{A}^{(s)})^\dagger f$;

3 Calculate the orthogonal projection of g on the columns of $\tilde{A}^{(s)}$, $g^{(s)} = \tilde{A}^{(s)} c$;

4 Form the matrix $A_*^{(s)} = [f_\epsilon(x_*, x_{s_1}) \ldots f_\epsilon(x_*, x_{s_k})]$;

5 Calculate the extension $g_*^{(s)} = A_* c$;

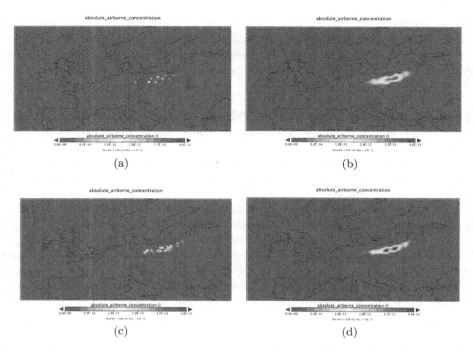

Fig. 1. Representative points of absolute airborne concentration (mg/m^3) out of 274 data points in the *physical space* at April 16 1200 UTC level 2000 m. The adjacency matrix of physical space graph was defined using $\epsilon_s = 2^{(-s)}$ a) For $s = 1$ there are 55 representative points b) Interpolation $RMSE = 0.027$ c) For $s = 1$ there are 109 representative points d) Interpolation $RMSE = 0.013$

For the random sampling algorithm, one critical question is what importance sampling distribution should be used to construct the sample. For the random projection algorithms, one must decide how to implement the random projections. Due consideration must be given to important issues of data sparsity, the decay of the eigenvalues, and the nonuniformity properties of eigenvectors. Nevertheless, the method requires no grid. It automatically generates a sequence of adaptive grids according to the data distribution. It is based on the mutual distances between the data points and on a continuous extension of Gaussian functions. In addition, most of the costly computations are done just once during the process, independently of the number of the extended data points since they depend only in the data and on the given function.

4   Results

Our goal is to produce a map showing the probability of *absolute airborne concentration* $(mg/m^3) > 0$ on April 16 1200 UTC, at 2000 m at each location in the parcel, from a collection of simulator runs whose parameters are drawn from

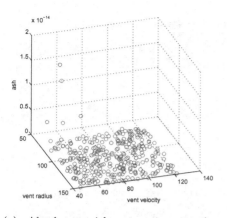
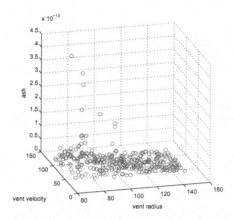

(a) Absolute airborne concentration (mg/m^3) at location (12, 55) lat, lon - 200 re-sample points

(b) Absolute airborne concentration (mg/m^3) at location (22, 48) lat, lon - 1000 re-sample points

Fig. 2. Absolute airborne concentration (mg/m^3) at a given location as a function of vent velocity and vent radius. Blue dots are LHS samples and red dots are re-samples data points (Color figure online)

a distribution that represents a volcanologist's best guess of the range of possible scenarios. We consider the study case for Eyjafjallajökull eruption on 14–18 April, 2010, for which ranges of the vent radius and vent velocity are available. For a good match of the ash volume range, the vent radius values were uniformly distributed between 65 and 150 m, while the vent velocity followed the same distribution with values between 45 and 124 m/s [34].

The 2-dimensional input parameter space is sampled using a simple space filling design like Latin Hypercube Sampling (LHS) to obtain 128 sets of input. Simulations are performed at each sample point using the PUFF model to generate a map of absolute airborne concentration, $abs_{air}(\mathbf{x})$ as function of position. In our approach, we first identify in the physical space the representative points (location in the parcel) for which we need to do out-of-sample extension of the absolute airborne concentration. Using the weighted graph approach, we generate an adjacency matrix as defined in where x_i and x_j represent the absolute airborne concentration at location i and j, respectively. By applying Algorithm 2 we identify representative data points at different scales: $s = 0, 1$ and 1.5. Out-of-sample extension will be performed at the same resolution (1°latitude by 1°longitude grid) as the original output. This allows us to evaluate the performance of the out-of-sample extension (interpolation in this case) by calculating the Root Mean Square Error (RMSE) (scaled). Based on the results presented in Fig. 1, we've decided that 55 points out of 274 (corresponding to $s = 1$) to be the chosen data points in the physical space for which we will perform evaluation in the parameter space.

In Fig. 2 is shown the absolute airborne concentration at two different location on the parcel as a function of the two parameters (the red dots are the LHS

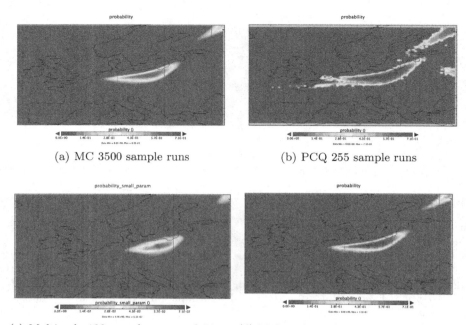

(a) MC 3500 sample runs   (b) PCQ 255 sample runs

(c) Multiscale 128 sample runs and 50 re- (d) Multiscale 128 sample runs and 200 re-
samples   samples

Fig. 3. Probability of having absolute airborne concentration $(mg/m^3) > 0$

sample). It can be observed that the absolute airborne concentration has not
only very small values, but the majority of the LHS sample give an absolute
airborne concentration equal to 0. In many situations these findings would create
a lot of computational challenges in order to obtain an out-of-sample extension
at re-sample points in the parameter space. Using a similar approach as for
the physical space, we define the adjacency matrix whose entries are defined
by: $f_\epsilon(x_i, x_j) = exp(-\|x_i - x_j\|^2/\epsilon_s)$. Here, x_i and $x_j \in [65\ 150] \times [45\ 124]$,
as given by the range of vent radius and vent velocity. This will results in a
39 representative points out of 128 LHS samples which are used in the out-of
sample extension at a larger number of re-sample points (red dots in Fig. 2).

Now for each re-sample point in parameter space we can generate a map
showing absolute airborne concentration and for each grid point find the fraction
of re-sample points with absolute airborne concentration > 0. The probability
map resulted is shown in Fig. 3(c, d). Our scheme is compared to MC when
3500 realizations of the parameter space are used and PCQ with 255 samples in
the parameter space. Both methods are in detailed explained by Dalbey et al.
[35]. Performing a qualitative analysis of the methods used, it can be seen that
our approach gives comparable results with MC and PCQ with much smaller
number of evaluations of both simulator and emulator.

5   Conclusions

We introduce a multiscale scheme to generate efficiently probabilistic hazard maps. Typical usage involves evaluating the fast surrogate at hundreds of thousands or millions of re-sample input points. The number of samples needed to generate the fast surrogate are exponential in the number of dimensions. Also when the output of the model has a predominant value, evaluation at re-sample points also becomes challenging. Our scheme relies on graph-based algorithms. Weighted graphs are employed to represent the "geometry" based on the local similarity or interaction between the data points. Since each of the data sample is represented by a collection of numerical attributes, the condition of two nodes to be connected is based on the proximity of the corresponding data points in the feature space. We also introduced a stochastic algorithm for computing a low rank approximation of the entire adjacency matrix of the graph. By performing a multiscale data sampling we identify a well-conditioned basis of a low rank Gaussian kernel matrix, which is used for out-of-sample extension.

References

1. Langmann, B., Folch, A., Hensch, M., Matthias, V.: Volcanic ash over Europe during the eruption of Eyjafjallajökull on iceland, April–May 2010. Atmos. Environ. 48, pp. 1–8 (2012)
2. Mastin, L., Guffanti, M., Servranckx, R., Webley, P., Barsotti, S., Dean, K., Durant, A., Ewert, J., Neri, A., Rose, W.: A multidisciplinary effort to assign realistic source parameters to models of volcanic ash-cloud transport and dispersion during eruptions. J. Volcanol. Geoth. Res. **186**(1), 10–21 (2009)
3. Dasgupta, S., Gupta, A.: An elementary proof of a theorem of Johnson and Lindenstrauss. Random Struct. Algorithm. **22**(1), 60–65 (2003)
4. Halko, N., Martinsson, P.-G., Tropp, J.A.: Finding structure with randomness: probabilistic algorithms for constructing approximate matrix decompositions. SIAM Rev. **53**(2), 217–288 (2011)
5. Searcy, C., Dean, K., Stringer, B.: PUFF: a high-resolution volcanic ash tracking model. J. Volcanol. Geoth. Res. **80**, 1–16 (1998)
6. Madankan, R., Pouget, S., Singla, P., Bursik, M., Dehn, J., Jones, M., Patra, A., Pavolonis, M., Pitman, E., Singh, T., et al.: Computation of probabilistic hazard maps and source parameter estimation for volcanic ash transport and dispersion. J. Comput. Phys. **271**, 39–59 (2014)
7. Apte, A., Hairer, M., Stuart, A., Voss, J.: Sampling the posterior: an approach to non-Gaussian data simulation. Physica D **230**, 50–64 (2007)
8. Doucet, A., de Freitas, N., Gordon, N.: Sequential Monte-Carlo Methods in Practice. Statistics for Engineering and Information Science. Springer, New York (2001)
9. Iyengar, R.N., Dash, P.K.: Study of the random vibration of nonlinear systems by the Gaussian closure technique. J. Appl. Mech. **45**, 393–399 (1978)
10. Lefebvre, T., Bruyninckx, H., Schutter, J.D.: Kalman filters of non-linear systems: a comparison of performance. Int. J. Control **77**(7), 639–653 (2004)
11. Lefebvre, T., Bruyninckx, H., Schutter, J.D.: Comment on a new method for the nonlinear transformations of means and covariances in filters and estimators. IEEE Trans. Autom. Control **47**(8), 1406–1409 (2002)

12. Archambeau, C., Cornford, D., Opper, M., Shawe-Taylor, J.: Gaussian process approximations of stochastic differential equations. J. Mach. Learn. Res. Workshop Conf. Proc. **1**, 1–16 (2007)
13. Scheidt, C., Caers, J.: Representing spatial uncertainty using distances and kernels. Math. Geosci. **41**(4), 397–419 (2009)
14. Stefanescu, E.: Multilevel-multiscale ensembles for uncertainty quantification with application to geophysical models. Ph.D. thesis, Mechanical and Aerospace Department, University at Buffalo (2014)
15. Hegde, C., Wakin, M., Baraniuk, R.: Random projections for manifold learning. In: Platt, J.C., Kolle, D., Singer, Y., Roweis, S.T. (eds.) Advances in Neural Information Processing Systems, vol. 20, pp. 641–648. MIT Press, Cambridge (2008)
16. Martinsson, P.-G., Rokhlin, V., Tygert, M.: A randomized algorithm for the decomposition of matrices. Appl. Comput. Harmon. Anal. **30**(1), 47–68 (2011)
17. Mahoney, M.: Randomized algorithms for matrices and data. Found. Trends Mach. Learn. **3**(2), 123–224 (2011)
18. Coifman, R., Lafon, S.: Diffusion maps. Appl. Comput. Harmon. Anal. **21**(1), 5–30 (2006)
19. Bermanis, A., Wolf, G., Averbuch, A.: Cover-based bounds on the numerical rank of Gaussian kernels. Appl. Comput. Harmon. Anal. **36**(2), 302–315 (2014)
20. Blum, A.: Random projection, margins, kernels, and feature-selection. In: Saunders, C., Grobelnik, M., Gunn, S., Shawe-Taylor, J. (eds.) SLSFS 2005. LNCS, vol. 3940, pp. 52–68. Springer, Heidelberg (2006)
21. Bermanis, A., Averbuch, A., Coifman, R.: Multiscale data sampling and function extension. Appl. Comput. Harmon. Anal. **34**(1), 15–29 (2013)
22. Williams, C.K.: Prediction with gaussian processes: from linear regression to linear prediction and beyond. In: Jordan, M.I. (ed.) Learning in Graphical Models. NATO ASI Series, pp. 599–621. Springer, Netherlands (1998)
23. Bernardo, J., Berger, J., Dawid, A., Smith, A., et al.: Regression and classification using gaussian process priors. In: Bernardo, J.M., Berger, J.O., Dawid, A.P., Smith, A.F.M. (eds.) Bayesian Statistics 6: Proceedings of the Sixth Valencia International Meeting, vol. 6, p. 475. Oxford University Press, Oxford (1998)
24. Quiñonero-Candela, J., Rasmussen, C.E.: A unifying view of sparse approximate gaussian process regression. J. Mach. Learn. Res. **6**, 1939–1959 (2005)
25. Banerjee, S., Gelfand, A.E., Finley, A.O., Sang, H.: Gaussian predictive process models for large spatial data sets. J. Roy. Stat. Soc.: Ser. B (Stat. Methodol.) **70**(4), 825–848 (2008)
26. Seeger, M., Williams, C., Lawrence, N.: Fast forward selection to speed up sparse gaussian process regression. In: Artificial Intelligence and Statistics 9, no. EPFL-CONF-161318 (2003)
27. Rasmussen, C.E.: Gaussian Processes for Machine Learning. MIT Press, Cambridge (2006)
28. Nguyen-Tuong, D., Seeger, M., Peters, J.: Model learning with local gaussian process regression. Adv. Robot. **23**(15), 2015–2034 (2009)
29. Banerjee, A., Dunson, D.B., Tokdar, S.T.: Efficient gaussian process regression for large datasets. Biometrika, p. ass068 (2012)
30. Lázaro-Gredilla, M., Quiñonero-Candela, J., Rasmussen, C.E., Figueiras-Vidal, A.R.: Sparse spectrum gaussian process regression. J. Mach. Learn. Res. **11**, 1865–1881 (2010)
31. Maillard, O.-A., Munos, R.: Linear regression with random projections. J. Mach. Learn. Res. **13**(1), 2735–2772 (2012)

32. Donoho, D.L.: Compressed sensing. IEEE Trans. Inf. Theor. **52**(4), 1289–1306 (2006)
33. Candès, E.J.: Compressive sampling. In: Proceedings of the International Congress of Mathematicians, Madrid, Invited Lectures, pp. 1433–1452, 22–30 August 2006
34. Bursik, M., Jones, M., Carn, S., Dean, K., Patra, A., Pavolonis, M., Pitman, E., Singh, T., Singla, P., Webley, P.: Estimation and propagation of volcanic source parameter uncertainty in an ash transport and dispersal model: application to the Eyjafjallajokull plume of 14–16 April 2010. Bull. Volcanol. **74**(10), 2321–2338 (2012)
35. Dalbey, K., Patra, A., Pitman, E., Bursik, M., Sheridan, M.: Input uncertainty propagation methods and hazard mapping of geophysical mass flow. J. Geophys. Res. **113**, 5203–5219 (2008). doi:10.1029/2006JB004471

Coupled Dynamic Data-Driven Framework for Forest Fire Spread Prediction

Carlos Brun, Ana Cortés$^{(\boxtimes)}$, and Tomàs Margalef

Computer Architecture and Operating Systems Department,
Universitat Autònoma de Barcelona,
Edifici Q, 08193 Cerdanyola V., Spain
carlos.brun@caos.uab.cat, {ana.cortes,tomas.margalef}@uab.cat
http://caos.uab.es

Abstract. Predicting the potential danger of a forest fire is an essential task of wildfire analysts. For that reason, many scientists have focused their efforts on developing propagation models that predict forest fire evolution to mitigate the consequences of such hazards. These propagation models require a precise knowledge of the whole environment where the fire is taking place. In the context of natural hazards simulation, it is well known that, part of the final forecast error comes from the uncertainty in the input data. In this work, we use a Dynamic Data-driven methodology to overcome such problem. The core of the methodology is a calibration stage previous to the forecast where complementary models, data injection and intelligent systems are working in a symbiotic way to reduce the forecast errors at real time. This approach has been tested using a forest fire that took place in Arkadia (Greece) in 2011.

Keywords: Forest fire · Simulation · Data uncertainty · Dynamic data-driven

1 Introduction

Forest fires involve serious consequences from the environmental, economic and social point of view. For that reason, the scientific community has developed simulation tools with the aim of providing useful information about forest fire spread evolution to the people in charge of managing extinction resources. Most of the existing forest fire spread simulators [1–7] implement the spread kernel equations based on the Rothermel's model [8]. However, it is well known that the forecast fire evolutions provided by existing fire spread simulators do not exactly reproduce the real behaviour of the fire. The reason for such a difference ranges from the input parameters uncertainty to the imprecision of the model itself. In previous works [9–11], it has been stated that a pre-processing of the simulator input parameters based on a steering loop driven by real data acquisition and fire behaviour observation, could lead to enhanced forecast fire evolutions. This prediction scheme is the so call Two-Stage prediction system.

© Springer International Publishing Switzerland 2015
S. Ravela and A. Sandu (Eds.): DyDESS 2014, LNCS 8964, pp. 54–67, 2015.
DOI: 10.1007/978-3-319-25138-7_6

The Two-Stage strategy performs a forest fire prediction by previously executing a Calibration stage, which involves the most sensitive parameters. In this stage, the actual evolution of the forest fire is observed and a Genetic Algorithm (GA) is carried out to determine the set of parameters that best reproduces the recent evolution of the fire. This set of values is then used as input parameters in the Prediction stage. Since forest fires are a dynamic phenomena, which is quite affected by changing data such as meteorological information, the mentioned pre-processing data phase has been designed as a feedback loop where gathered data guides the simulation and, the simulation results at a time, could eventually drive the data collection. This way of work feeds the so called Dynamic Data Driven Application System [12, 13]. A key point in this process is the evaluation of the simulation's quality, because it has a direct impact in both the Calibration stage and in the Prediction stage. The Calibration stage consists of a Genetic Algorithm (GA), which tries to minimize a predetermined fitness function. In the context of forest fire propagation, this fitness function is the difference between the real burnt area and the burnt area obtained by simulation. Eventually, a perfect match should be reflected into the fitness function as a global minimum/maximum value according to its definition. Up to now, the Two-Stage prediction system relies on the symmetric difference between sets as a fitness function (also called error function). This error function has been proven to provide good results when applied to predict forest fire to a maximum of regional size. However, when moving to forest fire classified as "dangerous" at European level, this fitness function was detected to be not enough accurate and, for that reason, an alternative error has been defined. However, not all the information needed by the prediction system could be considered in the calibration process. In particular, those data considered as static information such as elevation maps and fuel data, is typically obtained from public repositories. There is not an unique source of this kind of data and, consequently, the fire behaviour prediction delivered by a given forest fire spread model could vary according to the selected static data sources. Furthermore, gathering dynamic data such as real fire perimeter evolution and meteorological data could be a bottleneck to the system if there is no a clear way to proceed. For that reason, at European level, EFFIS (European Forest Fire Information System) raises as the EU common platform to provide all input data required in a forest fire simulation system (FFSS). Therefore, relying on the EFFIS data, one can design FFSS at European level based on standard basis. However, the resolution of these information is not always at the desired precision, so, it becomes mandatory to include complementary models to the forest fire spread model in order to obtain high resolution data, which takes into account the environment where the hazard is occurring. For that reason, the basic Two-Stage forest fire simulation system was enhanced by coupling two different models, a wind field model (WindNinja [14]), which takes into account the wind speed and wind direction variation due to the underlying topography and, a meteorological model (WRF [15]) to evaluate the time evolution of the meteorological variables. The resulting coupled prediction framework has been tested using a study case retrieved from the EFFIS database. In Sect. 2, the data uncertainty problem related to forest fire spread forecast is introduced. The coupled dynamic data-driven prediction framework (DDD-FFSS) is described in Sect. 3, as well as, the proposed error equation for events at paneuropean level. The described DDD-FFSS is then applied to a forest fire that took place in Arkadia (Greece) in 2011 in Sect. 4. Finally, Sect. 5 summarizes the main conclusions of this work.

2   Data Uncertainty in Forest Fire Simulation

As it has been mentioned, fire behavior models require accurate input data to provide fire spread forecast as reliable as possible. Although the model sensitivity to the input data clearly depends on the nature of each required parameter, the precision and quality of all of them are not dismissible. In general, the data needed to perform the predictions can be divided into two main groups: static and dynamic data. The static input data is the one that keeps constant during the whole prediction interval, and the dynamic data changes during the fire spread simulation. According to this feature (static/dynamic), the way of gathering and processing the information to obtain the corresponding input files is quite different. In the case of static data, the pre-processing and organization of the required layers in the proper format could be done previously to the hazard occurrence. There are certain constraints related to the terrain dimension that should be considered in an accurate way, but the process of homogenize the precision, projection and datum could be done off-line, and have this data characterized and ready to be used when a crisis occurs. If the static data of a region is available before a fire occurrence, the efforts must be focused on those parameters that vary dynamically during the simulation or depend on the fire scenario studied. In this case, it is necessary to collect them in real-time, thanks to the different data sources and services that can provide this information. Obviously, this case is the most critical since we depend on third-parties frequency of data arrival, and data format. Therefore, the conversions and the injection must be done in an on-line mode, while the simulation is being carried out. As we have previously mentioned, at European level, the reliable third-party is EFFIS (European Forest Fire Information System) and, therefore, this is the data source we have used to perform this study. Subsequently, we shall describe how static and dynamic data related to forest fire evolution is considered by EFFIS.

2.1   Topography

This data is obtained by processing Digital Elevation Maps (DEMs). A DEM defines the height of the terrain in every cell of the map. This is a discretization of a continuous surface, taking into account measures in certain points of the terrain. Those maps are obtained from the ASTER (Advanced Spaceborne Thermal Emission and Reflection Radiometer) imaging instrument onboard NASAs Terra satellite that takes high-resolution images of the earth. These images are processed and raster files are extracted with the information needed to perform the fire spread simulations (elevation, aspect and slope). The ASTER map resolution is 30 m.

2.2 Fuel Map

The vegetation map (or fuel map) is a raster file that describes the predominant vegetation in every cell. The fuel model used for fire simulation purposes, is the standard fuel model defined by [14]. This information has been obtained from the fuel type map of Europe developed at the JRC. The classification scheme adopted for the fuel map encompasses 42 fuel types representing the variety of fuel complexes found in European landscapes. A cross-walk to the original set of 13 fire behaviour fuel models tabulated by Anderson fire spread model is done at the JRC [14].

2.3 Meteorological Data

The meteorological data used is the ECMWF (European Centre for Medium-Range Weather Forecasts) operational high-resolution single global deterministic model (ec16), with a horizontal resolution of about 16 km [16]. The model is initiated on both the 00 and 12 UTC analysis reaching to a 24-hour forecast horizon with archived time-step of 3 hour. It is worth mentioning, that this is the configuration used in this work for experimental purposes, but it is not the unique source of meteorological data processed at the JRC.

2.4 Fire Perimeter

A key point in any forest fire simulation system is the capability to feed the system with either a real initial fire perimeters or a precise ignition point. The EFFIS Burnt Area Map module is in charge of this data. To obtain the fire perimeter information, the JRC relies on the MODIS (Moderate Resolution Imaging Spectroradiometer) sensors systems, which are on board both the NASAs Terra and Aqua satellites. Each satellite requires to complete 3 orbits (approximately 3 h) to cover the whole Europe area, so it could be possible to obtain fire perimeters twice a day, one from each satellite. The image resolution provided by the MODIS system is of 250 m.

3 Dynamic Data-Driven Forest Fire Simulation System

As it has been mentioned, the Two-Stage prediction scheme uses the Calibration stage to search for those input parameters setting that, fitted to the underlying simulator, better reproduces the recent observed forest fire spread. The obtained parameter configuration will then be used to fit the simulator in the Prediction stage to forecast the near future evolution of the fire. As a search technique in the Calibration stage, a Genetic Algorithm (GA) is applied, where a random initial population of individuals (input parameter setting) is generated. Each individual is simulated using FARSITE [6] (the underlying forest fire spread simulator) and the resulting forest fire spread is compared to the real observed fire evolution to compute the GA's fitness function (called error in this case).

Then, according to the quality of the prediction, the individuals are ranked and the genetic operators are applied to generate the new population. The process is repeated a certain number of iterations and the best individual at the end of the process is selected to run the prediction at the Prediction stage. Since evaluating the prediction quality is a key point in this scheme, in the following subsection, we shall describe the selected fitness function (error) and, subsequently, we will introduce how the DDD-FFSS has been improved by coupling complementary models.

3.1   Quality Prediction Evaluation

In order to compare the obtained predictions with the real fire behavior, it is necessary to define metrics in order to determine the quality of the simulations what enables the capacity of ranking them. There exist several metrics to compare real and predicted values [17] and each one weights the events involved differently. The event notation used to define those error functions is depicted in Fig. 1.

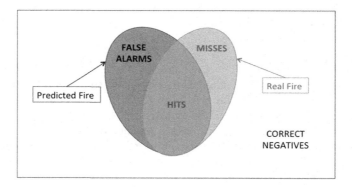

Fig. 1. Events involved in metrics related to forecast verification.

The cells around the map that have not been burnt by neither the real fire nor the predicted map are considered *Correct Negatives* (CN). Those cells that have been burnt in both maps are called *Hits*. The cells that are only present in the real fire and are not burnt by the predicted fire are called *Misses*. Finally, in the opposite case, the cells that the simulator predicts as burnt area but the real fire does not actually reach, are called *False Alarms* (FA). Besides these factors, some equations take into account the real map ($RealCell$), the simulated or predicted map ($SimCell$), the ignition map ($ICell$) or the total number of cells of the terrain ($TotalCell$). This notation may vary but the meaning remains the same.

Up until now, we have been using the *symmetric difference* between maps as error function. The values given by this error function are positive, but not in a closed interval, with the best value being 0 without an upper limit. We use the concept of $UCell$ (all cells belonging to both real fire and simulated fire) and $InterCell$ (cells belonging to both real fire and simulated fire) as factors in the equation. To better understand and to simplify the equations, the initial fire is considered a point and, therefore, it can be removed from the original equations what simplifies the translation of Eq. 1 to the notation previously described.

$$
\begin{aligned}
Error &= \frac{(UCell - ICell) - (InterCell - ICell)}{RealCell - ICell} = \\
&= \frac{(Hits + Misses + FA) - (Hits)}{RealCell} = \\
&= \frac{Misses + FA}{RealCell}
\end{aligned} \tag{1}
$$

In fact, both real and simulated maps can also be transformed as a combination of $Hits$, $Misses$, and FA events as is shown in Eq. 2

$$
\begin{aligned}
RealCell &= Hits + Misses \\
SimCell &= Hits + FA
\end{aligned} \tag{2}
$$

Equation 1 equally penalizes the $misses$ and the $false\ alarms$. Another metric that was used to rank individuals was the $Critical\ Source\ Index$ (CSI), which gives us the rate of $hits$ achieved from 0 to 1, with 1 being the perfect match between maps. It also weight $misses$ and $false\ alarms$ in the same way.

$$
Error = \frac{InterCell}{UCell} = \frac{Hits}{Hits + Misses + FA} \tag{3}
$$

The fact of equally penalizing both factors is not suitable in our field because it is much more important to minimize the $misses$ than to reduce the $false\ alarms$. The consequences of $misses$ can cause severe damage, both to the environment and in human lives, while the $false\ positives$ may represent an extra effort in fire-fighting resources.

The main problem of these metrics when applied to the Two-Stage methodology is concentrated into the Calibration stage. In this part of the methodology, we evaluate several scenarios, then we rank them using the error function, and finally, we select the best parameter set to perform the prediction. We have detected that when dealing with large forest fires at paneuroepan level, the individuals with less spread, tend to provide the best error values. Analyzing the shape of the other individuals, we observe that potential good predictions were discarded from the calibration process due to the high penalty generated by the $false\ alarms$. In order to solve this undesired effect, we changed Eq. 1 in order to minimize the effect of $false\ alarms$. The new error function is shown in Eq. 4.

$$
\begin{aligned}
Error &= \frac{\frac{(UCell-ICell)-(InterCell-ICell)}{RealCell-ICell} + \frac{(UCell-ICell)-(InterCell-ICell)}{SimCell-ICell}}{2} = \\
&= \frac{\frac{Misses+FA}{Real} + \frac{Misses+FA}{Sim}}{2}
\end{aligned} \tag{4}
$$

The latest equation has shown better behavior in the Calibration stage than the other metrics. In those cases where the difference between the predicted burnt area and the real burnt are is the same in terms of magnitude but opposite according to the event related (*misses* or *false alarms*), the individuals that provide overestimated predictions have a better error than those individuals that underestimated the fire evolution. Therefore, the new error function was incorporated to the Dynamic Data-Driven Forest Fire Simulation System (DDD-FFSS) describe below.

3.2   Coupling Models to the DDD-FFSS

As it was previously introduced, we rely on DDD-FFSS to perform forest fire spread predictions. This system encapsulates the Two-Stage prediction scheme with the possibility of coupling/uncoupling complementary models to better consider available environmental conditions (wind, humidity,...). The basic scheme of the Two-Stage approach is depicted in Fig. 2 (2ST-BASIC). It is well known that one of the parameters that most affect fores fire propagation is the wind, for that reason, the efforts has initially been concentrated on this parameter. The complementary models included in DDD-FFSS are: a wind field model to consider the effect of the terrain on wind speed and wind direction and, a meteorological model whose output has been post-processed to deliver a meteorological wind speed and wind direction at the pinpointed centroid of the fire. Since the objective of this work is to test the DDD-FFSS approach at European level, it is unrealistic to consider that the data injected in the Calibration stage will only come from meteorological stations. In fact, the data fitted into the steering loop is provided by a metereological model but it also can be improved with real data obtained from meteorological stations and sensors. This information can be directly fitted into the Calibration stage of the forest fire spread prediction system. However, during the prediction stage such values are not available beforehand. So, it is necessary to introduce a meteorological model that can provide the expected values for the meteorological wind speed and wind direction used at the prediction stage (see Fig. 3, 2ST-MM). The last enhancement included in the system was to consider the influence of the topography on the wind components as it is shown in Fig. 4 (2ST-MM-WF). In this case, the information related to wind speed and wind direction used at the Calibration stage is introduced to the wind field model before running all forest fire spread simulations. In the Prediction stage, the meteorological data is provided by a certain meteorological model and then introduced to the wind field model to provide the corresponding wind field.

These prediction schemes have been tested at European level using fire cases from the EFFIS repository. In the following section, we show the results obtained in terms of quality improvement for a particular study case.

4   Experimental Study

The Mediterranean area is one of the European regions most affected for forest fires during high risk seasons. As we have previously mentioned, we rely on

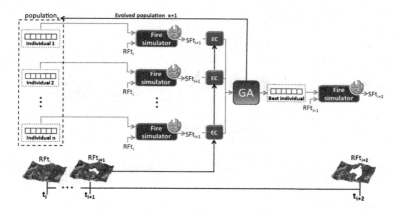

Fig. 2. 2ST-BASIC prediction scheme

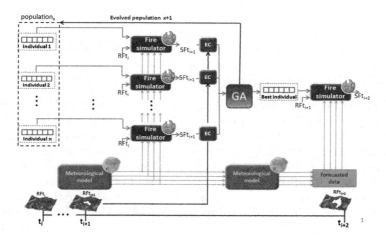

Fig. 3. 2ST-MM prediction scheme

EFFIS and JRC (Joint Research Centre) data sources to fit the dynamic data-driven prediction system described in the previous section. Therefore, we have selected as study case one event stored in the database of EFFIS. In particular, we have retrieved the information of a past fire that took place in Greece during the summer season of 2011 in the region of Arkadia, one of the seven prefectures of the Peloponnese peninsula in Greece. The forest fire began on the 26th of August and the total burnt area was 1,761 ha. The experimental results shown in this section were obtained using a computing platform, which consists of two PowerEdge C6145 nodes, each one including 4 AMD OpteronTM6376 with 16 cores each (128 cores).

In Fig. 5(a), the images provided by the MODIS system are shown for three different time instants:

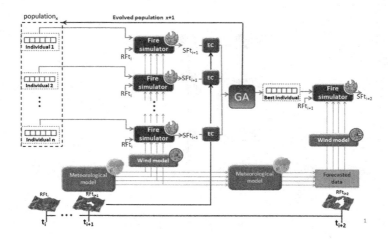

Fig. 4. 2ST-MM-WF prediction scheme

- t_0: August 26th at 09:43am obtained from the Terra satellite.
- t_1: August 26th at 11:27am obtained from the Aqua satellite.
- t_2: August 27th at 08:49am obtained from the Terra satellite.

The corresponding burnt areas (shapes) once the images have been processed, are shown in Fig. 5(b). These shapes are the information available at EFFIS. From these shapes, we obtain the real fire perimeters as are shown in Fig. 6.

In order to simplify the initial tests, the forecast meteorological data used for the simulations are the wind components (wind speed and wind direction), dew point and temperature of the pinpointing centroid of the observed fire. These meteorological data is provided with an frequency of 3 h, for that reason, the injection time step within the forest fire spread simulator has been set to 3 h. The prediction time horizons have been set according to the exact time the MODIS images have been obtained to be as fair as possible to the reality. In order to compare the prediction results in terms of quality when applying the DDD-FFSS coupling different complementary models, the system has been set to the three following configurations: 2ST-BASIC, 2ST-MM and 2ST-MM-WF. Keeping in mind that any configuration of the DDD-FFSS always implies the execution of the Calibration stage and then, the execution of the Prediction stage, it is necessary to describe how both stages use the available data perimeters. For calibration purposes, we used as initial perimeter *perimeter*1 from Fig. 6 and, as a reference perimeter, *perimeter*2 from Fig. 6. So, the simulations involved in the Calibration stage have been set to a time horizon around 2 h. In the case of the Prediction stage, the perimeter to be predicted is *perimeter*3 from Fig. 6 and, the initial perimeter is *perimeter*2. Therefore, the time horizon for the simulation at this stage has been set to 22 h. All these data inputs have been harmonized to fit a simulation grid map with a basic cell of $100\,\text{m} \times 100\,\text{m}$ square.

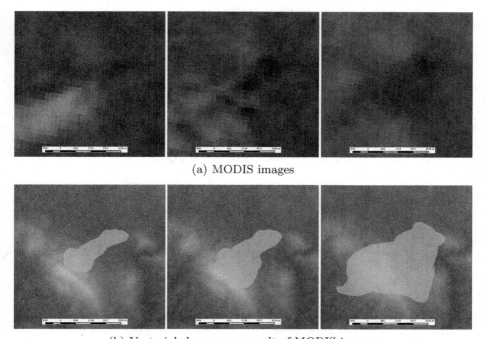

(a) MODIS images

(b) Vectorial shapes as a result of MODIS images

Fig. 5. MODIS images and their corresponding extracting shapes

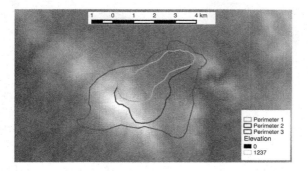

Fig. 6. Fire perimeters corresponding to Arkadia fire

The obtained results are shown in Fig. 7. As it can be observed, the 2ST-BASIC configuration is the one that provides the best error at the Calibration stage. Despite seeming this result contradictory to the claim of coupling models to obtain enhanced predictions, it is necessary to highlight that the prediction error in this case is the worst. To understand this, it is noteworthy that the interval between the first and second perimeters is around two hours, and there is only a single meteorological data sample in this interval. This lack of knowledge has a direct impact on the quality of the calibration. Figure 8 shows an example

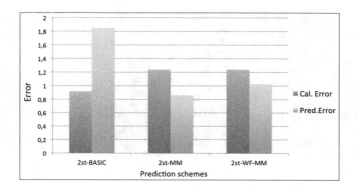

Fig. 7. Calibration and prediction errors for every prediction scheme

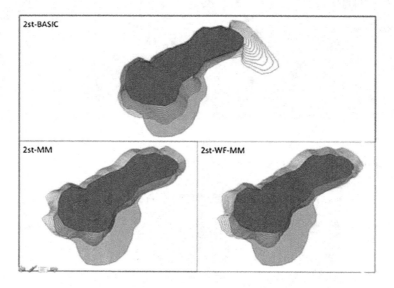

Fig. 8. Calibration stage perimeters for each prediction scheme

of the best calibrated perimeter for each scheme. All three methods under-predict the fire behavior, and there are some possible causes for this fact. The measured wind could be less than the reality, and the schemes could not tune the other parameters to minimize this effect. This fact arise another potential problem related to the fuel models used. It is possible that the fuel model conversion from the European cover uses to the standard fire models resulted in low-propagation types. The main reason to support this idea was the behavior of the 2ST-BASIC scheme. Although not sensitive to sudden changes, this method usually finds calibrated winds that make the fire spreading quite close to the real fire, although the final shape can differ due to its uniform conditions.

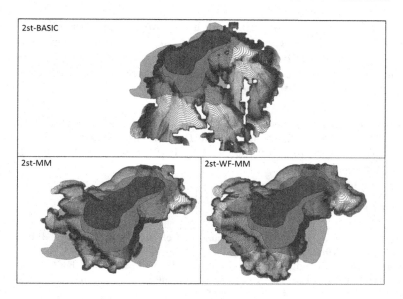

Fig. 9. Prediction stage perimeters for each prediction scheme

As it has been mentioned, this situation changes when we analyze the prediction stage that lasts around 22 h. In this case, the best prediction errors are the ones given by the 2ST-MM and 2ST-WF-MM schemes. The dynamic injection of meteorological data seems to be positive to the system and to provide good prediction shapes, as we can see in Fig. 9. Although in numerical terms the 2ST-MM is the best scheme, the 2ST-WF-MM gives back better perimeters and better covers the real burnt area. The 2ST-BASIC scheme uses the tuned weather values obtained in the calibration stage, which present a high wind speed value. This causes to excessively over-predict the real fire behavior.

5   Conclusions

Natural hazards, such as forest fire, are phenomena that require complex models to predict their evolution. In the particular case of forest fire, propagation models require input parameters that in some cases present a high degree of uncertainty. So, a Dynamic-Data Driven system was introduced to calibrate the input parameters based on the observation of the actual evolution of the fire. Moreover, some parameters are dynamic and present a temporal evolution that require the coupling of complementary models such as meteorological models to the Dynamic Data-Driven Forest Fire Framework. Finally it must be considered that all the input parameters must be introduced to the model at the same resolution what in some cases require the coupling of complementary models such as wind field models. The coupled Dynamic Data-Driven Forest Fire Framework has been used on the context of the European Forest Fire Information System to analyse the potential improvement in forest fire spread prediction and it has demonstrate a quite significant improvement. In this context, a new error equation has been proposed to evaluate the prediction quality for large forest fires taking into account the factor of overestimated/underestimated predictions compared to the real forest fire spread.

Acknowledgements. This research has been supported by MICINN-Spain under contract TIN2011-28689-C02-01 and by the Catalan Government under grant 2014-SGR-576. We also want to thank the member of EFFIS team at the JRC (Ispra) for their valuable collaboration.

References

1. Rothermel, R.C.: Behave and you can predict fire behavior. Fire Manag. Notes **44**(4), 11–15 (1983)
2. Finney, M.A., McHugh, C.W., Grenfell, I.C., Riley, K.L., Short, K.C.: A simulation of probabilistic wildfire risk components for the continental united states. Stoch. Env. Res. Risk Assess. **25**(7), 973–1000 (2011)
3. Andrews, P.L., Bevins, C.D., Seli, R.C., et al.: BehavePlus fire modeling system: version 2.0: user's guide. US Department of Agriculture (Forest Service), Rocky Mountain Research Station Fort Collins (2003)
4. Finney, M.A., et al.: An overview of flammap fire modeling capabilities. In: Proceedings of the Fuels Management-How to Measure Success, pp. 213–220 (2006)
5. Bevins, C.D.: Firelib user manual and technical reference (1996)
6. Finney, M.A., et al.: Farsite, fire area simulator-model development and evaluation (2004)
7. Lopes, A., Cruz, M., Viegas, D.: Firestationan integrated software system for the numerical simulation of fire spread on complex topography. Environ. Model. Softw. **17**(3), 269–285 (2002)
8. Rothermel, R.C.: A mathematical model for predicting fire spread in wildland fuels. Director (INT-115), 40 p. (1972)
9. Cencerrado, A., Rodríguez, R., Cortés, A., Margalef, T.: Urgency versus accuracy: dynamic driven application system natural hazard management. Int. J. Numer. Anal. Model. **9**, 432–448 (2012)
10. Abdalhaq, B., Cortés, A., Margalef, T., Luque, E.: Enhancing wildland fire prediction on cluster systems applying evolutionary optimization techniques. Future Gener. Comput. Syst. **21**(1), 61–67 (2005)
11. Bianchini, G., Denham, M., Cortés, A., Margalef, T., Luque, E.: Wildland fire growth prediction method based on multiple overlapping solution. J. Comput. Sci. **1**(4), 229–237 (2010)
12. Darema, F.: Dynamic data driven applications systems: a new paradigm for application simulations and measurements. In: Bubak, M., van Albada, G.D., Sloot, P.M.A., Dongarra, J. (eds.) ICCS 2004. LNCS, vol. 3038, pp. 662–669. Springer, Heidelberg (2004)
13. Darema, F.: Grid computing and beyond: the context of dynamic data driven applications systems. Proc. IEEE **93**(3), 692–697 (2005)
14. Potter, B., Butler, B.: Using wind models to more effectively manage wildfire. Fire Manage. **69**(2), 40–46 (2009)

15. Group, W.W.: Weather Research and Forecasting (WRF) model. Director (INT-115) (2008)
16. Molteni, F., Buizza, R., Palmer, T.N., Petroliagis, T.: The ECMWF ensemble prediction system: methodology and validation. Q. J. R. Meteorol. Soc. **122**(529), 73–119 (1996)
17. Bennett, N.D., Croke, B.F., Guariso, G., Guillaume, J.H., Hamilton, S.H., Jakeman, A.J., Marsili-Libelli, S., Newham, L.T., Norton, J.P., Perrin, C., et al.: Characterising performance of environmental models. Environ. Model. Softw. **40**, 1–20 (2013)

iSPUW: A Vision for Integrated Sensing and Prediction of Urban Water for Sustainable Cities

Dong-Jun Seo[1]([⊠]), Branko Kerkez[2], Michael Zink[3], Nick Fang[1],
Jean Gao[4], and Xinbao Yu[1]

[1] Department of Civil Engineering,
The University of Texas at Arlington, Arlington, TX, USA
{djseo,nickfang,xinbao,gao}@uta.edu
[2] Department of Civil and Environmental Engineering,
University of Michigan, Ann Arbor, MI, USA
bkerkez@umich.edu
[3] Department of Electrical and Computer Engineering,
University of Massachusetts, Amherst, MA, USA
mzink@cas.umass.edu
[4] Department of Computer Science and Engineering,
The University of Texas at Arlington, Arlington, TX, USA

Abstract. Many cities face tremendous water-related challenges in this Century of the City. Urban areas are particularly susceptible not only to excesses and shortages of water but also to impaired water quality. Even moderate rainfall can quickly fill and overflow urban water courses. To addresses these challenges, we will over the coming 4 years synergistically integrate advances in computing and cyber-infrastructure, environmental modeling, geoscience, and information science to develop integrative solutions for urban water challenges that will change the way municipalities and stakeholders plan and manage their actions, resources and civil infrastructure for sustainable cities. We will develop a system empowered by distributed computing and cyber-infrastructure for integrative sensing, high-resolution modeling and uncertainty-assessed prediction of water quantity and quality for a large urban area. The resulting system will enable multi-scale and multi-dimensional risk-based decision making related to threats and risks associated with urban water to a wide spectrum of users and stakeholders, and advance general understanding of urban sustainability and associated challenges through environmental, social and economic response of a large city as an uncertain dynamic system to extreme precipitation, urbanization and climate change. This paper details this vision by providing a blueprint for the development of iSPUW: Integrated Sensing and Prediction of Urban Water for sustainable cities.

1 Introduction

Many cities face tremendous water-related challenges in this Century of the City [1]. Urban areas are particularly susceptible not only to excesses and shortages of water but also to impaired water quality. Even moderate rainfall can quickly fill and overflow

© Springer International Publishing Switzerland 2015
S. Ravela and A. Sandu (Eds.): DyDESS 2014, LNCS 8964, pp. 68–78, 2015.
DOI: 10.1007/978-3-319-25138-7_7

urban water courses. Flash washoff of large impervious areas can quickly contaminate storm water. Urban water challenges are exacerbated by the fact that they tend to be approached in isolation rather than in concert [2–5].

With urbanization and climate change, water-related hazards and risks play an increasingly large role in people's lives and the economy. The Intergovernmental Panel on Climate Change (IPCC) reports [6] that it is likely that the number of heavy precipitation events over land has increased, that, over most of the mid-latitude land masses, extreme precipitation events will very likely be more intense and more frequent in a warmer world, and that there is high confidence that, as the climate warms, extreme precipitation rates (e.g. on daily time scales) will increase faster than the time average. Given these increased risks, cities must develop and implement strategies to adapt to the "new normal" of extremes. To make informed short- and long-term decisions in proactive response to water-related hazards and risks, the municipalities, the industries and the residents need impact-specific warning and planning information that is time- and location-specific, accurate and uncertainty-quantified.

The importance of accurate high-resolution precipitation information in urban hydrology and hydraulics is well recognized [7]. Currently, many cities rely on rain gauge-based flash flood warning systems for water-related emergency management and hire consultants for sustainability studies. While there are a number of models and modeling tools available, such as the US Army Corps of Engineers (USACE) Hydrologic Engineering Center's Hydrologic Modeling System (HEC-HMS) and River Analysis System (HEC-RAS) and the US Environmental Protection Agency's (EPA) Storm Water Management Model (SWMM), most cities do not have the expertise or resources to use them effectively. Also, modeling and analysis practices are often compartmentalized. Assessing flooding risks, for example, is generally handled separately from assessing long-term impact of urbanization and/or climate change. Because such analyses and studies are not widely shared by the professional community, it is difficult to build and expand shareable knowledge base and cyberinfrastructure to address urban sustainability challenges very effectively.

To addresses these challenges, over the coming 4 years we will leverage the synergistic integration of advances in computing and cyber-infrastructure, environmental modeling, geoscience, and information science to develop integrative solutions for urban water challenges that will change the way municipalities and stakeholders plan and manage their actions, resources and civil infrastructure for sustainable cities. We will develop a prototype system empowered by distributed computing and cyber-infrastructure for integrative sensing, high-resolution modeling and uncertainty-assessed prediction of water quantity and quality for a large urban area. We anticipate that the resulting system will enable multi-scale and multi-dimensional risk-based decision making related to threats and risks associated with urban water to a wide spectrum of users and stakeholders, and advance general understanding of urban sustainability and associated challenges through environmental, social and economic response of a large city as an uncertain dynamic system to extreme precipitation, urbanization and climate change. Specifically, we will (1) develop a cyber-based solution that integrates advanced sensing, modeling and prediction, both in terms of quantity and quality, of urban water, (2) support its early adoption by a spectrum of users and stakeholders, and (3) educate a new generation of future sustainability scientists and engineers. This paper details this vision by providing a blueprint for the future construction of iSPUW.

2   Vision

Our vision is to synergistically integrate cloud computing, crowdsourcing, advanced environmental sensing, computer modeling, data fusion and assimilation, causal inference and decision support to develop a prototype system for advanced sensing, high-resolution modeling and uncertainty-assessed prediction of water quantity and quality for a large urban area. Figure 1 depicts our system and the encompassing activities; they are collectively referred to herein as **I**ntegrated **S**ensing and **P**rediction of **U**rban **W**ater for sustainable cities, or iSPUW.

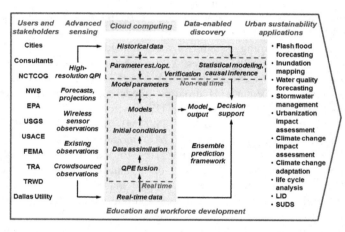

Fig. 1. Integrative sensing and prediction of urban water for sustainable cities (iSPUW).

2.1   Precipitation Sensing

Currently, a network of CASA X-band radars, referred to as the Dallas-Fort Worth Metroplex (DFW) Urban Demonstration Network, is being deployed in the area (Fig. 2). So far, four radars have been installed at UT Arlington, University of North Texas, Midlothian and Addison. Four radars will be added later this year for a planned 8-radar network in Phase 1. The radar quantitative precipitation estimates (QPE) from the network is KDP-based (R = 18.15 KDP$^{0.791}$ where R and KDP denote the rainrate in mm/hr and specific differential phase in deg/km, respectively, applicable for southern OK and North TX) [8–10]. This data will be used to provide real-time feeds for very high-resolution precipitation information to the modules described in the sections below.

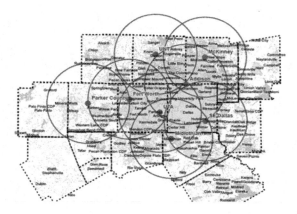

Fig. 2. DFW Urban Demonstration Network of eight CASA X-band radars.

2.2   Water Flow and Water Quality Sensing

While real-time streamflow data are available for most major cities, their spatial sparsity does not permit effective decoupling of flow from various urban runoff or point sources. We will deploy a wireless sensor network to measure both water level and quality. Each measurement location will comprise a cellular-enabled wireless sensor node. Approximately 25 or more such nodes will be deployed in the study areas in DFW. The complete selection of the study areas will be determined by the joint demonstration projects with the stakeholders but will include the Sycamore Creek and Forest Park-Berry Catchments in Fort Worth. The proposed sensor nodes leverage the latest generation of IP-enabled cellular modules to enable bi-directional communications with cloud-based services.

Designed for *smart-meter* applications, these modules are modified to permit extreme network configurability and ease of deployment. Embedded intelligence will permit each node to adjust its sampling frequencies to capture and predict events of interest (such as sudden rises in the hydrograph), rather than sampling at even intervals. This will significantly reduce power consumption at each node, enabling long-term (years) deployments on battery power. The sensor node technology has been vetted in the past year though a pilot deployment in an urban watershed in southeast Michigan [11]. These sensors will complement the existing precipitation and flow sensors deployed and operated by the cities (see Fig. 3).

2.3   Soil Moisture Sensing

To evaluate high-resolution hydrologic modeling and to resolve the urban water cycle, accurate sensing of soil moisture is critical. In-situ soil moisture measurement has advanced significantly in the last decade. Among the many available techniques, the Time Domain Reflectometry (TDR) moisture sensors have proven to be the most reliable [12]. TDR sensors utilize guided electromagnetic waves to measure dielectric constant and electrical conductivity of soils which are directly related soil moisture and

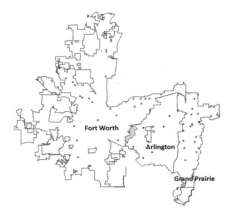

Fig. 3. Locations of High Water Warning System (HWWS) in the study areas.

density. We have developed a new strip type of TDR sensor to sense moisture distribution profile along the sensor length (US patent 20090273352). This sensor is capable of sensing wetting front migration in soil during a rainfall event. We will install strip-type TDR sensors using two different types of data acquisition: stand-alone and wireless sensor network.

2.4   Crowd Sourcing of Water Observations

To improve the accuracy and effective resolution of model prediction over a large area via calibration and validation, large-sample on-the-ground observations are necessary. We will crowd-source hydrologic and hydraulic observations by developing applications for cell phones and computers, and by deploying staff gauges and similar rugged devices for water level and other observations that can be made quickly and easily at strategic locations.

The observations targeted by the former are those of water level and presence/absence of ponded water at the time and location of reporting. Figure 4 shows two examples. The information gathered in this way will be generally qualitative in nature and limited to those times of the day and locations where people are active.

2.5   Data Fusion for Quantitative Precipitation Information

We will explore multisensor extension of conditional bias-penalized kriging [13] for improved estimation of heavy-to-extreme precipitation from multiple sources. We will exploit the fact that, in CBPK or its generalization of Fisher-like optimal linear estimation [14, 15], the additional quadratic penalty for Type-II conditional bias provides natural regularization. In addition to real-time QPE, high-quality, high-resolution, multi-year historical QPE are necessary for applications that require long-term simulations, such as verification of model-simulated streamflow following long-term

Fig. 4. Example crowd sourcing of water levels (Left, from http://i.bnet.com/blogs/crowdhydrology.jpg) and water level, flow rate and reporting (Right, from https://itunes.apple.com/us/app/creek-watch/id398420434?mt=8)

changes in land cover conditions, which is a requisite for making long-range projections. We will apply data fusion described above to produce a multi-year high-resolution precipitation reanalysis data set for DFW that will support a wide spectrum of applications by the research and operational communities.

2.6 Water Flow and Quality Modeling

The NWS Hydrology Laboratory Research Distributed Hydrologic Model (HLRDHM) [16] will be used for hydrologic modeling over a large area. The EPA's Storm Water Management Model (SWMM) [17] will be used for hydraulic and water quality modeling. HLRDHM will be used to provide a large-area view of flooding threats and risks in real-time prediction and long-term sustainability studies. Figure 5 shows an example of HLRDHM simulation at 1-min 250-m resolution of surface runoff (left) forced by the CASA QPE at 1-min 500-m resolution (right). In the real-time mode, the HLRDHM results will allow time-critical initial assessment of flooding threats over a large area for adaptive delineation of the hydraulic modeling domain as part of the intelligent system design.

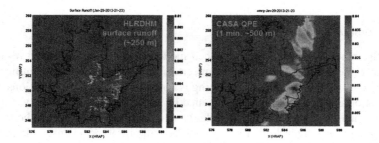

Fig. 5. Example of HLRDHM-simulated surface runoff forced by CASA QPE.

While HLRDHM operating at a high resolution is computationally only modestly expensive, it may become expensive if the model domain needs to be expanded to incorporate inflow from the upstream contributing areas. SWMM solves coupled 1-D flow through the channels and storm drains, and 2-D surface flow due to surcharge and overbank flow. For those areas identified as having increased flooding or water quality threats, SWMM will be used to dynamically delineate inundation extent and to predict water quality. However, 2-D simulation of SWMM is computationally expensive. Since SWMM and its family of models have been developed and used primarily for design or post analysis, inadequate attention has been paid to computational challenges associated with real-time applications and long-term continuous simulations. With high-resolution QPE, the computational challenges are greater.

2.7   Data Assimilation, Parameter Optimization and Uncertainty Analysis

To estimate the model dynamically-consistent, up-to-date state of the uncertain system, we will use advanced DA techniques to fuse all available information, i.e., the hydrologic and water quality observations from the cellular-enabled wireless sensor nodes, those from the HWWSs, the crowd-sourced observations, and the model predictions. It is well known that such DA-aided updating of model ICs significantly improves prediction accuracy over short lead times and hence the credibility of the inundation maps and other products. For this purpose, we will consider ensemble Kalman filter (EnKF) [18], and maximum likelihood ensemble filter (MLEF) [19].

Many of the parameters used in the hydrologic, hydraulic and water quality models are derived from a wide range of physiographic and biochemical data of varying degree of accuracy. Some are prescribed based on a priori knowledge. As such, the model parameters are subject to varying degrees of uncertainty. Estimation of the parameters and their refinement, or model calibration, generally requires considerable effort by experts as well as significant computing resources. For this reason, calibration is usually carried out only intermittently. Given the a priori estimates of the parameters, we will optimize a limited number high-impact parameters globally by adjusting them up or down while keeping the spatial patterns unchanged. Such an approach, which keeps the inverse problem reasonably well-posed, has been used successfully in hydrologic modeling [20].

2.8   Ensemble Prediction

Even with improved sensing and advanced modeling and DA, the model results will always be subject to varying levels of uncertainty. Without reliable quantification of this uncertainty, risk-based decision making is not possible. Hence, predictions, e.g., of the inundation extent should be accompanied by an estimate of uncertainty. Ensemble forecasting has been fast gaining popularity and acceptance as the methodology of choice in operational hydrologic forecasting. We will prototype an ensemble prediction system for urban water (see Fig. 6). An important distinction of our work from ensemble streamflow forecasting is that, in our system, complex statistical post processing is not viable due to lack of historical data and to nonstationarities arising from climate change and urbanization. For that, We will consider parsimonious stochastic error models for the ensemble post processor [13].

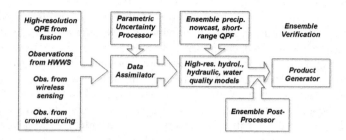

Fig. 6. Schematic of enable prediction system for urban water. Adapted from [21].

2.9 Causal Inferences

Causal inference or causal relationship discovery explores the causes of the phenomena of interest such as flooding and flash flooding to improve prediction and our abilities to response to natural hazards. The causal relationship among different hydrologic quantities, such as QPE, soil moisture, streamflow, etc., reveals the internal links among different factors that may contribute to modeling and prediction. Unlike generic causality studies in which the discovery of causal relations may suffice, modeling and prediction of extreme hydrological conditions demand not only the construction of a causal graph to reveal the contributing factors, but also the provision of the lead time of each cause to its effect, where the lead time refers to the time difference between the occurrence of lead and effect. The most commonly used computational algorithms for causality discovery can be categorized as regression [22, 23] or Bayesian approaches [24, 25]. No existing approaches incorporate lead time estimation in causal relationship discovery.

To explore the causal relationships among different hydrometeorological, hydrologic, hydraulic and water quality observations of the urban water cycle, we will use a new approach, referred to herein as mutual information causal (MI-Causal), for causal relationship discovery in point or spatial time series data. The MI-Causal approach embodies the advantages of the existing approaches and overcomes their limitations. For example, the traditional applications of mutual information verify causal Markov conditions and estimate Markov blankets without being able to determine the direction of causality. The proposed MI-Causal approach, on the other hand, investigates different causes for individual point or spatial time series data and discovers how the information will be transferred, if applicable, to its effect. As a result, we can create a causal graph without a large number of independency tests and causal relation calculations.

As an example of our preliminary work, we applied MI-Causal to discover the causality relationships among the 32 hydrologic variables within 90 days in the 30-yr hydrologic model simulation output produced by NOAA/NWS. The simulation period covers Jan 2, 1979, through Dec 31, 2008, with spatio-temporal resolution of ~ 4 km and 1 h. The 32 hydrologic variables include soil moisture (soilm) at four different depths, soil temperature (soilt), liquid water storage (liqw), snowfall (snow), and others. Figure 7 shows the causal relationships among the 32 variables and the lead time from causes to effects. Note the reasonable discovery of causality in the graph. For example, the water content in the top soil layer (smliq1 and soilm) is affected by rain and the amount of water it had on the previous day. Rain also causally affects the subsurface flow (subflow) and the upper zone tension water content (uztwc). Snow does not have as much effect as rain because snow is present only for one to two days a year on average in the study area. The causal relationship of soil temperature at four different layers is also consistent with what one may expect. The temperature of the top soil layer is affected by potential evaporation (pevap), air temperature (tem) and soilt1 itself. We will explore data-enabled discovery via causal inference to advance under-standing of the urban water cycle, identify model deficiencies and improve prediction of high-impact events. This task is expected to yield a causal inference-based assess-ment and prediction tool that will provide additional input for decision support inde-pendent of the numerical model output (see Fig. 1). We will comparatively assess the information content and evaluate the skill of the two predictions for a possible com-bined use in decision support.

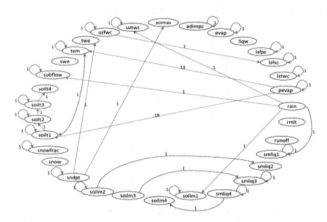

Fig. 7. Causal relationship graph for NOAA/NWS 30-yr hydrologic model simulation output.

3 Conclusions

This paper has laid out a vision for iSPUW, a system for integrative sensing, high-resolution modeling and uncertainty-assessed prediction of water quantity and quality for a large urban area. By synergistically integrating advances in computing and cyber-infrastructure, environmental modeling, geoscience, and information science, iSPUW is expected to allow impact-specific multi-scale and multi-dimensional risk-based decision making related to threats and risks associated with urban water to a wide spectrum of users and stakeholders, and advance general understanding of urban sustainability and associated challenges through environmental, social and economic response of a large city as an uncertain dynamic system to extreme precipitation, urbanization and climate change. We anticipate that this study will provide a blueprint for the integrated capabilities for sensing, modeling, prediction and decision support necessary for municipalities and stakeholder to plan and manage their actions, resources and civil infrastructure from water-related hazards and unintended consequences for sustainable cities.

Acknowledgments. This material is based upon work supported by the National Science Foundation under Grant No. IIP-1237767 and CyberSEES-1442735.

References

1. Peirce, N.R., Johnson, C.W.: Century of the City: No Time to Loose. Rockefeller Foundation, New York (2009)
2. Brown, P.: The changing face of urban water management. Water **21**, 28–30 (2009)
3. Daigger, G.T.: A vision for urban water and wastewater management in 2050. In: Grayman, W.M., Loucks, D.P., Saito, L. (eds.) Toward A Sustainable Water Future: Visions For 2050, pp. 113–121. American Society of Civil Engineers, Washington (2012)
4. Grigg, N.: Water Finance: Public Responsibilities and Private Opportunities. Wiley, Hoboken (2011)
5. Tucci, C.E.M.: Integrated urban water management in large cities: a practical tool for assessing key water management issues in the large cities of the developing world. World Bank (2009)
6. Stocker, T.F., et al.: Technical summary. In: Stocker, T.F., et al. (eds.) Climate Change 2013: The Physical Science Basis. Contribution of Working Group I to the Fifth Assessment Report of the Intergovernmental Panel on Climate Change. Cambridge University Press, Cambridge and New York (2013)
7. National Research Council: Weather Radar Technology Beyond NEXRAD. The National Academies Press, Washington (2002)
8. Chandrasekar, V., Lim, S.: Retrieval reflectivity in a networked radar environment. J Atmos. Oceanic Technol. **25**(10), 17555–17567 (2008). doi:10.1175/2008JTECHA1008.1
9. Wang, Y.T., Chandrasekar, V.: Algorithm for estimation of the specific differential phase. J Atmos Oceanic Technol. **26**(12), 2565–2578 (2009). doi:10.1175/2009JTECHA1358.1
10. Cifelli, R., Chandrasekar, V., Lim, S., Kennedy, P.C., Wang, Y., Rutledge, S.A.: A new dual-polarization radar rainfall algorithm: application in Colorado precipitation events. J Atmos Oceanic Technol. **28**(3), 352–364 (2011). doi:10.1175/2010JTECHA1488.1
11. Kerkez, B., Zhao, Y.: A machine-to-machine architecture for the real-time study of urban watersheds. In: AGU Fall meeting 2013, San Francisco, CA (2013)
12. Robinson, D.A., Campbell, C.S., Hopmans, J.W., Hornbuckle, B.K., Jones, S.B., Knight, R., Ogden, F., Selker, J., Wendroth, O.: Soil moisture measurement for ecological and hydrological watershed-scale observatories: a review. Vadose Zone J. **7**(1), 358 (2008)
13. Seo, D.-J., Herr, H., Schaake, J.: A statistical post-processor for accounting of hydrologic uncertainty in short-range ensemble streamflow prediction. Hydrol. Earth Syst. Sci. Discuss. **3**, 1987–2035 (2006)
14. Seo, D.-J., Seed, A., Delrieu, G.: Radar-based rainfall estimation. In: Testik, F., Gebremichael, M. (eds.) AGU Book Volume on Rainfall: State of the Science. Wiley, Hoboken (2010)

15. Seo, D.-J., Siddique, R., Zhang, Y., Kim, D.: Improving real-time estimation of heavy-to-extreme precipitation using rain gauge data via conditional bias-penalized optimal estimation. J. Hydrol. **519**, 1824–1835 (2014)
16. Koren, V., Reed, S., Smith, M., Zhang, Z., Seo, D.-J.: Hydrology laboratory research modeling system (HL-RMS) of the US national weather service. J. Hydrol. **291**(3–4), 297–318 (2004)
17. Rossman, L.A.: Storm Water Management Model User's Manual, EPA/600/R-05/040. U.S Environmental Protection Agency, Cincinnati, OH (2007)
18. Evensen, G.: Sequential data assimilation with nonlinear quasi-geostrophic model using Monte Carlo methods to forecast error statistics. J. Geophys. Res. **99**(C5), 143–162 (1994)
19. Zupanski, M.: Maximum likelihood ensemble filter: theoretical aspects. Mon. Weather Rev. **133**, 1710–1720 (2005)
20. Pokhrel, P., Yilmaz, K.K., Gupta, H.V.: Multiple-criteria calibration of a distributed watershed model using spatial regularization and response signatures. J. Hydrol. **418–419**, 49–60 (2012)
21. Weerts, A.H., El Serafy, G.Y.H.: Particle filtering and ensemble Kalman filtering for state updating with hydrological conceptual rainfall-runoff models. Water Resour. Res. **42**, W09403 (2006)
22. Granger, C.W.J.: Testing for causality: a personal viewpoint. J. Econ. Dyn. Control **2**, 329–352 (1980)
23. Liu, Y., Niculescu-Mizil, A., Lozano, A.C., Lu, Y.: Learning temporal causal graphs for relational time-series analysis. In: Proceedings of the 27th International Conference on Machine Learning, pp. 687–694 (2010)
24. Pearl, J.: Causality: Models, Reasoning and Inference. Cambridge University Press, Cambridge (2009)
25. Claassen, T., Heskes, T.: A bayesian approach to constraint based causal inference. In: Proceedings of the 28th Annual Conference on Uncertainty in Artificial Intelligence, pp. 207–216 (2012)

Local-Scale Assessment of Tropical Cyclone Induced Storm Surge Inundation over the Coastal Zones of India in Probabilistic Climate Risk Scenario

A.D. Rao[(⊠)], Jismy Poulose, Puja Upadhyay, and Sachiko Mohanty

Centre for Atmospheric Sciences,
Indian Institute of Technology Delhi, New Delhi, India
adrao@cas.iitd.ernet.in

Abstract. India is frequently affected by coastal flooding due to storm surges which has a significant impact on human life. The quantitative analysis of coastal flooding depends on accurate simulation of storm surges and its inundation. The analysis is imperative in coastal risk evaluation in terms of rise of water levels and its extent of inundation. In this study, risk analysis is made at the smallest geographical scale, particularly, for Andhra Pradesh which is one of the maritime states along the east coast of India often caused by coastal flooding. The ADCIRC model is used for calculating maximum possible total water elevation and associated inundation considering the non-linear interaction with the local tide as well. The simulations also include the risk assessment in the climate change scenario based on the IPCC reports. A detailed analysis of additional coastal regions which are prone to inundation in response to climate change is also made.

Keywords: Tropical cyclone · Storm surges · Risk analysis · Coastal inundation

1 Introduction

Quantitative risk analysis of consequences of a natural disaster like a tropical cyclone is extremely important for planning, preparedness and mitigation processes by the coastal authorities. The acceptability of the risk analysis depends on the judicious decisions made based on some risks that can be prevented at all costs and some can be disregarded because of low consequence, low frequency, or both. East coast of India experiences more number of cyclones compared to that of west coast of India. Most of the coastal regions along the east coast are more exposed to larger coastal vulnerability in terms of inundation due to storm surges. There are some coastal stretches, particularly river deltaic and other low-lying regions along the coast are known for higher risk. Identification of these regions are primary concern for many reasons that also includes for long-term planning of coastal development.

In *Climate Change 2007* [1], the Fourth Assessment Report of the United Nations Intergovernmental Panel on Climate Change (IPCC), a high probability of major

© Springer International Publishing Switzerland 2015
S. Ravela and A. Sandu (Eds.): DyDESS 2014, LNCS 8964, pp. 79–88, 2015.
DOI: 10.1007/978-3-319-25138-7_8

changes in tropical cyclone activity across the various ocean basins is highlighted. The Indian Ocean including the Arabian Sea and the Bay of Bengal are of particular concern because of the high population density along their low-lying coastline and deltas. These coastal populations are vulnerable to the negative impact of these projected extreme events. Using IPCC 2007 report, Thomas et al. [2] studied the future projections based on theory and high-resolution dynamical models consistently indicate that greenhouse warming will cause the globally averaged intensity of tropical cyclones to shift towards stronger storms, with intensity increases of 2–11 % by 2100. The tropical Indian Ocean is characterized by surface warming trends that are more statistically significant, compared to model-simulated internal variability, than those in many other tropical basins including in the Northeast Pacific and North Atlantic. This raises the possibility that tropical cyclone trends resulting from global warming could emerge in the Indian Ocean as well although these basins so far have been experiencing some of the intense tropical cyclones in the recent past like Mala (2006), Gonu (2007), Sidr (2007), Nargis (2008), Giri (2010), Phet (2010), Thane (2011), Phailin (2013) without any apparent increase in the frequency of the tropical storms itself.

In addition to this, there is a possibility of increase in size and duration/life cycle of the storm that would definitely affect the surge generation potential and hence changes the coastal inundation scenario. It is therefore interesting to study coastal vulnerability assessment in response to climate change. In this paper, it is focussed on the coastal risk analysis at smallest geographical scale associated with inland inundation due to storm surges in all the coastal districts of Andhra Pradesh which is often affected by tropical cyclones. Moreover, this region is particularly important for assessing coastal inundation in the context of two major rivers systems (Krishna and Godavari) joining the Bay of Bengal. It is expected larger extent of inundation through these river systems whenever a cyclone impinging in these regions that would be of immense important. Due to climate change, the water levels and the extent of inundation are recomputed based on the projections made on the intensity and size of the storm. These simulations would help for planning and policy making in view of the climate change.

2 Data Analysis and Methodology

The information of past cyclone data (1891–2013) that includes cyclone track along with its intensity (strength of wind stress or pressure-drop) and size of the cyclone (radius of maximum winds), surges and associated inundation are used from various sources (India Meteorological Department, JTWC, etc.) for all the coastal districts of Andhra Pradesh. This data is reconciled, to make a uniform data base for cyclones and its surges. From the data base, we can identify the maximum pressure-drop prevailed among all the cyclones that crossed each district during past more than 120 years.

The finite-element ADCIRC model [3] framework is configured for the coast with very high resolution near the coast to compute storm surges and associated inundation. The model uses onshore topography from the very high-horizontal resolution of 90 m data from the Shuttle Radar Topography Mission (SRTM). The model bathymetry is obtained from the General Bathymetric Chart of the Oceans (GEBCO) 30 s global bathymetric grid. The model is applied with the maximum pressure-drop value for a set of synthetic tracks which are generated by composing actual tracks as well as from theoretical ones, ensuring that each coastal district is covered. The model also incorporates the tides so that the non-linear interaction of tide and surge is comprehensively taken care of. The water levels can be finally computed in the affected region by making use of the precise onshore topography data. This information along with the extent of inundation is vital for mitigation and planning of coastal risk management.

The model simulations are calibrated with observed surge data for each region of the coast. Particularly, the extent of inundation is very large when a storm hits in the river deltaic region as the surge waters penetrate longer distances through the river causing more vulnerability. In order to study the climate change scenario, the cyclonic wind stress is increased by 7 % (an average value) and of 11 % (extreme value). It is also studied the effect of storm size in terms of enhancing the radius of maximum winds from 20 % to 40 % on the development of surges and hence coastal inundation.

3   Results and Discussion

The analysis of the model comprises the geographic domain from 79°E to 88°E and 12°N to 19.5°N, covering the entire Andhra coast. The finite-element mesh is constructed using the software package, Surface Modeling System (SMS). The program generates a grid with a low-resolution in the deeper region, and high-resolution when approaching near the coast. The node-spacing varies between 200 m near the coast and about 20 km in the open ocean. The distance from the coast to the off-shore is about 500 km, whilst, the north-south distance is about 750 km. The model mesh showing the variable grid resolution is shown in Fig. 1a. The model domain extends up to 15 m topographic line from the coast in order to estimate the landward inundation due to the storm surges. An explicit scheme is used in time discretization with a time-step of 2 s. The wind forcing is provided in terms of pressure drop and radius of maximum winds as input. The wind stress of the cyclone is computed using the scheme described in Jelesnianski and Taylor [4]. Minimum depth of 0.5 m is pre-set to delineate the wet and dry elements with a horizontal eddy viscosity coefficient of 5 m^2s^{-1}.

The model is initially validated with the past cyclone data. From the reconciled data base of past cyclones crossed along the coastal districts, it is identified the maximum pressure-drop of 80 mb is prevailed among all the cyclones that crossed the region during past more than 120 years. Using cyclone tracks information for each district, synthesized tracks are computed for each district which is shown in Fig. 1b. The boxes in the figure gives the coastline length for each coastal district. It may be noted that Srikakulam district has the longest coastline of about 160 km. The experiments have been carried out by shifting the synthesized track of a particular district by every 10 km along the coast considering the maximum pressure drop and radius of maximum winds as 80 mb and 30 km respectively. Using the ADCIRC model, the water levels and associated inundation is computed for each track. Finally, a composite depiction of maximum water levels and inundation is shown for each district as a combined response of all the possible cyclone tracks crossing the region concerned without and with climate change option.

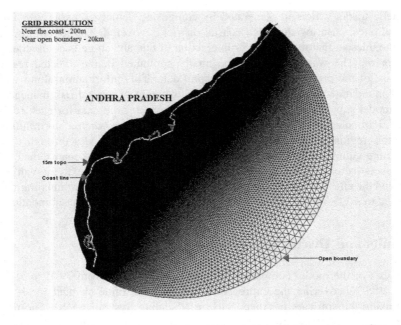

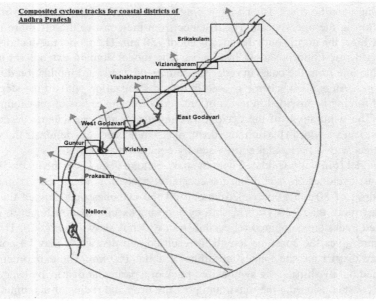

Fig. 1. a. Model mesh for Andhra coast with a resolution ranging from 200 m near the coast to 20 km near the open boundary. **b.** Synthesized cyclone tracks for each coastal district of Andhra Pradesh.

Figure 2a gives the model bathymetry and onshore topography of the region of Krishna district using both the data sets of GEBCO and SRTM. The model computes storm surges and associated inundation at each grid using the synthesized tracks. The storm surge in the model is always referred to the mean sea level. After computation of storm surges, the water levels at each grid are computed by subtracting local topography. A total of 10 tracks have been used for this district and computed the surges/water levels and associated extent of coastal inundation for each track. It is depicted in the Fig. 2b, the composite scenario of water levels and extent of landward inundation due to all possible cyclonic tracks crossing along the Krishna district in all the cases including normal scenario (without climate change), and enhancing wind forcing by 7 % and 11 % respectively in response to climate change. It is found, the maximum water levels simulated along the Krishna River that results a larger extent of inundation in all the scenarios. The maximum extent of inundation of about 50 km is computed in the vicinity of the Krishna River. The total area of inundation is about 2750 km^2. The model calculations suggest that many areas/regions covered with additional water levels ranging from 0.5 m to 3.5 m just as a response of enhanced forcing of 7 %. Similarly, additional water levels are also seen due to 11 % increase. It is depicted in Fig. 2c the possible extent of coastal vulnerability in each possible scenario. About 28 % of additional area of inundation is simulated which is subjected to 7 % enhancement of wind stress. However, only about 13 % further inundation is noticed due to extreme climate change scenario of 11 % enhancement of wind stress. Since the high water levels cause more catastrophe in the region, the area covered with more than a meter water level is calculated for each event of climate change scenario. In case of extreme climate change scenario, about 75 % of the total inundated area is exposed to above one meter water levels.

Similar experiments are carried out for Guntur district using synthetic cyclone tracks. Figure 3a shows the model bathymetry and onshore topography of the district. The composited maximum water level computed for normal scenario is about 6.2 m with an area of inundation of about 2300 km^2. Climate change scenario with 11 % increase in wind stress provides an additional 5 % in the total water level which is about 6.5 m (Fig. 3b). Most of the area of the district has got inundated in the vicinity of Krishna River. The maximum extent of inundation computed for this area is about 40 km as shown in Fig. 3c. In terms of total area of inundation, climate change scenario has an impact of about 16 % on this district which is little compared to that of Krishna district.

As shown in the Fig. 4a, East Godavari district includes three main branches of Godavari River which is connected to the open ocean. The length of the coastline is ~ 140 km. This district has many small river tributaries in addition to the Godavari estuary joining the adjacent bay and hence it is expected larger extent of coastal inundation. The maximum water level of about 8.5 m is concentrated along the banks of Godavari River with an inundated area of about 1500 km^2 (Fig. 4b). The composited maximum water level is increased by 9 % with extreme climate change scenario. Figure 4c depicts about 34 % additional area has got inundated for 7 % increase of wind stress and 19 % due to extreme occurrence of 11 % wind intensification. The total extent of inundation is about 40 km in all the cases.

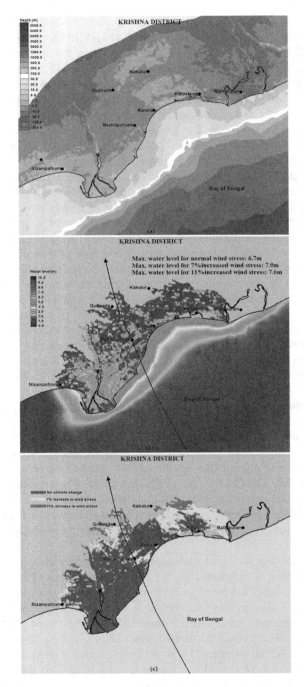

Fig. 2. a. Bathymetry and onshore topography **b.** Total depiction of maximum water level **c.** Extent of coastal inundation for different scenarios for Krishna District

Fig. 3. a. Bathymetry and onshore topography **b.** Total depiction of maximum water level **c.** Extent of coastal inundation for different scenarios for Guntur District

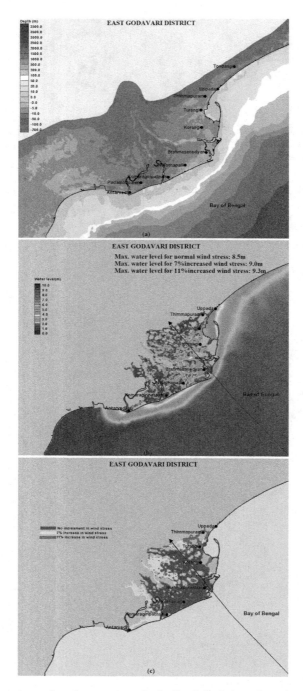

Fig. 4. a. Bathymetry and onshore topography **b.** Total depiction of maximum water level **c.** Extent of coastal inundation for different scenarios for East Godavari District

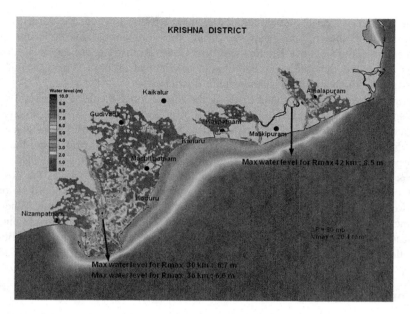

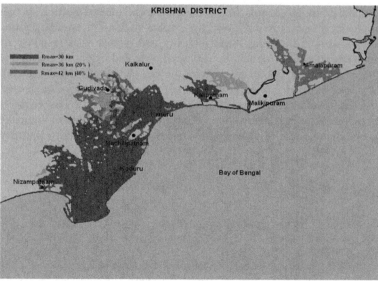

Fig. 5. a. Total depiction of maximum water level with peak surge locations for all possible Cyclones crossing Krishna district due to enhancement of R_{max} by 20 % & 40 % in no wind enhancement due to climate change. **b.** Total depiction of extent of coastal inundation for all possible Cyclones crossing Krishna district due to enhancement of R_{max} by 20 % & 40 % in no wind enhancement due to climate change

The simulations are also made for all the other districts, however, the corresponding figures are not shown. Our analysis of all the simulations due to wind stress enhancement shows that the Krishna and East Godavari districts are the most affected regions compared that of any other coastal districts of Andhra. The least affected regions are Srikakulam and Visakhapatnam districts.

Further experiments are made to study the impact on the coastal vulnerability by increasing the radius of maximum wind (R_{max}) by 20 % and 40 % respectively. The computations are only made for Krishna district for which the results are discussed. Figure 5a describes total depiction of maximum water level with peak surge locations for all possible cyclones crossing Krishna district due to an enhancement of R_{max} by 20 % & 40 % respectively with no wind enhancement. Figure 5b gives the possible extent of coastal vulnerability due to storm surges for the scenarios, viz., normal scenario, 20 % and 40 % increase in R_{max} as a response of climate change. When the R_{max} increases by 40 %, the maximum water level is not only shifts to the right but also enhances by 30 % which is considered to be very high for causing additional inundation.

4   Conclusions

ADCIRC model is used to demonstrate risk vulnerability due to storm surge generated by any tropical cyclone crossing along the coastal regions of Andhra Pradesh. The simulations are also made using storm intensity and its size as a response of future climate change scenario. Computation of water levels and extent of inundation at the smallest grid size of about 200 m are used for the assessment of coastal vulnerability of each district. The experiments suggest that the maximum risk associated with higher water levels are found along the banks of Krishna and Godavari rivers. In the possible event of extreme climate change, an area of about 75 % is exposed to inundation with more than one meter water level which is considered to be extremely alarming.

References

1. Solomon, S., Qin, D., Manning, M., Chen, Z., Marquis, M., Averyt, K.B., Tignor, M., Miller, H.L. (eds.): Climate Change 2007: The Physical Science Basis. Cambridge Univ. Press, Cambridge (2007)
2. Knutson, T.R., Mcbride, J.L., Chan, J., Emanuel, K., Holland, G., Landsea, C., Held, I., Kossin, J.P., Srivastava, A.K., Sugi, M.: Tropical cyclones and climate change. Nat. Geosci. 3, 157–163 (2010)
3. Luettich Jr., R.A. , Westerink, J.J., Scheffner, N.W.: ADCIRC: an advanced three dimensional circulation model for shelves coasts and estuaries, report 1: theory and methodology of ADCIRC-2DDI and ADCIRC-3DL. Dredging Research Program Technical Report DRP-92-6, Army Engineers Waterways Experiment Station, Vicksburg, MS, p. 137 (1992)
4. Jelesnianski, C.P., Taylor, A.D.: A preliminary view of storm surges before and after storm modification. NOAA Technical Memorandum. ERL, WMPO-3, p. 33 (1973)

A Data Driven Scientific Approach to Environmental Probes

Craig C. Douglas[1](✉), Tainara Mendes de Andrade Soares[2],
and Maurício Vieira Kritz[2]

[1] Mathematics Department, School of Energy Resources, University of Wyoming,
Laramie, WY 82071-3036, USA
cdougla6@uwyo.edu
[2] Laboratório Nacional de Computação Científica, Av. Getúlio Vargas,
333 - Quitandinha, Petrópolis, RJ 25651-075, Brazil
{tainara,kritz}@lncc.br

Abstract. The development of an Environmental Science is strongly connected with the long term observation of wild environmental systems, which are usually situated far from immediate reach. Environmental systems have as basic elements ecosystems that are difficult to delineate since their boundaries and dynamical regime change over time. This paper discusses the concept of environmental probes and their use in inaccessible regions, e.g., remote sites in the Amazon forest. The focus is on their ability to track environmental systems for long periods and produce useful scientific data. A dynamic data scientific approach is essential to our concept due to (a) the remote location of sensors and the many years span of observation processes, (b) the necessary dynamical creation and adaptation of environmental models to uncover environmental features, and (c) the partial substitution of human abilities concerning maintenance and the identification of novelties.

1   Introduction

We introduced the concept of environmental probes in [5], where we described the difficulties in delineating the concepts of environmental systems and of players. In this paper we provide more details in the concepts and introduce ways of implementing environmental probes.

The difficulties in studying environmental phenomena arise from several sources. Some are intrinsic to environmental phenomena, others come from our epistemological and discursive limitations. The former are of relevance here. Both are crucial in environmental management. Little is to be found in the scientific literature about the long term integrated observation of landscapes along the lines proposed.

Natural phenomena are caused by a collection of "things" that interact and interacting change the features we observe in them. The "things" giving rise to environmental phenomena are ecosystems, which are the smallest environmental standalone units. This means that pathways of mass and energy in ecosystems

© Springer International Publishing Switzerland 2015
S. Ravela and A. Sandu (Eds.): DyDESS 2014, LNCS 8964, pp. 89–99, 2015.
DOI: 10.1007/978-3-319-25138-7_9

are almost closed, requiring only solar energy, and that changes in dynamical behavior driven by signals and information do not severely depart from homeostatic regime domains under non-exceptional natural stresses. Nevertheless, they remain open and exchange mass, energy, and information with their surrounding siblings. This concept of ecosystem [17, Preface], pioneered by G.E. Hutchinson and H.T. Odum, requires the ability to identify a standalone unit in an ever changing landscape to be of practical use.

This identification problem cannot be solved by traditional modeling and theory construction alone since new interacting "things" may come and leave the modeled landscape and maintain strong interactions with local components for non-trivial periods [12]. External long range factors like large scale climate changes, a fortiori not represented in the model, may impose non-neglectable qualitative changes in dynamical regimes. An example where this behavior occurs naturally is the flooded Amazon landscape. Annually, the river water level rises and falls, causing flooding in extensive areas. In this region, there are two distinct ecosystems during the low water season and a hybrid aquatic-terrestrial ecosystem during the flooding period. Aquatic and terrestrial systems are quite different and their elements barely interact, with the possible exception of insects, alligators, and similar species at the water border. However, during the Amazon high water season plants may be partially or completely submersed for long periods of time and a lot of interactions between aquatic and terrestrial species happen that are not present or possible during the low water season [9]. Moreover, distinct species may be carried into a flooded ecosystem each year.

These characteristics of ecosystems indicate that no parameter indexed class of models can be established for them in advance, nor will any model obtained by parameter identification be representative for long periods of time, due to the migration of components in and out of the ecosystem and the formation of new connections. Hence, the modeling of environmental systems needs to encompass active and concurrent acquisition of observations to identify newcomers, new dynamical regimes, or new interactions that alter equations and parameter sets to be estimated. This necessity fully integrates the steps of the knowledge producing scientific process, which cycles from observation, to representation, to assertion of truths or predictions, and back to collecting observations [13].

The dynamic data scientific (DDS) approach integrates simulation with dynamically assimilated data, multiscale modeling, computation, in a two way interaction between the model execution and the data acquisition methods [4]. DDS methods and object-orientation offer a natural framework to address this problem, either as an intellectual paradigm or a development platform, allowing the individual modeling of components at an organizational level and their further assemblage into higher level models. We address problems related to the conceptualization and realization of environmental probes based on this approach.

The paper is organized as follows. In Sect. 2, we discuss the nature and the characteristics of environmental systems considered important by ecologists and environmentalists. In Sect. 3, we delineate environmental probes and describe their functioning. In Sect. 4, we describe how the data driven scientific (DDS) framework is essential for creating new environmental models and probes for regions that are in wild environments far from civilization. In Sect. 4, we discuss DDS and provide some thoughts on future directions.

2   Environmental Systems

In this section, we advance an operational definition for environmental systems and show how it pertains to the development of an environmental science. The way ecologists and environmental scientists look at ecological and environmental phenomena is of special relevance to reason about environmental probes. We highlight some aspects that are difficult to observe, e.g., the identification of especies and novelties, indirect effects, plasticity, redundancy, preferences, trophic channels, etc. that play essential roles in discussions concerning the monitoring and managing of extreme landscapes.

In Sect. 2.1, we describe the different spheres in the relatively thin slab around the Earth's surface where life is confined. In Sect. 2.2, we describe the nature of environmental systems and their characteristics known to be relevant to answer ecological, environmental, and sustainability questions. In Sect. 2.3, we discuss the observation of ecosystems and environments. We pay special attention to points that may be hard in nearly inaccessible or untouched regions such as in remote Amazon forest sites.

2.1   Spheres

Life on Earth is confined in a relatively thin slab 16 km thick embracing the Earth's non-gaseous surface. This slab is delimited inbound by the Earth's magma and outbound by the interplanetary void. Driven by solar energy, a thermodynamic turmoil incessantly goes on in this slab maintaining every portion of it far from equilibrium and hosting organized matter: the fifth state of matter [5]. In this slab, a peculiar collection of chemical substances in distinct physical states persists and evolves.

A substantial portion of the present characteristics and composition of the collection of "things", interactions, and processes in this slab that form the Earthly environment is known to be a consequence of evolving and evolutionary processes intrinsic to its living portion. The elements in this collection are usually grouped in spheres named after the physical state of the majority of its elements:

– the *pedosphere* **P** (mostly solid or grained soil),
– the *hydrosphere* **H** (that may be saline or fresh),
– the *cryosphere* **C** (either solid or powdered),
– the *atmosphere* **A** (mostly gaseous, sometimes liquid), and
– the *biosphere* (formed by living matter).

These spheres are tightly intertwined. No matter how they are delimited, there is no point in this Slab where they can be topologically disentangled. Therefore, we consider as an *environmental phenomenon* what happens in any portion of the Earthly environment that contains ecosystems and takes into account interactions between components of the biosphere (organisms and biomes) and elements of the other spheres, highlighting the effects that biosphere elements may have on phenomena in the other spheres. An *environmental system* is any semi-formal delimitation of an environmental phenomena that includes ecosystems and, therefore, trophical webs. This implies considering effects induced by the less organized phases in the other spheres upon biosphere components of the system. However, the exact delimitation of ecosystems or environmental systems is a difficult task. The sound establishment of environmental systems can only be achieved gradually [12].

As stated in Sect. 1, an *ecosystem* is the first entity in the hierarchy of biological organization that is complete [17, Preface]. It can sustain itself based solely on the input of solar energy, nevertheless allowing exchanges with surrounding components and factors. To conform to this definition, it needs to embrace all components (biological and physical), interactions, and processes necessary for survival. For instance, it needs to have photosynthetic components, detritivore and catabolic pathways restoring the basic nutrients, and any anabolic paths needed to reconstruct its components. It is pointless to have all these components if they do not interact and evolve supporting each other. Ecosystems are the environmental counterpart of cells that are the first organizations able to sustain life processes and reproduce. Contrary to cells, ecosystems have no well defined, readily recognizable, boundary leaving clear what belongs and what does not belong to the system. The pertinence of a component or process to an ecosystem can only be determined through the evaluation of the strength and quality of its interactions with other ecosystem elements.

2.2 Factors and Behavior

In this section, we discuss the nature and known relevant aspects of environmental systems.

The identification and study of ecosystems and environmental systems is a difficult task due to several ingredients. The first ingredient is the strong dependence of biological and ecological behavior on interactions and intercomponent relations as much as on the interacting components proper. Ecological interactions fall into three general classes: (1) classical (predator-prey), (2) mutualistic, and (3) parasitic/parasitoid, but have an enormous grade of variation. Relations concern the nature of interaction and are not easily classified. Those more relevant to the identification of trophic networks are energy/mass related, informational (driven mainly by biochemical signaling and genetic material), and functional, although the "function" of any ecosystem component can only be fully appreciated after understanding its behavior [18]. Interactions enchain forming networks and paths that are often circular [7,19]. Circular paths tend to be self correcting (homeostatic) within certain limits. They may nevertheless break down producing violent oscillations and changes in ecosystem homeostatic regimes when any intervening variable reaches values beyond the safe limits [7].

The second ingredient relates to the magnitudes of scales intrinsic to ecosystems which extend from the molecular scale to large geographical areas and fro smaller than a second intervals to centuries. Ecological interactions connect components at all scales, where processes have rather distinct characteristic times. For instance, energy-capturing (photosynthetic) and many catabolic processes occur both at sub-cellular and molecular scales and at supra-organismic scales (prey-predator games).

The third ingredient is the diversity of "things" and interactions; what refers both to the strength and the nature of interactions (what is exchanged and how the exchange occurs). Components of a phenomenon as well as its interactions can be classified into distinct types and associated with different behaviors within the ecosystem at various scales. Ecological diversity generally implies that different components and trophic chains have the same dynamical or functional role in the ecosystem and that interactions of different kinds and strengths may perform alike in ecosystems, favoring stability.

Living entities and ecosystems are open dynamical entities that are highly sophisticated in their organization. Detecting boundaries and revealing organization are not the only nonstandard characteristics associated with ecosystem observation. Due to the enormous importance of interactions in its behavior, crucial aspects of ecosystems that affect its long term behavior cannot be directly observed in short periods of time and need the intervention of models to be perceived and observed or estimated. The following aspects require the explicit use of models to be observed: indirect effects, interaction strength, phenotypic, plasticity, food preferences, influence of traits, behavior modification of elements at various levels of organization, and many more factors. These factors determine the length of trophic chains, the adaptability and flexibility of a trophic network, the onset of trophic cascades, ecosystem storage capacity, biodiversity, resilience potential, etc. The exactness and fidelity of their records are closely intertwined with how well the model represents the phenomenon, requiring several iterations to retract reality. Models in the present case are also the final output of an environmental probe, or *ecoscope*.

2.3   Observation of Ecosystems and Environmental Systems

In this section, we discuss how to do long term observations of ecosystems within an environmental system.

It would be clumsy to represent and understand ecosystems in their finest level of detail: considering all molecules, even individuals, and tracking their fate. Ecologists resort to aggregation directed by the biological organisation hierarchy and to an account of possible interactions to address ecosystems and environmental systems. Furthermore, the Amazon floodplains phenomenon [9] points to the fact that measurable and quantifiable data alone are not enough to model and foresee and ecosystem's fate [12].

Ecosystems are usually represented by networks or *webs* that deploy ecosystem components, the relations among them, and the possibilities of interaction between any two components. Webs describe components and how they might interact. Connections in an ecological network represent permissible interaction channels and constrain the ecosystem's dynamical behavior [14]. Interaction channels may convey mass, energy, or information (in the form of biochemical signals and pollination) and are of utmost importance in understanding ecosystems [20]. Whenever information is conveyed, the effect is generally much stronger than just the stimuli.

Aggregation goes from individuals to collectivities. Substances, populations and communities are aggregations respectively of molecules, organisms or populations [8]. Organisms themselves vary in scale and organizational complexity extending from unicellular organisms to large mammals. Each aggregation or organization level has its own spatial and temporal scales. Although not frequent, nodes of the same trophic web may represent elements at various aggregation-levels, as when individuals interact with populations.

Often, more than one web (each one is a subnetwork) is needed to sensibly represent all aspects and interactions relevant in a study. Their use reflects different *perspectives* of study and affect how observations are collected. Depending on the focus of observation, there are *source*, *sink*, and *community* food webs that can be topological, energetic, or functional depending on what interactions are represented. Many issues in the observation of ecosystems, e.g., the source, sink, community, population, and individual approaches depend on human choices about emphasis and observation procedures and are not attached intrinsically to the nature of the ecosystem. Moreover, it is important to inspect an ecosystem from several perspectives and aggregation levels to filter and compensate impacts on the model caused by decisions of constrains in the observation process, as well as to enlarge the model representativeness. This can only be achieved with long term, continual monitoring of ecosystems.

To register conditions, resources and signals [3,8,15] the observation of environmental systems needs to acquire:

- basic physico-chemical data (e.g., temperature, luminosity, (relative) humidity, acidity, salinity, fluid flows, concentration of nutrients, pollutants, etc.);
- determine (dynamical) patterns (e.g., soil structure, floral and faunal distribution and maturity, trophic preferences etc.);
- and identify novelties arising from invaders, extinctions, and long range changes in "external" conditions;
- changes in the trophic web.

Moreover, all of this data-gathering effort has to be accompanied by a thorough evaluation of the indirect, dynamical characteristics [6,22,23], to unveil several relevant aspects that cannot be directly observed because they depend on how each directly observed component interacts with others.

3   Environmental Probes

In this section, we define an environmental probe. In Sect. 3.1, we relate the probes to the Internet of Things (IoT) concept [2] and enlargen this concept to accommodate computational objects and human beings. In Sect. 3.2, we discuss tracking trophic changes and recognizing interactions, novelties, and imbalances.

An *environmental probe* is a collection of interconnected sensors, actuators, computational models, and human beings that produces data and observations in natural or artificial milieus that forms a picture of an ecosystem or an environmental system. Sensors are not tied to one specific computational model and may rearrange or re-group dynamically. A computational model attached to a group of sensors represents the behavior of an ecosystem dynamical entity: an individual, a population, a community, or elements of other environmental spheres interacting with the ecosystem, like rivers, lakes, soils, etc. When bound to a model, sensors adjust parameters and simulations preventing the latter to depart from observations in the long run. The ecosystem is represented by a collection of interconnected computational models that interact by exchanging signals, matter, and energy abstracted into data flows between computational objects. The human beings provoke rearrangements, insert novelties, valuate observations and create new perspectives. They eventually introducing new sensors and classes of models and submodels in the probe.

Environmental probes should capture most (ideally all) features of ecosystems and environmental systems. As discussed in Sect. 2, these features may not be readily apparent and require models to be perceived. Analogously to natural ecosystems, these secondarily observable aspects emerge from the interactions and the collective execution of interconnected computational models and sensors. Component models and connections need to change and adapt as new ecological elements appear or disappear or as interactions between ecosystem entities change, to better match simulations to aspects considered important by the human components of the probe.

The concept advanced in this section tries to better delineate these characteristics and show that current technologies make it possible to build environmental probes. For the sake of simplicity, we abstract from the energy and resource dependence of sensors and actuators, since technological advances in batteries and circuits may quickly void any assertion about those issues.

3.1 An Adaptive Network of Things

Internet of Things (IoT) is still a moving concept. This term first appeared in 1999 and is due to Kevin Ashton [1]. As presently stated this concept allow all sensors to be connected to the Internet, to communicate without human intervention, and to build useful databases automatically. If the IoT philosophy is successful, many of the major hurdles of data gathering and mining will be automated, freeing up humans to do things that computers are not good at.

An ecosystem is grounded on a collection of interacting organisms or organizations of organisms that use physical, chemical, and biological resources to recreate and reorganize themselves. Therefore, using IoT as a basis to discuss environmental probes, *Things* should include anything that can mimic, duplicate, or implement organisms' behavior and capabilities, and be attached to the Internet. This includes the usual things in a Internet of Things (e.g., sensors, actuators, communicators, RFID tags etc.), as well as autonomous transporters, objects able to report about themselves, implementable Turing Machines, communicating processes, and so on.

There are many factors in ecosystems that may change communication paths within it. Things that previously interacted become isolated and stop communicating and vice versa due to displacements or modifications in their surroundings. Among these factors we find distance modifications, obstacles, temperature changes, flooding, variegated displacements, and loss of power. In an environmental probe there is not just information transfer and exchange between nodes, as in a standard IoT, since energy and mass may also be transferred between ecosystem nodes. In living systems, however, the existence of an interaction channel does not guarantee an interaction (mass or energy transfer) like in physical and chemical phenomena since a game may mediate the interaction (e.g., during predator-prey interactions). Hence, the network idea in the *Internet* component of an IoT must be generalized to an organization represented as a whole-part graph [10], where connections are computationally active. Whole-part graphs may be roughly described as a tree where each fork is a hypergraph [11].

In the present context, an IoT is an organisation of information-capable nodes that is reorganizable and can adapt to internal and external stimuli. Operationally, an environmental probe is such an IoT.

3.2   Monitoring Environments

Ecosystems are open systems with fuzzy, imprecise, and moving boundaries that can only be delineated along intervals of time. They are living systems in the sense that their inner relations change often, adapting to present conditions, and a fraction of their components are substituted by equivalent ones over long enough periods. In Subsect. 3.1, we described environmental probes as adaptive IoTs in our extended sense. In this subsection, we discuss their behaviour and operation by sketching the dynamical characteristics of environmental probes. Ideally, an environmental probe must reproduce the state of ecosystems as accurately as possible since the state of a system allows foreseeing its behavior in the immediate future [16].

However, due to the necessity of tracking changes in interactions and in the possibilities of interactions, the state of ecosystems and environmental systems need to include its trophic web [12] that is mathematically represented by the interaction graph of dynamical systems [14]. The state of an environmental probe at a given moment, therefore, must include the current organization of its underlying IoT, which shall represent the ecosystem's trophic web, together with all observed values and features. Thus, the actual observation of an ecosystem by the ecoscope is an organization composed of the present state of the underlying IoT, together with the states of each of its sensor, actuator, and computational nodes.

Changes in the relations of an ecosystem's trophic web can be tracked by changes in the organization of the probe's underlying network. This is a consequence of rearrangements of sensors in space and time and the ability to create virtual subnetworks for communication and interaction among the environmental IoT nodes.

Many components of real ecosystems are living entities and adapt to nearby changes by changing their own organization. To track this, some portions of the environmental IoT must adapt. Modern sensors can be remotely controlled and reprogrammed to sense a different collection of aspects. Their flexibility is limited. Computational objects that model both components and interactions are quite flexible, as are the programming connections among them. Computational models can represent from individuals and populations to communities and higher organizations by means of appropriate program schemas. They can also intelligently alter themselves or be reprogrammed by humans when needed.

Therefore, the operation of an environmental probe may be summarized as follows:

- Sensors provide data that is available at appropriate intervals, relocating and regrouping themselves grounded on the observations made.
- Computational objects receive sensor data comparing observations with simulations based on previous observations taken as initial conditions.

Whenever simulations depart from observations, they correct themselves and sensors in the following manner:

- They may reprogram sensors and reprioritize their associations.
- They adapt themselves by adjusting parameters, by altering their own instructions through the many technologies available, by creating and destroying computational objects, by altering connections between computational object and between those and sensors and actuators, and by calling for human assistance.
- Humans may intervene in creative and unpredictable ways.

4 DDS and Future Directions

Natural phenomena are recognized though changes in attributes associated with their interacting elements and interactions. The interdependent, ever changing nature of environmental systems challenge our understanding of their *normal* or *unstressed* behavior. Identifying homeostasis related states of ecological and environmental phenomena is crucial and will greatly enhance and deepen our understanding of environmental change and the associated rates. To accomplish this, we need long term observations of wild environments that usually sit far from human settlements where observational and scientific knowledge is normally found.

Monitoring regions of difficult access, like remote sites in the Amazon region, is of utmost importance for the establishment of an Environmental Science. This kind of monitoring provides information about which changes are "acceptable" and which lead to *environmental change* (good, bad, and noncommittal). The probe sketched above is not a final solution. Maintenance of equipment, even "self repairing" and resilient ones, and the ultimate recognition of novelties still depend on human intervention and presence. The proposed probe can reduce this dependence and lessen all sorts of costs associated with field excursions.

Available robot and automatization technologies allow for remote inspection and intervention to a certain level. The role of DDS methodologies and paradigms extends far beyond the mere automation or telescoping of existing observation procedures. It has the potential to transform a network of sensors, computational objects, hybrid systems, and humans into a symbiotic whole able to automatically repeat decisions and foresee the majority of environmental aspects known to be relevant. The goal is to able to mimic the behavior of the environment to an extent capable of supporting sustainable decisions.

In this sense, DDS methodologies allow us to build *modeling machines* that leverage the role of human beings in this process to a meta-level. Science has proceeded through a cycle of observation, representation (modeling), and assimilation (reasoning and knowledge enhancement) since the scientific revolution in 17th century, where observations were gathered either as passive recordings of changes in nature or with (wet) experiments in laboratories. Observation always required the construction of artifacts to collect observations and perform experiments. The advent of computers largely widened this process by introducing a virtual (computational) environment where virtual artifacts can be easily constructed and virtual experiments can be performed in formerly unthinkable situations. The possibilities underlying this attributed a new role to models that once simply represented observations in a comprehensible, synthetic, and manipulable manner. Virtual experiments opened new ways to re-think observation and re-engineer its methods, particularly with respect to what was formerly passive recordings.

DDS methodologies and computational modeling techniques allow us to go further in improving the scientific process. By intelligently introducing adaptation and decision abilities in computational objects and sensors it is possible to leverage the observation process by building probes that adapt their behavior to what is being observed and then modelg it more accurately. Such probes are even able to identify novelties to a certain extent. They allow for observing interactions for their strengths and other aspects of nature that are crucial in understanding complex phenomena [21] that are not observable without the intervention of (partial) models. This includes ecological and environmental phenomena and phenomena at other scales that have living entities as components.

Combining DDS and environmental probes allows us to model an environment over a very long timeframe, predict future changes, and shepard its changes to some degree. Unlike in a conventional DDS where we change physical models to suit the data, here we are using DDS techniques to derive and modify the environmental model over long periods of time based on the data collected to date. Environments that are far from cities and people, such as in the Amazonal regions, will be much better modeled using this technique.

References

1. Ashton, K.: That 'internet of things' thing. RFID J., 22 June 2009. http://www.rfidjournal.com/articles/view?4986. Accessed 9 October 2014
2. Atzori, L., Iera, A., Morabito, G.: The internet of things: a survey. Comput. Netw. **54**(15), 2787–2805 (2010)

3. Caramaschi, E.P., Scarano, F.R., Vieira, M.V., Monteiro, R.F.: Populações, Comunidades e Conservação, vol. 2. Fundação CECIERJ, Rio de Janeiro (2010)
4. Douglas, C.C.: This is a scientific web site with contributions from about 100 people. http://www.dddas.org. Accessed 9 October 2014
5. Douglas, C.C., Kritz, M.V.: A glimpse on environmental probes. In: Guo, Q., Douglas, C.C. (eds.) Proceedings of DCABES 2012, Guilin, China, 2012, pp. 473–476. IEEE Computer Society CPS, Los Alamitos (2012)
6. Faria, L.D.B., da Silveira Costa, M.I.: The interplay between predator's prey preference and environmental heterogeneity in food web long-term stability. J. Theor. Biol. **258**(3), 339–343 (2009)
7. Hutchinson, G.: Circular causal systems in ecology. Ann. N. Y. Acad. Sci. **50**(4), 221–246 (1948)
8. Jones, A.M.: Environmental Biology. Routledge Introductions to Environment Series. Routledge, London (1997)
9. Junk, W.J. (ed.): The Central Amazon Floodplain: Ecology of a Pulsating System. Ecological Studies, vol. 127. Springer, New York (1997)
10. Kritz, M.V.: On biology and information. P&D Report 25/91, LNCC/MCT, Petrópolis, December 1991
11. Kritz, M.V.: Biological information and knowledge. Relatório de P&D 23/2009, LNCC/MCT, Petrópolis, December 2009
12. Kritz, M.V.: Boundaries, interactions and environmental systems. Mecánica Computacional **XXIX**, 2673–2687 (2010), http://www.cimec.org.ar/ojs/index.php/mc/article/viewFile/3183/3110
13. Kritz, M.V., Dias, C.M., da Silva, J.M.: Modelos e Sustentabilidade nas Paisagens Alagáveis Amazônicas. Notas em Matemática Aplicada, SBMAC - Sociedade Brasileira de Matemática Aplicada e Computacional, São Carlos (2008)
14. Kritz, M.V., dos Santos, M.T.: Dynamics, systems, dynamical systems and interaction graphs. In: Peixoto, M.M., Rand, D., Pinto, A.A. (eds.) Dynamics, Games and Science, in honour of Maurício Matos Peixoto and David Rand. Proceedings in Mathematics, vol. 2. Springer, Berlin (2011)
15. Ricklefs, R.E.: The Economy of Nature, 6th edn. W.H. Freeman and Company, New York (2008)
16. Rosen, R.: Life Itself: A Comprehesive Inquiry into the Nature, Origin, and Fabrication of Life. Complexity in Ecological Systems Series. Columbia University Press, New York (1991)
17. Sala, O.E., Jackson, R.B., Mooney, H.A., Howarth, R.W. (eds.): Methods in Ecosystem Science. Springer, New York (2000)
18. Shrager, J.: The fiction of function. Bioinformatics **19**(15), 1934–1936 (2003)
19. Ulanowicz, R.E.: Identifying the structure of cycling in ecosystems. Math. Biosci. **65**, 219–237 (1983)
20. Ulanowicz, R.E.: On the nature of ecodynamics. Ecol. Complex. **1**(4), 341–354 (2004)
21. Weaver, W.: Science and complexity. Am. Sci. **36**, 536–544 (1948)
22. Wootton, J.T.: Indirect effects in complex ecosystems: recent progress and future challenges. J. Sea Res. **48**(2), 157–172 (2002)
23. Wootton, J.T., Emmerson, M.: Measurement of interaction strength in nature. Annu. Rev. Ecol. Evol. Syst. **36**(1), 419–444 (2005)

Towards Intelligent Closed-Loop Workflows
for Ecological Research

JD Knapp[1]([⊠]), Matias Elo[2], James Shaeffer[1], and Paul G. Flikkema[1]

[1] Northern Arizona University, Flagstaff, AZ 86001, USA
jdk85@nau.edu
[2] Nokia Networks, Espoo, Finland

Abstract. Spurred by needs related to research on the effects of climate change on ecological systems, distributed facilities for ecological research are of growing importance. While software infrastructure for low-level networking services are well-established, experiments using these facilities will demand real time data-driven workflows for monitoring, model inference, and control of environmental processes. In this paper, we motivate and present a middleware-based approach that enables construction and deployment of workflows that assimilate real-time streaming data and, if necessary, command and control streams. We demonstrate the approach by developing and deploying a workflow for characterizing the round-trip delays incurred by increasing levels of software infrastructure, and using the workflow to assess time delay performance in laboratory, campus, and remote scenarios.

Keywords: Closed loop · Real-time · Workflows · Ecology · Middleware · Experiments · Design · Delay

1 Introduction

Evidence is strong and growing that the rate of climate change is such that many ecosystems will not be able to adapt rapidly enough to survive if they are not assisted by human intervention. If we can synthesize predictive performance models for these systems from experiments, we can improve understanding of how they will respond to climate change and develop a scientific basis for ecosystem restoration, and more broadly, ecological engineering. Thus there is a need for experimental platforms that will enable data-driven modeling of the effects of climate on these systems.

Experiments of this type require the establishment of garden plots across geographically-distributed climate gradients and the ability to manipulate environmental processes, such as plant water availability, to provide a spectrum of potential future climates. We have been developing a facility that combines an array of gardens distributed over an elevation gradient with engineered infrastructure for sensing, networking, computation, and actuation of key environmental processes to support multiple, concurrent, long-term experiments.

© Springer International Publishing Switzerland 2015
S. Ravela and A. Sandu (Eds.): DyDESS 2014, LNCS 8964, pp. 100–111, 2015.
DOI: 10.1007/978-3-319-25138-7_10

In this paper, we describe on-going work at the intersection of scientific workflows and closed-loop real-time control. This work builds on foundational sensing, computation, networking and actuation infrastructure to enable development workflows for management of complex experiments. These workflows are necessarily closed-loop since efficient sensing, learning, reasoning, and decision-making will rely on the interplay of streaming data and evolving models.

We first present our middleware-based architecture for integration of modular algorithms into closed-loop workflows. We then describe a specific diagnostic workflow for data-driven modeling of the delays associated with the distributed infrastructure; such workflows can be used to monitor the performance of the overall system and provide services to support delay-sensitive dynamic workflows at the experiment application level. Finally, we use this workflow to characterize the delay performance of our deployed infrastructure that incorporates processing modules and cellular data links to remote garden sites.

2 Previous and Related Work

Different approaches to the development of scientific workflows [4] have been explored [3,6–9], but they have not addressed the requirements of real-time, closed-loop systems. A workflow is a data flow graph [12–14], with tasks and their software implementations as nodes and their connectivity specified by directed edges. The graph may reflect a simple processing chain or a more complex structure that supports closed-loop control. Graphical representations at this level are well-established across many disciplines, and are used in many engineering design and simulation tools that can support real-time and closed-loop workflows, e.g., Simulink, LabVIEW, and Ptolemy [11]. These tools, with their focus on initial engineering design, are primarily desktop applications. However, our approach is network-centric, with processing blocks executing on any Internet-connected host that are interconnected via Java-based middleware. In our approach, processing blocks can be designed and tested in simulation environments prior to deployment. For example, Simulink can be used for algorithm design and generation of C/C++ code that can be integrated into the real-time workflow using Java/C++ interfaces.

3 Overview

The Southwest Experimental Garden Array (SEGA) is a facility that allows researchers to study the ecological and evolutionary responses of individual plants, species, and communities to a range of climate regimes. SEGA consists of ten gardens, each of which can support multiple experiments, each consisting of multiple plots. Each SEGA garden is instrumented with a network of wireless sensor/actuator nodes for sensing and control of environmental processes. Each garden is also equipped with a central data logger that captures garden-scale weather/climate data and a garden server; the garden servers, along with the on-campus SEGA Real-Time Data Center (RTDC), form a network that supports experiments across multiple gardens. The RTDC provides a range of services that support both experiments and SEGA operations, including real-time data processing, generation of actuation commands, data validation and quality assurance, streaming data visualization, and performance monitoring.

Streaming data middleware [2,10] connects the SEGA garden servers and the RTDC, providing networking abstractions that hide lower-level networking layers by offering services such as stream naming, publish/subscribe semantics, and local persistent storage. The SEGA project uses DataTurbine [1], an open-source middleware package written in Java, to stream data between garden servers and the RTDC.

DataTurbine abstracts TCP/IP connections so that streams can be routed to and from other Java programs regardless of their locations. Data can be inserted into, or extracted from any instance of a DataTurbine Ring-Buffered Network Bus —or simply RBNB—using a client program called a Source/Sink that invokes DataTurbine methods via the DataTurbine API. Source/Sinks are written in Java and can include code that implements arbitrary data processing, including learning, reasoning, and decision-making. Source/Sinks can both produce and/or consume data streams both to and from DataTurbine instances. For this reason, here we refer to DataTurbine clients as *processors*.[1]

Each garden server executes a processor that gathers incoming data packets from the garden's sensor network and central data logger and inserts them into a local DataTurbine instance. A processor running on the RTDC server uses a request/response protocol [16] to fetch data and insert it into a local RBNB. Other processors further parse and process the raw streaming data, e.g., transforming them to engineering units or performing sensor fault detection.

4   Closed-Loop Control of Ecological Experiments

The middleware-based architecture and cyber-infrastructure described in the previous section allows for the introduction of any number of modular processors that are able to consume and/or produce RBNB data streams. Processors can be composed into directed graphs to construct processing chains that implement streaming data workflows. For example, a particular experiment may require the fusion of *in situ* streaming data with external streams (e.g. models of insolation) for inference of parameters or state. Perhaps more importantly, closed-loop real-time control can be implemented. An example of one possible configuration of a closed-loop workflow is illustrated by Fig. 1. The shaded block represents the physical environment as well as the sensors and actuators that interact directly with the physical system or, in this case, the garden plot environment. Signals from the sensors are processed and fed to a model inference processor. The model is used to synthesize a control system which can, in turn, make decisions and send commands to actuators that manipulate the environment.

---

[1] The authors thank J. Eberle, J.-P. Calbimonte, and A. Marjovi for helpful discussions around this concept and for this label.

The modeling processors can be viewed as comprising the second-highest level of a layered architecture (Fig. 2) in the SEGA infrastructure. At the lowest level is the garden plot; this is the physical environment being sensed and manipulated via sensors and actuators at the second-lowest level. In the SEGA implementation, the sensors generate data streams that are transported to the RTDC via the layers shown in Fig. 2 and assimilated by a data-driven model of the environmental system. This model then drives the synthesis and tuning of a control algorithm which closes the loop by manipulating the *in situ* actuators. Each logical entity in the workflow can be represented as a block in a dataflow graph and implemented as a processor. Because of the layered model, a researcher designing an experiment using the platform needs to only be familiar with the highest level of abstraction.

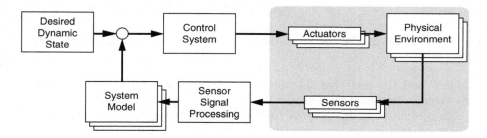

Fig. 1. An example of a closed-loop workflow using interconnected processors

Using a block based approach to designing closed-loop workflows also enables the rapid design and testing of the modular system within a simulated environment. Software such as Simulink can be used to interconnect multiple processor designs in order to validate basic interactions used by the model. The interplay of high-level algorithms can be tested using the simulated models and the results can then be used as the basis for generating Java/C++ code for incorporation into the real-time workflow.

A typical example of such a closed-loop workflow is control of plant water availability in one experimental plot as a function of soil moisture observations at another plot, perhaps in a different garden. An array of soil moisture sensors and a solenoid controlling a irrigation system valve comprise the sensing/actuation layer. The soil moisture observations are assimilated by a system identification (or model calibration) processor that infers the parameters of a state space soil moisture model [17]. This model is then used to estimate the system state and tune a control algorithm that, using the sensed and processed data, determines when to toggle the solenoid and closes the sense, learn, reason, decide loop. This workflow is implemented as processors for sensor signal processing, system identification, state estimation, and control.

At the highest abstraction level, the SEGA Web Portal is hosted on the RTDC and provides a user interface that includes a set of tools for interacting with experiment workflows. The SEGA web portal is a broker between the

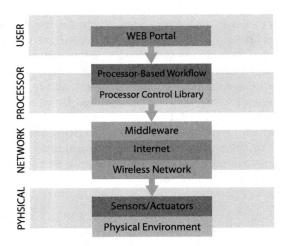

Fig. 2. A representation of the abstraction layers used in the SEGA cyber-infrastructure

workflow and the user that allows the monitoring of system status, real-time data visualization, and data export for exploratory data analysis.

The system is designed such that an arbitrary number of processors can be plugged in and interconnected via the middleware. These processors might implement modular algorithms that ingest data streams and generate commands based on a set of parameters or they might simply sniff data and create a log of potentially corrupted data points or even assess system performance across networks. Any given processor has access to nearly any other entity within the workflow and can therefore serve a wide variety of purposes. The Web Portal facilities the relationship between processor and workflow.

The Web Portal's interactions with the workflow are governed by a set of support libraries. SEGA users have access to some of these support libraries that are utilized when creating and designing new processors. This approach further abstracts the users' experience from the complexities of the underlying workflow design. One such support library facilitates adding processors that read and analyze incoming data and generate control commands that can be used to trigger actuation events in the environmental plot.

4.1   SEGA Processor Construction Library

We have designed a Processor Construction Library (PCL) that supports rapid creation of processors with parameters that can be exposed to the user via the Web Portal, enabling on-line editing of parameters or operating modes. Modular control algorithms implemented using the PCL can be added or removed from the Web Portal on-the-fly. The web interface gives users with administrator privileges the ability to upload *Java* class files to the RTDC server via a form submission. The server then uses the system compiler to attempt to generate a compiled instance of the uploaded class file within the same virtual space that is running other processors. The RTDC creates a parent class wrapper for the uploaded file and attempts to assign the newly compiled instance as the child class to determine if the processor can be safely inserted into the currently running workflow. At this point, if everything has been successful, the RTDC can verify that the uploaded processor class file meets all the system design requirements. If the processor fails to pass any of these tests at any point during the upload and compilation process, it will not be added to the workflow and the user is informed as to why the processor failed the tests.

The PCL enables processors to interact directly with the middleware by providing high-level convenience methods to flush and fetch streaming data to and from DataTurbine instances without requiring the user to manually handle DataTurbine connections. The PCL includes an environment that also abstracts error-handling and thread-safe processes from the user. The high-level function calls are made using the PCL API that provides access to streaming data, given the RBNB stream names are known. For example, a workflow might consist of a chain of processors that assimilate temperature measurements. The sensor reading is inserted into the workflow as a raw value; in this case, there might be a processor that converts the raw measurement into engineering units and subsequently flushes this converted value into a DataTurbine instance, making it available to other processors.

5   Case Study: Measuring Round-Trip Delays

Workflows facilitate monitoring and modeling the performance of the SEGA cyber-system itself in addition to control of ecological experiments. Here we describe the design and use of a workflow to measure round-trip network delays that enables inference of a predictive model of the delays in closed-loop work-flows. We employ a client/server model, where a client processor sends message packets to a server processor, receives a response message, and records the inter-vening time. The server processor simply listens for packets from the client and generates response packets on a one-to-one basis.

In this case study, we were interested in the potential overhead effects of the DataTurbine middleware and the use of processors. In the latter case, we wanted to quantify delays associated with implementing algorithms using processors built using the PCL. To estimate these effects, we used both 'raw' UDP and TCP packet exchange as a reference system. In the following sections, we describe three distinct modes of operation to characterize the corresponding delays.

In long-term ecological experimentation applications, the cyber-infrastucture should detect, report and log system performance and events, and attempt to improve performance or recover from failures. As part of this effort, we are enabling the creation of processors that can monitor overall system performance as well as the performance of the workflow they are part of. Although the case study presented here employs stand-alone processors, we intend to make this capability available in the PCL so that other processors in all experimental workflows can monitor delays.

Figure 5 provides a graphical representation of the network interactions that occur in each of the available operational modes. These round-trip delay tests are run on the operational SEGA hardware in an effort to estimate system performance as accurately as possible. The following sections describe the operational modes in more detail (Fig. 3).

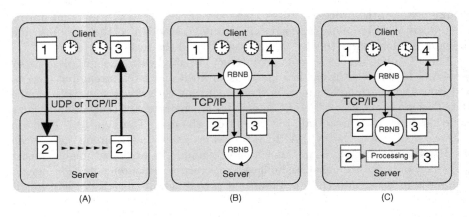

Fig. 3. (A) Raw-Packet exchange mode, (B) DataTurbine-Packet exchange mode, and (C) DataTurbine with processor control packet exchange

5.1   UPD and TCP Raw-Packet Exchange

Raw-packet mode can operate using UDP or TCP and does not include either DataTurbine middleware or processors that perform data processing algorithms built on top of the PCL. A simple client processor on the garden server creates either a UPD or TCP socket connection to a server processor running at the data center. Packets containing a sequence number are echoed back to the client processor by another processor across a network interface that is running in server mode.

Internally, a packet generation thread creates message payloads containing unique message sequence numbers and buffered to reach a desired packet payload size. A custom object class is used to store the time when data is sent across the socket connection. The object stores the sequence number, a timestamp of Java system time, and a time-sent value. A user-defined time interval is used to run a timer that continually creates packets that contain the sequence number.

The received packet thread monitors the socket for data packets from the server and, when a packet is received, the client processor fetches the original message and compares the time sent with time received to calculate the round-trip delay for that particular message. Sent and received time measurements use Java's System.nanoTime() method which has a nanosecond resolution relative to an arbitrary but fixed point in time [15].

5.2   DataTurbine Packet Exchange

This mode uses DataTurbine instead of a basic UDP or TCP socket and therefore includes the overhead of the DataTurbine middleware. In DataTurbine, data streams are called channels. The server processor establishes a DataTurbine connection to the client and configures itself to listen for incoming data on one channel while producing outgoing data on another. The processor then monitors the client channel; when a new packet arrives it is repackaged and returned to the client via the source channel.

The client processor also has source and sink channels but both connections are made to the local instance of DataTurbine. The client uses two threads and operates in a similar fashion to the raw packet mode client. The same time-delay measurement object is created when a packet is sent. The packet itself is constructed identically to the process described by the raw packet mode, but in this mode the packet is flushed to the local DataTurbine instance. This is the source channel that is being monitored by the server's sink. The client locally inserts packets and the server remotely fetches data on this channel when it becomes available. This process is done to mimic the actual interactions between garden server and data center in the SEGA cyber-infrastructure. When the server returns the data packets, the client then runs the same check as the raw mode and calculates the round trip delay.

5.3   DataTurbine with Processor Control Packet Exchange

This mode aims to mimic an experiment control workflow; however, minimal computational processing is used to enable quantification of the delay cost of using processors constructed using the PCL. The client runs exactly as it does in the DataTurbine Implementation mode, but the server is slightly different in this mode. A very simple server processor was built using the PCL that monitors the client source channel and performs a simple arithmetic operation on the data. The server still repackages the received packet and flushes it back to the client, but this occurs after the arithmetic operation is performed.

5.4   Measuring the Effects of Locality

To test the effects of locality on round-trip delay (RTD), we conducted testing under three scenarios:

LAN - A loop between a garden server and a development RTDC server in our laboratory are connected via a common LAN provided using a single Ethernet switch.

Campus - The garden server in our laboratory connects to a server at our Real-time Data Center about 1 km away.

Remote - A garden server at a remote site about 10 Km from campus is linked to the RTDC, requiring a cellular data link, the Internet and the campus network.

Identical Java-based software for the client and server is created and deployed on both SEGA servers that are to be tested. The round-trip delay processor is configured so that the same software package can be executed using the different modes described in Sect. 5 as well as being run as either a server or client.

6   Numerical Results

In each of our tests, we transmitted 1000 64-byte packets at a rate of one per second for each of the three scenarios and four modes described above. All tests were performed back-to-back to minimize the effects processor loading and of the diurnal variation of network congestion. Results of the RTD testing are summarized in Table 1. To visualize the results, we also generated beanplots of the round-trip time distribution, as seen in Fig. 4. Beanplots combine a distribution with a scatterplot [19]. The distribution is drawn in a solid color and is overlaid by individual observations represented as short horizontal lines. The thick horizontal line indicates the mean of each distribution, while the dotted horizontal line across each plot is the overall mean of the delays measured.

In the LAN and Campus scenarios, TCP/IP significantly improved performance over UDP, with average RTD reduction of approximately 140 ms and a considerable reduction of the frequency of extreme delay values. Also for the LAN and Campus scenarios the RTD for TCP/IP was under 1 ms. The introduction of the DataTurbine middleware gives rise to an increase in the average delay of 6 to 8 ms. Again, in the LAN and Campus scenarios, the increased computational burden of the processors (Experiment mode) appears to introduce a further delay of about 1.5 to 5 ms. Finally, note that the remote data connection involves the Internet, the cellular provider's private network, and the wireless link. The results are somewhat surprising: on average, UDP has better average performance, but a broader distribution of outliers. The DataTurbine

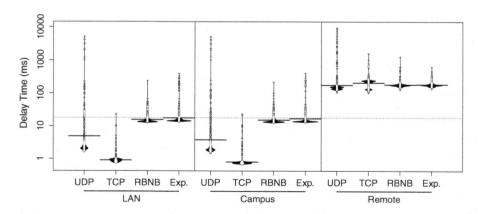

Fig. 4. A beanplot representation of network round-trip times across different SEGA servers

Table 1. Round trip delay measurements for raw packet, middleware-based delivery using DataTurbine, and closed-loop experiment control.

Scenario	Results (ms)	Raw (UDP)	Raw (TCP)	DataTurbine	Experiment
LAN	Mean	144.4	0.958	16.69	22.59
	Std. Dev	693.8	0.857	9.55	33.67
Campus	Mean	142.2	0.905	15.97	21.83
	Std. Dev	694.89	1.23	6.69	34.45
Remote	Mean	330.7	221.4	184.9	186.4
	Std. Dev	881.2	114.75	52.93	35.63

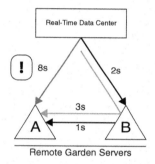

Fig. 5. Example decision process to reroute packet traffic based on real-time delay measurement.

and Experimental Control modes had better performance than Raw TCP/IP, perhaps due to sub-hourly variations in traffic congestion.

7 Towards Operational Performance Monitoring

The round-trip delay measurement workflow could be executed periodically across a set of servers, enabling other workflows that could analyze the results and adjust decision-making processes. For example, if we know that garden server A is experiencing major delays in communications with the RTDC but communication between garden server B and the RTDC are within the expected range we can attempt to identify a faster route for packets destined for garden server A. We might then perform delay tests between garden servers A and B. If these tests show that redirecting traffic intended for garden server A through garden server B from the RTDC would be faster than transmitting directly to garden server A, we might choose to temporarily reroute traffic through garden server B. This example is illustrated in Fig. 5.

8 Concluding Remarks

We have introduced an architecture and implementation to build and deploy complex workflows that operate in real-time. These can be open- or closed-loop depending on the application-level need. In future work, we plan to further refine the PCL so that processors can invoke complex algorithms implemented in languages familiar to scientists, such as Mathematica, Matlab, and R. We also plan to explore supporting a simulation capability so that experimenters can develop, test, and refine workflows before deploying them to ecological experiments.

References

1. Fountain, T., et al.: The open source dataturbine initiative: empowering the scientific community with streaming data middleware. Bull. Ecol. Soc. Am. **93**(3), 242–252 (2012)
2. Aberer, K., Hauswirth, M., Salehi, A.: A middleware for fast and flexible sensor network deployment, In: Proceedings of the 32nd International Conference on Very Large Databases, pp. 1199–1202 (2006)
3. Deelman, E., Singh, G., Su, M.H., Blythe, J., Gil, Y., Kesselman, C., Katz, D.S.: Pegasus: a framework for mapping complex scientific workflows onto distributed systems. Sci. Program. **13**(3), 219–237 (2005)
4. Deelman, E., et al.: Workflows and e-Science: an overview of workflow system features and capabilities. future Gener. Comput. Syst. **25**(5), 528–540 (2009)
5. Freire, J.: Making computations and publications reproducible with Vistrails. Comput. Sci. Eng. **14**(4), 18–25 (2012)
6. Barseghian, D., Altintas, I., Jones, M.B., Crawl, D., Potter, N., Gallagher, J., Hosseini, P.R.: Workflows and extensions to the Kepler scientific workflow system to support environmental sensor data access and analysis. Ecol. Inf. **5**(1), 42–50 (2010)
7. Wolstencroft, K., Haines, R., Fellows, D., Williams, A., Withers, D., Owen, S., Goble, C.: The Taverna workflow suite: designing and executing workflows of Web Services on the desktop, web or in the cloud. Nucleic Acids Res. **41**(W1), W557–W561 (2013)
8. Zhang, J., Kuc, D., Lu, S.: Confucius: a tool supporting collaborative scientific workflow composition. IEEE Trans. Serv. Comput. **7**(1), 2–17 (2014)
9. Ekanayake, J., Gunarathne, T., Fox, G., Balkir, A.S., Poulain, C., Araujo, N., Barga, R.: Dryadlinq for scientific analyses. In: Fifth IEEE International Conference on e-Science (e-Science 2009), pp. 329–336, December 2009
10. Andriescu, E., Speicys Cardoso, R., Issarny, V.: AmbiStream: a middleware for multimedia streaming on heterogeneous mobile devices. In: Kon, F., Kermarrec, A.-M. (eds.) Middleware 2011. LNCS, vol. 7049, pp. 249–268. Springer, Heidelberg (2011)
11. Eker, J., et al.: Taming heterogeneity-the Ptolemy approach. Proc. IEEE **91**(1), 127–144 (2003)
12. Lee, E., Messerschmitt, D.G.: Static scheduling of synchronous data flow programs for digital signal processing. IEEE Trans. Comput. **C-36**(1), 24–35 (1987)
13. Kavi, K.M., Buckles, B.P., Bhat, Narayan, U.: A formal definition of data flow graph models. IEEE Trans. Comput. **C-35**(11), 940–948 (1986)
14. Boose, E., Ellison, A., Osterweil, L., Clarke, L., Podorozhny, R., Hadley, J., Wise, A., Foster, D.: Ensuring reliable datasets for environmental models and forecasts. Ecol. Inform. **2**(3, Sp. Iss. SI), 237–247 (1986)
15. Java Platform, Standard Edition 7 API Specification. http://docs.oracle.com/javase/7/docs/api/java/lang/System.html#nanoTime()

16. Shaeffer, J., Knapp, J.D., Miller, M., Flikkema, P.G.: A middleware-based approach to the design of interconnected sensor/actuator networks. In: 2014 IEEE International Workshop on Real-Time Cyber-Physical Systems, June 2014
17. Ghosh, S., Bell, D.M., Clark, J.S., Gelfand, A.E., Flikkema, P.: Process modeling for soil moisture using sensor network data. Stat. Methodol. (Special Issue on Modern Statistical Methods in Ecology) **17**, 99–112 (2014)
18. Kampstra, P.: Beanplot: a boxplot alternative for visual comparison of distributions. J. Stat. Softw. **28**(Code Snippet 1), 1–9 (2008)

Reduced Representations and Features

Objective Detection of Lagrangian Vortices in Unsteady Velocity Data

George Haller$^{(\boxtimes)}$

Institute of Mechanical Systems, ETH Zürich, Zurich, Switzerland
georgehaller@ethz.ch

Abstract. Lagrangian Coherent Structures (LCSs) are special material surfaces that delineate tracer patterns in unsteady flows. The recently developed variational theory of LCSs enables their objective (frame-invariant) detection in numerical and experimental velocity data. Here we review the main results of this variational theory for elliptic LCSs (i.e., perfectly coherent material vortices) and show how such structures can be extracted from geophysical data sets.

Keywords: Lagrangian mixing · Invariant manifolds · Transport · Turbulence

1 Background

Fluid flows tend to display coherent structures in passive tracer fields they carry. The centerpieces of such tracer patterns are well known in the case of steady, time-periodic and quasi-periodic flows: fixed points, periodic orbits, invariant tori, as well as stable and unstable manifolds [1]. These invariant structures are influential material points and lines with distinguished asymptotic behavior. They form a skeleton of fluid particle motion that creates a profound signature in tracer distributions over long enough time intervals. We collectively refer to such key material objects in the flow as Lagrangian coherent structures (LCSs).

Observational, experimental and numerical flow data, however, tend to be temporally aperiodic and finite in time. None of the classic invariant objects mentioned above is expected to exist in such flows. Yet signs of sustained material coherence are ubiquitous in models and observations of turbulent flows. Geophysical examples include stretching and folding of biological surfactants in the ocean reminiscent of stable and unstable manifolds; mesoscale phytoplankton patterns reminiscent of center-type regions filled with periodic orbits; and ring-type tracer patterns of volcanic steam reminiscent of Kolmogorov-Arnold-Moser (KAM) invariant tori (see Fig. 1). All this suggests that appropriately defined LCSs continue also exist in temporally aperiodic finite-time flow data. A mathematical challenge is to identify and extract such structures in a systematic and self-consistent way, without any assumption on temporal recurrence or asymptotic features.

Substantial progress has been made in the theory and computation of LCSs over the past decade (see [2–5] for reviews). Here we focus on recent results on elliptic LCSs, which provide an objective (frame-invariant) way of defining coherent Lagrangian vortices in turbulent flows.

© Springer International Publishing Switzerland 2015
S. Ravela and A. Sandu (Eds.): DyDESS 2014, LNCS 8964, pp. 115–120, 2015.
DOI: 10.1007/978-3-319-25138-7_11

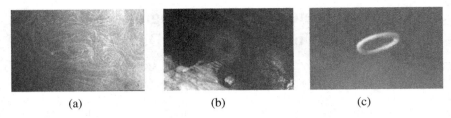

Fig. 1. (a) Spiral eddies in the Mediterranean Sea (Paul Scully-Power/NASA) (b) Phytoplankton patch in the Agulhas leakage (Jeff Schmaltz/NASA) (c) Steam rings over Mount Etna (Tom Pfeiffer/www.volcanodiscovery.com).

2   Coherent Lagrangian Vortices in Two-Dimensional Flows

We consider a typical closed material curve in a two-dimensional unsteady flow. This curve will generically stretch and fold, evolving into a closed but filamented shape. The evolution of the enclosed fluid volume will then show no coherence, occupying an irregular and elongated shape.

By contrast, elliptic-type coherent regions familiar from KAM theory [5] will be observed inside exceptional closed curves. The time t_0 position of such a closed curve, denoted by γ, translates and rotates under the flow but shows no smaller-scale filamentation. We express this coherence property of the material line evolving from γ over a finite time interval $[t_0, t_1]$ by requiring the averaged Lagrangian strain to admit a stationary value along the initial elliptic LCS position γ [6]. Later positions of this LCS at a general time $\tau \in [t_0, t]$ are the obtained by advecting γ under the flow map $F_{t_0}^\tau$.

Specifically, we consider a closed curve $\gamma \subset \mathbb{R}^2$ at time $t = t_0$, which is mapped forward by a flow map $F_{t_0}^t : x_0 \mapsto x_i$ of a two-dimensional unsteady velocity field $\dot{x} = v(x, t)$. Let γ be parametrized as $r(s)$ and let $C_{t_0}^t = [DF_{t_0}^t]^T DF_{t_0}^t$ denote the Cauchy-Green strain tensor. In line with our discussion above, we seek positions of elliptic LCSs as stationary curves of the material-line-averaged Lagrangian strain functional computed over the time interval $[t_0, t_1]$. In other words, the time t_0 position of the LCS is a closed curve γ satisfying the variational principle

$$\delta \oint_\gamma \sqrt{\left\langle r', C_{t_0}^t(r)r' \right\rangle / \langle r', r' \rangle} \, ds = 0. \tag{1}$$

The Euler-Lagrange equations arising from the variational problem (1) are complicated, but turn out to be equivalent to a geodesic problem under a metric generated by the deformation field [6]. Solving this geodesic problem gives that the curves satisfying Eq. (1) are precisely the limit cycles of the planar direction field family.

$$\eta_\lambda^\pm(x) = \sqrt{\frac{\lambda_2(x) - \lambda^2}{\lambda_2(x) - \lambda_1(x)}} \xi_1(x) \pm \sqrt{\frac{\lambda^2 - \lambda_1(x)}{\lambda_2(x) - \lambda_1(x)}} \xi_2(x), \tag{2}$$

where $\lambda > 0$ is a free parameter and $0 < \lambda_1(x) \leq \lambda_2(x)$ are the eigenvalues of the Cauchy-Green strain tensor field $C_{t_0}^{t_1}(x)$ with corresponding orthonormal eigenvectors $\xi_i(x)$.

The limit cycles of the direction field family (2) are therefore the initial positions of elliptic LCSs. They tend to exist for λ parameter values near one. As obtained in [6], each such elliptic LCS remains remarkably coherent under advection. While it may translate and rotate, any of its subsets is stretched in length precisely by the same factor λ over the time interval $[t_0, t_1]$. In nested families of elliptic LCSs, the outermost limit cycle serves as a coherent Lagrangian vortex boundary.

The limit cycles of (3) also turn out to be two-dimensional analogues of photon spheres arising in general relativity [6]. As a consequence, elliptic LCSs necessarily encircle metric singularities, which facilitate their automated detection in large-scale velocity data [6, 7].

Figure 2 shows coherent Lagrangian vortices extracted from a two-dimensional direct numerical simulation of Navier-Stokes turbulence [8]. The initial positions of the vortices were located as outermost elliptic LCSs, i.e., outermost limit cycles of a differential equation whose right-hand side is given by Eq. (1).

Figure 3 shows the application of the same analysis to the detection of coherent Lagrangian eddies in the Agulhas leakage, a vortex shedding process in the South

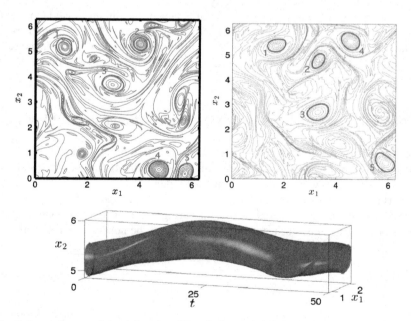

Fig. 2. Coherent Lagrangian vortices in a 2D turbulence simulation [8]. Upper left: initial vortex boundary positions detected as outermost limit cycles of (1). Upper right: final limit cycle positions obtained by advecting their initial positions as material lines. Note the complete absence of filamentation. Bottom: Time history of vortex #1 under advection.

Fig. 3. Families of coherent Lagrangian vortices computed from satellite-detected surface velocities in the Agulhas leakage [6].

Atlantic originating from the southern tip of Africa [6]. The velocity field used in this study was obtained from satellite altimetry under the geostrophic assumption. Seven mesoscale Lagrangian eddies emerged as limit cycles of the direction field (1), with the length of the extraction interval $[t_0, t_1]$ chosen as 3 months. These coloured material patch-families translate and rotate in the northwest direction without noticeable deformation for 3 months. Several of them remain materially coherent for substantially longer.

3   Coherent Lagrangian Vortices in Three-Dimensional Flows

In three-dimensional flows, both surface-based and curve-based variational principles have been developed to define and extract analogues of steady vortex tubes and vortex rings in finite-time flows with general time-dependence.

A surface-based approach developed in [9] seeks coherent Lagrangian vortex boundaries as outermost members of most shearing material tubes or material. Initial positions of such material surfaces at time t_0 turn out to be normal to the direction field

$$n_\pm(x_0) = \sqrt{\frac{\sqrt{\lambda_1(x_0)}}{\sqrt{\lambda_1(x_0)} + \sqrt{\lambda_3(x_0)}}} \xi_1(x_0) \pm \sqrt{\frac{\sqrt{\lambda_3(x_0)}}{\sqrt{\lambda_1(x_0)} + \sqrt{\lambda_3(x_0)}}} \xi_3(x_0), \quad (3)$$

where $\lambda_i(x_0)$, $i = 1, 2, 3$ again denote the eigenvalues of the three-dimensional Cauchy-Green strain tensor in increasing order, and $\xi_i(x_0)$ denote the corresponding orthonormal eigenvectors.

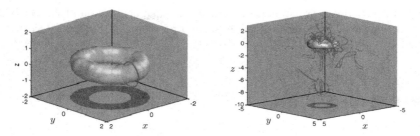

Fig. 4. Left: Initial position of a coherent Lagrangian vortex ring (green) extracted from the chaotically forced ABC flow [9]. Also shown for reference is a nearby closed material line (red) encircling the vortex ring. Right: Evolution of the vortex ring and the reference material line in the flow, showing the sharpness of the identification of the material ring as a coherent vortex boundary (Color figure online).

Figure 4 shows a coherent Lagrangian vortex in the chaotically forced Arnold-Beltrami-Childress (ABC) low. The boundary of this vortex was extracted in [9] as a surface orthogonal to the direction field (3).

A more recent variational approach [10] seeks coherent material vortices in three dimensions as smooth sets of curves satisfying an appropriate extension of the

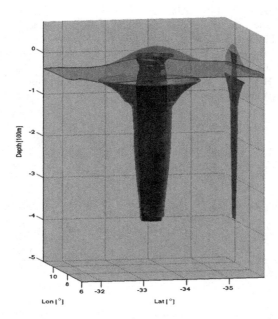

Fig. 5. Coherent material vortex (blue) and its inner coherent core (red) in the SOSE data set. Also shown is the sea surface obtain from the same model. (Image: Daniel Blazevski, reproduced from [4]) (Color figure online).

curve-based variational principle (1). Figure 5 shows an application of this method to the extraction of a three-dimensional Agulhas ring from the Southern Ocean State Estimate data set [11].

References

1. Ottino, J.M.: The Kinematics of Mixing: Stretching Chaos and Transport. Cambridge University Press, Cambridge (1989)
2. Shadden, S.C.: Lagrangian coherent structures. In: Grigoriev, R. (ed.) Transport and Mixing in Laminar Flows: From Microfluidics to Oceanic Currents, pp. 59–89. Wiley-VCH, Berlin (2012)
3. Peacock, T., Haller, G.: Lagrangian coherent structures: the hidden skeleton of fluid flows. Phys. Today **66**, 41–47 (2014)
4. Haller, G.: Lagrangian Coherent Structures. Ann. Rev. Fluid Mech. **47**, 62–137 (2015). http://www.annualreviews.org/toc/fluid/47/1
5. Arnold, V.I.: Mathematical Methods of Classical Mechanics. Springer-Verlag, NY (1989)
6. Haller, G., Beron-Vera, F.J.: Coherent Lagrangian vortices: The black holes of turbulence. J. Fluid Mech. **731**(R4), 1–10 (2013)
7. Karrasch, D., Huhn, F., Haller, G.: Automated detection of coherent Lagrangian vortices in two-dimensional unsteady flows (2014) http://arxiv.org/abs/1404.3109
8. Farazmand, M. Haller, G.: How coherent are the vortices of two-dimensional turbulence? (2014). http://arxiv.org/abs/1402.4835
9. Blazevski, D., Haller, G.: Hyperbolic and elliptic transport barriers in three-dimensional unsteady flows. Physica D **273–274**, 46–64 (2014)
10. Öttinger, D., Blazevski, D., Haller, G.: Geodesic approach to transport barriers in 3D unsteady flows (2014). (preprint)
11. Mazloff, M.R., Heimbach, P., Wunsch, C.: An eddy-permitting southern ocean state estimate. J. Phys. Oceanogr. **40**, 99–880 (2010)

Statistical Inference for Coherent Fluids

Sai Ravela[✉]

Earth Signals and Systems Group, Earth, Atmospheric and Planetary Sciences,
Massachusetts Institute of Technology, Cambridge, USA
ravela@mit.edu

Abstract. A non-parametric perceptual organization for coherent fluids is proposed, motivated by the observation that ignoring coherence can be disastrous for inference. Detecting coherence features and establishing correspondence can be challenging for sparse measurements and complex structures in fluid fields. Therefore, a non-parametric representation using deformation (geometry) and amplitude (appearance) is developed. It is first applied to Data Assimilation and Ensemble analysis problems for coherent fluids, following which new methods for Principal Modes, Random Fields, Variational Blending and Reduced Order Modeling are introduced. Simple examples illustrating application suggest broad utility in environmental inference, verification, representation and modeling.

Keywords: Data assimilation · Uncertainty quantification · Reduced modeling · Field alignment · Field coalescence · Principal Appearance and Geometry modes · Coherent random fields

1 Introduction

Localized geophysical phenomena can often be visualized as dynamically deformable objects. For example, hurricanes appear to be steered by the background even as they intensify or decay. Coherence in localized phenomena can be represented by amplitude, scale and shape descriptors in addition to their position. This includes lagrangian descriptors of flows, e.g., Lagrangian Coherent Structures, but so are, for the inference problems studied in this paper, vortex elements, tracer texture, filaments and contours.

The prediction and predictability of coherent fluids is of great interest and accounting for coherence is critical in inference methodology. To see why, consider the prototypical challenges shown in Fig. 1. The optimal estimate (red) from sparse, noisy measurements (dots) and an imperfect prediction (green) with position error is distorted instead of being coherent (Fig. 1(a)); a well-documented problem [11]. In the unsupervised case (Fig. 1(b)), the ensemble mean of coherent fields can be incoherent, and not an exemplar of the ensemble [8,14,15]. The principal modes (Fig. 1(c)) of a Gauss-Markov Random Field (GMRF) estimated from the ensemble produces incoherent random realizations even at full rank (Fig. 1(d)).

© Springer International Publishing Switzerland 2015
S. Ravela and A. Sandu (Eds.): DyDESS 2014, LNCS 8964, pp. 121–133, 2015.
DOI: 10.1007/978-3-319-25138-7_12

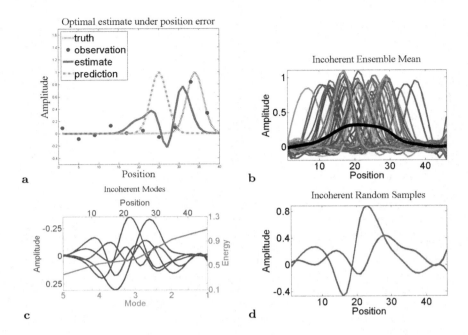

Fig. 1. Unaccounted coherence attributes can lead to incoherent estimates (top-left), statistics (top-right), and reduced models (bottom-right) of coherent fields (Color figure online).

It is easy to see why the estimates in Fig. 1 are poor. A simple translation of the predicted feature $X \circ q \equiv X(p - q(p))$[1] with Taylor expansion $X \circ q \approx X(p) - q_0 \frac{\partial X}{\partial p}$ for a translation $q(p) = q_0$ has covariance $C_q = C + q_0^2 E[\frac{\partial X}{\partial p} \frac{\partial X}{\partial p}^T]$. For non-zero perturbations, C_q has less information and sparse observations cause further loss.

Augmenting feature information could solve the problem in an analysis-synthesis paradigm. Preferred locations, scales, shapes and amplitudes with embedded dynamical relationships can be detected. They can be adjusted by assimilating measurements, then resynthesizing physical fields. For example, Tagade et al. [16] detect position-amplitude features in chaotic solitons to enable non-linear filtering. Features can also facilitate reduced models or serve as sampling "hot spots." We call this a Perceptual Organization for Coherent Fluids (POCF), intended for verification, inference, and modeling.

However, POCF faces detection difficulties in multidimensional, sparsely observed and noisy fields. It faces representational difficulties for complex shapes and deformations. One way to resolve these problems is to account for coherence without explicit feature detection. Since location, scale and shape can be controlled through a deformation of a field, i.e. $X(p - q(p))$, a non-parametric representation of vector-field q leads to a generalized error model for spatial fields, to be sure both in amplitude and deformation.

---

[1] Gridded spatial fields are interchanged as vectors by rasterizing.

A variety of problems are amenable to non-parametric POCF. Among them, data assimilation [7,11,13,15,17] ensemble statistics [8,9,15], random fields, reduced modeling, downscaling, nowcasting [8,10] and mapping [8,10,12], and forecast error [6] decomposition. Many others are emerging.

In this paper, solutions to two fundamental and four derived problems are discussed. The first fundamental problem is supervised inference using distribution $P(X, q|Y)$ on sparse, noisy measurements Y to recover *gridded* fields X and q respectively. Second, we recover the coherent ensemble mean $\bar{X}$ using $P(\bar{X}, \{q\}|\{X^f\})$ by solving an N-body problem that we call *Field Coalescence* [8,9]. Solutions to these problems help solve others. In particular, we develop Principal Appearance and Geometry modes (PAG), a Coherent Random Field model (CRF), a new Reduced order Model by Alignment (ROMA), and a Field-Alignment based Blending algorithm (FABle). Together, they lead us towards a statistical theory of inference for coherent structures.

The remainder of this paper is organized as follows; Field Alignment is developed in Sect. 2, Field Coalescence in Sect. 3, and PAG and CRF in Sect. 4. FABle and ROMA are presented in Sect. 5, with conclusions in Sect. 6.

2   Supervised Spatial Inference: Field Alignment

Consider, for simplicity, the deformation $X \circ q = X(p - q(p))$ of gridded scalar field X (vector fields are easily handled [7]) deformed by a dense vector field q. Also consider a second field Y related to the first field by the linear observation operator $Y = H(X \circ q) + n$. Both fields have uncertainties. To solve for X and q, consider a Bayesian expansion of the posterior $P(X, q|Y) \propto P(Y|X, q)P(X|q)P(q)$ with three terms: the likelihood, the appearance (or amplitude) prior conditioned on grid geometry, and the deformation prior. Using a deformation prior in the form of differential [7] or turbulence [18] motion constraints, the negative log likelihood of the posterior yields a quadratic objective [15]:

$$J(X,q) := \frac{1}{2}\delta X^T \{C(X^f \circ q)\}^{-1}\delta X + \frac{1}{2}\delta Y^T R^{-1}\delta Y + \Lambda(q) \qquad (1)$$

The term $\delta X \equiv [X \circ q - X^f \circ q]$ and $\delta Y \equiv [Y - H(X \circ q)]$, C is the amplitude error covariance, X^f is the prior estimate, forecast or first guess, Λ a scalar potential function on deformation, and R is the observation error covariance. Solutions to J that directly depend on evaluating gradients of C^{-1} with respect to deformation q in Eq. 1 are, however, not tractable. An ensemble to implicitly represent C in reduced rank square-root form with iterated minimization [11] or Expectation Maximization (EM) [15] can be used. In this iterative approach, C is updated from the estimate of the deformation ensemble $\{q\}$ at the current iteration and held fixed when the objective is solved. Even so, the dimensionality of this optimization problem remains large.

Another, simplified approach can be used. In this iterated alternating optimization approach, setting $X = X^f$ as the most recent amplitude estimate leads to Field Alignment (FA):

$$J_q(q|X^f) = \frac{1}{2}\left[Y - H(X^f \circ q)\right]^T R^{-1}\left[Y - H(X^f \circ q)\right] + \Lambda(q) \qquad (2)$$

Using the solution $\hat{q}$, define $\hat{X}^f \equiv X^f \circ \hat{q}$, $\delta X \equiv X - \hat{X}^f$, $\delta Y \equiv [Y - HX]$, we solve the second objective:

$$J_x(X|\hat{q}) = \frac{1}{2}\delta X^T \hat{C}^{-1}\delta X + \frac{1}{2}\delta Y^T R^{-1}\delta Y \qquad (3)$$

J_q and J_x must be iteratively alternated [15], generalizing the earlier *two-step* [7]. Like the two-step, this formulation is also amenable as a *pre-processor* to current practice and applicable *with or without* an ensemble. J_q does not need C and flow-dependent $\hat{C}$ can be constructed with the aligned amplitude field. With an ensemble, the objective $J_{qs} = \sum_{s=1}^{S} J_q(q_s|X_s^f)$ is solved with ensemble member s. Similarly, amplitude J_{xs} can be constructed with $\hat{C} \equiv C(\{\hat{X}_s^f\})$.

Nominal Solution: We solve J_q and J_x via their Euler-Lagrange equations. J_q can nominally be solved iteratively. The solution is initialized with $X^{f(0)} = X^f$ and $q^{(0)} = \underline{0}$. At each iteration i, update $X^{f(i)} = X^{f(i)} \circ q^{(i-1)}$, define $Z^{(i)} \equiv H^T R^{-1}(Y - HX^{f(i)})$ and $\tilde{q}^{(i)} \equiv L^{(i)}q^{(i)}$ then solve:

$$\tilde{q}^{(i)}(r) = [\nabla X^{f^{(i)}}(r)]^T Z^{(i)}(r) \equiv f^{(i)}(r) \qquad (4)$$

Here, $L^{(i)}q^{(i)} = d\Lambda/dq^{(i)}$, the gradient of the potential. Note that Eq. 4 is evaluated for each component of $\tilde{q}^{(i)}$ at pixel or grid point r. The final solution is $\hat{q} = \sum_i q^{(i)}$. The objective J_x (Eq. 3) becomes defined and we get:

$$\hat{X}^a = \hat{X}^f + \hat{C}H^T(H\hat{C}H^T + R)^{-1}(Y - H\hat{X}^f) \qquad (5)$$

Deformation Scale Space and Scale Cascade: Ravela et al. [11,13] suggested differential smoothness and non-divergence constraints to construct Λ. For some choice of weights w_1 and w_2, Eq. 4 becomes:

$$Lq^{(i)} \equiv w_1\nabla^2 q^{(i)} + w_2\nabla\left(\nabla \cdot q^{(i)}\right) = f^{(i)} \qquad (6)$$

Ravela et al. [7] use a multiresolution framework for large deformations. They extend FA to multivariate and vector fields [11], including dynamical balance [15]. The control of smoothness is important. Although weights could be viewed as length scale D, e.g. $w_1\nabla^2 q^{(i)} = \nabla^2(q^{(i)}/D)$, however, neither the deformation spectrum's shape changes nor lower wavenumber deformations are resolved. Largely, the rate of convergence adjusts [7]. Thus, Ravela [11] control smoothness in two ways. First, by padding the domain to resolve smaller wave number deformations but without changing the order of the differential constraint. This is generally computationally expensive. Second, by alternately reformulating the constraint. Yang and Ravela [18] assume power-laws for deformation spectra and represent them as a weighted sum of Gabor scale-space basis.

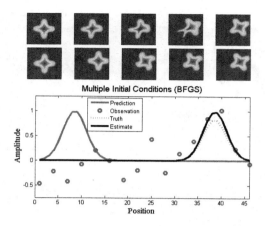

Fig. 2. SCA uses a Gabor basis to recover dominant deformation modes. It provides a more parsimonious explanation in contrast to classical differential constraints, see Yang and Ravela [18]. The correct deformation is recovered (top plot, second row) in contrast to naive diffeomorphic alignment [3,4] (top plot, first row). Stochastic optimization (bottom plot) is performed from random initial deformations sampled from the deformation prior using BFGS with sparse noisy observations.

Deformation modes are estimated sequentially by *cascading* from DC (translation) to higher wave number bases, and call it Scale-Cascaded Alignment (SCA). SCA controls deformation by seeking the most parsimonious solution (see Fig. 2). It can be iteratively solved for each basis in the cascade, or through an optimization approach discussed next. Supporting examples are shown at http://stics.mit.edu.

Deep Minima: Stochastic Optimization. Ravela et al. [15] also provide a non-local stochastic minimization procedure for J_q. Since the instantaneous deformation is of the form $Lq = f$, therefore, $q = L^{-1}f$. A random f produces a random deformation field with structure consistent with L. This leads to a sampling approach, and the following algorithms are used. 1. Multiple starting points: Solve J_q from multiple initial perturbations $\{q_0\}$ generated by sampling $q_0 = L^{-1}\eta$ for a random i.i.d. vector η. 2. MCMC: Generate a perturbation; accept if it improves the objective or accept with a probability if it does not [15]. As shown in Fig. 2 (bottom panel), the multiple initialization with BFGS converges to the correct solution in response to sparse, noisy measurements and a large initial error (12 sigma away). A stochastic non-local SCA approach is desirable. It is robust, capable of handling up to about 30 % noise, whereas local minima problems plague the local iterative approach [15].

3   Unsupervised Inference: Field Coalescence

The solution to the unsupervised problem for the mean from an ensemble, in contrast to the supervised assimilation problem, is based on observations that the

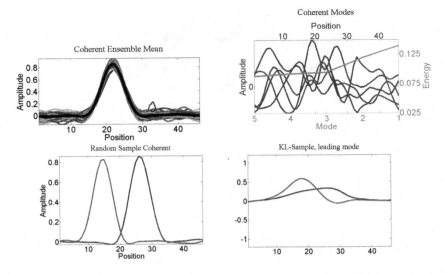

Fig. 3. Field Coalescence automatically to recover the mean (top-left). The recovered coherent principal appearance modes (top right), and random coherent realizations with just one leading appearance and geometry mode (bottom left), in contrast to classical synthesis (bottom right).

statistics of coherent fields can become incoherent. Formulating this as inference on $P(\bar{X}, \{q\} | \{X^f\})$ [8], an objective is developed and solved using stochastic-EM. Each ensemble member experiences a *body force* from the other in this formulation, and the resulting N-body problem discovers the coherent mean field as its solution [9].

In the ith EM iteration $(i > 0)$ ensemble members are deformed $X_s^{f(i)} = X_s^{f(i-1)} \circ q_s^{(i-1)}$, also implicitly updating the ensemble covariance C_i. Omitting subscript i for simplicity by writing $X_s^f \equiv X_s^{f(i)}$, $q_s \equiv q_s^{(i)}$ and $C \equiv C_i$, the E-step forms an updated objective:

$$J(\bar{X}, \{q_s\} | \{X_s^f\}) = \sum_{s=1}^{S} (\bar{X} - X_s^f \circ q_s)^T C^{-1} (\bar{X} - X_s^f \circ q_s) + \Lambda_s(q_s) \qquad (7)$$

The first normal equation that emerges is an expression for the amplitude mean, $\bar{X} = \frac{1}{S} \sum_s X_s^f \circ q_s$. Substituting it in the objective again produces a pure alignment problem eliminating $\bar{X}$. This problem is solved iteratively as discussed for J_q, however, in the large sample limit the instantaneous deformation $q_s^{(j)}$ of ensemble member s in the inner iteration j of alignment (not EM) satisfies:

$$\tilde{q}_s^{(j)}(r) = \frac{2}{S} \sum_{t \neq s} \nabla X_s^{f(j)T}(r)\, Z_{ts}^{(j)}(r) \qquad (8)$$

where $Z_{ts}^{(j)} \doteq \left[C^{-1}(X_t^{f(j)} - X_s^{f(j)}) \right]$, $\tilde{q}_s^{(j)} \doteq L_s q_s^{(j)} = d\Lambda_s/dq_s^{(j)}$ and $X_s^{f(j)} \doteq X_s^{f(j-1)} \circ q_s^{(j-1)}$, $j > 0$ and $q_s^{(0)} = 0$. Note that the normalization becomes

$(S-1)/S^2$ instead of $1/S$ in the small case. Naturally, both MCMC and stochastic BFGS versions can also be used with SCA. Once Eq. 8 converges, $q_s^* \doteq \sum_j q_s^{(j)}$ provides for $q_s^{(i)} = q_s^*$ in the outer iteration. The next iteration of the E-step commences. Naturally, $\bar{X}^* = \frac{1}{S}\sum_{s=1}^S X_s^{f(N-1)} \circ q_s^N$ results from the last outer iteration N. In many practical situations, only one outer iteration is required, but this is not generally true. Several may be required for C to converge to an accurate representation of amplitude uncertainty.

Equation 8 shows that every ensemble member experiences a *body force* from the others. In this way, all *coalesce* to a mean. Both synchronous and asynchronous solutions exist. The coherent structures in Fig. 3 (top left) are coalesced from Fig. 1 (top right) which contain foreground and background variability [8,15]. Also, see http://stics.mit.edu.

4   Coherent Random Fields

A natural application of Field Coalescence is to generate deformation statistics that can be used to produce random field models for coherent structures without explicit feature detection. Let's assume that $X = \bar{X} + US\eta$ is the Karhunen Loeve (KL) expansion representing a Gauss-Markov spatial process with covariance $C = US^2U^T$, and η is i.i.d. sample from a Normal distribution with unit variance. Such decompositions find ready use, for example, in the Proper Orthogonal Decomposition or Empirical Orthogonal Functions. Data or model simulations are often used to construct reduced models using few modes of U.

However, coherent structures do not necessarily distribute in amplitude as a Gauss Markov process! The sampling problem on distribution $P(X, q)$ is modeled as $X \circ q \sim P(X|q)P(q)$, decomposed here in what we call the Coherent Random Field (CRF)

$$X \circ q = (\bar{X} + U_{xx}S_{xx}\eta_x) \circ (\bar{q} + U_{qq}S_{qq}\eta_q) \tag{9}$$

Here, $\bar{X}$ and $\bar{q}$ are the appearance and geometry mean fields respectively, U_{xx} and U_{qq} are their principal modes, S_{xx} and S_{qq} their spectra, and η_x and η_q are amplitude and phase stochastic variables. We call these Principal Appearance

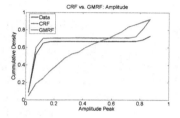 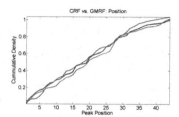

Fig. 4. Comparison of the distribution of coherent feature amplitude and positions. PAG preserves the statistics better.

and Geometry modes (PAG). In Fig. 3, the coherent random fields are synthesized from the coalesced ensemble (top right). Random realizations with even just one leading PAG mode (bottom-left) is superior to either all or one leading normal modes without. To confirm, we check the peak amplitude distribution and peak amplitude's position distribution in Fig. 4. As suspected, peaks distributed across the domain contain incorrect amplitudes in the classical approach. PAG produces coherent features and reproduces the data statistics it was trained from. The implication for reduced modeling of coherent structures is immediate.

5   Applications

We consider two applications in this section. The first uses FA and Coalescence to construct a reduced forward model and its backward propagator, which we use to solve the *blending problem* between two sources of data. The second application uses PAG, FA and Coalescence to adapt classical reduced order modeling (here, POD/EOF) to be dynamic and data-driven. Both are illustrated on simple problems.

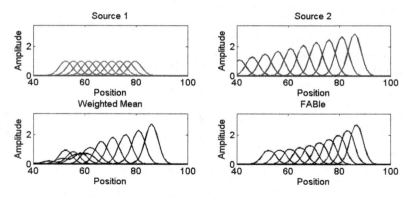

Fig. 5. FABle application two sources. The fields are superposed to show evolution of a coherent structure. Source 1 (top left) and Source 2 (top right) predictions are blended by weighted averaging (bottom left) and using FABle (bottom right).

5.1   Field Alignment-Based Blending (FABle): An Illustration

Applications of Nowcasting, for example for Aviation [8,10,15], seek 0–8 h storm forecasts. One way is data-driven model. The apparent motion, growth and decay of observed radar image time series of vertically integrated liquid in the recent past, assuming some persistence timescale, is extrapolated from the current time to the $[0,8]hr$ interval. Another way is to assimilate data to reinitialize a numerical model (e.g., the High Resolution Rapid Refresh Rate model) for a $0-8$ h forecast. Neither is perfect. The confidence in extrapolation decreases exponentially over time and the confidence in HRRR appears to increase as the

Algorithm 1. FABle: Field Alignment-based Blending Illustration

Input: $X_1 \ldots X_N$, $Y_1 \ldots Y_N$, α, $\beta_1 \ldots \beta_N$
Output $X_1^* \ldots X_N^*$
for $i := 1 : N$ **do** $\hat{X}_i = X_i$
end for % Initialize Left Boundary
while .not. Converged **do**
    for $i := 1 : N - 1$ **do** % Identify a Deformation-Growth/Decay model.
      $q_i = argmin J_q(\hat{X}_i, \hat{X}_{i+1})$; $q_i^{\#} = argmin J_q(\hat{X}_{i+1}, \hat{X}_i)$;
      $\delta \hat{X}_i = (\hat{X}_{i+1} - \hat{X}_i \circ q_i) \circ q_i^{\#}$
    end for
    $\lambda = argmin J_q(\hat{X}_N, Y_N)$; $\lambda_{N-1} = (\lambda \circ q_{N-1}^{\#})$ % Assert right boundary point.
    for i:=N:2 **do** $\lambda_{i-1} = (\lambda_i \circ q_{i-1}^{\#})$; % Adjoint deformation error propagation.
    end for
    $\hat{X}_1 = X_1$; % Assert left boundary point.
    $\delta q_1 \leftarrow \lambda_1$ % Incremental deformation.
    for i=1:N-1 **do** % Forward adjustment of coherent field.
      $q_i \leftarrow q_i + \alpha \delta q_i$
      $\hat{X}_{i+1} = (\hat{X}_i + \delta \hat{X}_i) \circ q_i$
      $\delta q_{i+1} \leftarrow (1 - \alpha) \delta q_i \circ q_i$ %
    end for
end while % Time/phase adjusted coherent fields
$\forall i$ Align $\hat{X}_i \rightarrow \hat{X}_N =: \check{X}_i$ % Done partially in parallel
$\forall i$ Align $Y_i \rightarrow Y_N =: \check{Y}_i$ % Done partially in parallel
$\forall i$ Blend: $\check{X}_i \leftarrow \beta_i \check{X}_i + (1 - \beta_i) \check{Y}_i$ % Amplitude adjustment
$\forall i$ Restore time line: $X_i^* \leftarrow \check{X}_i \circ q_{N-1}^{\#} \circ \ldots q_i^{\#}$

model equilibrates after initial assimilation shocks [8] and then saturates. From a methodological perspective, the two forecasts are to be blended. At one end point (left), radar extrapolation is preferred and at the right, HRRR. A weighted average seems natural, preferring source 1 on the left and source 2 on the right. It does not work (see Fig. 5), for obvious reasons of position error.

The Field Alignment-based blending (FABle) solves this as a two-point boundary value problem (see Algorithm 1), matching Source 1 (radar) on the left and Source 2 on the right. FA establishes a deformation, growth and decay model going forward and backward (FA-adjoint) for Source 1. The error with Source-2's right boundary is back-propagated through Source-1 snapshots, "stretching an accordion" without letting its left boundary budge. Forward adjustment of coherent fields and backward error propagation continues iteratively to remove misalignment. Both fields are coalesced to their right boundary, whence weighted amplitude average corresponding fields can be correctly taken. The average is "opened up" using FA-adjoint revealing a perfectly blended output (see Fig. 5, bottom right). To be sure, no features are detected in this process. The ability to propagate information across time for coherent fluid fields in this way has wide application for time-dependent problems.

5.2   Reduced Order Models by Alignment (ROMA): Compensating for Model Error

FA, Coalescence and CRMs via PAG modes also enables robust reduced modeling in a more classical sense. A popular approach is to use an offline model to generate samples (snapshots, lagged forecasts, ensemble forecasts), and characterize the dynamical regime with a reduced linear model that requires a few (possibly stochastic) variables to represent system's evolution. During runtime (or online), predictions made by the propagated reduced variable are corrected using data and the process repeats. The modes may or may not themselves slowly adapt (Fig. 6).

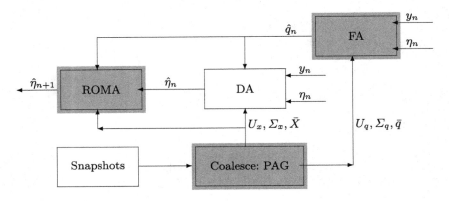

Fig. 6. Using FA and Coalescence, a Reduced Order Model by Alignment (ROMA) is constructed so that the principal modes can adapt to model error.

The problem, of course, is the presence of model error which, for a variety of reasons, puts the coherent structure in the wrong place. In a simple tracer transport problem, for example, velocity, timing, boundaries, and forcing errors can be culprits. As our preceding discussion shows, state estimates can become poor when the tracer is coherent. The reduced variable updates will lead to incoherent realizations. Using FA on the full-state is meaningful to resolve this problem [11], but when phase (position, scale, shape) error is systematic, i.e., has a mean deformation component or a slow variation, a deformable reduced model proposed herein may be more suitable. Using POD/EOF as an example, we show dynamic data-driven model adaption; we call this Reduced Order Modeling by Field Alignment (ROMA).

In the ROMA approach, the reduced variable consists of the reduced appearance variable $\nu_x = \Sigma_{xx}\eta_x$ and reduced geometry variable $\nu_q = \Sigma_{qq}\eta_q$ (formulation works with η_x and η_q), and the principal appearance and geometry statistics, $\bar{X}, U_{xx}, \Sigma_{xx}$ and $\bar{q}, U_{qq}, \Sigma_{qq}$ respectively, with terms as in Sect. 4. These terms are calculated by *Coalescing* snapshots offline.

During runtime, predicted coherent mean (due to coalescence) is used to solve J_q (a partial state reconstruction can also be used). The incremental $\hat{q}$ over iterations deform the statistics, producing $\bar{X} \leftarrow \bar{X} \circ \hat{q}$, such that $U_{xx} \leftarrow Orth(U_{xx} \circ \hat{q})$

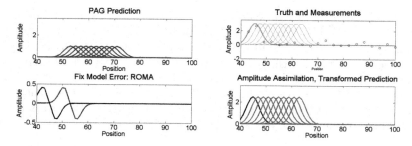

Fig. 7. Automatic deformation of reduced models using PAG modes and Field Alignment demonstrates the ability to fix model errors for coherent fluids (Color figure online).

where $U_{xx} \circ \hat{q} \equiv [U_{xx}(:,i) \circ \hat{q}]$. That is, the incremental deformation is used to deform the reduced basis and mean, with re-orthogonalization (*Orth*) to assert the conditions on U_{xx}. The reduced model is adapted by the deformation component upon convergence.

In Fig. 7, the reconstructions from reduced predictions from PAG modes are shown (top-left). The sparse measurements (dots) are shown at the assimilation time (top right) with truth (green). The automatically deformation adjusted modes (only first mode is shown, bottom left) transforms the predictions to have correct phase while the amplitude assimilation restores the amplitude. The reduced model is now phase synchronized which offers exciting possibilities for data driven corrections to flow errors. Without doing this, the assimilation and subsequent predictions are simply incoherent.

6 Conclusion

A non-parametric perceptual organization of coherent fluids solves several inference problems in data assimilation, uncertainty quantification, and reduced modeling better. Error between spatial fields is reduced in position and amplitude subspaces without explicit detection of features. Thus, sparse observations or features difficult to specify (e.g., fronts, complex storm shapes) can be accounted for. A weakened covariance primarily plagues effective estimation for coherent structures [11,13]. Equation 1 differs from prior work [5] that assumes C was fixed to after alignment, thus ignoring the dependence of amplitude errors on position errors. An ensemble approach with EM [11,15] addresses this problem as well as incorrect independence or jointly Gaussian assumptions in work that followed [2]. A two-step approximation enables an alignment preprocessor [11] in ensemble and variational modes. Williams applies this to the WRF model [17], and Jankov et al. to decomposing forecast errors [6]. The latter application is not viable using other direct approaches. Iterative deformation-amplitude adjustment [15] generalizes the two-step.

Ravela et al. use spectral resolution [11] to control deformation smoothness, avoiding ad-hoc constraints [5], and use a multi-resolution solution [7] for large deformations. For multivariate/vector fields, FA incorporates balance constraints [15]. Yang and Ravela's [18] SCA automatically and parsimoniously recovers dominant spectral modes without explicit parameterization. In contrast to [1], it can be generally applied without learning. Together with a stochastic optimization method [15] for FA/SCA, these characteristics distinguish FA and Coalescence from other image-based, large deformation kinematics approaches [3,4]. In addition to Field Coalescence [8,9,15], we propose CRF, PAG, FABle and ROMA which, to the best of our knowledge, have not been reported.

References

1. Amit, Y., Grenander, U., Piccioni, M.: Structural image restoration through deformable templates. J. Am. Stat. Assoc. **86**(414), 376–387 (1991)
2. Beezily, J.D., Mandel, J.: Morphing ensemble Kalman filters. Tellus A **60**, 130–140 (2008)
3. Charpiat, G., Faugeras, O., Keriven, R.: Image statistics based on diffeomorphic matching. In: ICCV, pp. 852–857 (2005)
4. Christensen, G.E., Rabbitt, R.D., Miller, M.I.: Deformable templates using large deformation kinematics. IEEE Trans. Image Process. **5**(10), 1435–1447 (1996)
5. Hoffman, R.N., Liu, Z., Louis, J., Grassotti, C.: Distortion representation of forecast errors. Mon. Weather Rev. **123**, 2758–2770 (1995)
6. Jankov, I., Gregory, S., Ravela, S. Toth, Z.: A field alignment technique for forecast errors estimation and decomposition (2014, submitted)
7. Ravela, S.: Two new directions in data assimilation by field alignment. Lect. Notes Comput. Sci. **4487**, 1147–1154 (2007)
8. Ravela, S.: Quantifying uncertainty for coherent structures. Procedia Comput. Sci. **9**, 1187–1196 (2012)
9. Ravela, S., Chatdarong, V.: How do we deal with position errors in observations and forecasts annual? Geophys. Res. Abs. (EGU), **8**(09557) (2006)
10. Ravela, S., Dupree, W.J., Langlois, T.R., Wolfson, M.M., Yang, C.M.: Method and apparatus for generating a forecast weather image. US Patent 8,625,840, Janary 2014
11. Ravela, S., Emanuel, K., McLaughlin, D.: Data assimilation by field alignment. Phys. D **230**, 127–145 (2007)
12. Ravela, S., Sleder, I., Salas, J.: Mapping coherent atmospheric structures with small unmanned aircraft systems. In: AIAA Infotech@Aerospace (I@A) Conference, pp. 1–11 (2013)
13. Ravela, S.: Amplitude-position formulation of data assimilation. In: Alexandrov, V.N., van Albada, G.D., Sloot, P.M.A., Dongarra, J. (eds.) ICCS 2006. LNCS, vol. 3993, pp. 497–505. Springer, Heidelberg (2006)
14. Ravela, S.,Yang, C., William, J., Emanuel, K.: An objective framework for assimilating coherent structures. In: WMO Symposium on Nowcasting (2009)
15. Ravela, S.: Spatial inference for coherent geophysical fluids by appearance and geometry. In: Winter Conference on Applications of Computer Vision, pp. 925–932 (2014)
16. Tagade, P., Seybold, H., Ravela, S.: Mixture ensembles for data assimilation in dynamic data-driven environmental systems. Procedia Comput. Sci. **29**, 1266–1276 (2014)

17. Williams, J.K.: WRF-Var implementation for data assimilation experimentation at MIT. Master's thesis, Massachusetts Institute of Technology (2008)
18. Yang, C., Ravela, S.: Deformation invariant image matching by spectrally controlled diffeomorphic alignment. In: Proceedings of International Conference on Computer Vision, vol. 1, pp. 1303–1310 (2009)

Reduced Order Probabilistic Prediction of Rogue Waves in One-Dimensional Envelope Equations

Will Cousins$^{(\boxtimes)}$ and Themistoklis P. Sapsis

Department of Mechanical Engineering, Massachusetts Institute of Technology,
Cambridge, MA, USA
{wcousins,sapsis}@mit.edu

Abstract. We describe a method for prediction of rogue waves in
the one-dimensional Nonlinear Schrodinger and Modified Nonlinear
Schrodinger equations. This method is based on distinguishing the unstable wave groups likely to generate rogues out of a complex background
field. After a careful study of the evolution of isolated wave groups, we
then apply an automatic scale selection algorithm to pick out these individual wave groups that will trigger the formation of rogue waves. We
demonstrate the skill of our scheme for Reduced Order Prediction of
Extremes (ROPE), predicting rogues well in advance of their formation
with low rates of false positives/negatives.

1 Introduction

Rogue or extreme waves are ocean waves whose height is abnormally large for a
particular sea state. Often described as an enormous "wall of water", such waves
have caused catastrophic damage to ships and coastal structures. For example,
in 1978 the German super-tanker *Munchen* vanished, along with her 26 crew
members. Searches for the ship recovered little, but a lifeboat was recovered
whose attachment pins showed evidence of being subjected to a great force. As
this lifeboat was stowed 20 m above the water line, some have conjectured that
the *Munchen* may have been struck by an extremely large wave [12]. In this
work, we describe a reduced order method for reliably predicting these rogue
waves before they occur, which we term Reduced Order Prediction of Extremes
(ROPE).

The large, steep nature of these extreme waves, combined with recent evidence that they can occur more likely than Gaussian statistics would suggest,
imply that nonlinear models are necessary to fully understand their dynamics.
Thus, we focus our attention on models that incorporate this nonlinearity while
remaining simple enough to be tractable. A high-fidelity approach for modeling
surface waves in deep water is to use the Navier-Stokes equations, assuming irrotational flow with neglible viscosity and surface tension. Neglecting these effects
is deemed reasonable due to the large scale of typical ocean waves (wavelength
$\mathcal{O}(100)$ meters). Enforcing a pressure and kinematic condition on the free surface
gives the following system:

© Springer International Publishing Switzerland 2015
S. Ravela and A. Sandu (Eds.): DyDESS 2014, LNCS 8964, pp. 134–143, 2015.
DOI: 10.1007/978-3-319-25138-7_13

$$\nabla^2 \phi = 0, \qquad\qquad\qquad\qquad z \leq \eta$$

$$\frac{\partial^2 \phi}{\partial t^2} + g\eta + \frac{1}{2}|\nabla \phi|^2 = 0, \qquad\qquad\qquad z = \eta$$

$$\frac{\partial \eta}{\partial t} + \nabla \phi \cdot \nabla \eta = \frac{\partial \phi}{\partial z}, \qquad\qquad\qquad z = \eta$$

in the above ϕ is the velocity potential, $\eta(x, y)$ is the surface eleveation, and z is the vertical coordinate. Although this system has been shown to faithfully model the evolution of deep water waves well, it is complicated to investigate numerically and anlytically. Thus, for simplification purposes here we consider fields with no variation along the y direction. Even with this simplification, the model remains quite complicated. Thus, we consider simplified envelope equations. These equations govern the evolution of the envelope $u(x, t)$ of a slowly modulated carrier wave and may be derived, for example, by a perturbation approach. The simplest such envelope equation which incorporates nonlinear dynamics is the nonlinear Schrodinger equation (NLS) [18], which reads (in nondimensionalized form)

$$\frac{\partial u}{\partial t} + \frac{1}{2}\frac{\partial u}{\partial x} + \frac{i}{8}\frac{\partial^2 u}{\partial x^2} + \frac{i}{2}|u|^2 u = 0 \tag{1}$$

u is the envelope of the modulated carrier wave–to leading order $\eta = \Re[ue^{i(x-t)}]$. By considering higher order terms, Dysthe derived the modified Nonlinear Schrodinger Equation (MNLS) [8]:

$$\frac{\partial u}{\partial t} + \frac{1}{2}\frac{\partial u}{\partial x} + \frac{i}{8}\frac{\partial^2 u}{\partial x^2} - \frac{1}{16}\frac{\partial^3 u}{\partial x^3} + \frac{i}{2}|u|^2 u \tag{2}$$
$$+ \frac{3}{2}|u|^2\frac{\partial u}{\partial x} + \frac{1}{4}u^2\frac{\partial u^*}{\partial x} + iu\frac{\partial \phi}{\partial x}\Big|_{z=0} = 0$$

In simulations presented in this paper we consider (1) and (2) in a coordinate frame moving with group velocity 1/2. That is, we neglect the $(1/2)\partial u/\partial x$ term in each equation. The reason for this is that in this moving coordinate frame, localized groups of waves are roughly stationary, which makes visualization of the evolution of these groups clearer. Although NLS and MNLS are not without their limitations, they have shown reasonable agreement with laboratory experiments of rogue waves [3,4] and MNLS has faithfully reproduced the appropriate $k^{-2.5}$ spectrum observed in deep water [7]. Furthermore, these waves also admit intermittently appearing large-amplitude, localized coherent structures and heavy tailed statistics [9,14].

Here, we describe a simple, computationally cheap approach for predicting rogue waves with a high degree of spatiotemporal skill. This work can be viewed as an extension of our previous extreme event prediction scheme for the model of Majda-McLaughlin-Tabak (MMT) [5], which is another one dimensional nonlinear dispersive wave equation where large amplitude coherent structures form due to a soliton collapse mechanism [1,2,13]. We showed that MMT equation posesses a type of localized energy instability, where only a small amount of

highly localized energy is sufficient to initiate an extreme event. We then showed
how there was a most sensitive length scale for triggering extreme event, and projecting the field to a Gabor wavelet basis at this scale yielded a reliable predictor
of upcoming extreme events.

Although like MMT, the NLS and MNLS equations do admit extreme events,
there is no single critical length scale, meaning we have to considerably modify
our prior approach to predict extremes in this setting. For NLS and MNLS we
have successfully developed an extreme wave prediction scheme based on identifying, in a general wave field, structures that are likely to trigger an extreme
wave. These triggers are localized wave groups, whose isolated evolution we study
in detail in Sect. 2. In Sect. 3, we describe how we use existing scale selection algorithms to detect the existence and characteristics of wave groups embedded in
irregular wave fields. Finally, we combine the results from Sects. 2 and 3 to create a method to predict extreme waves before they occur. This ROPE (Reduced
Order Prediction of Extremes) approach reliably predicts extreme waves with
spatiotemporal skill while maintaining a low rate of false positives and false
negatives. Furthermore, although simulation is used to tune the ROPE scheme
the "live" implementation is far cheaper than performing any simulation, only
requiring the computation of a few integrals to project the field onto a carefully
chosen set of modes.

2   Evolution of Localized Wave Groups

We first consider solutions of NLS (1) and MNLS (2) using for initial data a sum
of complex exponentials with random phases with spectrum given by a Gaussian
function of wavenumber:

$$F(k) = \frac{\epsilon^2}{\sigma\sqrt{2\pi}} e^{-\frac{k^2}{2\sigma^2}}$$

initial data for u are then given by

$$u(x,0) = \sum_{k=-N}^{N} \sqrt{2\Delta_k F(k\Delta_k)} e^{i(k\Delta_k x + \theta)}$$

where L_x is the width of the spatial domain, $\Delta_k = 2\pi/L_x$, and θ_k are independent random variables distributed uniformly between 0 and 2π. The use of
periodic boundary conditions in space is, of course, completely nonphysical. We
merely use them so boundary effects are not important, as is the case in the deep
ocean far from land. Furthermore, the phenomena we focus on occur on a much
smaller scale than the chosen domain size and results are insensitive to increases
in L_x. Numerically, we solve NLS and MNLS via a Fourier method in space and
a 4th order Runge-Kutta exponential time differencing scheme (ETDRK4) [6].
We performed detailed grid refinement studies and chose our spatiotemporal
resolution to ensure accuracy to four decimal places.

The Benjamin Feir Index, $\epsilon\sqrt{2}/\sigma$, provides a measure of how unstable a particular wave field is with respect to nonlinear interactions–at larger BFI the spectrum broadens (particularly BFI > 1), large amplitude coherent structures are formed, and the statistics of the surface elevation are highly non-Gaussian [9,15]. In this work, we consider $\epsilon = 0.05, \sigma = 0.1$, which corresponds to a moderately high BFI where some spectral broadening takes place. We choose these values since very large BFI are rare in realistic ocean scenarios [16] and we wish to demonstrate that our method posesses skill in regimes where extreme waves are not ubiquitous.

Our key observation is the following: extreme waves are preceded by the formation of particular types of localized wave groups (see Fig. 1). This localization initiates dramatic energy transfers to smaller scales, creating an extreme wave. Of course, not all wave groups initiate an extreme event. Certain wave groups do focus, triggering an extreme wave, while others merely disperse, broadening and decreasing in amplitude. We now precisely characterize the dynamics of these wave groups as a function of their amplitude and length scale.

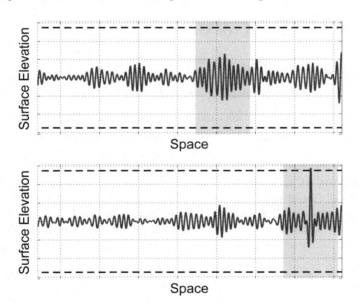

Fig. 1. A localized wave group (top) focuses energy to smaller scales, generating an extreme event (bottom).

Specifically, we suppose $u(x,0) = A\exp\left(-x^2/2L^2\right)$. What is the value of the next local maximum (in space and time) of $|u|$? We answer this question via direct numerical simulation. For the NLS equation, for any length scale L there is a critical value A^* where, if $A > A^*$, the wave group focuses and increases in amplitude. This increase, measured as a percentage increase growth in the wave group amplitude, becomes more dramatic as the initial amplitude grows. For example, if $L = 1$ a wave group with $A = 0.8$ grows negligibly, while a wave group with $A = 1.5$ doubles in amplitude. Due to the scale invariance of solutions to NLS, this behavior remains qualitatively unchanged for differing values of L.

The MNLS equation, however, does not posses a scale invariance and displays considerable differences as L is changed. For larger L, the MNLS wave group dynamics agree closely with NLS until the initial amplitude becomes large. However, for small L (such as $L = 1$), we see that regardless of initial amplitude the wave group does not increase in elevation (this fact has been confirmed via numerical simulation using a much broader range of amplitudes than that pictured in Fig. 2).

The differences in wave group evolution under NLS and MNLS are important, however, here we emphasize the following: in each equation there is a family of wave groups which evolve by dramatically transferring energy to smaller scales, increasing in amplitude and creating a wave (or group thereof) of considerable height. Furthermore, by performing an ensemble of simulations, we have catalogued the precise evolution of (A, L) pairs–we will use this data in Sect. 4 to drive our predictive scheme.

3   Identification of Wave Groups (Scale Selection)

Given a particular (perhaps irregular) wave field, we would like to determine the location, length scale, and amplitude of the various wave groups comprising that field. For example, let $f(x) = A_0 \exp\left(-(x - x_0)^2/2L_0^2\right) + A_1 \exp\left(-(x - x_1)^2/2L_1^2\right)$. In this case the envelope f consists of 2 wave groups, one centered at x_0 with length scale L_0 and amplitude A_0 and another centered at x_1 with length scale L_1 and amplitude A_1 (assuming x_0 and x_1 are sufficiently separated). To identify these wave groups algorithmically, we use the scale space representation of $|u|$, an approach that goes back to the work of Witkin [17] and Koenderink [10] (see also recent work by Lindeberg [11]). Given a function f, this algorithm determines the most significant length scales by finding local minima and maxima of *scale-normalized derivatives* s_m, which are properly normalized derivatives of the function f convolved with the heat kernel $g(x, L)$. That is,

$$s_m(x, L) = L^{m/2} \frac{\partial^m}{\partial x^m} (f * g)$$

where $g(x, L)$ is the heat kernel:

$$g(x, L) = \frac{1}{\sqrt{2\pi L}} e^{-\frac{x^2}{2L}}$$

Note here that g is the heat kernel in space x and scale L. We briefly review a simple example showing why the quantity s_m is meaningful (from [11]). Consider $f(x) = \cos(\omega x)$. Recalling that g is the heat kernel, we have (for even m)

$$s_m(x, L) = L^{m/2} \frac{\partial^m}{\partial x^m} \cos(\omega x) e^{-\omega^2 L/2}$$

$$= L^{m/2}(-1)^{m/2} \cos(\omega x) e^{-\omega^2 L/2}$$

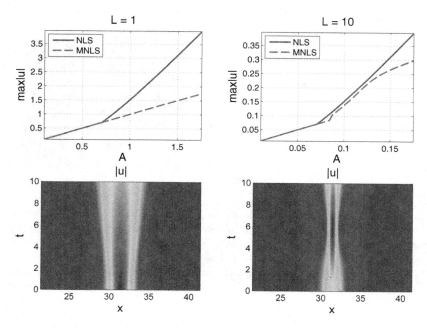

Fig. 2. Growth of localized waves in NLS and MNLS for $L = 1$ (top left) and $L = 10$ (top right). Spatiotemporal solution of NLS with $L = 1$ for a small amplitude, dispersive group (bottom left) and larger amplitude, focusing group (bottom right).

It is straightforward to show that the local maxima/minima of s_m occur when $L = m/\omega^2$ and $x = n\pi$, where n is an integer. Thus the scale normalized derivative s_m correctly picks the centers of the localized blobs, and the scale space maxima occur at a value of L proportional to the square of the length scale $1/\omega$.

If $f(x) = A \exp\left[-\frac{x^2}{2L0^2}\right]$, s_m again performs well as a wave group detector. For $m = 2$, we have

$$s_2(x, L) = -A \frac{L_0 L(L_0^2 + L - x^2)}{(L_0^2 + L)^{5/2}} e^{-\frac{x^2}{2(L_0^2 + L)}}$$

For the $f(x) = \cos(\omega x)$, example, local minima of s_2 correspond to the peaks of f and local maxima of s_2 correspond to valleys of f. For the Gaussian case it is straightforward to show that the unique local minimum of s_2 occurs at $x = 0, L = 2L_0^2$. Thus, if we did not know that the length scale of f was L_0, we could compute s_2 and find the value of x and L where the s_2 attains its minimum. Calling these values x^*, L^*, we would then say that f has a wave group of length scale $\sqrt{L^*/2}$ centered at $x = x^*$. Values of s_2 for the case $f(x) = \exp\left[-\frac{x^2}{2L_0^2}\right]$ with $L_0 = 10$ are displayed in Fig. 3. Clearly s_2 is able to pick out the correct scale of 10.

Finally, we demonstrate the scale-selection algorithm on a wave field generated as a sum of complex exponentials with Fourier coefficients of random phase

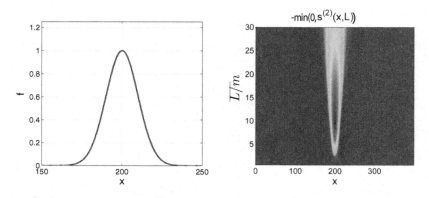

Fig. 3. Left: Gaussian function with length scale $L = 10$. Right: $-\min(0, s^{(2)})$ as function of space and scale. Notice that a local maximum occurs at $L = 10$, identifying the appropriate length scale.

and Gaussian amplitude. To identify the wave groups, we identify local minima of $s^{(2)}$. For each local minimum we compute the relative $\mathcal{L}^2$ error between the field and the local Gaussian approximation. We treat a relative error of less than 0.3 as evidence that the field $|u|$ can be well represented locally as a Gaussian wave group. In Fig. 4, we display an example field $|u|$ along with the identified wave groups, showing the successful performance of the scale selection algorithm in identifying wave groups.

The computational cost involved with this algorithm is small. If N is the number of spatial grid points in the domain, computing the scale space representation requires convolution and subsequent computation of second derivatives in space. The convolution requiires $\mathcal{O}(N \log N)$ work via FFT and the differentiation is $\mathcal{O}(N)$. This process must be repeated for a variety of values of L. For the simulations performed in this work, 50 points distributed between $L = 0$ and $L = 25$ are sufficient.

4   Reduced Order Prediction of Extremes

We now combine the ideas from Sects. 2 and 3 to create a scheme to predict extreme waves in advance. This relatively simple procedure is as follows: given a wave field $u(x,t)$ at a particular time, we use the automated scale selection algorithm to identify coherent wave groups, as well as their amplitude and length scale. In Sect. 2, we performed an exhaustive set of simulations where, given a wave group with a particular amplitude and length scale, we determined whether or not this group will increase in amplitude, and, if so, what its maximal focused amplitude will be. That is, we have numerically constructed the map $F(A, L)$, where A is the amplitude of the group, L is its length scale, and F is its maximal *future* amplitude. After we identify wave groups in the irregular field, we then use the controlled numerical experiments from Sect. 2 to determine how large these groups will grow via a simple table lookup. If the predicted maximal amplitude

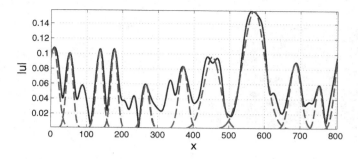

Fig. 4. Wave field generated by a Gaussian spectrum with random phases (blue) and the identified wave groups (red, dashed) (Color figure online).

is greater than the particular rogue wave threshold (twice the significant wave height) for a particular sea state, then we predict that a rogue wave is imminent.

We have tested this scheme on 50 simulations of MNLS using a Gaussian spectrum. Each simulation spanned 500 nondimensionalized time units and 128π nondimensionalized spatial units. For these simulations, a rogue wave occurs when $|u|$ exceeds 0.2 (significant wave height is 0.1). In this ensemble of simulations there were 123 distinct rogue waves, all of which were predicted in advance by our scheme. The average advance warning time was 105 time units, which corresponds to approximately 16 temporal wave periods. With a typical ocean wave period of 8–10 s, this would correspond to a warning time on the order of minutes in dimensional time. We do mention that there were 27 instances were we predicted a rogue wave and one did not occur, yielding a false positive rate of 18 %. An example simulation result alongside the output of the predictive scheme is displayed in Fig. 5.

As a final note, we mention that although the procedure described above is computationally inexpensive, the computational cost could be driven down further. In the ensemble of simulations discussed above, we computed the joint density of A and L for each of the wave groups (Fig. 6). Based on our numerical study of Sect. 2, we can partition each of these groups into stable groups unlikely to cause a rogue wave, and those that we predict would in fact trigger rogues. On the right of Fig. 6 we then plot the probability density of the length scales of these unstable wave groups. We see that, for the chosen spectrum, there is a critical scale that is the most likely length scale where rogue waves will be triggered (roughly $L = 9$). Rather than performing the scale selection algorithm, we could merely project the field onto a set of Gabor wavelets, *fixing* the length scale at this critical scale $L = 9$, and use this coefficient as a measure of the likelihood of an upcoming rogue wave. Such an approach may be less precise, but we successfully used a similar scheme previously to predict extreme events in the model of Majda-McLaughlin-Tabak (MMT) [5]. This approach would serve to simplify the scheme and reduce the computational cost. Although in one-dimension the cost of the automated scale selection algorithm is extremely minimal, these cost savings could become meaningful in two-dimensional settings.

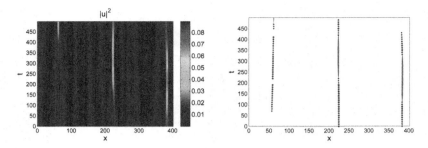

Fig. 5. Left: squared modulus of the amplitude (squaring is to accentuate the extreme waves). Right: red sections denote spatiotemporal regions where rogue wave is occurring. Blue dots denote rogue wave predictions (Color figure online).

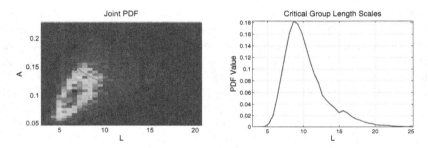

Fig. 6. Left: Joint (A, L) density for the wave groups identified in MNLS simulations. Right: density function for the length scales of the rogue inducing groups

5   Discussion

We have described a scheme to predict rogue waves in the NLS and MNLS equations, which are one dimensional nonlinear dispersive waves governing the evolution of the envelope of a modulated carrier wave on the surface of deep water. Our scheme is intuitive, computationally cheap, and reliable, successfully predicting all rogue waves in the cases considered with a low rate of false positives.

Such a scheme could be quite valuable, as predicting rogue waves in the vicinity of a vessel or structure could allow those in the wave's path to at least take some action to prepare for the oncoming impact. Thus, we are now working to extend our scheme to more realistic ocean settings, which involves two major modifications to the scenario presented here. First, two-dimensional models must be used. Secondly, we must account for the fact that in a realistic setting only noisy, incomplete data regarding the ocean surface would be available via measurements. Thus, we are currently investigating filtering schemes to estimate the wave group properties which serve as inputs to our predictive scheme.

References

1. Cai, D., Majda, A., McLaughlin, D., Tabak, E.G.: Dispersive wave turbulence in one dimension. Physica D **152–153**, 551–572 (2001)
2. Cai, D., Majda, A.J., McLaughlin, D.W., Tabak, E.G.: Spectral bifurcations in dispersive wave turbulence. Proc. Nat. Acad. Sci. **96**(25), 14216–14221 (1999)
3. Chabchoub, A., Hoffman, N., Onorato, M., Akhmediev, N.: Super rogue waves: observation of a higher-order breather in water waves. Phys. Rev. X **2**, 011015 (2012)
4. Chabchoub, A., Hoffman, N., Akhmediev, N.: Rogue wave observation in a water wave tank. Phys. Rev. Lett. **106**, 204502 (2011)
5. Cousins, W., Sapsis, T.: Quantification and prediction of extreme events in a one-dimensional nonlinear dispersive wave model. Physica D **280–281**, 48–58 (2014)
6. Cox, S., Matthews, P.: Exponential time differencing for stiff systems. J. Comput. Phys. **176**(2), 430–455 (2002)
7. Dysthe, K., Trulsen, K., Krogstad, H.E., Socquet-Juglard, H.: Evolution of a narrow-band spectrum of surface gravity waves. J. Fluid Mech. **478**, 1–10 (2003)
8. Dysthe, K.B.: Note on a modification to the nonlinear schrodinger equation for application to deep water waves. Proc. Roy. Soc. London. A Math. Phys. Sci. **369**(1736), 105–114 (1979)
9. Janssen, P.: Nonlinear four-wave interactions and freak waves. J. Phys. Oceanogr. **33**, 863–884 (2003)
10. Koenderink, J.J.: The structure of images. Biol. Cybern. **50**(5), 363–370 (1984)
11. Lindeberg, T.: Feature detection with automatic scale selection. Int. J. of Comput. Vis. **30**(2), 79–116 (1998)
12. Liu, P.C.: A chronology of freaque wave encounters. Geofizika **24**(1), 57–70 (2007)
13. Majda, A., McLaughlin, D.W., Tabak, E.: A one-dimensional model for dispersive wave turbulence. J. Nonlinear Sci. **6**, 9–44 (1997)
14. Onorato, M., Osborne, A., Serio, M., Bertone, S.: Freak waves in random oceanic sea states. Phys. Rev. Lett. **86**(25), 5831 (2001)
15. Onorato, M., Osborne, A., Serio, M., Cavaleri, L.: Modulational instability and non-gaussian statistics in experimental random water-wave trains. Phys. Fluids **17**, 078101 (2005)
16. Ruban, V.P.: Rogue waves at low benjamin-feir indices: numerical study of the role of nonlinearity. JETP Lett. **97**(12), 686–689 (2013)
17. Witkin, A.P.: Scale-space Filtering: A New Approach To Multi-scale Description. Ablex, Norwood (1984)
18. Zakharov, V.E.: Stability of periodic waves of finite amplitude on the surface of a deep fluid. J. Appl. Mech. Tech. Phys. **9**(2), 190–194 (1968)

Analytical Approximation of the Heavy-Tail Structure for Intermittently Unstable Complex Modes

Mustafa A. Mohamad[✉] and Themistoklis P. Sapsis

Massachusetts Institute of Technology, Cambridge, USA
{mmohamad,sapsis}@mit.edu

Abstract. In this work, we consider systems that are subjected to intermittent instabilities due to external, correlated stochastic excitation. These intermittent instabilities, though rare, give rise to heavy-tailed probability distribution functions (pdf). By making appropriate assumptions on the form of these instabilities, we formulate a method for the analytical approximation of the pdf of the system response. This method relies on conditioning the pdf of the response on the occurrence of an instability and the separate analysis of the two states of the system, the unstable and stable state. In the stable regime we employ steady state assumptions, which lead to the derivation of the conditional response pdf using standard methods. The unstable regime is inherently transient and in order to analyze this regime we characterize the statistics under the assumption of an exponential growth phase and a subsequent decay phase until the system is brought back to the stable attractor. We illustrate our method to a prototype intermittent system, a complex mode in a turbulent signal, and show that the analytic results compare favorably with direct Monte Carlo simulations for a broad range of parameters.

1 Introduction

A wide range of dynamical systems describing physical and technological processes are characterized by intermittency. This intermittent response is usually formulated through the interplay of stochastic excitation, which can trigger internal system instabilities, deterministic restoring forces and dissipation terms. It is often the case that, despite the high dimensionality of the stable attractor, an extreme response of short duration is due to an intermittent instability occurring over a single mode. This scenario does not exclude the case of having more than one intermittent mode, as long as the extreme responses of these modes are statistically independent. For this case, it may be possible to analytically approximate the probabilistic structure of these modes and understand the effect of the unstable dynamics on the heavy-tails.

Instabilities of this kind are common in dynamical systems with uncertainty. Popular examples are modes in turbulent fluid flows and nonlinear water waves subjected to nonlinear energy exchanges that occur in an intermittent fashion

© Springer International Publishing Switzerland 2015
S. Ravela and A. Sandu (Eds.): DyDESS 2014, LNCS 8964, pp. 144–156, 2015.
DOI: 10.1007/978-3-319-25138-7_14

and result in intermittent responses [1–7]. Recently, it has been shown that these properly designed single mode models can describe intermittent responses, even in very complex systems characterized by high dimensional attractors [8–10].

In all of these systems, the complexity of the unstable dynamics is often combined with stochasticity introduced by persistent instabilities that lead to chaotic dynamics as well as by the random characteristics of external excitations. The structure of the stochasticity introduced by these factors plays an important role on the dynamics of the system response. In particular, for a typical case the stochastic excitation is colored noise. Due to the possibility of large excursions by the correlated stochastic excitation from its mean value into an "unsafe-region", where hidden instabilities are triggered, extreme events can be particularly severe. Therefore, it is essential to develop analytical methods that capture the effects of the correlation in the excitation processes for intermittent modes. However, analytical modeling in this case is particularly difficult since standard methods that describe the pdf of the response are not available.

In this work, our goal is the development of a method that will allow for the analytical approximation of the pdf of modes associated with intermittent instabilities and extreme responses due to parametric excitation by colored noise, using an analytic approach that provides a direct link between dynamics and response statistics. The results presented have important significance in the context of reduced order modeling of complex systems with intermittent instabilities, in particular for extreme event detection and prediction (e.g. oceanic rouge waves [9]). In addition, it also offer a method for the inverse estimation of system parameters in a data driven context, for dynamical systems featuring heavy-tailed distributions arising from instabilities.

2   Problem Setup and Method

Let $(\Theta, \mathcal{B}, \mathcal{P})$ be a probability space, where Θ is the sample space with $\theta \in \Theta$ denoting an elementary event of the sample space, $\mathcal{B}$ the associated σ-algebra of the sample space, and $\mathcal{P}$ a probability measure. We are interested in describing the statistical characteristics of modes subjected to intermittent instabilities and thus consider a general dynamical system

$$\dot{\boldsymbol{x}} = G(\boldsymbol{x}, t), \quad \boldsymbol{x} \in \mathbb{R}^n. \tag{1}$$

The presented analysis will rely on the following assumptions related to the form of the extreme events:

A1 The instabilities are rare enough so that they can be considered statistically independent and have finite duration.

A2 During an extreme event the influenced modes have decoupled dynamics. Moreover, for each one of these modes, during the growth phase, the instability is the governing mechanism.

A3 After each extreme event there is a relaxation phase that brings the system back to its stable stochastic attractor.

Under these assumptions we may express each intermittent mode, denoted by $u(t; \theta) \in \mathbb{R}$, where $\theta \in \Theta$, as a dynamical system of the form

$$\dot{u} + \alpha(t; \theta)u + \varepsilon\zeta(u, \boldsymbol{v}) = \varepsilon\xi(t; \theta), \qquad (2)$$

where $\varepsilon > 0$ is a small quantity and $\zeta(u, \boldsymbol{v})$ is a nonlinear function with zero linearization with respect to u, which may also depend on other system variables $\boldsymbol{v} \in \mathbb{R}^{n-1}$. Since ε is a small quantity, we can assume that the nonlinear term is important only in the stable regime. The stochastic processes α and ξ are assumed stationary with known statistical characteristics. For α we will make the additional assumption that its statistical mean is positive i.e. $\bar{\alpha} > 0$ so that the above system has a stable attractor.

The objective of this work is to derive analytical approximations for the pdf of the system response, taking into account intermittent instabilities that arise due to the effect of the stochastic process α. In particular, these instabilities are triggered when $\alpha < 0$, and force the system to depart from the stable attractor. Therefore, the system has two regimes where the underlying dynamics behave differently: the stable regime where $\alpha > 0$ and the unstable regime that is triggered when $\alpha < 0$ (Fig. 1). Motivated by this behavior, we quantify the system's response by conditioning the pdf of the response on stable regimes and unstable events,

$$\mathcal{P}[u] = \mathcal{P}[u \mid \text{stable regime}]\mathcal{P}[\text{stable regime}]+$$
$$\mathcal{P}[u \mid \text{unstable regime}]\mathcal{P}[\text{unstable regime}], \quad (3)$$

thereby separating the two regions of interest so they can be individually studied. The method we employ relies on the derivation of the pdf for each of the terms in (3) and then the reconstruction of the full distribution of the system. Essentially, we decouple the response pdf into two parts: a probability density function with rapidly decaying tails (typically Gaussian) and a heavy tail distribution with very low probability close to zero.

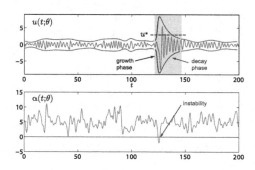

Fig. 1. An intermittent system. Green lines denote the envelope in the stable regime, blue and red lines correspond to the growth and decay phase of an instability, respectively (Color figure online).

2.1   Stochastic Description of the Stable Regime

During the stable regime we have by definition $\alpha > 0$ and therefore the considered mode is stable. Note that this condition is also true during the relaxation (decay) phase after an extreme event, when the system has entered a regime where $\alpha > 0$. To this end, we cannot directly relate the duration of being on the stable attractor with the probability $\mathcal{P}[\alpha > 0]$, but a correction should be made, which we present in Sect. 2.3. Here we focus on characterizing the probability density function of the system under the assumption that it has relaxed to the stable attractor and moreover we have $\alpha > 0$.

As a first-order estimate of the stable dynamics we approximate the original dynamical system for the intermittent mode by the stable system

$$\dot{u} + \bar{\alpha}|_{\alpha > 0} u + \varepsilon \zeta(u, v) = \varepsilon \xi(t; \theta), \tag{4}$$

where $\bar{\alpha}|_{\alpha > 0}$ denotes the conditional average of the process α given that this is positive. The determination of the statistical structure of the stable attractor for (4) can be done with a variety of analytical and numerical methods, such as the Fokker-Planck equation if the process ξ is white noise (see e.g. [11,12]) or the joint response-excitation equations otherwise [13,14]. Using one of these methods we can obtain the the conditionally stable pdf $\mathcal{P}[u \mid \text{stable regime}]$.

2.2   Stochastic Description of the Growth Phase

In contrast to the stable regime, the unstable regime is far more complicated due to its inherently transient nature. In addition, the unstable regime consists of two distinct phases: a growth phase where $\alpha < 0$ and a decay phase where $\alpha > 0$. We first consider the growth phase, where we rely on assumption A2, according to which the dominant mechanism is the term related to the instability. Under this assumption, to first-order, the growth phase is governed by the system

$$\dot{u} + \alpha(t; \theta)u = 0 \implies u(t; \theta) = u_0 e^{\Lambda T}, \tag{5}$$

where u_0 is a random initial condition described by the probability measure in the stable regime, T is the random duration of the upcrossing event $\alpha < 0$, and Λ is the growth exponent, which for each extreme event can be approximated by

$$\Lambda \simeq -\frac{1}{T} \int_T \alpha(t; \theta) \, dt \simeq -\alpha(t; \theta), \tag{6}$$

due to the rapid nature of the growth phase. Therefore, during the growth phase we have

$$\mathcal{P}[u > u^* \mid \alpha < 0] =$$
$$\mathcal{P}[u_0 e^{\Lambda T} > u^* \mid \alpha < 0] = \mathcal{P}[u_0 e^{\Lambda T} > u^* \mid \alpha < 0, u_0] \mathcal{P}[u_0]. \tag{7}$$

The right hand side of (7) is a derived distribution depending on the probabilistic structure of Λ and T. The initial value u_0 is a random variable with statistical characteristics corresponding to the stable regime of the system, i.e. by $\mathcal{P}[u \mid \text{stable regime}]$. Hence, to determine the required pdf we seek $\mathcal{P}[\alpha, T \mid \alpha < 0]$, i.e. the joint pdf for the value of α (given that this is negative) and the duration of the time interval over which α is negative. This distribution involves only the excitation process α, and for the Gaussian case it can be approximated analytically (see Sect. 3). Alternatively, one can compute this distribution using numerically generated random realizations that respect the statistical characteristics of the process.

2.3   Stochastic Description of the Decay Phase

The decay phase is also an inherently transient stage. It occurs right after the growth phase of an instability, when α has an upcrossing of the zero level, and is therefore characterized by positive values of α, with the effect of driving the system back to the stable attractor. To provide a statistical description for the relaxation phase, we first note the strong connection between the growth and decay phase. In particular, as shown in Fig. 1, for each extreme event there is a one-to-one correspondence for the values of the intermittent variable u between the growth phase and the decay phase. By focusing on an individual extreme event, we note that the probability of u exceeding a certain threshold during the growth phase is equal with the probability of u exceeding the same threshold during the decay phase. Thus over the total instability have

$$\mathcal{P}[u > u^* \mid \text{unstable regime}] =$$
$$\mathcal{P}[u > u^* \mid \text{instability} - \text{decay}] = \mathcal{P}[u > u^* \mid \text{instability} - \text{growth}], \quad (8)$$

where the conditional distribution for the growth phase is given by (7).

2.4   Probability of the Stable and the Unstable Regime

In the final step we determine the relative duration of the stable and unstable regimes. This ratio will define the probability of a stable event and an unstable event. The probability of having an instability is simply $P[\alpha < 0]$, however, due to the decay phase the duration of an instability will be longer than the duration of the event $\alpha < 0$. To determine the typical duration of the decay phase, we first note that during the growth phase we have

$$u_p = u_0 e^{-\bar{\alpha}|_{\alpha<0} T_{\alpha<0}}, \tag{9}$$

where $T_{\alpha<0}$ is the duration for which $\alpha < 0$, and u_p is the peak value of u during the instability. Similarly, for the decay phase we utilize system (4) and obtain

$$u_0 = u_p e^{-\bar{\alpha}|_{\alpha>0} T_{\text{decay}}}. \tag{10}$$

Combining (9) and (10) we have $T_{\alpha<0}/T_{\text{decay}} = -\bar{\alpha}|_{\alpha>0}/\bar{\alpha}|_{\alpha<0}$, which expresses the typical ratio between the growth and the decay phase. Thus, the total duration of an unstable event is given by the sum of the duration of these two phases

$$T_{\text{inst}} = \left(1 - \frac{\bar{\alpha}|_{\alpha<0}}{\bar{\alpha}|_{\alpha>0}}\right) T_{\alpha<0}. \tag{11}$$

Using this result, we can express the total probability of being in an unstable regime by

$$\mathcal{P}[\text{unstable regime}] = \left(1 - \frac{\bar{\alpha}|_{\alpha<0}}{\bar{\alpha}|_{\alpha>0}}\right)\mathcal{P}[\alpha < 0]. \qquad (12)$$

Note that since we have assumed in A1 that instabilities are sufficiently rare so that instabilities do not overlap and that instabilities are statistical independent, we have $\mathcal{P}[\text{unstable regime}] < 1$. Hence $\mathcal{P}[\text{stable regime}] = 1 - \mathcal{P}[\text{unstable regime}]$, where $\mathcal{P}[\text{unstable regime}]$ is given in (12).

3   Instabilities Driven by Gaussian Processes

Here we recall relevant statistical properties associated with a Gaussian stochastic parametric excitation.

The zero level of the stochastic process α defines the boundary of the two states for our system. For convenience, let $\alpha(t; \theta) = m + k\gamma(t; \theta)$, where γ is also an ergodic and stationary Gaussian process, but with zero mean and unit variance, so that α has mean m and variance k^2. Thus the threshold of a rare event in terms of γ is given by the parameter $\eta \equiv -m/k$. We assume that second order properties, such as the power spectrum, of γ are known. In such a case, the correlation of the process is given by $R_\gamma(\tau) = \int_{-\infty}^{\infty} S_\gamma(\omega)e^{i\omega\tau}\,d\omega$.

Since γ is a stationary Gaussian process, the probability that the stochastic process is in the two states $\mathcal{P}[\alpha < 0]$ and $\mathcal{P}[\alpha > 0]$ are, respectively, $\mathcal{P}[\gamma < \eta] = \Phi(\eta)$ and $\mathcal{P}[\gamma > \eta] = 1 - \Phi(\eta)$ (where $\phi(\cdot)$ denotes the standard normal pdf and $\Phi(\cdot)$ the standard normal cumulative pdf).

3.1   Average Time Below and Above the Zero Level

Here we determine the average length of the intervals that α spends above and below the zero level. For the case $\alpha < 0$, that is $\gamma < \eta$, the expected number of upcrossings of this threshold per unit time is given by Rice's formula [15, 16]

$$\overline{N^+}(\eta) = \int_0^\infty u f_{\gamma\dot{\gamma}}(\eta, u)\,du = \frac{1}{2\pi}\sqrt{-R_\gamma''(0)}\exp(-\eta^2/2), \qquad (13)$$

where $\overline{N^+}(\eta)$ is the average number of upcrossings of level η per unit time, which is equivalent to the average number of downcrossings $\overline{N^-}(\eta)$. The expected number of crossings is finite if and only if γ has a finite second spectral moment [16].

The average length of the interval that γ spends below the threshold η can then be determined by noting that this probability is given by the product of the number of downcrossings of the threshold per unit time and the average length of the intervals for which γ is below the threshold η [17]. Thus using (13) we have

$$\bar{T}_{\alpha<0}(\eta) = \frac{\mathcal{P}[\gamma < \eta]}{\overline{N^-}(\eta)} = \frac{2\pi\exp(\eta^2/2)}{\sqrt{-R_\gamma''(0)}}\Phi(\eta). \qquad (14)$$

3.2 Distribution of Time Below the Zero Level

In general, it is not possible to derive an exact analytical expression for the distribution of time intervals given $\gamma < \eta$, in other words the distribution of the length of time between a downcrossing and an upcrossing. However, the asymptotic expression in the limit $\eta \to -\infty$ is given by [17] (henceforth we denote $\bar{T}_{\alpha<0}$ by $\bar{T}$ for clarity)

$$\mathcal{P}_T(t) = \frac{\pi t}{2\bar{T}^2} \exp\left(-\pi t^2/4\bar{T}^2\right), \tag{15}$$

which is a Rayleigh distribution with scale parameter $\sqrt{2\bar{T}^2/\pi}$, and $\bar{T}$ is given by (14).

4 Application: Intermittently Unstable Complex Mode

Here we present an example application of the method formulated in Sect. 2, to that of a complex scalar Langevin equation that models a single mode in a turbulent signal, where multiplicative stochastic damping γ and colored additive noise b, both specified as Ornstein-Uhlenbeck (OU) processes, replace interactions between various modes. The nonlinear system is given by

$$\frac{du(t)}{dt} = (-\gamma(t) + i\omega)u(t) + b(t) + f(t) + \sigma\dot{W}(t), \tag{16}$$

$$\frac{db(t)}{dt} = (-\gamma_b + i\omega_b)(b(t) - \hat{b}) + \sigma_b\dot{W}_b(t), \tag{17}$$

$$\frac{d\gamma(t)}{dt} = -d_\gamma(\gamma(t) - \hat{\gamma}) + \sigma_\gamma\dot{W}_\gamma(t), \tag{18}$$

where $u(t) \in \mathbb{C}$ physically describes a resolved mode in a turbulent signal and f is a prescribed deterministic forcing. The process γ models intermittency due to the (hidden) nonlinear interactions between $u(t)$ and other unobserved modes. In other words, intermittency in $u(t)$ is primarily due to the action of γ, with $u(t)$ switching between stable and unstable regimes when γ switches signs.

The nonlinear system (17) was introduced for filtering of multiscale turbulent signals with hidden instabilities [18,19], and has since been used for various applications [8,10,20–22]. The system features rich dynamics that closely mimics turbulent signals in various regimes of the turbulent spectrum. The three physically relevant regimes are described by [20] (reproduced for completeness):

R1 A regime where the dynamics are dominated by frequent, short-lasting transient instabilities; characteristic of the turbulent energy transfer range.

R2 Here the dynamics are characterized by large-amplitude intermittent instabilities followed by a relaxation phase; representative of modes in the dissipative range.

R3 A regime described by dynamics where transient instabilities are very rare, and fluctuations in rapidly decorrelate; corresponding to the laminar modes.

We apply the method described in Sect. 2, to approximate the pdf for the dynamics of $u(t)$ in the special case with no additive noise $b = 0$ and no external forcing $f = 0$. This is the simplest case that incorporates intermittency, driven by the state of OU process γ. The system we consider is given by

$$\frac{du(t)}{dt} = (-\gamma(t) + i\omega)u(t) + \sigma\dot{W}(t), \tag{19}$$

$$\frac{d\gamma(t)}{dt} = -d_\gamma(\gamma(t) - \hat{\gamma}) + \sigma_\gamma\dot{W}_\gamma(t), \tag{20}$$

In this case, the dynamics of $u(t)$ are such that it oscillates at a fixed frequency ω. For this system, we derive the system response pdf and compare the analytical result for the three regimes R1–R3.

4.1   Probability Distribution in the Stable Regime

Here we derive approximation of the pdf for $u(t)$ given that we are in the stable regime and, moreover, that we have statistical stationarity. In the stable regime, following Sect. 2.1, we replace γ by the conditional average $\bar{\gamma}|_{\gamma>0} = \hat{\gamma} + k\phi(\eta)/(1 - \Phi(\eta))$. Thus the governing equation in the stable regime becomes

$$\frac{du(t)}{dt} = (-\bar{\gamma}|_{\gamma>0} + i\omega)u(t) + \sigma\dot{W}(t), \tag{21}$$

Since this is a Gaussian system, we can fully describe the pdf for $u(t)$ in this regime by its stationary mean $\overline{u(t)} = 0$, and stationary variance

$$\text{Var}(u(t)) = \text{Var}(u_0)e^{-2\bar{\gamma}|_{\gamma>0}t} + \frac{\sigma^2}{2\bar{\gamma}|_{\gamma>0}}(1 - e^{-2\bar{\gamma}|_{\gamma>0}t}) \rightarrow \frac{\sigma^2}{2\bar{\gamma}|_{\gamma>0}}, \quad \text{as } t \rightarrow \infty. \tag{22}$$

Therefore, we have the following pdf for the real part of $u(t)$ in the stable regime

$$\mathcal{P}[\text{Re}(u) = x \mid \text{stable}] = \sqrt{\frac{2\bar{\gamma}|_{\gamma>0}}{\pi\sigma^2}}\exp\left(-\frac{2\bar{\gamma}|_{\gamma>0}}{\sigma^2}x^2\right). \tag{23}$$

4.2   Probability Distribution in the Unstable Regime

In the unstable regime we describe the pdf in terms of the envelope, *treating the system response as a narrow band process*. The envelope of $u(t)$ is given by

$$\frac{d|u|^2}{dt} = 2\text{Re}\left[\frac{du}{dt}u^*\right] \implies \frac{d|u|^2}{dt} = -2\gamma(t)|u|^2 + \sigma^2. \tag{24}$$

Following assumption A2 we ignore σ^2, which does not have a large probabilistic impact on the instability strength, and therefore substituting the representation $|u| = e^{\Lambda T}$ into (24) we get $\Lambda \simeq -\gamma$. Now since $\mathcal{P}[\Lambda] = \mathcal{P}[-\gamma \mid \gamma < 0]$ we have

$$\mathcal{P}_\Lambda(\lambda) = \frac{1}{\Phi(\eta)}\mathcal{P}_\gamma(-\lambda) = \frac{1}{k\Phi(\eta)}\phi\left(-\frac{\lambda + \hat{\gamma}}{k}\right), \quad \lambda > 0 \tag{25}$$

To proceed, we set $U = u_0 \exp(\Lambda T)$ (for clarity denote $T_{\gamma<0}$ by T) and $Y = \Lambda$, then from a change of variables

$$\mathcal{P}_{UY}(u,y) = \mathcal{P}_{\Lambda T}(\lambda,t)|\det[\partial(\lambda,t)/\partial(u,y)]|. \tag{26}$$

Next, we assume that T and Λ are independent, which gives

$$\mathcal{P}_{UY}(u,y) = \frac{\mathcal{P}_\Lambda(\lambda)\mathcal{P}_T(t)}{u_0\lambda\exp(\lambda t)} = \frac{1}{uy}\mathcal{P}_\Lambda(y)\mathcal{P}_T\left(\frac{\log(u/u_0)}{y}\right), \quad u > u_0, \, y > 0. \tag{27}$$

Taking the marginal density gives

$$\mathcal{P}_U(u) = \frac{1}{u}\int_0^\infty \frac{1}{y}\mathcal{P}_\Lambda(y)\mathcal{P}_T\left(\frac{\log(u/u_0)}{y}\right)dy. \tag{28}$$

Hence, using (25) and (15) we have the following pdf for the envelope in the unstable regime

$$\mathcal{P}[u \mid \gamma < 0, u_0] =$$

$$\frac{\pi\log(u/u_0)}{2k\bar{T}^2\Phi(\eta)u}\int_0^\infty \frac{1}{y^2}\phi\left(-\frac{y+\hat\gamma}{k}\right)\exp\left(-\frac{\pi}{4\bar{T}^2y^2}\log(u/u_0)^2\right)dy, \quad u > u_0. \tag{29}$$

In addition, using (11), the average length of an extreme event is given by

$$\frac{T_{\text{decay}}}{T_{\alpha<0}} = -\frac{\hat\gamma - k\frac{\phi(\eta)}{\Phi(\eta)}}{\hat\gamma + k\frac{\phi(\eta)}{1-\Phi(\eta)}} \equiv \mu \implies T_{\text{inst}} = (1-\mu)T_{\alpha<0}. \tag{30}$$

Finally, to construct the full distribution for the envelope of $u(t)$ in the unstable regime, we need to incorporate the distribution of the initial point of the instability, which is described by the envelope of $u(t)$ in the stable regime. Since the conditionally stable regime is described by a stationary Gaussian process the envelope pdf can be easily derived [12], which for the current case we have

$$\mathcal{P}[u_0] = \frac{4\bar\gamma|_{\gamma>0}}{\sigma^2}u_0\exp\left(-\frac{2\bar\gamma|_{\gamma>0}}{\sigma^2}u_0^2\right). \tag{31}$$

We note that the oscillatory character during an instability has be taken into account. However, to avoid the additional integral that would result, we refer to the narrow band approximation made. This will give approximately $u = |u|\cos\varphi$, where φ is a uniform random variable distributed between 0 and 2π. The probability density function for $z = \cos\varphi$ is given by $\mathcal{P}[z] = 1/(\pi\sqrt{1-z^2})$, $z \in [-1,1]$, which we approximate by $\mathcal{P}[z] = \frac{1}{2}(\delta(z+1) + \delta(z-1))$. This approximation allows us to formulate the pdf for $\text{Re}(u)$ in terms of its envelope:

$$\mathcal{P}[\text{Re}(u) = x \mid \gamma < 0] = \frac{1}{2}\mathcal{P}[u = |x| \mid \gamma < 0]. \tag{32}$$

We show in Sect. 4.4 that this approximation compares favorably with direct numerical simulations.

4.3   Summary of Analytical Results for the Complex Mode

Combining (23), (29), (31), and (30) into the Bayes' decomposition (3) and utilizing the approximation (32) gives the following heavy-tailed, symmetric pdf for the complex mode, for $x \in \mathbb{R}$,

$$
\mathcal{P}[\mathrm{Re}(u) = x] = (1 - (1 - \mu)\Phi(\eta))\sqrt{\frac{2\bar{\gamma}|_{\gamma>0}}{\pi\sigma^2}}\exp\left(-\frac{2\bar{\gamma}|_{\gamma>0}}{\sigma^2}x^2\right) + (1 - \mu)\frac{\sqrt{2\pi}\bar{\gamma}|_{\gamma>0}}{2\sigma^2 k\bar{T}^2}
$$
$$
\int_0^{|x|}\int_0^{\infty}\frac{\log(|x|/u_0)}{y^2(|x|/u_0)}\exp\left(-\frac{(y+\hat{\gamma})^2}{2k^2} - \frac{\pi}{4\bar{T}^2 y^2}\log(|x|/u_0)^2 - \frac{2\bar{\gamma}|_{\gamma>0}}{\sigma^2}u_0^2\right)dy\,du_0. \qquad (33)
$$

4.4   Comparisons with Direct Monte Carlo Simulations

Here we compare the analytic results (33) with direct Monte Carlo simulations for the three regimes R1–R3. In Fig. 2, the results for Regime 1 are presented alongside a sample realization. As previously mentioned, this regime is characterized by frequent short-lasting instabilities. Despite the weak violation of assumption A1, the analytical results are still able to capture the the heavy tails of the response. However, due to the frequency of these short-lasting instabilities and the fact that our analytic results neglects phase information in the conditionally unstable pdf, a cusp is observed near the mean state. In contrasts, in Regime 2 (see Fig. 3), we have large-amplitude instabilities that occur less frequently. Therefore, the analytical results in this regime are able to capture the response extremely accurately even near the mean state, despite no phase information. Again, this is due to the fact that this regime is characterized by less frequent large-amplitude instabilities, which push the conditionally unstable pdf further towards larger magnitude responses, and hence impact the pdf of the conditionally stable regime less severely than in Regime 1. In Fig. 4 we present the results for Regime 3 for completeness, even though this regime is nearly Gaussian, since in the laminar regime intermittent events are extremely rare.

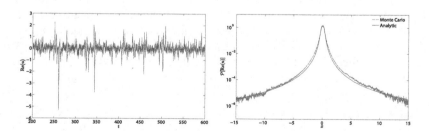

Fig. 2. Regime 1: Sample path (left) and analytic pdf (33) compared with results from Monte Carlo simulations (right), for: $\omega = 1.78$, $\sigma = 0.5$, $\hat{\gamma} = 1.2$, $d_\gamma = 10$, $\sigma_\gamma = 10$.

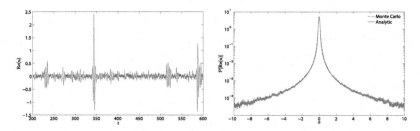

Fig. 3. Regime 2: Sample path (left) and analytic pdf (33) compared with results from Monte Carlo simulations (right), for: $\omega = 1.78$, $\sigma = 0.1$, $\hat{\gamma} = 0.55$, $d_\gamma = 0.5$, $\sigma_\gamma = 0.5$.

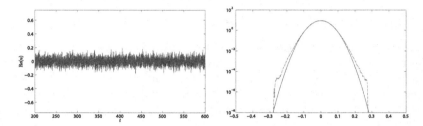

Fig. 4. Regime 3: Sample path (left) and analytic pdf (33) compared with results from Monte Carlo simulations (right), for: $\omega = 1.78$, $\sigma = 0.25$, $\hat{\gamma} = 8.1$, $d_\gamma = 0.25$, $\sigma_\gamma = 1$.

5   Conclusions

We have formulated a general method to analytically approximate the pdf of intermittently unstable systems excited by correlated stochastic noise. The method developed in this paper relies on conditioning the system response on stable regimes and unstable events according to Bayes' rule, and then reconstruction of the full probabilistic response after analysis of the conditional pdf in the two regimes. Thus, we have demonstrated how the system's response can be decomposed into a statistically stationary part and an essentially transient part. And have shown that this decomposition provides a direct link between the character of the intermittent instabilities and the form of the heavy-tail statistics of the response. We then provide an application of the formulated method to a prototype intermittently unstable system: a complex mode that represents intermittent modes of a turbulent system, where we show that the analytic results compare favorably with Monte Carlo simulations for a broad range of parameters.

Acknowledgments. This research has been partially supported by the Naval Engineering Education Center (NEEC) grant 3002883706 and by the Office of Naval Research (ONR) grant ONR N00014-14-1-0520. The authors thank Dr. Craig Merrill (NEEC Technical Point of Contact), Dr. Vadim Belenky, and Prof. Andrew Majda for numerous stimulating discussions.

References

1. Pedlosky, J.: Ocean Circulation Theory. Springer, Heidelberg (1996)
2. Salmon, R.: Lectures on Geophysical Fluid Dynamics. Oxford University Press, Oxford (1998)
3. DelSole, T.: Stochastic models of quasigeostrophic turbulence. Surv. Geophys. **25**, 107–149 (2004)
4. Majda, A.J., Abramov, R.V., Grote, M.J.: Information Theory and Stochastics for Multiscale Nonlinear Systems. CRM Monograph Series, vol. 25. American Mathematical Society, Providence (2005)
5. Majda, A.J., McLaughlin, D.W., Tabak, E.G.: A one-dimensional model for dispersive wave turbulence. J. Nonlinear Sci. **6**, 9–44 (1997)
6. Dysthe, K., Krogstad, H., Muller, P.: Oceanic rogue waves. Annu. Rev. Fluid Mech. **40**, 287 (2008)
7. Xiao, W., Liu, Y., Wu, G., Yue, D.K.P.: Rogue wave occurrence and dynamics by direct simulations of nonlinear wave-field evolution. J. Fluid Mech. **720**, 357–392 (2013)
8. Majda, A.J., Harlim, J.: Filtering Complex Turbulent Systems. Cambridge University Press, Cambridge (2012)
9. Cousins, W., Sapsis, T.P.: Quantification and prediction of extreme events in a one-dimensional nonlinear dispersive wave model. Physica D **280**, 48–58 (2014)
10. Chen, N., Majda, A.J., Giannakis, D.: Predicting the cloud patterns of the Madden-Julian Oscillation through a low-order nonlinear stochastic model. Geophys. Res. Lett. **41**, 5612–5619 (2014)
11. Sobczyk, K.: Stochastic Differential Equations. Kluwer Academic Publishers, Dordrecht (1991)
12. Soong, T., Grigoriu, M.: Random Vibration of Mechanical and Structural Systems. PTR Prentice Hall, Englewood Cliffs (1993)
13. Sapsis, T.P., Athanassoulis, G.A.: New partial differential equations governing the joint, response-excitation, probability distributions of nonlinear systems, under general stochastic excitation. Probab. Eng. Mech. **23**(2-3), 289–306 (2008)
14. Venturi, D., Sapsis, T.P., Cho, H., Karniadakis, G.E.: A computable evolution equation for the joint response-excitation probability density function of stochastic dynamical systems. Proc. Roy. Soc. A **468**, 759 (2012)
15. Blake, I.F., Lindsey, W.C.: Level-crossing problems for random processes. IEEE Trans. Inf. Theor. **19**, 295–315 (1973)
16. Kratz, M.F.: Level crossings and other level functionals of stationary Gaussian processes. Probab. Surv. **3**, 230–288 (2006)
17. Rice, S.O.: Distribution of the duration of fades in radio transmission: Gaussian noise model. Bell Syst. Tech. J. **37**, 581–635 (1958)
18. Gershgorin, B., Harlim, J., Majda, A.J.: Test models for improving filtering with model errors through stochastic parameter estimation. J. Comput. Phys. **229**(1), 1–31 (2010)
19. Gershgorin, B., Harlim, J., Majda, A.J.: Improving filtering and prediction of spatially extended turbulent systems with model errors through stochastic parameter estimation. J. Comput. Phys. **229**(1), 32–57 (2010)

20. Branicki, M., Gershgorin, B., Majda, A.J.: Filtering skill for turbulent signals for a suite of nonlinear and linear extended Kalman filters. J. Comput. Phys. **231**, 1462–1498 (2012)
21. Branicki, M., Majda, A.J.: Quantifying uncertainty for predictions with model error in non-Gaussian systems with intermittency. Nonlinearity **25**, 2543 (2012)
22. Majda, A.J., Branicki, M.: Lessons in uncertainty quantification for turbulent dynamical systems. Discrete continuous Dyn. Syst. **32**, 3133–3221 (2012)

Multiscale Stochastic Representation in High-Dimensional Data Using Gaussian Processes with Implicit Diffusion Metrics

Charanraj Thimmisetty[1], Arman Khodabakhshnejad[1], Nima Jabbari[1],
Fred Aminzadeh[1], Roger Ghanem[1]([✉]), Kelly Rose[2], Jennifer Bauer[2],
and Corinne Disenhof[2,3]

[1] University of Southern California, Los Angeles, CA, USA
ghanem@usc.edu
[2] Department of Energy, National Energy Technology Laboratory,
Albany, OR, USA
[3] URS Corporation, National Energy Technology Laboratory, Albany, OR, USA

Abstract. We develop a stochastic representation of a scalar function defined on a high-dimensional space conditional on marginal statistics of the function at a finite set of localities and a high-dimensional correlation structure. The representation leverages a particular structure of the functional dependence that exhibits scale separation. In the process, we construct a polynomial chaos representation for the scalar quantity of interest (QoI) whose coefficients are themselves random. The intrinsic randomness of the polynomial chaos expansion (PCE) reflects local uncertainty and captures dependence on a subset (say S_1) of the parameters, while randomness in the PCE coefficients captures a global structure of the uncertainty and dependence on the remaining parameters (say S_2) in the high-dimensional space (let $S = S_1 \cup S_2$). This construction is demonstrated by predicting wellbore signatures in the Gulf of Mexico (GoM) where 100 tabulated data values are available at several thousand wellbore locations throughout the GoM. Reservoir simulators describing the physics of multiphase flow in porous media are used to calculate the PCE representations at the sites where data is available. In this context, random parameters describing the subsurface define the parameter set S_1. A Gaussian process model is then developed for each coefficient in these representations, construed as a function on S_2 over which an intrinsic diffusion metric is defined.

1 Introduction

We address the problem of conditional density regression of a stochastic process $q(x, \underline{y}, \underline{\theta})$ based on available marginal densities of $q_i(x_i, \underline{y}_i, \underline{\theta}_i)$ at highly sparse locations $i = 1, 2, ..n$. Here $x \in \mathbb{R}^3$ refers to spatial locations, and $\underline{y}$ and $\underline{\theta}$ are, respectively, deterministic and stochastic inputs to underlying physical process. Our interest is in estimating the marginal density of $q(s, \underline{y}_s, \underline{\theta}_s)$ at location "s" with partial or no data on $\underline{y}_s$ and marginal densities at n highly sparse locations.

© Springer International Publishing Switzerland 2015
S. Ravela and A. Sandu (Eds.): DyDESS 2014, LNCS 8964, pp. 157–166, 2015.
DOI: 10.1007/978-3-319-25138-7_15

Methods for simulating conditional Gaussian and non-Gaussian process have been proposed in the literature using series expansions [12, 13] or density regression techniques using Dirichlet process [3, 10].

In this paper, stochastic processes of interest describe wellbore signatures in the Gulf of Mexico (GoM) and exhibit different character of statistical fluctuations at different spatial scales. These wellbore signatures are governed by micro (reservoir) scale, meso (field) scale and macro (GoM) scale processes. Our objective is to develop methods for density regression which leverage this multiscale dependence on available information. Such a hierarchical model will enhance our understanding of the role different scales of uncertainty play in reducing predictability as well as the value of reducing each of these uncertainties and the worth of associated information. We achieve this density regression, using a polynomial chaos representation in conjunction with a Gaussian process (GP) representation of the PCE coefficients. The GP representation itself is carried out relative to a diffusion metric which learned from the data.

2   Motivation and Challenges

The recent Deepwater Horizon oil spill highlighted the uncertainty associated with predictions of wellbore signatures due to anthropogenic events in hydrocarbon production. During this event attempts were made to control and cease the blowout. Scarcity of data as well as uncertainty in leakage and seepage mechanisms made associated predictions challenging. Several investigations have been conducted to model the blowout and estimate the damage. It took almost two months to get reliable wellbore signatures which were used to estimate the degree of contamination in the GoM [9]. To address challenges associated with these events, a ROM to rapidly estimate wellbore signatures or Quantity of Interests (QoI) based on database of wellbore data over the GoM is developed. This ROM serves as rapid risk assessment tool in case of anthropogenic events such as Deepwater Horizon oil spill, anomaly detection tool by doing hypothesis testing with normal conditions and also a prior model for the sites with limited data.

A repository of wellbore data from the Gulf of Mexico is curated by the Bureau of Ocean and Energy Management (BOEM) and can be queried online (http://www.boem.gov). The data pertains both to reservoirs that are no longer in production and to currently producing reservoirs. Figure 1 shows a spatial distribution of one of such available databases. This data is sparse and features different types of uncertainty at reservoir, field and GoM scales. Our interest is to develop a ROM to estimate a QoI at sites where partial or no data has been collected. As a first step, the QoI is computed at sites where data is available by evaluating a reservoir simulation code that takes as input a subset of the data with predominantly local influence, such as permeability. Typically, measurements are taken from multiple wellbores within a reservoir and a model for permeability as a stochastic process is constructed using geostatistical methods. We rely on a Karhunen-Loéve construction for that purpose which diagonalizes an assumed covariance function leading to an optimal representation

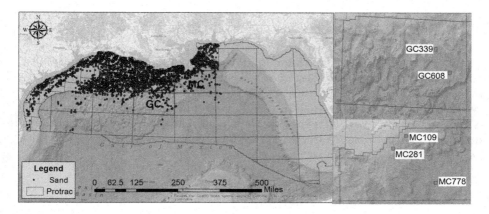

Fig. 1. Spatial location of boreholes over the Gulf of Mexico, and location of study areas in the GoM; Source of data [5]

of the permeability field in terms of uncorrelated random variables. These stochastic interpolation schemes lead to uncertain QoI within each reservoir site. Although permeability data with higher resolution is available to private operators throughout the Gulf of Mexico, publicly available data is limited to the BOEM data set which provides a single permeability value, averaged along the length of the wellbore. Such uncertainty levels associated with the measured data, coupled with sparsity of the data makes our task of density regression quite challenging.

3 Summary of the Methodology

For a number of operational reasons, we focus our attention on a QoI that consists of cumulative production after one day. Uncertainty associated with permeability values renders the QoI at each site random. To represent these random quantities, PCE of QoI are constructed at all sites where data is available by carrying out numerical reservoir simulations with permeability fields described as lognormal stochastic processess. The PCE represents the QoI, q, as a multidimensional polynomial in the input random variables [4, 14] with deterministic coefficients. We augment this standard construction by interpolating the PCE coefficients using GP over a parameter space defined by the content of the database. Gaussian Process (GP) regression [2, 6–8, 11] is a supervised learning algorithm. Interpolation using GP makes PCE coefficients random at all locations where no data was collected, including spatial locations where only partial data is available. This leads to a stochastic expansion (PCE) with random coefficients. If some of the data is not available at a spatial site of interest, this data is itself interpolated using GP over the spatial domain, thus adding another level of uncertainty in the model leading to a stochastic expansion with three levels of uncertainty. Denoting the number of sites where data is available by R we thus have,

$$q(r, \underline{\xi}_r) = \sum_j q_j(r) \Psi_j(\underline{\xi}_r), \quad r = 1, 2, 3, ...R, \tag{1}$$

where ξ_r are iid $\mathbb{R}^d$-valued Gaussian random variables (d is equal to the number of random variables used to describe the lognormal process for the permeability over each reservoir), and ψ_i are multidimensional Hermite polynomials. The zeroth order polynomial is equal to 1, signifying that the zeroth order coefficient is the average of q. We will assume in the sequel that the fine scale uncertainty, described by the random variables ξ_r are identical across all reservoirs. At site "s", knowing $\{q_j(s)\}$, then we can estimate of $q(s)$ as

$$q(s, \underline{\xi}_r) = \sum_j q_j(s) \Psi_j(\underline{\xi}_r). \tag{2}$$

To get $\{q_j(s)\}$, an interpolatory model is constructed over the parameter set S_2. Since S_2 is not observed at site "s", its content is interpolated over GoM with respect to the parameters in the set S_1 and with respect to geospatial references (referred to as set D_2. This interpolation task is denoted symbolically by,

$$\hat{S}_2(s, S_1, D_2) = \mathcal{I}_g(s, S_1 | S_1, D_2), \tag{3}$$

where $\mathcal{I}_g$ is an interpolation operator, which in our case is the Gaussian process regression. This leads to a PCE representation of entries in $\hat{S}_2$,

$$\hat{S}_2(s, \underline{\xi}_g) = \sum_j S_{2j}(s) \Psi_j(\underline{\xi}_g), \tag{4}$$

where $\underline{\xi}_g$ are new Gaussian random variables that reflect fundamental uncertainty that controls variability at the scale of the Gulf. These random variables are assumed to be independent of the set $\underline{\xi}_r$. The PCE coefficients $q_j(s)$ are thus interpolated as function of the interpolated $\hat{S}_2$ and the PCE coefficients obtained at all the observed reservoir sites $q_j(r)$. This is expressed as,

$$\hat{q}_j(\hat{D}_{s_2}(s, \underline{\xi}_g), q_j(r)) = \mathcal{K}_g \left(q_j(s) | \hat{D}_{s_2}(s, \underline{\xi}_g), q_j(r) \right) \tag{5}$$

where $\mathcal{K}_g$ is an interpolation operator, which in this case is again given as Gaussian process regression over parameter space. This can be described in the following PCE,

$$\hat{q}_j \left(D_{s_2}(s, \underline{\xi}_g), \xi_f \right) = \sum_i q_{ij} \left(D_{s_2}\left(s, \underline{\xi}_g \right) \right) \Psi_i(\underline{\xi}_f) \tag{6}$$

in which a new set of, $\underline{\xi}_f$, "fundamental" random variables is introduced. Putting all the representations together leads to

$$\hat{q} \left(s, \underline{\xi}_r, \underline{\xi}_f, \underline{\xi}_g \right) = \sum_{i,j} q_{ij} \left(\sum_k D_{s_{2k}}(s) \Psi_k(\underline{\xi}_g) \right) \Psi_i(\underline{\xi}_r) \Psi_j(\underline{\xi}_f), \tag{7}$$

where the parentheses on the right hand side refer to functional dependence which can further be unfolded yielding the following expression,

$$\hat{q}\left(s, \underline{\xi}_r, \underline{\xi}_f, \underline{\xi}_g\right) = \sum_{i,j,k} q_{ijk} \; \Psi_k(\underline{\xi}_g) \; \Psi_i(\underline{\xi}_r) \; \Psi_j(\underline{\xi}_f). \tag{8}$$

This model has three levels of uncertainty, which arise from three different physical scales. The first level of uncertainty is in the reservoir model because of the lack of detailed information of the microscale features such as permeability. This uncertainty can be reduced by having detailed information of microscale features, i.e. by having more wellbores inside the reservoir. The second level of uncertainty is due to the uncertainty of local geological features such as initial pressure, which can be reduced by having an understanding of geology and variability of the parameter set D_2 in local scale, i.e. inside the field where the reservoir "s" is located. The third level of uncertainty is attributed to geological fluctuations across the GoM, which can be reduced by detailed information of the geology of the entire GoM.

If we know S_2 at site "s" the above model reduces to

$$\hat{q}\left(s, \underline{\xi}_r, \underline{\xi}_g\right) = \sum_{i,j} q_{ij}(s)\Psi_i(\underline{\xi}_r)\Psi_j(\underline{\xi}_f). \tag{9}$$

4   Numerical Simulations

In order to show the capability of the developed procedure, simulations are carried at a few locations in the GoM. Figure 1 shows location of lease blocks used in this in GoM which are located in Green Canyon (GC) and Mississippi Canyon (MC). The lease blocks are identified as MC109, MC281, MC778, GC339 and GC608, and serve to demonstrate the predictive value of our ROM methodologies. More specifically, we will demonstrate how, given data from various wells located in MC109, MC281, MC778 and GC339 we can anticipate flows at some arbitrary well, "s" in GC608. The credibility of our predictions will depend on the type of information available within MC109, MC281, MC778, GC339 as well as on the information available for well "s" in GC608. Information about "s" consists of spatial coordinates, but could also include additional geological, geophysical and subset of parameters of D_2. Fields MC109, MC778, MC281, GC339, GC608 have 13, 14, 9, 28 and 1 sands identified in the BOEM dataset. Each sand is assumed to have one reservoir with the parameters listed in BOEM database.

4.1   PCE of QoI

Since BOEM data do not have detailed enough information to carry out numerical simulation of the reservoir, additional assumptions are made to enable numerical reservoir simulation. Thus each reservoir is assumed to be bounded by a cube with dimensions specified by the area of the reservoir and average thickness (both available in the BOEM dataset), which is consistent with our stated QoI which is related to flow rates at early times. Since BOEM data consists of only average permeability along each wellbore, the permeability field is assumed to be log-normal process with mean specified from the BOEM dataset and assumed coefficient of variation and correlation length. With these assumptions, numerical reservoir simulations are carried out at each of the 65 reservoirs to get PCE representations of the QoI at these reservoirs. Figure 2(a) shows probability density functions for all 65 reservoirs and Fig. 2(b) shows the combined pdf of QoI obtained by collecting samples of QoI from pdf's of QoI at all 65 reservoirs. This pdf is considered as describing a prior model. Our aim is to improve on this estimate of wellbore signatures as we specialize it to a spatial location in the GoM. It is clear in subfigure (a) of this figure that reducing the uncertainty at each reservoir has a limited effect since that would result in a collection of delta functions whose scatter reflects uncertainty about the geology of the GoM.

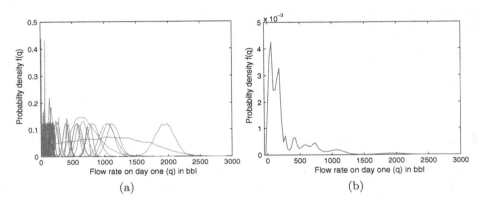

Fig. 2. (a) Probability density functions of flow rate on day one (q) in bbl for all 65 reservoirs (b) Combined pdf of flow rate on day one in bbl for all 65 reservoirs.

4.2   Diffusion Metric

In the above analysis, a Euclidean metric was adopted between points in set S_2. This precludes any intrinsic structure whereby S_2 may be embedded in a manifold within this Euclidean space. Given the fact that the large dataset we are dealing with is the result of a number of complex physical phenomena taking place at different scales in time and space, we do expect a certain hidden structure to emerge in response to these interactions. We thus compute a diffusion metric that defines the shortest path between points within S_2 as the path traversed by a Markov chain wandering on S_2 with constrained jumps sizes. We thus introduce the kernel,

$$k(x, y) = e^{-\frac{||x-y||^2}{\alpha}}, \tag{10}$$

which defined the diffusion matrix in the form,

$$L_{i,j} = k(x_i, x_j). \tag{11}$$

The normalized graph Laplacian, which acts as a transition matrix is then constructed using

$$M = D^{-1}L, \tag{12}$$

where

$$D = \sum_l L(x_i, x_j). \tag{13}$$

An eigen decomposition of M then leads to a representation of M in the form,

$$M_{i,j}^t = \sum_l \lambda_l^t \psi_l(x_i)\phi_l(x_j). \tag{14}$$

The distance between any two points on the manifold can then be evaluated using Euclidean distance between so called diffusion coordinates $\{\psi_i\}$. A map from the diffusion coordinates to the Euclidean distance is thus given in the form,

$$D_t(x_i, x_j)^2 = \sum_l \lambda_l^{2t}(\psi_l(x_i) - \psi_l(x_j))^2. \tag{15}$$

4.3   Prediction of QoI

Assuming we have only partial information of attributes regarding well "s" in GC608, QoI at this site is predicted by using PCE coefficients from reservoirs in MC109, MC281, MC778 and GC339. GP of PCE coefficients is performed over the subset of S_2 parameter space, since these parameters are used in numerical

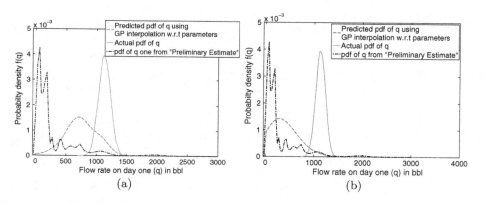

Fig. 3. QoI: Flow rate on day one in bbl; Solid green line indicates pdf of QoI at prediction location obtained from available data at that location; Dashed red line indicates predicted pdf of QoI using Gaussian Process regression over parameter space; Dotted and dashed black line indicates pdf of QoI from Preliminary Estimate (a) With known parameters at target site (b) With unknown parameters at target site (Color figure online).

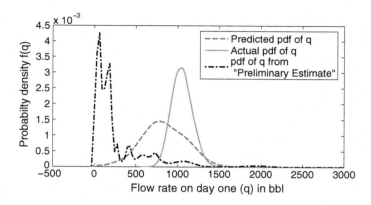

Fig. 4. QoI: Flow rate on day one in bbl; Solid green line indicates pdf of QoI at prediction location obtained from available data at that location; Dashed red line indicates predicted pdf of QoI using Gaussian Process regression over parameter space; Dotted and dashed black line indicates pdf of QoI from Preliminary Estimate. S_2 has dimension 36 (Color figure online).

Table 1. List of parameters included in the construction of the diffusion metric.

Spatial references X	Spatial references Y	RKB Elevation
Bore hole total measured depth	True vertical depth	Surface North/South distance
Surface East/West distance	Bottom North/South distance	Bottom East/West distance
Depth of water	Surface longitude	Bottom longitude
Surface latitude	Bottom latitude	Discovered BOE
Subsea Depth	Total average net thickness	Total area
Total volume	Oil average net thickness	Oil total area
Oil total volume	Gas average net thickness	Gas total area
Gas total volume	Porosity	Water saturation
Initial pressure	Initial temperature	Sand pressure gradient
Sand temperature gradient	Initial solution gas-oil ratio	Gas specific gravity
Oil API gravity	Initial gas formation volume factor	Initial oil formation volume factor

reservoir simulations. In one case we use as members of S_2 the five parameters given by porosity, water saturation, initial pressure, thickness of the reservoir and area of the reservoir. In a second instance we use a subset consisting of 36 parameters. If these parameters are known at well "s" they are used directly

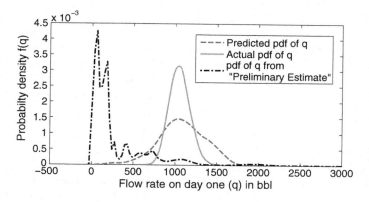

Fig. 5. QoI: Flow rate on day one in bbl; Solid green line indicates pdf of QoI at prediction location obtained from available data at that location; Dashed red line indicates predicted pdf of QoI using Gaussian Process regression over diffusion parameter space; Dotted and dashed black line indicates pdf of QoI from Preliminary Estimate. S_2 has dimension 36 (Color figure online).

for interpolation, otherwise they are interpolated over spatial reference and used for the interpolation of PCE coefficients. Figure 3 shows predicted pdf for the cases both with known and unknown parameters, for the case where S_2 is five-dimensional.

Figure 3 shows that predicted QoI using proposed stochastic interpolation methodology is better than the preliminary estimates obtained by pooling available data into a single pdf. Also, predictions are close to actual QoI if few parameters are available directly at the target site.

Figure 4 shows the pdf then the size of S_2 is increased to 36 (thus using a GP in 36 dimensional space). Figure 5 shows the results obtained by constructing the GP in 36 dimensions using the diffusion metric instead of the euclidean metric used in Fig. 4. The diffusion metric is constructed according to standard procedures for diffusion on a graph constructed by the data [1]. The diffusion metric is adapted to the data and discovers nonlinear intrinsic structure that is clearly relevant to the present case as demonstrated by the improvement in the match of the pdf. In the present problem, the diffusion map in 36 dimensional parameter space shown in Table 1 was computed. Connectivity between one data point and any another data point was defined by a Gaussian kernel with $\sigma = 1$. Based on the eigenvalues decay of the corresponding normalized graph laplacian, the dimension is reduced to 15.

5   Conclusions

A procedure has been developed for conditional density regression which produced a reduced order model useful for interpolating wellbore signatures over the Gulf of Mexico. These are useful for rapid risk assessment in case of anthropogenic events such as Deepwater Horizon oil spill. The construction uses polynomial chaos expansion in conjunction with a Gaussian process regression and a database of wellbore data over the GoM. The final model has three levels of uncertainties which are arising from three different physical scales. Despite these uncertainties the proposed model has the potential to provide improved probabilistic estimates of wellbore signatures at unobserved sites. This is demonstrated by carrying out numerical simulations in Mississippi Canyon and Green Canyon within the Gulf of Mexico.

References

1. Coifman, R.R., Lafon, S.: Diffusion maps. Appl. Comput. Harmonic Anal. **21**(1), 5–30 (2006). http://www.sciencedirect.com/science/article/pii/S1063520306000546, special Issue: Diffusion Maps and Wavelets
2. Cressie, N.: The origins of kriging. Math. Geol. **22**(3), 239–252 (1990)
3. Dunson, D.B., Pillai, N., Park, J.H.: Bayesian density regression. J. Roy. Stat. Soc. Ser. B (Stat. Methodol.) **69**(2), 163–183 (2007)
4. Ghanem, R.G., Spanos, P.D.: Stochastic Finite Elements: A Spectral Approach, vol. 41. Springer, New York (1991)
5. Graham, J., Rose, K., Bauer, J., Disenhof, C., Jenkins, C., Nelson, J., Ringo, C., Sim, L., VanAckeren, K.: Integration of spatial data to support risk and impact assessments for deep and ultra-deepwater hydrocarbon activities in the Gulf of Mexico. EPAct Technical report Series, Morgantown, WV; p. 36, NETL-TRS-4-2012 (2012)
6. Isaaks, E., Srivastava, R.: Applied Geostatistics. Oxford University, London (2011)
7. Krige, D.: A statistical approach to some basic mine valuation problems on the Witwatersrand. Jnl. C'hem. Met. and Min. Soc. S. Afr. **52**, 119–139 (1951)
8. Matheron, G.: Principles of geostatistics. Econ. Geol. **58**(8), 1246–1266 (1963)
9. McNutt, M.K., Camilli, R., Crone, T.J., Guthrie, G.D., Hsieh, P.A., Ryerson, T.B., Savas, O., Shaffer, F.: Review of flow rate estimates of the Deepwater Horizon oil spill. Proc. Nat. Acad. Sci. **109**(50), 20260–20267 (2012)
10. Müller, P., Erkanli, A., West, M.: Bayesian curve fitting using multivariate normal mixtures. Biometrika **83**(1), 67–79 (1996)
11. Rasmussen, C.E.: Gaussian Processes for Machine Learning. MIT Press, Cambridge (2006)
12. Sakamoto, S., Ghanem, R.: Simulation of multi-dimensional non-gaussian non-stationary random fields. Probab. Eng. Mech. **17**(2), 167–176 (2002)
13. Shinozuka, M., Deodatis, G.: Simulation of stochastic processes by spectral representation. Appl. Mech. Rev. **44**(4), 191–204 (1991)
14. Xiu, D., Karniadakis, G.E.: The Wiener-Askey polynomial chaos for stochastic differential equations. SIAM J. Sci. Comput. **24**(2), 619–644 (2002)

Recent Advances in Scaling Up Gaussian Process Predictive Models for Large Spatiotemporal Data

Kian Hsiang Low[1](✉), Jie Chen[2], Trong Nghia Hoang[1], Nuo Xu[1], and Patrick Jaillet[3]

[1] National University of Singapore, Singapore, Singapore
{lowkh,nghiaht,xunuo}@comp.nus.edu.sg
[2] Singapore-MIT Alliance for Research and Technology, Singapore, Singapore
chenjie@smart.mit.edu
[3] Massachusetts Institute of Technology, Cambridge, USA
jaillet@mit.edu

Abstract. The expressive power of *Gaussian process* (GP) models comes at a cost of poor scalability in the size of the data. To improve their scalability, this paper presents an overview of our recent progress in scaling up GP models for large spatiotemporally correlated data through parallelization on clusters of machines, online learning, and nonmyopic active sensing/learning.

1 Introduction

Gaussian process (GP) models are a rich class of Bayesian non-parametric models that can perform probabilistic regression by providing Gaussian predictive distributions with formal measures of predictive uncertainty. Unfortunately, the expressive power of a *full-rank GP* (FGP) model comes at a cost of poor scalability (i.e., cubic time) in the data size, which hinders its practical use for large data generated from environmental sensing and monitoring applications. To boost its scalability, two research trends are prevalent:

Model Approximation. To improve the time efficiency of training with all the given data, structural assumptions have been imposed on the FGP model to yield two different classes of sparse GP approximation methods: (a) Low-rank approximate representations [7, 27, 31] of the FGP model are especially suitable for modeling smoothly-varying environmental phenomena with high spatiotemporal correlation (i.e., long length-scales) and they utilize all the data for predictions like FGP; and (b) localized regression and covariance tapering methods (e.g., local GPs [6, 25] and compactly supported covariance functions [11]) are capable of modeling highly-varying phenomena with low correlation (i.e., short length-scales) but they use only local data for predictions, hence predicting poorly in areas with sparse data. Recent sparse GP approximation methods [3, 28, 30] have attempted to unify the best of both worlds.

© Springer International Publishing Switzerland 2015
S. Ravela and A. Sandu (Eds.): DyDESS 2014, LNCS 8964, pp. 167–181, 2015.
DOI: 10.1007/978-3-319-25138-7_16

Data/Information Gathering. Alternatively, the GP model can be trained with considerably less but highly informative data that are actively (as opposed to passively) gathered by optimizing some active sensing/learning[1] criterion defined using mean-square error, entropy, or mutual information [1,16,18,19]. This is particularly desirable in environmental sensing applications and tasks constrained by some sampling budget.

This paper presents an overview of our recent progress in scaling up GP models for large spatiotemporally correlated data along the two research directions discussed above. The specific contributions of our three recent works [3,12,32] include:

Parallel GP Models. Though existing sparse GP approximation methods utilizing low-rank representations (i.e., including the unified approaches) [7,27,28,30,31] have improved the scalability of GP models to linear time in the data size, they remain computationally impractical for performing real-time predictions necessary in many time-critical environmental sensing and monitoring applications and decision support systems (e.g., precision agriculture [19], sensing and monitoring of ocean, freshwater, and traffic phenomena [1,2,4,5,10,17,18,20,21,26], GIS) that need to process and analyze huge quantities of data collected over short time durations (e.g., in traffic, meteorology, surveillance). To resolve this, our first work considers exploiting clusters of parallel machines to achieve efficient predictions in real time. The local GPs method [6] appears most straightforward to be "embarrassingly" parallelized but they suffer from discontinuities in predictions on the boundaries of different local GPs. The work of [25] rectifies this problem by imposing continuity constraints along the boundaries in a centralized manner. But, its use is restricted strictly to data with 1D and 2D input features.

Different from the parallel local GPs method, our proposed parallel GP models [3] (Sect. 3), which exploit low-rank approximate representations for distributing the computational load among parallel machines to achieve time efficiency and scalability, do not suffer from boundary effects, work with multi-dimensional input features, and exploit all the data for predictions but do not incur the cubic time cost of FGP model. We theoretically guarantee the predictive performances of our parallel GP models to be equivalent to that of some centralized sparse GP approximation methods and implement them using the *message passing interface* (MPI) framework to run in a cluster of 20 computing nodes for empirically evaluating their predictive performances, time efficiency, scalability, and speedups on a dataset featuring a real-world traffic phenomenon. Interestingly, our parallel GP models can be adapted to GP-based decentralized data fusion algorithms to be run on a network of mobile sensors for cooperative perception of spatiotemporally varying environmental phenomena, as detailed in [4,5].

Online GP Model. When the data is expected to be streaming in over a (possibly indefinitely) long period of time, it is computationally impractical to

---

[1] Active sensing/learning in machine learning is also known as adaptive sampling in oceanography and control [17].

repeatedly use existing offline sparse GP approximation methods [7, 27, 28, 30, 31] or online FGP model [9] for training at each time step because they incur, respectively, linear and quadratic time in the data size per time step. Our next work proposes a novel online sparse GP approximation method [22, 32] (Sect. 4) that, in contrast to existing works mentioned above, is capable of achieving *constant* time and memory (i.e., independent of data size) per time step. We provide a theoretical guarantee on its predictive performance to be equivalent to that of the offline sparse *partially independent training conditional* (PITC) approximation method. Our proposed method [32] generalizes the sparse online GP model of [9] by relaxing its conditional independence assumption significantly, hence potentially improving the predictive performance. We empirically demonstrate the practical feasibility of using our generalized online sparse GP model through a real-world persistent mobile robot localization experiment.

Nonmyopic Active Sensing/Learning. Its objective is to derive an optimal sequential policy that plans the most informative locations to be observed for minimizing the predictive uncertainty of the unobserved areas of a spatially varying environmental phenomenon given a sampling budget (e.g., number of deployed sensors, energy consumption). To achieve this, many existing active sensing algorithms [1, 4, 5, 16, 18–20] have assumed the spatial correlation structure of the phenomenon modeled by GP (specifically, the parameters defining it) to be known, which is often violated in real-world applications. The predictive performance of the GP model in fact depends on how informative the gathered observations are for both parameter estimation and spatial prediction given the true parameters. Interestingly, as revealed in [23], policies that are efficient for parameter estimation are not necessarily efficient for spatial prediction with respect to the true model parameters. Thus, active sensing/learning involves a potential trade-off between sampling the most informative locations for spatial prediction given the current, possibly incomplete knowledge of the parameters (i.e., exploitation) vs. observing locations that gain more information about the parameters (i.e., exploration). To address this trade-off, one principled approach is to frame active sensing as a sequential decision problem that jointly optimizes the above exploration-exploitation trade-off while maintaining a Bayesian belief over the model parameters. Solving this problem then results in an induced policy that is guaranteed to be optimal in the expected active sensing performance [12]. Unfortunately, such a nonmyopic *Bayes-optimal active learning* (BAL) policy cannot be derived exactly due to an uncountable set of candidate observations and unknown model parameters. As a result, existing works advocate using greedy policies [24] or performing exploration and exploitation separately [15] to sidestep the difficulty of solving for the exact BAL policy. But, these algorithms are sub-optimal in the presence of budget constraints due to their imbalance between exploration and exploitation [12].

Our final work proposes a novel nonmyopic active sensing/learning algorithm [12, 13] (Sect. 5) that can still preserve and exploit the principled Bayesian sequential decision problem framework for jointly optimizing the exploration-exploitation trade-off and hence does not incur the limitations of existing works.

In particular, although the exact BAL policy cannot be derived, we show that it is in fact possible to solve for a nonmyopic ϵ-*Bayes-optimal active learning* (ϵ-BAL) policy given an arbitrary loss bound ϵ. To meet real-time requirement in time-critical applications, we then propose an asymptotically ϵ-optimal anytime algorithm based on ϵ-BAL with performance guarantee. We empirically demonstrate using a dataset featuring a real-world traffic phenomenon that, with limited budget, our approach outperforms state-of-the-art algorithms.

2   Modeling Environmental Phenomena with Gaussian Processes

The GP^2 can be used to model an environmental phenomenon as follows: The phenomenon is defined to vary as a realization of a GP. Let $\mathcal{X}$ be a set of sampling units representing the domain of the phenomenon such that each sampling unit $x \in \mathcal{X}$ denotes a d-dimensional feature vector and is associated with a realized (random) measurement z_x (Z_x) if x is observed (unobserved). Let $\{Z_x\}_{x \in \mathcal{X}}$ denote a GP, that is, every finite subset of $\{Z_x\}_{x \in \mathcal{X}}$ has a multivariate Gaussian distribution. The GP is fully specified by its *prior* mean $\mu_x \triangleq \mathbb{E}[Z_x]$ and covariance $\sigma_{xx'|\lambda} \triangleq \mathrm{cov}[Z_x, Z_{x'}|\lambda]$ for all locations $x, x' \in \mathcal{X}$, the latter of which characterizes the spatial correlation structure of the phenomenon and can be defined using a covariance function parameterized by λ. When λ is known and a set $z_{\mathcal{D}}$ of realized measurements is observed for some set $\mathcal{D} \subset \mathcal{X}$ of sampling units, the FGP model can exploit these observations to predict the unobserved measurement for any sampling unit $x \in \mathcal{X} \setminus \mathcal{D}$ as well as provide its predictive uncertainty using a Gaussian predictive distribution $p(z_x|x, \mathcal{D}, z_{\mathcal{D}}, \lambda) = \mathcal{N}(\mu_{x|\mathcal{D}, \lambda}, \sigma_{xx|\mathcal{D}, \lambda})$ with the following *posterior* mean and variance, respectively:

$$\mu_{x|\mathcal{D},\lambda} \triangleq \mu_x + \Sigma_{x\mathcal{D}|\lambda} \Sigma_{\mathcal{D}\mathcal{D}|\lambda}^{-1} (z_{\mathcal{D}} - \mu_{\mathcal{D}}) \quad \text{and} \quad \sigma_{xx|\mathcal{D},\lambda} \triangleq \sigma_{xx|\lambda} - \Sigma_{x\mathcal{D}|\lambda} \Sigma_{\mathcal{D}\mathcal{D}|\lambda}^{-1} \Sigma_{\mathcal{D}x|\lambda} \tag{1}$$

where, with a slight abuse of notation, $z_{\mathcal{D}}$ is to be perceived as a column vector, $\mu_{\mathcal{D}}$ is a column vector with prior mean components $\mu_{x'}$ for all $x' \in \mathcal{D}$, $\Sigma_{x\mathcal{D}|\lambda}$ is a row vector with prior covariance components $\sigma_{xx'|\lambda}$ for all $x' \in \mathcal{D}$, $\Sigma_{\mathcal{D}x|\lambda}$ is the transpose of $\Sigma_{x\mathcal{D}|\lambda}$, and $\Sigma_{\mathcal{D}\mathcal{D}|\lambda}$ is a matrix with components $\sigma_{x'x''|\lambda}$ for all $x', x'' \in \mathcal{D}$. When λ is not known, a probabilistic belief $b_{\mathcal{D}}(\lambda) \triangleq p(\lambda|z_{\mathcal{D}})$ is maintained over all possible λ and updated using Bayes' rule to the posterior belief $b_{\mathcal{D} \cup \{x\}}(\lambda) \propto p(z_x|x, \mathcal{D}, z_{\mathcal{D}}, \lambda) b_{\mathcal{D}}(\lambda)$ given a new measurement z_x. Then, using belief $b_{\mathcal{D}}$, the predictive distribution is obtained by marginalizing out λ: $p(z_x|x, \mathcal{D}, z_{\mathcal{D}}) = \sum_{\lambda \in \Lambda} p(z_x|x, \mathcal{D}, z_{\mathcal{D}}, \lambda) b_{\mathcal{D}}(\lambda)$.

---

[2] GP regression in machine learning is equivalent to the data assimilation scheme called objective analysis or optimal interpolation or 3DVAR in oceanography and meteorology [2,17] when the domain is reduced to a finite set of grid points and all observations are at the grid points. It is also equivalent to kriging in geostatistics [8].

3 Parallel GP Models

In this section, we will present a class of parallel GP models (pPITC and pPIC) that distributes the computational load among parallel machines to achieve efficient and scalable approximate GP prediction by exploiting the notion of a support set. The key idea of the *parallel partially independent training conditional* (pPITC) approximation of FGP model is as follows: After distributing the data evenly among N machines (Step 1), each machine encapsulates its local data, based on a common prior support set $\mathcal{S} \subset \mathcal{X}$ where $|\mathcal{S}| \ll |\mathcal{D}|$, into a local summary that is communicated to the master[3] (Step 2). The master assimilates the local summaries into a global summary (Step 3), which is then sent back to the N machines to be used for predictions distributed among them (Step 4). These steps are detailed below. For simplicity, we omit the use of the known GP model parameters λ in our notations.

STEP 1: DISTRIBUTE DATA AMONG N MACHINES.
The data $(\mathcal{D}, y_{\mathcal{D}})$ is partitioned evenly into N blocks, each of which is assigned to a machine, as defined below:

Definition 1 (Local Data). *The local data of machine n is defined as a tuple* $(\mathcal{D}_n, y_{\mathcal{D}_n})$ *where* $\mathcal{D}_n \subseteq \mathcal{D}$, $\mathcal{D}_n \bigcap \mathcal{D}_i = \emptyset$ *and* $|\mathcal{D}_n| = |\mathcal{D}_i| = |\mathcal{D}|/N$ *for* $i \neq n$.

STEP 2: EACH MACHINE CONSTRUCTS AND SENDS LOCAL SUMMARY TO MASTER.

Definition 2 (Local Summary). *Given a common support set* $\mathcal{S} \subset \mathcal{X}$ *known to all N machines and the local data* $(\mathcal{D}_n, y_{\mathcal{D}_n})$*, the local summary of machine n is defined as a tuple* $(\dot{y}_{\mathcal{S}}^n, \dot{\Sigma}_{\mathcal{S}\mathcal{S}}^n)$ *where* $\dot{y}_{\mathcal{S}}^n \triangleq \Sigma_{\mathcal{S}\mathcal{D}_n} \Sigma_{\mathcal{D}_n \mathcal{D}_n | \mathcal{S}}^{-1} (y_{\mathcal{D}_n} - \mu_{\mathcal{D}_n})$ *and* $\dot{\Sigma}_{\mathcal{S}\mathcal{S}}^n \triangleq \Sigma_{\mathcal{S}\mathcal{D}_n} \Sigma_{\mathcal{D}_n \mathcal{D}_n | \mathcal{S}}^{-1} \Sigma_{\mathcal{D}_n \mathcal{S}}$ *such that* $\mu_{\mathcal{D}_n}$ *is defined in a similar manner as* $\mu_{\mathcal{D}}$ *in* (1) *and* $\Sigma_{\mathcal{D}_n \mathcal{D}_n | \mathcal{S}}$ *is a matrix with posterior covariance components* $\sigma_{xx'|\mathcal{S}}$ *for all* $x, x' \in \mathcal{D}_n$*, each of which is defined in a similar way as* (1).

Remark. Since the local summary is independent of the outputs $y_{\mathcal{S}}$, they need not be observed. So, the support set $\mathcal{S}$ does not have to be a subset of $\mathcal{D}$ and can be selected prior to data collection. Predictive performances of pPITC and pPIC are sensitive to the selection of $\mathcal{S}$. An informative support set $\mathcal{S}$ can be selected from domain $\mathcal{X}$ using an iterative greedy active selection procedure [16] prior to observing data.

STEP 3: MASTER CONSTRUCTS AND SENDS GLOBAL SUMMARY TO N MACHINES.

Definition 3 (Global Summary). *Given a common support set* $\mathcal{S} \subset \mathcal{X}$ *known to all N machines and the local summary* $(\dot{y}_{\mathcal{S}}^n, \dot{\Sigma}_{\mathcal{S}\mathcal{S}}^n)$ *of every machine $n = 1, \ldots, N$, the global summary is defined as a tuple* $(\ddot{y}_{\mathcal{S}}, \ddot{\Sigma}_{\mathcal{S}\mathcal{S}})$ *where* $\ddot{y}_{\mathcal{S}} \triangleq \sum_{n=1}^{N} \dot{y}_{\mathcal{S}}^n$ *and* $\ddot{\Sigma}_{\mathcal{S}\mathcal{S}} \triangleq \Sigma_{\mathcal{S}\mathcal{S}} + \sum_{n=1}^{N} \dot{\Sigma}_{\mathcal{S}\mathcal{S}}^n$.

---

[3] One of the N machines can be assigned to be the master.

Step 4: Distribute predictions among N machines.
To predict the unobserved measurement for any set $\mathcal{U}$ of sampling units, $\mathcal{U}$ is partitioned evenly into disjoint subsets $\mathcal{U}_1, \ldots, \mathcal{U}_N$ to be assigned to the respective machines $1, \ldots, N$. So, $|\mathcal{U}_n| = |\mathcal{U}|/N$ for $n = 1, \ldots, N$.

Definition 4 (pPITC). *Given a common support set $\mathcal{S} \subset \mathcal{X}$ known to all N machines and the global summary $(\ddot{y}_{\mathcal{S}}, \ddot{\Sigma}_{\mathcal{S}\mathcal{S}})$, each machine m computes a predictive Gaussian distribution $\mathcal{N}(\widehat{\mu}_x, \widehat{\sigma}_{xx})$ of the unobserved measurement for all sampling units $x \in \mathcal{U}_n$ where $\widehat{\mu}_x \triangleq \mu_x + \Sigma_{x\mathcal{S}} \ddot{\Sigma}_{\mathcal{S}\mathcal{S}}^{-1} \ddot{y}_{\mathcal{S}}$ and $\widehat{\sigma}_{xx} \triangleq \sigma_{xx} - \Sigma_{x\mathcal{S}} \left(\Sigma_{\mathcal{S}\mathcal{S}}^{-1} - \ddot{\Sigma}_{\mathcal{S}\mathcal{S}}^{-1} \right) \Sigma_{\mathcal{S}x}$.*

Theorem 1. *Let a common support set $\mathcal{S} \subset \mathcal{X}$ be known to all N machines. Let $\mathcal{N}(\mu_{x|\mathcal{D}}^{\mathrm{PITC}}, \sigma_{xx|\mathcal{D}}^{\mathrm{PITC}})$ be the predictive Gaussian distribution computed by the centralized PITC approximation of FGP model [27] for all sampling units $x \in \mathcal{U}$ where*

$$\mu_{x|\mathcal{D}}^{\mathrm{PITC}} \triangleq \mu_x + \Gamma_{x\mathcal{D}} \left(\Gamma_{\mathcal{D}\mathcal{D}} + \Lambda \right)^{-1} \left(y_{\mathcal{D}} - \mu_{\mathcal{D}} \right) \text{ and } \sigma_{xx|\mathcal{D}}^{\mathrm{PITC}} \triangleq \sigma_{xx} - \Gamma_{x\mathcal{D}} \left(\Gamma_{\mathcal{D}\mathcal{D}} + \Lambda \right)^{-1} \Gamma_{\mathcal{D}x}$$
(2)

such that $\Gamma_{\mathcal{B}\mathcal{B}'} \triangleq \Sigma_{\mathcal{B}\mathcal{S}} \Sigma_{\mathcal{S}\mathcal{S}}^{-1} \Sigma_{\mathcal{S}\mathcal{B}'}$ for all $\mathcal{B}, \mathcal{B}' \subset \mathcal{X}$ and Λ is a block-diagonal matrix constructed from the N diagonal blocks of $\Sigma_{\mathcal{D}\mathcal{D}|\mathcal{S}}$, each of which is a matrix $\Sigma_{\mathcal{D}_n \mathcal{D}_n | \mathcal{S}}$ for $n = 1, \ldots, N$ where $\mathcal{D} = \bigcup_{n=1}^{N} \mathcal{D}_n$. Then, $\widehat{\mu}_x = \mu_{x|\mathcal{D}}^{\mathrm{PITC}}$ and $\widehat{\sigma}_{xx} = \sigma_{xx|\mathcal{D}}^{\mathrm{PITC}}$.

Remark. Since PITC generalizes the Bayesian Committee Machine (BCM) of [29], pPITC generalizes parallel BCM [14], the latter of which assumes the support set $\mathcal{S}$ to be $\mathcal{U}$ [27]. As a result, parallel BCM does not scale well with large $\mathcal{U}$. Similarly, since PITC reduces to the *fully independent training conditional* (FITC) approximation method when Λ is a diagonal matrix constructed from $\sigma_{x'x'|\mathcal{S}}$ for all $x' \in \mathcal{D}$ (i.e., $N = |\mathcal{D}|$), pPITC generalizes parallel FITC.

Though pPITC scales very well with large data [3], it can predict poorly due to (a) loss of information caused by summarizing the realized measurements and correlation structure of the original data; and (b) sparse coverage of $\mathcal{U}$ by the support set. We propose a novel *parallel partially independent conditional* (pPIC) approximation of FGP model that combines the best of both worlds, that is, the predictive power of FGP and time efficiency of pPITC. pPIC is based on the following intuition: A machine can exploit its local data to improve the predictions of unobserved measurements that are highly correlated with its data. At the same time, pPIC can preserve the time efficiency of pPITC by exploiting its idea of encapsulating information into local and global summaries. The predictive Gaussian distribution computed by pPIC on each machine is (a) more complicated mathematically because, to avoid exploiting the local data twice, its contribution to the summary information has to be removed, and (b) proven to be equivalent to that of the centralized PIC approximation of FGP model [30]. Interested readers are referred to [3] for more details.

Remark 1. The above equivalence results imply that the computational load of the centralized PITC and PIC approximations of FGP can be distributed among N parallel machines, hence improving the time efficiency and scalability of approximate GP prediction. Supposing $|\mathcal{U}| < |\mathcal{D}|$ and $|\mathcal{S}| < |\mathcal{D}|$ for simplicity, the $\mathcal{O}(|\mathcal{S}|^2|\mathcal{D}| + |\mathcal{D}|(|\mathcal{D}|/N)^2)$ time incurred by PITC and $\mathcal{O}(|\mathcal{S}|^2|\mathcal{D}| + |\mathcal{D}|(|\mathcal{D}|/N)^2 + N|\mathcal{D}|)$ time incurred by PIC can, respectively, be reduced to $\mathcal{O}(|\mathcal{S}|^2(|\mathcal{S}| + N + |\mathcal{U}|/N) + (|\mathcal{D}|/N)^3)$ incurred by pPITC and $\mathcal{O}(|\mathcal{S}|^2(|\mathcal{S}| + N + |\mathcal{U}|/N) + (|\mathcal{D}|/N)^3 + |\mathcal{D}|)$ time incurred by pPIC, the latter of which scale better with increasing data size $|\mathcal{D}|$. The speedups of pPITC and pPIC over their centralized counterparts (a) deviate further from ideal speedup with more machines N due to their additional $\mathcal{O}(|\mathcal{S}|^2N)$ time, and (b) grow with increasing data size $|\mathcal{D}|$ because, unlike the additional $\mathcal{O}(|\mathcal{S}|^2|\mathcal{D}|)$ time of PITC and PIC that increase with more data, they do not have corresponding $\mathcal{O}(|\mathcal{S}|^2|\mathcal{D}|/M)$ terms.

Remark 2. The equivalence results also shed some light on the underlying properties of pPITC and pPIC based on the structural assumptions of PITC and PIC, respectively: pPITC assumes that $Y_{\mathcal{D}_1}, \ldots, Y_{\mathcal{D}_M}, Y_{\mathcal{U}_1}, \ldots, Y_{\mathcal{U}_M}$ are conditionally independent given $Y_{\mathcal{S}}$. In contrast, pPIC can predict the unobserved measurements $Y_{\mathcal{U}}$ better since it imposes a less restrictive assumption of conditional independence between $Y_{\mathcal{D}_1 \cup \mathcal{U}_1}, \ldots, Y_{\mathcal{D}_M \cup \mathcal{U}_M}$ given $Y_{\mathcal{S}}$. Experimental results on two real-world datasets [3] show that pPIC achieves predictive accuracy comparable to FGP and significantly better than pPITC, thus justifying the practicality of such an assumption.

Remark 3. Predictive performances of pPITC and pPIC are improved by increasing size of $\mathcal{S}$ at the expense of greater time, space, and communication complexity [3].

Experiments and Discussion. This section empirically evaluates the predictive performances, time efficiency, scalability, and speedups of our proposed parallel GPs against their centralized counterparts and FGP on a dataset of size $|\mathcal{D}| = 41850$ featuring a real-world traffic phenomenon, which contains traffic speeds (km/h) along 775 road segments of an urban road network (including highways, arterials, slip roads, etc.) during the morning peak hours on April 20, 2011. The traffic speeds are the measurements. The mean speed is 49.5 km/h and the standard deviation is 21.7 km/h. Each sampling unit (i.e., road segment) is specified by a 5-dimensional vector of features: length, number of lanes, speed limit, direction, and time. The time dimension comprises 54 five-minute time slots. This spatiotemporal traffic phenomenon is modeled using a relational GP (previously developed in [5]) whose correlation structure can exploit both the road segment features and road network topology information. 10 % of the data is randomly selected as test data for predictions (i.e., as $\mathcal{U}$). Our experimental platform is a cluster of 20 computing nodes connected via gigabit links: Each node runs a Linux system with Intel® Xeon® CPU E5520 at 2.27 GHz and 20 GB memory. More details of our experimental setup can be found in [3].

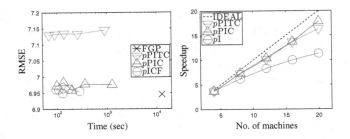

Fig. 1. Performance of parallel GP models with varying number $N = 4, 8, 12, 16, 20$ of machines, data size $|\mathcal{D}| = 32000$, and support set size $|\mathcal{S}| = 2048$. The *ideal* speedup of a parallel algorithm is defined to be the number N of machines running it.

Figure 1 shows that, with $N = 20$ machines and data size $|\mathcal{D}| = 32000$, pPITC and pPIC incur 2–4 orders of magnitude less time than FGP while achieving comparable predictive performances (respectively, *root mean square error* (RMSE) differences of less than 0.2 km/h and 0.05 km/h). Specifically, pPITC and pPIC incur only 1–2 min while FGP incurs more than 3.5 h. Also, the speedups of pPITC and pPIC over their centralized counterparts deviate further from ideal speedup with more machines, as explained earlier. We have in fact proposed another parallel GP model in [3] called pICF that exploits parallel incomplete Cholesky factorization. For implementation details of pICF and more extensive experimental results, interested readers are referred to [3].

4 Generalized Online Sparse GP (GOSGP) Approximation

The key idea of our GOSGP approximation method [32] is to summarize the newly gathered data at regular time intervals/slices, assimilate the summary information of the new data with that of all the previously gathered data/observations, and then exploit the resulting assimilated summary information to compute a Gaussian predictive distribution of the unobserved measurement for any sampling unit. For simplicity, we omit the use of the known GP model parameters λ in our notations. Let $x_{1:t-1} \triangleq \{x_1, \ldots, x_{t-1}\}$ denote a set of sampling units from time steps 1 to $t - 1$, each time slice n span time steps $(n-1)\tau + 1$ to $n\tau$ for some user-defined slice size $\tau \in \mathbb{Z}^+$, and the number of time slices available thus far up until time step t be denoted by N (i.e., $N\tau < t$).

Definition 5 (Slice Summary). *Given a support set $\mathcal{S} \subset \mathcal{X}$, a subset $\mathcal{D}_n \triangleq x_{(n-1)\tau+1:n\tau} \in x_{1:t-1}$ of sampling units associated with time slice n, and the column vector $z_{\mathcal{D}_n} = z_{(n-1)\tau+1:n\tau}$ of corresponding realized measurements, the slice summary of time slice n is defined as a tuple $(\mu_{\circledS}^n, \Sigma_{\circledS}^n)$ for $n = 1, \ldots, N$ where $\mu_{\circledS}^n \triangleq \Sigma_{\mathcal{S}\mathcal{D}_n} \Sigma_{\mathcal{D}_n\mathcal{D}_n|\mathcal{S}}^{-1} (z_{\mathcal{D}_n} - \mu_{\mathcal{D}_n})$ and $\Sigma_{\circledS}^n \triangleq \Sigma_{\mathcal{S}\mathcal{D}_n} \Sigma_{\mathcal{D}_n\mathcal{D}_n|\mathcal{S}}^{-1} \Sigma_{\mathcal{D}_n\mathcal{S}}$.*

Definition 6 (Assimilated Summary). *Given* $(\mu^n_{\circledS}, \Sigma^n_{\circledS})$, *the assimilated summary* $(\mu^n_{\circledA}, \Sigma^n_{\circledA})$ *of time slices* 1 *to* n *is updated from the assimilated summary* $(\mu^{n-1}_{\circledA}, \Sigma^{n-1}_{\circledA})$ *of time slices* 1 *to* $n-1$ *using* $\mu^n_{\circledA} \triangleq \mu^{n-1}_{\circledA} + \mu^n_{\circledS}$ *and* $\Sigma^n_{\circledA} \triangleq \Sigma^{n-1}_{\circledA} + \Sigma^n_{\circledS}$ *for* $n = 1, \ldots, N$ *where* $\mu^0_{\circledA} \triangleq 0$ *and* $\Sigma^0_{\circledA} \triangleq \Sigma_{SS}$.

Remark 1. After constructing and assimilating $(\mu^n_{\circledS}, \Sigma^n_{\circledS})$ with $(\mu^{n-1}_{\circledA}, \Sigma^{n-1}_{\circledA})$ to form $(\mu^n_{\circledA}, \Sigma^n_{\circledA})$, $\mathcal{D}_n = x_{(n-1)\tau+1:n\tau}$, $z_{\mathcal{D}_n} = z_{(n-1)\tau+1:n\tau}$, and $(\mu^n_{\circledS}, \Sigma^n_{\circledS})$ (Definition 5) are no longer needed and can be removed from memory. As a result, at time step t where $N\tau + 1 \leq t \leq (N+1)\tau$, only $(\mu^N_{\circledA}, \Sigma^N_{\circledA})$, $x_{N\tau+1:t-1}$, and $z_{N\tau+1:t-1}$ have to be kept in memory, thus requiring only constant memory (i.e., independent of t).

Remark 2. The slice summaries are constructed and assimilated at a regular time interval of τ, specifically, at time steps $N\tau + 1$ for $N \in \mathbb{Z}^+$.

Theorem 2. *Given* $\mathcal{S} \subset \mathcal{X}$ *and* $(\mu^N_{\circledA}, \Sigma^N_{\circledA})$, *our GOSGP approximation method computes a Gaussian predictive distribution* $p(z_t | x_t, \mu^N_{\circledA}, \Sigma^N_{\circledA}) = \mathcal{N}(\tilde{\mu}_{x_t}, \tilde{\sigma}_{x_t x_t})$ *of the measurement for any* $x_t \in \mathcal{X}$ *at time step* t *(i.e.,* $N\tau + 1 \leq t \leq (N+1)\tau$*) where*

$$\tilde{\mu}_{x_t} \triangleq \mu_{x_t} + \Sigma_{x_t S} \left(\Sigma^N_{\circledA} \right)^{-1} \mu^N_{\circledA} \quad and \quad \tilde{\sigma}_{x_t x_t} \triangleq \sigma_{x_t x_t} - \Sigma_{x_t S} \left(\Sigma^{-1}_{SS} - \left(\Sigma^N_{\circledA} \right)^{-1} \right) \Sigma_{S x_t}.$$

If $t = N\tau + 1, \tilde{\mu}_{x_t} = \mu^{\mathrm{PITC}}_{x_t | x_{1:t-1}} and \tilde{\sigma}_{x_t x_t} = \sigma^{\mathrm{PITC}}_{x_t x_t | x_{1:t-1}}.$ \hfill (3)

Remark 1. Theorem 2 implies that our GOSGP approximation method [32] is in fact equivalent to an online learning formulation/variant of the offline PITC [27]. Supposing $\tau < |\mathcal{S}|$, the $\mathcal{O}(t|\mathcal{S}|^2)$ time incurred by offline PITC can then be reduced to $\mathcal{O}(\tau|\mathcal{S}|^2)$ time (i.e., time independent of t) incurred by GOSGP [32] at time steps $t = N\tau + 1$ for $N \in \mathbb{Z}^+$ when slice summaries are constructed and assimilated. Otherwise, GOSGP [32] only incurs $\mathcal{O}(|\mathcal{S}|^2)$ time per time step.

Remark 2. The above equivalence result allows the structural property of GOSGP [32] to be elucidated using that of offline PITC: The measurements $Z_{\mathcal{D}_1}, \ldots, Z_{\mathcal{D}_N}, Z_{x_t}$ between different time slices are assumed to be conditionally independent given $Z_{\mathcal{S}}$. Such an assumption enables the data gathered during each time slice to be summarized independently of that in other time slices. Increasing slice size τ (i.e., less frequent assimilations of larger slice summaries) relaxes this conditional independence assumption (hence, potentially improving the predictive performance), but incurs more time at time steps when slice summaries are constructed and assimilated (see Remark 1).

Remark 3. Since offline PITC generalizes offline FITC, our GOSGP approximation method [32] generalizes the online learning variant of FITC (i.e., $\tau = 1$) [9].

When $N\tau + 1 < t \leq (N+1)\tau$ (i.e., before the next slice summary of time slice $N+1$ is constructed and assimilated), the most recent observations (i.e., $\mathcal{D}' \triangleq x_{N\tau+1:t-1}$ and $z_{\mathcal{D}'} = z_{N\tau+1:t-1}$), which are often highly informative, are not used to update $\tilde{\mu}_{x_t}$ and $\tilde{\sigma}_{x_t x_t}$ (3). This may hurt the predictive performance when τ is large. To resolve this, we exploit incremental update formulas

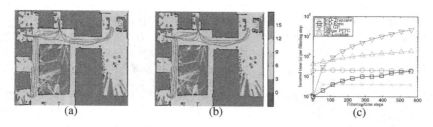

Fig. 2. (a) Pioneer 3-DX mobile robot trajectory of about 280 m in SMART FM IRG office/lab generated by AMCL package in ROS, along which (b) 561 relative light (%) observations/data are gathered at locations denoted by small colored circles. (c) Graphs of incurred time (s) per time step vs. number of time steps comparing different GP localization algorithms.

of Gaussian posterior mean and variance [32] to update $\widetilde{\mu}_{x_t}$ and $\widetilde{\sigma}_{x_t x_t}$ with the most recent observations, thereby yielding a Gaussian predictive distribution $p(z_t | x_t, \mu_@^N, \Sigma_@^N, \mathcal{D}', z_{\mathcal{D}'}) = \mathcal{N}(\widetilde{\mu}_{x_t | \mathcal{D}'}, \widetilde{\sigma}_{x_t x_t | \mathcal{D}'})$ where

$$\widetilde{\mu}_{x_t | \mathcal{D}'} \triangleq \widetilde{\mu}_{x_t} + \widetilde{\Sigma}_{x_t \mathcal{D}'} \widetilde{\Sigma}_{\mathcal{D}' \mathcal{D}'}^{-1} (z_{\mathcal{D}'} - \widetilde{\mu}_{\mathcal{D}'}) \text{ and } \widetilde{\sigma}_{x_t x_t | \mathcal{D}'} \triangleq \widetilde{\sigma}_{x_t x_t} - \widetilde{\Sigma}_{x_t \mathcal{D}'} \widetilde{\Sigma}_{\mathcal{D}' \mathcal{D}'}^{-1} \widetilde{\Sigma}_{\mathcal{D}' x_t} \tag{4}$$

such that $\widetilde{\mu}_{\mathcal{D}'}$ is a column vector with mean components $\widetilde{\mu}_x$ (i.e., defined similarly to (3)) for all $x \in \mathcal{D}'$, $\widetilde{\Sigma}_{x_t \mathcal{D}'}$ is a row vector with covariance components $\widetilde{\sigma}_{x_t x}$ (i.e., defined similarly to (3)) for all $x \in \mathcal{D}'$, $\widetilde{\Sigma}_{\mathcal{D}' x_t}$ is the transpose of $\widetilde{\Sigma}_{x_t \mathcal{D}'}$, and $\widetilde{\Sigma}_{\mathcal{D}' \mathcal{D}'}$ is a matrix with covariance components $\widetilde{\sigma}_{xx'}$ (i.e., defined similarly to (3)) for all $x, x' \in \mathcal{D}'$.

Theorem 3. *Computing* (4) *incurs* $\mathcal{O}(\tau |\mathcal{S}|^2)$ *time at time steps* $t = N\tau + 1$ *for* $N \in \mathbb{Z}^+$ *and* $\mathcal{O}(|\mathcal{S}|^2)$ *time otherwise. It requires* $\mathcal{O}(|\mathcal{S}|^2)$ *memory at each time step.*

So, GOSGP [32] incurs constant time and memory (i.e., independent of t) per time step.

Experiments and Discussion. In contrast to existing localization algorithms that train the GP observation model of a Bayes filter offline, GOSGP [32] is used to learn it *online* for persistent robot localization and the resulting algorithm is called *GP-Localize* [32]. The *adaptive Monte Carlo localization* (AMCL) package in ROS is run on a Pioneer 3-DX mobile robot mounted with a SICK LMS200 laser rangefinder to determine its trajectory (Fig. 2(a)) and the 561 locations at which the relative light measurements are taken using a weather board (Fig. 2(b)); these locations are assumed to be ground truth. For empirical evaluation of GP-Localize with other real-world datasets, refer to [32].

The localization error (i.e., distance between the robot's estimated and true locations) and scalability of GP-Localize are compared to that of two sparse GP localization algorithms [32]: (a) The *Subset of Data (SoD)-Truncate* method uses

$|\mathcal{S}| = 10$ most recent observations (i.e., compared to $|\mathcal{D}'| < \tau = 10$ most recent observations considered by GOSGP [32] besides the assimilated summary) as training data at each time step while (b) the *SoD-Even* method uses $|\mathcal{S}| = 40$ observations (i.e., compared to the support set of $|\mathcal{S}| = 40$ possibly unobserved locations selected *prior* to localization and exploited by GOSGP [32]) evenly distributed over the time of localization. The scalability of GP-Localize is further compared to that of GP localization algorithms employing full GP (FGP) and offline PITC. GP-Localize, SoD-Truncate, and SoD-Even achieve, respectively, localization errors of 2.1 m, 5.4 m, and 4.6 m averaged over all 561 time steps and 3 runs. Figure 2(c) shows the time incurred by GP-Localize, SoD-Truncate, SoD-Even, FGP, and offline PITC at each time step. GP-Localize is clearly much more scalable (i.e., constant time) than FGP and offline PITC. Though it incurs slightly more time than SoD-Truncate and SoD-Even, it can localize significantly better.

5 Nonmyopic ϵ-Bayes-Optimal Active Sensing/Learning

Problem Formulation. To cast active sensing as a Bayesian sequential decision problem, we define a sequential active sensing policy $\pi \triangleq \{\pi_n\}_{n=1}^{N}$ that is structured to sequentially decide the next location $\pi_n(z_{\mathcal{D}}) \in \mathcal{X} \setminus \mathcal{D}$ to be observed at each stage n based on the current observations $z_{\mathcal{D}}$ over a finite planning horizon of N stages (i.e., sampling budget). To measure the predictive uncertainty over unobserved areas of the phenomenon, we use the entropy criterion and define the value under a policy π to be the joint entropy of its selected observations when starting with some prior observations $z_{\mathcal{D}_0}$ and following π thereafter [12]. The work of [19] has established that minimizing the posterior joint entropy (i.e., predictive uncertainty) remaining in unobserved locations of the phenomenon is equivalent to maximizing the joint entropy of π. Thus, solving the active sensing problem entails choosing a sequential BAL policy $\pi_n^*(z_{\mathcal{D}}) = \arg\max_{x \in \mathcal{X} \setminus \mathcal{D}} Q_n^*(z_{\mathcal{D}}, x)$ induced from the following N-stage Bellman equations, as formally derived in [12]:

$$
\begin{aligned}
V_n^*(z_{\mathcal{D}}) &\triangleq \max_{x \in \mathcal{X} \setminus \mathcal{D}} Q_n^*(z_{\mathcal{D}}, x) \\
Q_n^*(z_{\mathcal{D}}, x) &\triangleq \mathbb{E}\left[-\log p(Z_x | x, \mathcal{D}, z_{\mathcal{D}})\right] + \mathbb{E}\left[V_{n+1}^*(z_{\mathcal{D}} \cup \{Z_x\}) | x, \mathcal{D}, z_{\mathcal{D}}\right]
\end{aligned}
\tag{5}
$$

for stage $n = 1, \ldots, N$ where $p(z_x | x, \mathcal{D}, z_{\mathcal{D}})$ is defined in Sect. 2 and the second expectation term is omitted from right-hand side expression of Q_N^* at stage N. Unfortunately, since the BAL policy π^* cannot be derived exactly, we instead consider solving for an ϵ-BAL policy π^ϵ whose joint entropy approximates that of π^* within $\epsilon > 0$.

ϵ-BAL Policy. The key idea of our nonmyopic ϵ-BAL policy π^ϵ is to approximate the expectation terms in (5) at every stage using truncated sampling. Specifically, given realized measurements $z_{\mathcal{D}}$, a finite set of τ-truncated, i.i.d. observations $\{z_x^i\}_{i=1}^{S}$ [12] is generated and exploited for approximating V_n^* (5)

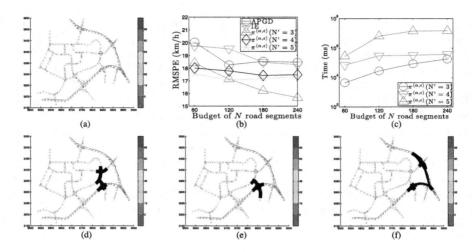

Fig. 3. (a) Traffic phenomenon (i.e., speeds (km/h) of road segments) over an urban road network, graphs of (b) *root mean square prediction error* (RMSPE) of APGD, IE, and $\langle \alpha, \epsilon \rangle$-BAL policies with horizon length $N' = 3, 4, 5$ and (c) total online processing cost of $\langle \alpha, \epsilon \rangle$-BAL policies with $N' = 3, 4, 5$ vs. budget of N segments, and (d–f) road segments observed (shaded in black) by respective APGD, IE, and $\langle \alpha, \epsilon \rangle$-BAL policies $(N' = 5)$ with $N = 60$.

through the following Bellman equations:

$$
\begin{aligned}
V_n^\epsilon(z_\mathcal{D}) &\triangleq \max_{x \in \mathcal{X} \setminus \mathcal{D}} Q_n^\epsilon(z_\mathcal{D}, x) \\
Q_n^\epsilon(z_\mathcal{D}, x) &\triangleq \frac{1}{S} \sum_{i=1}^{S} -\log p\left(z_x^i | x, \mathcal{D}, z_\mathcal{D}\right) + V_{n+1}^\epsilon\left(z_\mathcal{D} \cup \left\{z_x^i\right\}\right)
\end{aligned}
\tag{6}
$$

for stage $n = 1, \ldots, N$. The use of truncation is motivated by a technical necessity for theoretically guaranteeing the *expected* active sensing performance (specifically, ϵ-Bayes-optimality) of π^ϵ relative to that of π^* [12].

Anytime ϵ-BAL ($\langle \alpha, \epsilon \rangle$-BAL) Algorithm. Although π^ϵ can be derived exactly, the cost of deriving it is exponential in the length N of planning horizon since it has to compute the values $V_n^\epsilon(z_\mathcal{D})$ (6) for all $(S|\mathcal{X}|)^N$ possible states $(n, z_\mathcal{D})$. To ease this computational burden, we propose an anytime algorithm based on ϵ-BAL that can produce a good policy fast and improve its approximation quality over time. The key intuition behind our *anytime ϵ-BAL algorithm* ($\langle \alpha, \epsilon \rangle$-BAL) is to focus the simulation of greedy exploration paths through the most uncertain regions of the state space (i.e., in terms of the values $V_n^\epsilon(z_\mathcal{D})$) instead of evaluating the entire state space like π^ϵ. Interested readers are referred to [12] for more details.

Experiments and Discussion. This section evaluates the active sensing performance and time efficiency of our $\langle \alpha, \epsilon \rangle$-BAL policy $\pi^{\langle \alpha, \epsilon \rangle}$ empirically under using a real-world dataset of a large-scale traffic phenomenon (i.e., speeds of road segments) over an urban road network; refer to [12] for additional experimental results on a simulated spatial phenomenon. Figure 3(a) shows the urban road network $\mathcal{X}$ comprising 775 road segments in Tampines area, Singapore during lunch hours on June 20, 2011. Each road segment $x \in \mathcal{X}$ is specified by a 4D vector of features: length, number of lanes, speed limit, and direction. More details of our experimental setup can be found in [12].

The performance of our $\langle \alpha, \epsilon \rangle$-BAL policies with planning horizon length $N' = 3, 4, 5$ are compared to that of APGD and IE policies [15] by running each of them on a mobile robotic probe to direct its active sensing along a path of adjacent road segments according to the road network topology. Figure 3 shows results of the tested policies averaged over 5 independent runs: It can be observed from Fig. 3(b) that our $\langle \alpha, \epsilon \rangle$-BAL policies outperform APGD and IE policies due to their nonmyopic exploration behavior. Figure 3(c) shows that $\langle \alpha, \epsilon \rangle$-BAL incurs $< 4.5\,\mathrm{h}$ given a budget of $N = 240$ road segments, which can be afforded by modern computing power. To illustrate the behavior of each policy, Fig. 3 (d–f) show, respectively, the road segments observed (shaded in black) by the mobile probe running APGD, IE, and $\langle \alpha, \epsilon \rangle$-BAL policies with $N' = 5$ given a budget of $N = 60$. Interestingly, Fig. 3(d–e) show that both APGD and IE cause the probe to move away from the slip roads and highways to low-speed segments whose measurements vary much more smoothly; this is expected due to their myopic exploration behavior. In contrast, $\langle \alpha, \epsilon \rangle$-BAL nonmyopically plans the probe's path and direct it to observe the more informative slip roads and highways with highly varying traffic measurements (Fig. 3(f)) to achieve better performance.

Acknowledgments. This work was supported by the Singapore-MIT Alliance for Research & Technology Subaward Agreements No. 41 and No. 52.

References

1. Cao, N., Low, K.H., Dolan, J.M.: Multi-robot informative path planning for active sensing of environmental phenomena: a tale of two algorithms. In: Proceedings of AAMAS, pp. 7–14 (2013)
2. Chao, Y., Li, Z., Farrara, J.D., Hung, P.: Blending sea surface temperatures from multiple satellites and in situ observations for coastal oceans. J. Atmos. Ocean. Technol. **26**(7), 1415–1426 (2009)
3. Chen, J., Cao, N., Low, K.H., Ouyang, R., Tan, C.K.Y., Jaillet, P.: Parallel Gaussian process regression with low-rank covariance matrix approximations. In: Proceedings of UAI (2013)
4. Chen, J., Low, K.H., Tan, C.K.Y.: Gaussian process-based decentralized data fusion and active sensing for mobility-on-demand system. In: Proceedings of RSS (2013)
5. Chen, J., Low, K.H., Tan, C.K.Y., Oran, A., Jaillet, P., Dolan, J.M., Sukhatme, G.S.: Decentralized data fusion and active sensing with mobile sensors for modeling and predicting spatiotemporal traffic phenomena. In: Proceedings of UAI, pp. 163–173 (2012)

6. Choudhury, A., Nair, P.B., Keane, A.J.: A data parallel approach for large-scale Gaussian process modeling. In: Proceedings of SDM, pp. 95–111 (2002)
7. Cressie, N., Johannesson, G.: Fixed rank kriging for very large spatial data sets. J. R. Stat. Soc. B **70**(1), 209–226 (2008)
8. Cressie, N., Wikle, C.K.: Statistics for Spatio-Temporal Data. Wiley, Hoboken (2011)
9. Csató, L., Opper, M.: Sparse online Gaussian processes. Neural Comput. **14**, 641–669 (2002)
10. Dolan, J.M., Podnar, G., Stancliff, S., Low, K.H., Elfes, A., Higinbotham, J., Hosler, J.C., Moisan, T.A., Moisan, J.: Cooperative aquatic sensing using the tele-supervised adaptive ocean sensor fleet. In: Proceedings of SPIE Conference on Remote Sensing of the Ocean, Sea Ice, and Large Water Regions, vol. 7473 (2009)
11. Furrer, R., Genton, M.G., Nychka, D.: Covariance tapering for interpolation of large spatial datasets. JCGS **15**(3), 502–523 (2006)
12. Hoang, T.N., Low, K.H., Jaillet, P., Kankanhalli, M.: Nonmyopic ϵ-Bayes-optimal active learning of Gaussian processes. In: Proceedings of ICML, pp. 739–747 (2014)
13. Hoang, T.N., Low, K.H., Jaillet, P., Kankanhalli, M.: Active learning is planning: nonmyopic ϵ-Bayes-Optimal active learning of Gaussian processes. In: Calders, T., Esposito, F., Hüllermeier, E., Meo, R. (eds.) ECML PKDD 2014, Part III. LNCS, vol. 8726, pp. 494–498. Springer, Heidelberg (2014)
14. Ingram, B., Cornford, D.: Parallel geostatistics for sparse and dense datasets. In: Atkinson, P.M., Lloyd, C.D. (eds.) geoENV VII. Quantitative Geology and Geo-statistics, vol. 16, pp. 371–381. Springer, Netherlands (2010)
15. Krause, A., Guestrin, C.: Nonmyopic active learning of Gaussian processes: an exploration-exploitation approach. In: Proceedings of ICML, pp. 449–456 (2007)
16. Krause, A., Singh, A., Guestrin, C.: Near-optimal sensor placements in Gaussian processes: theory, efficient algorithms and empirical studies. JMLR **9**, 235–284 (2008)
17. Leonard, N.E., Palley, D.A., Lekien, F., Sepulchre, R., Fratantoni, D.M., Davis, R.E.: Collective motion, sensor networks, and ocean sampling. Proc. IEEE **95**(1), 48–74 (2007)
18. Low, K.H., Dolan, J.M., Khosla, P.: Adaptive multi-robot wide-area exploration and mapping. In: Proceedings of AAMAS, pp. 23–30 (2008)
19. Low, K.H., Dolan, J.M., Khosla, P.: Information-theoretic approach to efficient adaptive path planning for mobile robotic environmental sensing. In: Proceedings of ICAPS, pp. 233–240 (2009)
20. Low, K.H., Dolan, J.M., Khosla, P.: Active Markov information-theoretic path planning for robotic environmental sensing. In: Proceedings of AAMAS, pp. 753–760 (2011)
21. Low, K.H., Podnar, G., Stancliff, S., Dolan, J.M., Elfes, A.: Robot boats as a mobile aquatic sensor network. In: Proceedings of IPSN-09 Workshop on Sensor Networks for Earth and Space Science Applications (2009)
22. Low, K.H., Xu, N., Chen, J., Lim, K.K., Özgül, E.B.: Generalized online sparse gaussian processes with application to persistent mobile robot localization. In: Calders, T., Esposito, F., Hüllermeier, E., Meo, R. (eds.) ECML PKDD 2014, Part III. LNCS, vol. 8726, pp. 499–503. Springer, Heidelberg (2014)
23. Martin, R.J.: Comparing and contrasting some environmental and experimental design problems. Environmetrics **12**(3), 303–317 (2001)
24. Ouyang, R., Low, K.H., Chen, J., Jaillet, P.: Multi-robot active sensing of non-stationary Gaussian process-based environmental phenomena. In: Proceedings of AAMAS, pp. 573–580 (2014)

25. Park, C., Huang, J.Z., Ding, Y.: Domain decomposition approach for fast Gaussian process regression of large spatial data sets. JMLR **12**, 1697–1728 (2011)
26. Podnar, G., Dolan, J.M., Low, K.H., Elfes, A.: Telesupervised remote surface water quality sensing. In: Proceedings of IEEE Aerospace Conference (2010)
27. Quiñonero-Candela, J., Rasmussen, C.E.: A unifying view of sparse approximate Gaussian process regression. JMLR **6**, 1939–1959 (2005)
28. Sang, H., Huang, J.Z.: A full scale approximation of covariance functions for large spatial data sets. J. R. Stat. Soc. B **74**(1), 111–132 (2012)
29. Schwaighofer, A., Tresp, V.: Transductive and inductive methods for approximate Gaussian process regression. In: Proceedings of NIPS, pp. 953–960 (2002)
30. Snelson, E.: Local and global sparse Gaussian process approximations. In: Proceedings of AISTATS (2007)
31. Wikle, C.K.: Low-rank representations for spatial processes. In: Gelfand, A.E., Diggle, P., Guttorp, P., Fuentes, M. (eds.) Handbook of Spatial Statistics, pp. 107–118. Chapman and Hall, Boca Raton (2010)
32. Xu, N., Low, K.H., Chen, J., Lim, K.K., Özgül, E.B.: GP-Localize: persistent mobile robot localization using online sparse Gaussian process observation model. In: Proceedings of AAAI, pp. 2585–2592 (2014)

A Gaussian Process-Enabled MCMC Approach for Contaminant Source Characterization in a Sensor-Rich Multi-Story Building

Joon-Hong Seok[1]([⊠]), Su-Jin Lee[2], and Han-Lim Choi[2]

[1] Laboratory for Information and Control Systems,
Mechanical Engineering Research Institute, Korea Advanced Institute
of Science and Technology, Daejeon, Republic of Korea
seokjh@kaist.ac.kr
[2] Laboratory for Information and Control Systems,
Department of Aerospace Engineering, Korea Advanced Institute of Science
and Technology, Daejeon, Republic of Korea
sjlee@lics.kaist.ac.kr, hanlimc@kaist.ac.kr

Abstract. This paper presents contaminant source localization and characterization in a sensor-rich multi-story building with a large-scale domain. Bayesian framework infers the posterior distribution of source location and characteristics from the sensor network with the model uncertainty and inaccurate prior knowledge. A Markov Chain Monte Carlo method with a Metropolis-Hastings algorithm provides samples extracted from the posterior distribution. A computationally efficient Gaussian process emulator allows Markove Chain Monte Carlo sampling to use a physics-based model with tractable computational cost and time. The posterior distribution obtained by the proposed method through hypothetical contaminant release in a four-story building with total 156 subzones and sensors approaches true values of parameters of interest closely and shows the efficacy for parameter inference in a large-scale domain.

Keywords: Bayesian inference · Gaussian process emulator · Multizone model · CONTAM · Source localization and characterization · Sensor-rich multi-story building

1 Introduction

Modern building environments require proper evacuation plan to ensure occupants' safety against release of hazardous contaminant [1]. Deliberate release by terrorist organizations as well as accidental release causes significant influences on serious health conditions including death [2]. Therefore, it is necessary to perform source localization and characterization rapidly by using sensor networks that monitors contaminant concentration. As the building environments gets more complex, the detection and interpretation of the contaminant information

© Springer International Publishing Switzerland 2015
S. Ravela and A. Sandu (Eds.): DyDESS 2014, LNCS 8964, pp. 182–194, 2015.
DOI: 10.1007/978-3-319-25138-7_17

to localize and characterize the contaminant source requires heavier computational cost and time.

Multizone model focuses on the average characteristics of airflows and contaminant dispersion rather than their detailed distributions, then it needs much less computing load than computational fluid dynamics [3]. Multizone model considers a building as a network of zones with homogeneous air properties and contaminant concentration. Airflows pass through the paths representing doors, windows, and cracks, with their own leakage characteristics among zones. Although multizone model doesn't provide the accurate source location, due to the computational efficiency and the capability of modeling an entire large building, multizone model has been adopted for contaminant source characterization [4]. In this paper, a multizone model available with CONTAM [5] is used to simulate the contaminant fate and transport for a sensor-rich multi-story building.

Gaussian process emulator (GPE) for approximating dynamic simulators has emerged recently to predict behavior of complex system. It is impractical to perform simulation many times repeatedly due to computational cost and time when plentiful prediction samples and results are needed. Because structural complexity, aerodynamic characteristics, model uncertainty, and sensor measurement noise requires a number of simulation runs to obtain knowledge to infer unknown parameters accurately, it stands to reason that GPE is adopted for efficient computation of contaminant concentration in sensor-rich multi-story buildings.

Bayesian framework infers the posterior distribution of source location and characteristics based on sensor measurement data considering model uncertainty, inaccurate prior knowledge, and sensor measurement noise. Markov Chain Monte Carlo sampling is adopted to extract samples from the posterior distribution by using the Metropolis-Hastings algorithm. GPE accelerates sampling procedure by approximating the multizone model in CONTAM simulator.

Rest of the paper is organized as follows. Airflow model is briefly presented in Sect. 2. Problem formulation with a Bayesian framework is described in Sect. 3. Section 4 provides a Gaussian Process-enabled MCMC approach for source localization and characterization in a sensor-rich multi-story building. In Sect. 5, contaminant source location and characteristics is inferred through a hypothetical contaminant release in a four-story building with 156 subzones. The paper is concluded in Sect. 6.

2 Airflow Models

Multizone model calculates the airflow and contaminant concentration between the zones i and j of buildings through the flow path ij. Let P_i and P_j denote the total pressures in zone i and j respectively, and $\Delta P_{ij} = P_i - P_j$ denotes the pressure drop across the path ij. A power-law function provides F_{ij}, through the flow path ij can be represented as [7].

$$F_{ij} = c_{ij} \cdot \text{sgn}(\Delta P_{ij})|\Delta P_{ij}|^{n_{ij}} \tag{1}$$

where c_{ij} is flow coefficient, n_{ij} is flow exponent, $\text{sgn}(\Delta P_{ij})$ is a sign function of ΔP_{ij}, $\text{sgn}(\Delta P_{ij})=0$ for same total pressures of zones i and j. For each zone j, the steady state air mass balance equation is established for the multizone model.

$$\sum_i F_{ij} + F_j = \sum_i (c_{ij} \cdot \text{sgn}(\Delta P_{ij})|\Delta P_{ij}|^{n_{ij}}) + F_j = 0 \qquad (2)$$

where F_j is the air mass sources in the zone j. Contaminant steady state mass balance for a species α is similarly obtained by

$$\sum_i F_{ij}C_{\alpha_i} + \sum_i F_{ji}C_{\alpha_j} + S_j = 0 \qquad (3)$$

where S_j is the contaminant source in the zone j, C_{α_i} and C_{α_j} are the contaminant concentration in zone i and zone j, respectively.

3   Problem Formulation with Bayesian Framework

This section describes contaminant source localization and characterization problem in the Bayesian framework [6]. A multizone model T is represented as

$$y_j = T(x, \theta), \qquad (4)$$

where x is a set of deterministic inputs (rooms, flow path, wind conditions, etc.), y_j is the transient contaminant concentration in the jth zone, and θ is a set of unknown parameters of interest.

A contaminant source model used in the paper is an exponentially decaying model. The contaminant source model equation is expressed as

$$S(t) = g_0 e^{-kt}, \qquad (5)$$

where $S(t)$ is the transient contaminant concentration of a source, g_0 is an initial concentration, and k is an exponential decaying constant. Z is denoted as the zone including an active source. The method assumes the sources be active in a single zone. Finally, a set of unknown parameters for source localization and characterization is represented as $\theta = [Z, g_0, k]$.

Let $\hat{\theta}$ be the set of 'true' but unknown source location and characteristics. The simulator output is assumed to deviate from the 'true' system response even on specification of $\hat{\theta}$ due to the existence of smodel uncertainty. This deviation is modeled as

$$\zeta_j = T(x, \hat{\theta}) + \delta_j, \qquad (6)$$

where $\{\zeta_j(t); t \in \mathbb{R}^+\}$ is the 'true' system response, while $\{\delta_j(t); t \in \mathbb{R}\}$ is a discrepancy function.

Let the building be equipped with sensors in M zones that detect and measure the contaminant concentration for j^{th} zone at i^{th} time instance in given by

$$y_{e_j}(t_i) = \zeta_j(t_i) + \epsilon_j(t_i), \qquad (7)$$

where $\epsilon_j(t_i)$ denotes the sensor measurement uncertainty. Using $Y_e, \hat{\theta}$, and δ can be inferred through the Bayes theorem as

$$p(\hat{\theta}, \delta | Y_e) \propto p(Y_e | \hat{\theta}, \delta) p(\hat{\theta}, \delta), \tag{8}$$

where $p(\hat{\theta}, \delta)$ is the prior, $p(Y_e | \hat{\theta}, \delta)$ is the likelihood, and $p(\hat{\theta}, \delta | Y_e)$ is the posterior probability distribution. Using the probability distribution of ϵ and marginalization of δ, the posterior probability distribution is given by [6]

$$p(\hat{\theta} | Y_{e_j}, \sigma_\delta^2, \lambda) \propto |\sigma_j|^{-\frac{1}{2}} \prod_{j=1}^{M} \exp(-\frac{1}{2} d_j^T \Sigma_j^{-1} d_j) p(\hat{\theta}), \tag{9}$$

where $d_j = \{y_{e_j}(t_i) - T(x, \hat{\theta}; t_i); i = 1, \ldots, N; j = 1, \ldots, M\}, \sigma_\delta^2 = \{\sigma_{\delta_j}^2; j = 1, \ldots, M\}, \lambda = \{\lambda_j; j = 1, \ldots, M\}$, and $\Sigma_j = \Sigma_{\delta_j} + \Sigma_{\epsilon_j}$. Solution of Eq. (9) requires sampling from the posterior distribution using MCMC method with the Metropolis-Hastings algorithm. GPE provides tractable MCMC sampling from the multizone model in the CONTAM simulator.

4   Gaussian Process-Enabled MCMC Approach for Source Localization and Characterization

This section provide details of composing GPEs [6,8] for the multizone model $T(x, \cdot)$ in CONTAM simulator. Composed GPEs replace computationally expensive simulator and provide efficacy to calculate posterior probability for Bayesian inference about source localization and characterization with MCMC sampling using a Metropolis-Hastings algorithm [9,10].

4.1   Gaussian Process Emulator

The multizone model can be treated as a random function with a probability distribution using a q-dimensional Gaussian process

$$p(T(x, \cdot) | \mathcal{B}, \Sigma, \lambda) \sim \mathcal{N}_q(m(\cdot), c(\cdot, \cdot)\Sigma), \tag{10}$$

where $m(\cdot)$ is mean, $c(\cdot, \cdot)\Sigma$ is a covariance structure, and $\mathcal{B}, \Sigma$, and λ are hyperparameters of the Gaussian process. The mean, covariance, and correlation functions of the Gaussian process are modeled as

$$m(\theta_1) = \mathcal{B}^T h(\theta_1)$$
$$cov(T(x, \theta_1), T(x, \theta_2)) = c(\theta_1, \theta_2)\Sigma \tag{11}$$
$$c(\theta_1, \theta_2) = \exp(-(\theta_1 - \theta_2)^T \Lambda (\theta_1 - \theta_2)),$$

where $h(\cdot) = [h_1(\cdot), h_2(\cdot), \ldots, h_m(\cdot)]^T$ is a vector of m regression functions, while $\mathcal{B} \in \mathbb{R}^{m \times q}$ is a matrix of regression coefficients with each column given by

$\beta = [\beta_1, \beta_2, \ldots, \beta_m]^T$, Σ is a $q \times q$ positive definite matrix, and Λ is a diagonal matrix with length-scales $\lambda = [\lambda_1, \lambda_2, \ldots, \lambda_d]$.

A set of n simulation runs at design points $S = [\theta_1, \theta_2, \ldots, \theta_n] \subset \Theta$ is used to compose an emulator. Let $\mathcal{D} \in \mathbb{R}^{n \times q}$ define a $n \times q$ matrix of simulator outputs at design points. An emulator is defined as posterior distribution of the random function $T(x, \cdot)$ given a set of simulation runs $\mathcal{D}$. Conditional on hyper-parameters $\mathcal{B}, \Sigma$, and λ, probability distribution of $\mathcal{D}$ is given as

$$p(\mathcal{D}|\mathcal{B}, \Sigma, \lambda) \sim \mathcal{MN}_{n,q}(\mathcal{HB}, \mathcal{A}, \Sigma), \tag{12}$$

where $\mathcal{MN}_{n,q}$ is a matrix normal distribution, $\mathcal{H}^T = [h(\theta_1), h(\theta_2), \ldots, h(\theta_n)] \in \mathbb{R}^{m \times n}$ and $\mathcal{A} = [c(\theta_i, \theta_j)] \in \mathbb{R}^{n \times n}$ is a correlation matrix for a design set.

Standard Normal theory in addition to some matrix calculus manipulations hence leads to the following conditional posterior distribution for the simulator

$$p(T(x, \cdot)|\mathcal{B}, \Sigma, \lambda, \mathcal{D}) \sim \mathcal{N}_q(m^*(\cdot), c^*(\cdot, \cdot)\Sigma), \tag{13}$$

where

$$\begin{aligned} m^*(\theta) &= \mathcal{B}^T h(\theta) + (\mathcal{D} - \mathcal{HB})^T \mathcal{A}^{-1} r(\theta) \\ c^*(\theta_1, \theta_2) &= c(\theta_1, \theta_2) - r^T(\theta_1)\mathcal{A}^{-1} r(\theta_2), \end{aligned} \tag{14}$$

where $r^T(\cdot) = [c(\cdot, \theta_1), c(\cdot, \theta_2), \ldots, c(\cdot, \theta_n)] \in \mathbb{R}^n$.

First, marginalization of $\mathcal{B}$ gives

$$p(T(x, \cdot)|\Sigma, \lambda, D) \sim \mathcal{N}_q(m^{**}(\cdot), c^{**}(\cdot, \cdot)\Sigma; n - m), \tag{15}$$

where

$$\begin{aligned} m^{**}(\theta) &= \hat{\mathcal{B}}^T h(\theta) + (\mathcal{D} - \mathcal{H}\hat{\mathcal{B}})^T \mathcal{A}^{-1} r(\theta) \\ c^{**}(\theta_1, \theta_2) &= c^*(\theta_1, \theta_2) + [h(\theta_1) - \mathcal{H}^T \mathcal{A}^{-1} r(\theta_1)]^T \\ &\quad (\mathcal{H}^T \mathcal{A}^{-1} \mathcal{H})^{-1} [h(\theta_2) - \mathcal{H}^T \mathcal{A}^{-1} r(\theta_2)]. \end{aligned} \tag{16}$$

Here, $\hat{\mathcal{B}}$ is a generalized least square estimate of $\mathcal{B}$ given by

$$\hat{\mathcal{B}} = (\mathcal{H}^T \mathcal{A}^{-1} \mathcal{H})^{-1} \mathcal{H}^T \mathcal{A}^{-1} \mathcal{D}. \tag{17}$$

Second, marginalization of Σ gives

$$p(T(x, \cdot)|\lambda, D) \sim \mathcal{T}_q(m^{**}(\cdot), c^{**}(\cdot, \cdot)\hat{\Sigma}; n - m), \tag{18}$$

where $\mathcal{T}_q$ is a Students T process, while $\hat{\Sigma}$ is generalized least square estimator of Σ, which is given by

$$\hat{\Sigma} = \frac{(\mathcal{D} - \mathcal{H}\hat{\mathcal{B}})^T \mathcal{A}^{-1} (\mathcal{D} - \mathcal{H}\hat{\mathcal{B}})}{n - m} \tag{19}$$

Finally, marginalization of λ should be performed. However, analytical solution for the resultant integration is not available and requires use of sampling techniques [8]. The literature suggests fixing the values of length-scales using a

Maximum A Posteriori (MAP) estimate. Posterior distribution of λ is obtained by marginalization of $\mathcal{B}$ and Σ, which gives

$$p(\lambda|\mathcal{D}) \propto p(\lambda)|\mathcal{A}|^{\frac{-q}{2}}|\mathcal{H}^T\mathcal{A}^{-1}\mathcal{H}|^{\frac{-q}{2}}|\mathcal{D}^T\mathcal{Q}\mathcal{D}|^{\frac{-(n-m)}{2}}, \tag{20}$$

where

$$\mathcal{Q} = \mathcal{A}^{-1}(1 - \mathcal{H}(\mathcal{H}^T\mathcal{A}^{-1}\mathcal{H})^{-1}\mathcal{H}^T\mathcal{A}^{-1})$$
$$p(\lambda) = \prod_{i=1}^{d}(1 + \lambda_i^2)^{-1} \tag{21}$$

$p(\lambda)$ is defined as the product of squared reciprocal function [8]. Let $\hat{\lambda}$ be a MAP of λ obtained by maximizing Eq. (20) with respect to λ and $\hat{\lambda} = [\hat{\lambda}_1, \hat{\lambda}_2, \ldots, \hat{\lambda}_d]$. In the paper, a Genetic Algorithm(GA) [11] is used to estimate $\hat{\lambda}$ by maximizing Eq. (20) with avoidance of local optima as much as possible.

According to the MAP of λ, variables related with $c(\cdot, \cdot)$ are updated.

$$c_{\hat{\lambda}}(\theta_i, \theta_j) = \exp(-(\theta_i - \theta_j)^T\hat{\lambda}(\theta_i - \theta_j))$$
$$A_{\hat{\lambda}} = [c_{\hat{\lambda}}(\theta_i, \theta_j)] \in \mathbb{R}^{n \times n} \tag{22}$$
$$r_{\hat{\lambda}}^T = [c_{\hat{\lambda}}(\cdot, \theta_1), c_{\hat{\lambda}}(\cdot, \theta_2), \ldots, c_{\hat{\lambda}}(\cdot, \theta_n)] \in \mathbb{R}^n$$

Other hyper-parameters are updated by estimated correlation function.

$$\hat{\mathcal{B}}_{\hat{\lambda}} = (\mathcal{H}^T A_{\hat{\lambda}}^{-1}\mathcal{H})^{-1}\mathcal{H}^T A_{\hat{\lambda}}^{-1}\mathcal{D}$$
$$\hat{\Sigma}_{\hat{\lambda}} = (n - m)^{-1}(\mathcal{D} - \mathcal{H}\hat{\mathcal{B}}_{\hat{\lambda}})^T A_{\hat{\lambda}}^{-1}(\mathcal{D} - \mathcal{H}\hat{\mathcal{B}}_{\hat{\lambda}}) \tag{23}$$

The mean and correlation are updated by updated hyper-parameters.

$$m^{***}(\theta) = \hat{\mathcal{B}}_{\hat{\lambda}}^T h(\theta) + (\mathcal{D} - \mathcal{H}\hat{\mathcal{B}}_{\hat{\lambda}})^T A_{\hat{\lambda}}^{-1}r_{\hat{\lambda}}(\theta)$$
$$c^{***}(\theta_i, \theta_j) = c_{\hat{\lambda}}(\theta_i, \theta_j) - r_{\hat{\lambda}}^T(\theta_i)A_{\hat{\lambda}}^{-1}r_{\hat{\lambda}}(\theta_j) + [h(\theta_i) - \mathcal{H}^T A_{\hat{\lambda}}^{-1}r_{\hat{\lambda}}(\theta_i)]^T \tag{24}$$
$$(\mathcal{H}^T A_{\hat{\lambda}}^{-1}\mathcal{H})^{-1}[h(\theta_j) - \mathcal{H}^T A_{\hat{\lambda}}^{-1}r_{\hat{\lambda}}(\theta_j)]$$

Finally, the posterior distribution of simulator $T(x, \cdot)$ conditional on probability distribution of $\mathcal{D}$ is follows as

$$p(T(x, \cdot)|\mathcal{D}) \sim \mathcal{T}_q(m^{***}(\cdot), c^{***}(\cdot, \cdot)\hat{\Sigma}_{\hat{\lambda}}; n - m). \tag{25}$$

For the emulator, the mean $m^{***}(\cdot)$ works as an interpolator providing predictions at an unsampled θ, while $c^{***}(\cdot, \cdot)$ provide estimate of uncertainty in the predictions.

4.2 MCMC Sampling for GPE-Based Bayesian Inference

Consider a building with total N_z zones. For a given number of zones, a multizone model in CONTAM simulator provides averaged transient contaminant concentration in each zone. Each transient response of simulator is distinguished

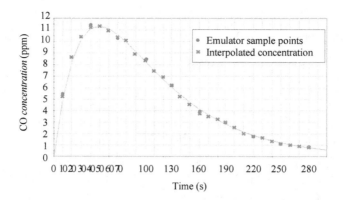

Fig. 1. The GPE sample points of the CONTAM simulation results (10 sample points for every thirty-second) and the interpolated concentration values of GPE-based Bayesian inference (27 interpolated points for every ten-second) (Color figure online).

by the zone in which source is active, $Z_a \in N_z$ and the zone in which contaminant concentration is measured, $Z_m \in N_z$. Separate GPEs $\varepsilon_{Z_a,Z_m}(x, \cdot)$ are composed for each possible combination of (Z_a, Z_m).

To compose GPEs $\varepsilon_{Z_a,Z_m}(x, \theta)$ for contaminant source characterization, an initial set of design points $S = [\theta_1, \theta_2, \ldots, \theta_n]$ is selected using Halton sequences [12]. Halton sequences are of low discrepancy, albeit deterministic sampling that uses a prime number as its base. It is a kind of quasi-random number sequence for variable number of samples [13]. The Halton sequence of g_0 is based on 2 and that of k is based on 3 without loss of generality. Total thirty design points (i.e. $n=30$) are selected by two sequences paired with each other. At each design point, contaminant concentration $\mathcal{D}$ at ten temporal locations (i.e. $q=10$) in the interval of thirty-second starting from ten seconds after the source activation time using the multizone model in the CONTAM simulator. Conditional on $\mathcal{D}$, the MAP of length-scales $\hat{\lambda}$ are estimated by maximizing Eq. (20) through GA. Conditional on $\hat{\lambda}, \hat{\mathcal{B}}_{\hat{\lambda}}$ and $\hat{\Sigma}_{\hat{\lambda}}$ are estimated. These estimate compose each GPE $\varepsilon_{Z_a,Z_m}(x, \theta)$ for the multizone model of contaminant transport and fate. The contaminant concentration of each GPE is calculated as $m^{***}(\theta)$ for any $\theta \in \Theta$ at the ten temporal locations which are used to compose GPEs. Based on the estimated values, contaminant concentrations of any time can obtained by interpolation methods (i.e., cubic spline interpolation method). Figure 1 depicts the example of sample points (blue circles) of the multizone model of CONTAM simulator to compose GPEs and the interpolated concentration (blue crosses) obtained from the composed GPE.

Location of an active source is assumed to be completely unknown with prior given by uniform distribution among N_z zones,

$$p(Z) = \frac{1}{N_z}. \tag{26}$$

Let g_0 and k are assumed to be completely unknown with the range of possible values as only available information. Let $g_0 \in I_g$ and $k \in I_k$ be the ranges of g_0 and k. Thus,

$$p(g_0, k) = \frac{1}{I_g I_k}. \tag{27}$$

Let the sensors be placed in $\mathcal{O} \subset \{Z; Z = 1, \ldots, N_o\}$ zones, where N_o represents total number of sensors, while the observations are collected at time instances $T_{\mathcal{O}} = \{t_i\}$. The observations are used in the Bayesian inference of the posterior distribution of unknown parameters given by Eq. (9), with prior defined using $p(Z)$ and $p(g_0, k)$.

In the MCMC implementation of the Bayesian inference, an appropriate GPE $\varepsilon_{Z_a, Z_m}(x, \cdot)$ replaces a computationally expensive multizone model in CONTAM simulator. MCMC method can be implemented to sample from the probability distribution of a Markov chain ϕ using the Metropolis-Hastings algorithms. N_{ini} is the number of samples for burn-in period and N_{smp} is the number of samples for posterior distribution estimation.

A set of Markov chain ϕ is represented as $\phi = \{\phi^i\} = \{Z, g_0, k\}$. The range of each unknown parameter is normalized into [0,1]. First, three parameters of the chain are initialized as

$$\phi \equiv \phi_0 = \{\phi_0^i\} \sim \mathcal{U}(0, 1), \tag{28}$$

where $\mathcal{U}$ is an uniform distribution and $i \in \{1, 2, 3\}$. A chain candidate ϕ_* is sequentially generated from the current chain ϕ_k and variation $\Delta = \{\Delta^i\} = \{\Delta_z, \Delta_{g_0}, \Delta_k\}$ as

$$\begin{aligned}\{\Delta^i\} &\sim \mathcal{U}(-1, 1) \\ \phi_* = \{\phi_*^i\} &\equiv \{\phi_k^i + \Delta^i\}.\end{aligned} \tag{29}$$

The zone in which source is active is assigned as

$$Z_a = round(\phi_*^1 N_z), \tag{30}$$

where $round(x)$ rounds off x to the nearest integer. Other parameters are denoted as

$$\theta = \{\phi_*^2, \phi_*^3\}, \tag{31}$$

For all $Z_m \in \mathcal{O}$, the emulator $\varepsilon_{Z_a, Z_m}(x, \theta)$ is used to predict contaminant concentration at time instances $T_{\mathcal{O}}$. Thus, the posterior probability $p(\phi_*)$ using Y_e and GPE prediction of contaminant concentration in Eq. (9). Acceptance probability is defined as

$$A(\phi_*, \phi_k) = \min \left\{1, \frac{p(\phi_*)}{p(\phi_k)}\right\} \tag{32}$$

Next chain ϕ_{k+1} is determined by the acceptance probability $A(\phi_*, \phi_k)$ and uniformly sampled variable u from [0,1] as

$$\phi_{k+1} = \begin{cases} \phi_* & \text{if } u < A(\phi_*, \phi_k) \\ \phi_k & \text{otherwise,} \end{cases} \tag{33}$$

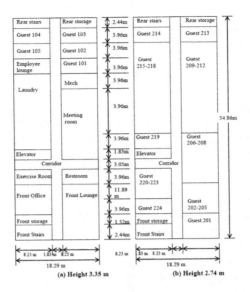

Fig. 2. A plan of the four-story target building. (a) First floor plan. (b) Upper (2–4) floor plan.

During an initial burn-in period, Eq. (29–33) are repeated by N_{ini} times and then all chains except for $\phi_{N_{ini}}$ are removed. After the initial burn-out period, with $\phi_{N_{ini}}$ as the initial chain, Eq. (29–33) are repeated by N_{smp} times. All chains $\phi_k, N_{ini} \leq k < N_{smp}$ are outputs of MCMC sampling and Bayesian inference. These chains are utilized to calculate the posterior distribution of unknown parameters Z, g_0, and k.

5   Simulation Results

Contaminant source localization and characterization is performed in a four-story building represent in Fig. 2 [14]. Based on the reference map and instructions in the CONTAM simulator, walls, windows, doors, and fans are implemented. Meanwhile, for the sake of convenience, air handling system and operation time scheduling are ignored. It is assumed that the air handling system is not operated and airflow path is not dependent on time of day. In the case of the multi-zone model, each zone is regarded as a well-mixed zone. Well-mixed means that a zone is characterized by a discrete set of state variables. For instance, temperature, pressure, and contaminant concentration is not varied within each zone spatially. Thus, long and narrow corridors are divided into many subzones for more accurate simulation [15]. Elevator, front stairs, and rear stairs are defined as phantom zones that are shared with all floors. On the contrary, other zones belong to only one of four floors. Components of the target building implemented by the CONTAM simulator are illustrated in Fig. 3. A released contaminant compound is carbon monoxide (CO). It is assumed that atmospheric pressure is 101.3kPa and

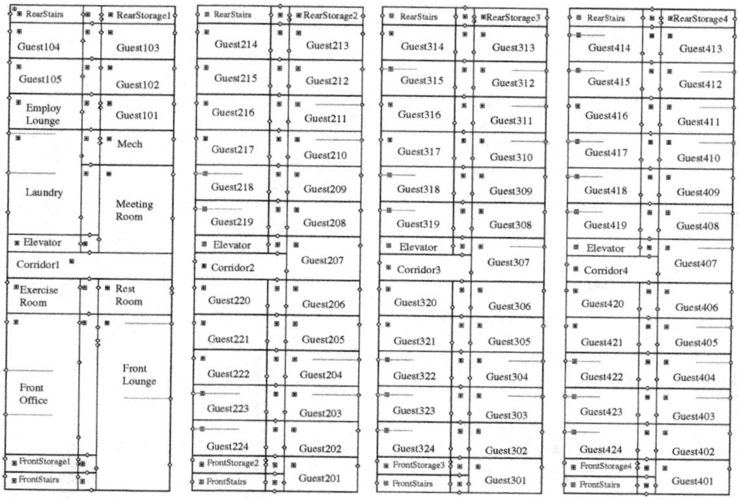

Fig. 3. Rooms, partitioned corridors and wind pressure applied to windows of the target building implemented by the CONTAM simulator

atmospheric temperature is $23°C$. Total 156 subzones over four floors are finally defined and used to perform simulation. One of the 156 subzones is selected as the location of the active sources. The range of initial concentration I_g is defined as $[0.5, 1]$, and the exponential decaying constant I_k is defined as $[0.8, 1.2]$. The number of burnout samples is 10000, and total number of samples is 20000. Sensor measurement uncertainty is assumed to be 1 %. The number of generated GPE is $156 \times 30 = 4680$.

Contaminant source localization and characterization is performed by six hypothetical contaminant release cases. Each test case has a single active contaminant source and has the different zone where the contaminant source is activated, respectively. The zones with the active source are Zone1, Zone33, Zone62, Zone98, Zone128, and Zone156, respectively. Figure 4 shows the final posterior distribution of contaminant location and characteristics of each test case. First, the posterior probability distribution of the location of contaminant active source is inferred. For the six test cases, the method exactly infers the zone where the contaminant source is activated with probability one. The posterior probability distribution of the initial concentration and the exponential decaying constant are also inferred. The posterior probabilities near the 'true' initial concentration and 'true' exponential decaying constant are high enough to match closely. In Fig. 4, blue and red vertical lines represent 'true' initial concentration and 'true' exponential decaying constant, respectively.

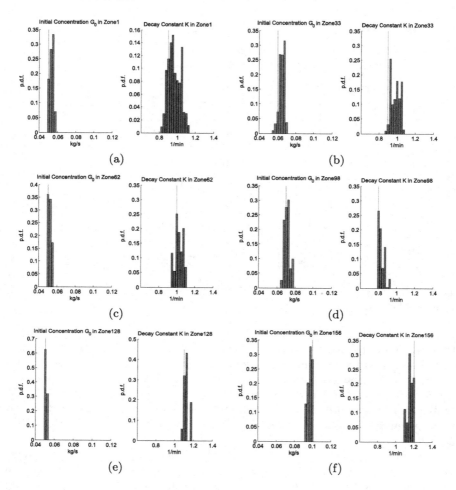

Fig. 4. The contaminant localization and characterization results for six hypothetical contaminant release cases, respectively. Active contaminant source is located (a) in Zone1. (b) in Zone33. (c) in Zone62. (d) in Zone98. (e) in Zone128. (f) in Zone156.

6   Conclusion

The paper focuses on contaminant source localization and characterization in a sensor-rich multi-story building with dozens of rooms using gaussian process-enabled MCMC approaches with a Bayesian inference architecture. The multi-zone model in CONTAM simulator is used to extract contaminant concentration considering the given deterministic inputs about the target building. A computationally efficient GPE allows a physics-based model in a large-scale problem domain for source location and characterization through Bayesian inference with tractable computational cost and time. The required number of simulation to infer unknown parameters of interest is clearly less than the required number of MCMC samples. MCMC sampling to infer the posterior distribution of source localization and characterization from the sensor network with the model uncertainty and inaccurate prior knowledge is archived by a Metropolis-Hasting algorithm, a Bayesian framework, and separate GPEs. The posterior distribution obtained by the proposed method through hypothetical contaminant release in a four-story building with total 156 subzones and sensors closely matches the true value of parameters of interest with fewer simulations exploiting physics-based model. The combination of GPE and MCMC implementation shows the efficacy for parameter inference in a large-scale domain.

Acknowledgement. This work was supported in part by Microsoft Research Asia Accelerating Urban Informatics with Azure Program, and in part by the KI Project via KI for Design of Complex Systems.

References

1. Chen, Y., Wen, J.: Comparison of sensor systems designed using multizone, zonal and CFD data for protection of indoor environments. Build Environ. **45**, 1061–1071 (2010)
2. Zhai, Z., Sebric, J., Chen, Q.: Application of CFD to predict and control chemical and biological agent dispersion in buildings. Int. J. Vent. **3**, 251–264 (2003)
3. Feustel, H.E., Dieris, J.: A survey of airflow models for multizone structures. Energy Build. **18**(2), 79–199 (1992)
4. Liu, X., Zhai, Z.J.: Prompt tracking of indoor airborne contaminant source location with probability-based inverse multi-zone modeling. Build. Environ. **44**, 1135–1143 (2009)
5. CONTAM: Multizone Airflow and Contaminant Transport Analysis Software (2013). http://www.bfrl.nist.gov/IAQanalysis/CONTAM/index.htm
6. Tagade, P.M., Jeong, B.-M., Choi, H.-L.: A Gaussian process emulator approach for rapid contaminant characterization with an integrated multizone-CFD model. Build. Environ. **70**, 232–244 (2013)
7. Wang, L.: Coupling of multizone and cfd programs for building airflow and contaminant transport simulations. Ph.D. dissertation, Purdue University, West Lafayette (2007)
8. Conti, S., O'Hagan, A.: Bayesian emulation of complex multi-output and dynamic computer models. J. stat. plann. infer. **140**(3), 640–651 (2010)
9. Metropolis, N., Rosenbluth, A.W., Rosenbluth, M.N., Teller, A.H., Teller, E.: Equation of state calculations by fast computing machines. J. chem. phys. **21**(6), 1087–1092 (1953)
10. Hasting, W.K.: Monte Carlo sampling methods using Markov chains and their applications. Biometrika **57**(1), 97–109 (1970)
11. Davis, L., et al.: Handbook of Genetic Algorithms. Van Nostrand Reinhold, New York (1991)
12. Halton, J.H.: On the efficiency of certain quasi-random sequences of points in evaluating multi-dimensional integrals. Numer. Math. **2**(1), 84–90 (1960)
13. Kuipers, L., Niederreiter, H.: Uniform Distribution of Sequences. Courier Dover Publications, Mineola (2012)

14. Ng, L.C., Musser, A., Persily, A.K., Emmerich, S.J.: Airflow and indoor air quality models of DOE reference commercial buildings. National Institute of Standards and Technology Technical Note, 1734 (2012)
15. Mora, L., Gadgil, A.J., Wurtz, E.: Comparing zonal and CFD model predictions of isothermal indoor airflows to experimental data. Indoor Air **13**(2), 77–85 (2003)

An Empirical Reduced Modeling Approach for Mobile, Distributed Sensor Platform Networks

Isaac J. Sledge[1], Liqian Peng[2], and Kamran Mohseni[1,2]([✉])

[1] Department of Electrical and Computer Engineering,
University of Florida, Gainesville 32611, USA
isledge@ufl.edu
[2] Department of Mechanical and Aerospace Engineering,
University of Florida,Gainesville 32611, USA
{liqianpeng,mohseni}@ufl.edu

Abstract. In this paper, we present an efficient means for both modeling phenomena in a mobile sensor context and determining where the sensors should travel to collect meaningful information. Our approach is based on offline-online model reduction, which is performed via a snapshot-weighted proper orthogonal decomposition/discrete empirical interpolation. That is, through collected observations, we construct and reduce empirical dynamical systems that characterize the evolution of the phenomena and determine those locations that can be visited and sensed to improve the model quality. To showcase the effectiveness of our contributions, we apply them to the tasks of estimating the concentration and location of plumes in two-dimensional environments.

1 Introduction

Reliable forecasting of natural phenomena typically requires extensive sensor observations of the environment; these observations form the foundation for empirically-derived models that can predict the progression of the events [1–3]. However, without spatially and temporally dense measurements, stark differences between the estimated states of the models and the underlying states of the events can materialize.

An increasingly popular means of addressing this concern is to pair the sensors with mobile agents that can adapt to the environment. While augmenting sensors in this way can permit quick responses to fleeting and unanticipated events, it is crucial that the sensors are targeted to information-rich locations. To aid in this task, a number of schemes have been proposed [4–10]. For example, Choi and How [4,5] proposed a mutual-information-based targeted observation scheme that attempts to position the sensing agents so that the forecast uncertainty of their model is minimized. In [6,7], Leonard et al. employed an objective analysis approach to determine both if their agents were optimally sampling the environment and how to adjust their locations if they were not. Additionally, Yilmaz et al. [8]

© Springer International Publishing Switzerland 2015
S. Ravela and A. Sandu (Eds.): DyDESS 2014, LNCS 8964, pp. 195–204, 2015.
DOI: 10.1007/978-3-319-25138-7_18

relied on techniques like error subspace statistical estimation to rank various spatial locations according to their potential information contribution.

In this paper, we propose a means for determining areas that could benefit from increased sensory inclusion. More specifically, we consider an adaptive proper orthogonal decomposition/discrete empirical interpolation approach for creating empirical dynamical systems from collected observations of the environment (see Sect. 2). When properly constructed, an advantage of these dynamical systems is that they should permit the efficient simulation of many types of phenomena. They also should allow the interpolation and extrapolation of the observations to times and places not examined. Additionally, due to the adaptive nature of the approach, the systems should generalize somewhat to changes in the background processes generating the phenomena and thus yield more accurate results than pure proper orthogonal decomposition.

There are numerous applications for such a methodology. To evaluate the capabilities of our contributions, we specialize them for describing the evolution of two-dimensional particulate plumes as they interact with both wind currents and the buffers formed by buildings (see Sect. 3). For this problem, our aim is to discern both the initial conditions and distributions of the plumes and thus their possible trajectories, based upon scant stores of observations. We also want to track the dominant modes of the plumes. Upon addressing both of these aspects, it can be determined where learning-beneficial observations might occur that can be incorporated to yield insight into the phenomena.

2   Methodology

The approach we employ for dynamical system learning and reduction relies on an offline-online splitting paradigm. In the offline phase, we sample various spatially-varying quantities about the phenomena and construct an initial system, which results in possible trajectories in which the phenomena could evolve. To keep the system relevant, in the online phase we assume that the sensor platforms will be traveling through the domain and collecting additional observations. As more observations are gathered, the dynamical system is iteratively revised, increasing its accuracy.

For what follows, we will have the phenomena be characterized by dynamical systems with time-dependent solutions. That is, we assume the phenomena are governed by parabolic partial differential equations, which have the form $\dot{u} = g(t, u; \alpha)$ after being spatially discretized. Here, $g : \mathcal{R}_+ \times \mathcal{R}^n \times \mathcal{R}^m$ is a smooth function for some time index $t \in \mathcal{R}_+$, a variable $u \in \mathcal{R}^n$, and an input parameter $\alpha \in \mathcal{R}^m$. The evolution of the phenomena can be considered as a mapping from the phase space to itself, which is parameterized by time. By definition, the state variable $u(t; \alpha) \in \mathcal{R}^n$ is a flow that yields an orbit in $\mathcal{R}^n$ as t varies over a monotonically increasing domain for a fixed initial condition $u(0; \alpha)$ and fixed input parameter α. The orbit contains a sequence of states, or state vectors, that follow from the initial condition.

In general, the latent partial differential equations defining the phenomena may possess redundant degrees of freedom. Since each of these irrelevant degrees of freedom increases the evaluation time, it is prudent to form accurate, abridged representations. We illustrate how this may be done via the Galerkin projection and a non-linear interpolation (see Sect. 2.1). Since the projection requires a factorization of the observed motions, we also describe how this can be performed in the context of an adaptive basis formulation (see Sect. 2.2).

2.1   Model Projection and Interpolation

The Galerkin projection can provide a lower-dimensional approximation by projecting the full system onto a linear subspace. For any linear subspace, there exists an orthonormal matrix $\Phi_k \in \mathcal{R}^{n \times k}$ whose columns form a complete basis associated with it. Any state $u(t; \alpha) \in \mathcal{R}^n$ can be projected onto a subspace by the mapping $v_k = \Phi_k^\top u(t; \alpha)$, where $v_k \in \mathcal{R}^k$ is the state variable in the subspace coordinate system. Assuming that a vector field $g_k(t, u)$ in the subspace is constructed by $g_k(t, u; \alpha) = \Phi_k^\top g(t, \Phi_k u; \alpha)$, then a model of the simplified system can be obtained: $\dot{v}_k = \Phi_k^\top g(t, \Phi_k v_k; \alpha)$, $v_0 = \Phi_k^\top u(0; \alpha)$.

It is important to note that the Galerkin projection has a low computational complexity only when a heavily abridged version of the analytical formula of the reduced vector field $\Phi_k^\top g(t, \Phi_k v_k; \alpha)$ exists. This is particularly crucial when the vector field is a linear, or possibly polynomial, function of the state variable $v_k \in \mathcal{R}^k$. Otherwise, an investigator will need to compute the state variable in the original system $\Phi_k v$, evaluate the non-linear vector field at each element, and then project the function onto the subspace. This three-part process can be more expensive to perform than evaluating the corresponding full-resolution models.

To preempt this wasteful computation, either the empirical interpolation method [11] or discrete empirical interpolation method [12] can be employed. These methods approximate the original model by constructing surrogates of the non-linear terms for the system of equations using a data-fitting approach. In particular, they work by splitting the original vector field into linear and non-linear parts: $g(t, u; \alpha) = g_1(t; \alpha)u + g_2(t, u; \alpha)$. Using the Galerkin projection, the reduced vector field can be written as $\dot{v}_k = \Phi_k^\top g_1(t; \alpha)\Phi_k v_k + \Phi_k^\top g_2(t, \Phi_k v_k; \alpha)$, where $\Phi_k^\top g_1(t; \alpha)\Phi_k$ is the linear operator and $\Phi_k^\top g_2(t, \Phi_k v_k; \alpha)$ is the non-linear term of the vector field. Unless the non-linear term can be analytically simplified, its computational complexity can still depend on the dimensionality of the state variable. An effective way to sidestep this difficulty is to approximate the non-linear term by embedding it in a lower-dimensional subspace. Considering that $u(t; \alpha)$ is a smooth function, we can define a non-linear snapshot $g_2(t, u(t; \alpha); \alpha)$. Then, the reduced vector field, restricted on $(t; \alpha)$ and $u = u(t; \alpha)$, can be calculated as $\Phi_k^\top g(t, u(t; \alpha); \alpha) = \Phi_k^\top g_1(t; \alpha)\Phi_k v_k + \Phi_k^\top \Psi_m (Q^\top \Psi_m)^{-1} Q^\top g_2(t, u(t; \alpha); \alpha)$. Here $\Psi_m \in \mathcal{R}^{n \times m}$ is a matrix denoting a collateral basis on a pre-computed, non-linear snapshot ensemble while $Q^\top \in \mathcal{R}^{n \times d}$ is an index matrix to project a vector of dimension n onto its d elements. The matrix $Q^\top$ can be computed by an offline, greedy algorithm and we refer to [12] for more details. Notice that $\Phi_k^\top \Psi_m (Q^\top \Psi_m)^{-1}$ is calculated only once and $Q^\top g_2(t, u(t; \alpha); \alpha)$ is solely evaluated on d elements of $g_2(t, u(t; \alpha); \alpha)$, which makes it very efficient when $d \ll n$.

The Galerkin projection and its empirical interpolation extensions can be used to construct efficient dynamical models of the reactive behaviors. However, the outputs of these models might not approximate the original motions with a high degree of accuracy unless the subspace is approximately invariant with respect to the solution $u(t; \alpha)$. A subspace $\mathcal{S}^*$ is said to be invariant of $u(t; \alpha)$ if $u(0; \alpha) \in \mathcal{S}^*$ and the solution orbit given by $u(t; \alpha)$ lies in $\mathcal{S}^*$, $(\Phi_k \Phi_k^\top)^* u(t; \alpha) = u(t; \alpha)$, where $(\Phi_k \Phi_k^\top)^* \in \mathcal{R}^{n \times n}$ is a projection operator corresponding to $\mathcal{S}^*$. In this case, the governing equations of the reduced and full models must be identical, which requires that $(\Phi_k \Phi_k^\top)^* g(t, u; \alpha) = g(t, u; \alpha)$. That is, an invariant projection operator must not only preserve the state vector, but also preserve the vector field and hence its dynamics. Since an invariant subspace is uniquely determined by its basis, we will need a means of constructing empirical eigenfunctions from motion data ensembles.

2.2   Empirical Basis Computation

An offline-online splitting scheme is used here for model reduction. If we let p be the observation size, in the offline stage, $\{(t_i; \alpha_i)\}_{i=1}^p$ are sampled in the parameter space. The corresponding solutions with their derivatives could then be used to induce a subspace, where the real solution approximately resides. Here, we are focused on forming a reduced model in the k-dimensional Lagrange subspace span($\{u_i\}_{i=1}^p$) [13].

One means of doing this is by the standard proper orthogonal decomposition method, which creates a global reduced model from all of the snapshots in the observation ensemble. More specifically, proper orthogonal decomposition [14] finds a basis Φ_k that solves $\min_{\Phi_k \in \{A \in \mathcal{R}^{n \times r} : A^\top A = I_{r \times r}\}} \|(I_{n \times n} - \Phi_k \Phi_k^\top) X\|_2$, where $X \in \mathcal{R}^{n \times p}$ is a snapshot matrix and each column represents a solution snapshot for the parameters $(t_i; \alpha_i)$. A closed-form solution to this minimization problem can be uncovered via a singular-value decomposition of the snapshot matrix.

Global reduction through proper orthogonal decomposition lends itself well to many applications. However, if a solution varies greatly with parameter changes, a relatively high-dimensional reduced space is needed to characterize the phenomena. The issue is further compounded when considering phenomena that undergo significant changes over time. Moreover, unless the reduced model of the phenomena has a significantly lower dimension, it is possible that the time needed to evaluate the reduced model will be on par with that of the full model.

To overcome these issues, we will compute adaptive reduced bases that can tolerate some parameter variation [18]. Letting u_* be the solution corresponding to the input parameter (α_*), we will assume that it is approximated by a linear combination $u_* \approx \sum_{i=1}^p a_i(\alpha_*) u_i$ of all of the solution snapshots in the ensemble. Here, the non-negative interpolation coefficient $a_i(\alpha_*)$ is a function of the parameter space and has at most unit magnitude. The projection of u_* onto a subspace is specified by a linear combination of the u_i: $\sum_{i=1}^p \eta_i a_i u_i$, where $|\eta_i| < \epsilon$ for some ϵ and $\eta_i = 0$ if $a_i = 0$.

Through this weighting scheme, we can define a weighted snapshot matrix for the input parameter α_*: $X(\alpha_*) = [a_1(\alpha_*) u_1, \ldots, a_p(\alpha_*) u_p]$. Using singular value decomposition, we could obtain reduced bases. However, it is not the most efficient approach: when the trajectories show high temporal variation over a long period, it will be necessary to maintain a large snapshot matrix. We instead construct the online bases from the first few modes returned by the proper orthogonal decomposition of some pre-computed trajectories [15], rather than the original snapshots.

By locally measuring various quantities of interest and learning reduced models, it becomes possible to estimate these quantities at times and spaces not observed. But, the quality of this estimation is highly dependent on where and when the observations are collected. In the worst case, if all of our sensor platforms are located in a region with sparse measurements, the inverse problem is ill-conditioned and the results will be determined by the stochastic measurement noise.

To help the mobile sensor platforms capture meaningful information, we will have them travel to locations that correspond to the dominant adaptive basis modes over some interval; the dominant modes are taken to be the eigenvectors with the largest corresponding eigenvalues [10]. In doing so, we can ensure that the Frobenius-normed error for the various quantities is minimized.

3   Plume Dynamics Estimation and Tracking

With this methodology in hand, we can now transition to assaying its virtues. In what follows, we flesh out our experimental protocols and report our discoveries for an application: plume monitoring.

Aside from the difficulties faced in understanding and exploiting information from the fume signatures, there were several factors that provoked us to tackle this problem. One of the principal motivators was Biowatch [16], a pathogen counter-terrorism program implemented in cities across the United States. While able to ostensibly function as a sound early warning system for airborne infectious agents in some situations, the methodology applied by BioWatch has failings that curtail its overall effectiveness in general. For starters, it relies on a relatively low number of survey stations and the transport of air particle samples to laboratories at daily intervals; despite this kind of monitoring being adequate for static events with a few temporal constraints, it is not in a rapid-response contexts. Moreover, one of the missing elements in programs like BioWatch is information sharing in an automated and meaningful way: even with scores of data available, identifying the underlying process producing the data is difficult.

In light of these concerns, we reiterate that, in our minds, one of the best methods for achieving wide coverage zones of detection are small mobile devices that can be networked and dispersed over a variety of domains. However, for these devices to be truly practical, they should be married with models, like the one we gave above, that are flexible enough to describe many events that can arise and anticipate how they might unfold.

As an analogue to the kinds of circumstances that might be encountered in the BioWatch program, we consider the transport of hypothetical contaminants through urban and suburban scenes. For what is to come, we will be taking the contaminants to adhere to the standard advection-diffusion equation, with homogeneous Dirichlet conditions ascribed to the inflow boundary and homogeneous Neumann conditions given to outflow boundary. Within this context, we will be examining the case where a Gaussian source releases a constant plume. The plume will be advected under the action of a velocity field, specified by discretizing and solving the incompressible Navier-Stokes equations, and dispersed due to diffusion.

3.1   Experimental Results

For our experiments, we consider the case of an urban setting where we have one or more plumes that are driven by hidden, fluctuating background wind velocity fields; the plume evolution is governed by the advection-diffusion protocols outlined above. To provide a reasonable challenge, neither the location nor the extent of the sources driving the phenomenon is given to our framework. As the simulations progress, our modeling strategy is able to identify and update the particulate magnitudes and other associated attributes. To drive the platforms to their locations, we use the path planning framework of [17].

For now, the wind velocity is calculated by effectively solving the Navier-Stokes equation over a two-dimensional, discretized spatial domain; once found, it is assumed to be a known quantity that is continuously revised. To further specify the problem, velocity boundary conditions are set on the left and right sides of the domain, while free-slip constraints are enforced on the remaining borders. Additionally, no-slip conditions are applied to all of the structure in the environment. The mobile sensors are assumed to have little effect on the progression of the plume at the scales we consider and therefore are ignored entirely.

As part of appraising our mobile sensor scheme and framing the results that it returns, we contemplate four alternatives. In the first, we consider a uniform random placement of the sensors throughout the environment, which offers a lower bound on the solution reconstruction quality. The second entails building models from varying numbers of observations and permanently affixing the sensors to structures near the global modes of the phenomenon. In this case, however, the models are constructed using the same data-based dynamics reduction technique used by our mobile sensor framework, which should yield comparable performance than many of the statistical schemes considered in the literature. The third alternative perfectly aggregates information from the whole domain and repositions the sensors every few iterations so that they record informative content. Lastly, we consider the situation where we have the mobile sensors construct a model of the plume using a non-adaptive proper orthogonal decomposition.

Some of our findings for these trials are spread across Figs. 1 and 2; our metric for comparison is the relative sum of squares error in the simulated concentration plume as a function of time. Overall, it is clear from the plots in Figs. 1(c) and 2(c) that our adaptive scheme has the least amount of discrepancies, regardless

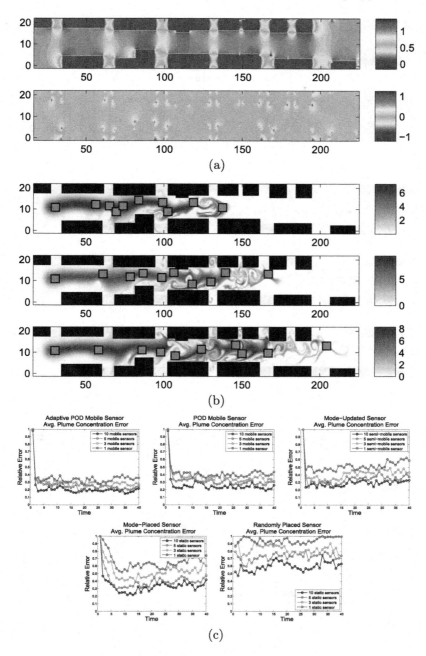

Fig. 1. (a) Plots of the horizontal and vertical velocities at the start of the simulation. (b) Plot of the plume concentration at different times. The gray squares correspond to the simulated sensor platforms at the moment they arrive at the dominant adaptive proper orthogonal decomposition modes. The black regions correspond to buildings. (c) Plots of the relative sensor error for the five test cases.

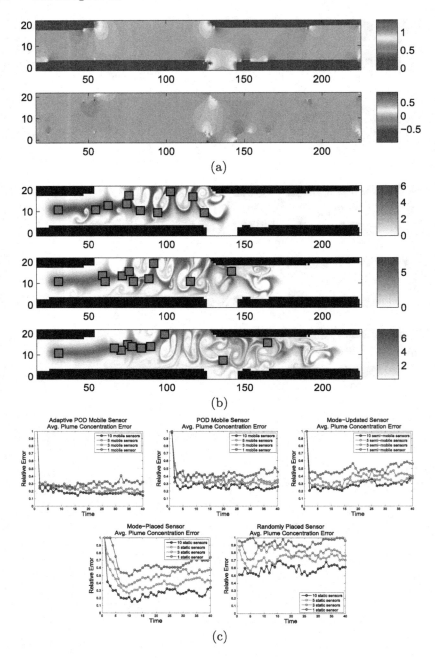

Fig. 2. (a) Plots of the horizontal and vertical velocities at the start of the simulation. (b) Plot of the plume concentration at different times. The gray squares correspond to the simulated sensor platforms at the moment they arrive at the dominant adaptive proper orthogonal decomposition modes. The black regions correspond to buildings. (c) Plots of the relative sensor error for the five test cases.

of the number of sensors that are used. This realization, however, is not surprising: in situations with widespread, continuously changing events, it can be particularly tricky to ensure sufficient coverage with static sensors.

To briefly comment on the outcomes themselves, for the first scheme, the relative errors are near unity, which is to be expected since randomly distributed sensors cannot hope to capture the nuances of such desultory phenomena. Moreover, adding sensors beyond a certain level fails to markedly enhance the models' prognostic capabilities. This can be explained by the fact that the remaining sensors are often relegated to non-informative sites. In the second approach, there are still fairly large amounts of inaccuracies due to the deviations in the wind patterns over time. For the third, the error drops dramatically, given that it is able to perfectly exploit signatures from the environment. Nevertheless, its performance is nowhere near that of our framework, unless the transitions occur very frequently. The fourth case with the non-adaptive proper orthogonal decomposition yields somewhat comparable performance. However, since the adaptive version is able to intelligently weight the observations in the offline stage, its error does not fluctuate as much. As well, error from the adaptive model never equals or exceeds that of the model produced by proper orthogonal decomposition.

Something else worth noting is that when a few mobile platforms are employed, the relative error can increase over time. This is due to the fact that there are dominant modes that have meaningful information but are unable to be visited since the platforms are collecting measurements at higher-energy modes. As the number of platforms increases, better coverage of the domain can be achieved, which permits the inclusion of information from these other modes. However, accounting for more than ten modes has a negligible impact on the model quality.

4   Conclusions

We have proposed a dynamic, data-driven application system for measuring and simulating plume concentration and estimating the origin of the plume. In order to assimilate incomplete and noisy state observations about the phenomena, an offline-online dynamical system learning scheme is used. In the offline stage, we build a database by sampling possible plume source regions and solving the governing equation to obtain possible trajectories for the plume concentration. We then use an adaptive reduced modeling approach to find a few dominant modes. In the online state, estimations of the concentration are restricted to the subspace of the adaptive modes to best match partial observations. Our simulation results verify the utility of our modeling scheme in the context of a mobile planning framework.

Acknowledgement. This work was funded via grants from the Air Force Office of Scientific Reasearch.

References

1. Caselton, W.F., Zidek, J.V.: Optimal monitoring networking designs. Stat. Probab. Lett. **2**, 223–227 (1984)
2. Wikle, C.K., Royle, J.A.: Space-time dynamic design of environmental monitoring networks. J. Agric. Biol. Environ. Stat. **4**, 489–507 (1999)
3. Salehi, M.: Optimal sampling design under a spatial correlation model. J. Stat. Plann. Infer. **118**, 9–18 (2004)
4. Choi, H.-L., How, J.P.: Coordinated targeting of mobile sensor networks for ensemble forecast improvement. IEEE Sens. J. **11**, 621–633 (2011)
5. Choi, H.-L., How, J.P.: Efficient targeting of sensor networks for large-scale systems. IEEE Trans. Control Syst. Technol. **19**, 1569–1577 (2011)
6. Leonard, N.E., Paley, D.A., Lekien, F., Sepulchre, R., Fratantoni, D.M., Davis, R.E.: Collective motion, sensor networks, and ocean sampling. Proc. IEEE **95**, 48–74 (2007)
7. Fiorelli, E., Leonard, N.E., Bhatta, P., Paley, D.A., Bachmayer, R., Fratantoni, D.M.: Multi-AUV control and adaptive sampling in Monterey Bay. IEEE Trans. Oceanic Eng. **31**, 935–948 (2007)
8. Yilmaz, N.K., Evangelinos, C., Lermusiaux, P.F.J., Patrikalakis, N.M.: Path planning of autonomous underwater vehicles for adaptive sampling using mixed integer linear programming. IEEE Trans. Oceanic Eng. **33**, 522–537 (2009)
9. Julian, B.J., Angermann, M., Schwager, M., Rus, D.: Distributed robotic sensor networks: an information theoretic approach. Int. J. Rob. Res. **31**, 1134–1154 (2012)
10. Peng, L., Lipinski, D., Mohseni, K.: Dynamic data driven application system for plume estimation using UAVs. J. Intell. Rob. Syst. **74**, 421–436 (2014)
11. Barrault, M., Maday, Y., Nguyen, N.C., Patera, A.T.: An empirical interpolation method: application to efficient reduced-basis discretization of partial differential equations. C. R. Math. **339**, 667–672 (2004)
12. Chaturantabut, S., Sorensen, D.C.: Nonlinear model reduction via discrete empirical interpolation. SIAM J. Sci. Comput. **32**, 2737–2764 (2010)
13. Porsching, T.A.: Estimation of the error in reduced basis method solution of nonlinear equations. Math. Comput. **45**, 487–496 (1985)
14. Rathinam, M., Petzold, L.R.: A new look at proper orthogonal decomposition. SIAM J. Numer. Anal. **41**, 1893–1925 (2003)
15. Maday, Y., Stamm, B.: Locally adaptive greedy approximations for anisotropic parameter reduced basis spaces. SIAM J. Sci. Comput. **35**, 2417–2441 (2013)
16. Shea, D.A., Lister, S.A.: The BioWatch program: detection of bioterrorism. Congressional Research Service, Congressional Research Service Report RL **32152**, Washington, DC, USA (2003)
17. Sledge, I.J., Mohseni, K.: Coordinating groups of sensing platforms in dynamic uncertain environments, IEEE Transactions on Automation Science and Engineering (2015) (under review)
18. Peng, L., Mohseni, K.: Nonlinear model reduction via a locally weighted POD method. Int. J. Numer. Methods Eng. (2015, accepted, in press)

Data Assimilation and Uncertainty Quantification

A One-Step-Ahead Smoothing-Based Joint Ensemble Kalman Filter for State-Parameter Estimation of Hydrological Models

Mohamad E. Gharamti[1], Boujemaa Ait-El-Fquih[2], and Ibrahim Hoteit[1,2](✉)

[1] Earth Sciences and Engineering, King Abdullah University of Science and Technology, Thuwal 23955, Saudi Arabia
ibrahim.hoteit@kaust.edu.sa
[2] Applied Mathematics and Computational Sciences, King Abdullah University of Science and Technology, Thuwal 23955, Saudi Arabia

Abstract. The ensemble Kalman filter (EnKF) recursively integrates field data into simulation models to obtain a better characterization of the model's state and parameters. These are generally estimated following a state-parameters joint augmentation strategy. In this study, we introduce a new smoothing-based joint EnKF scheme, in which we introduce a one-step-ahead smoothing of the state before updating the parameters. Numerical experiments are performed with a two-dimensional synthetic subsurface contaminant transport model. The improved performance of the proposed joint EnKF scheme compared to the standard joint EnKF compensates for the modest increase in the computational cost.

1 Introduction

Quantifying and addressing uncertainties in hydrological modeling, including surface and subsurface water flow, contaminant transport, and reservoir engineering, is important to obtain meaningful and useful outputs. This is driven by the uncertain and stochastic nature of hydrological systems. To reduce the modeling uncertainties, sequential data assimilation techniques such as ensemble Kalman filtering methods (EnKFs) were largely utilized. These provide an effective and robust estimation framework for state-parameters estimation with reasonable computational requirements [2,4,7,10].

EnKFs are sequential Monte Carlo techniques that aim at estimating the assumingly Gaussian probability distribution of the state and parameters of a dynamical system following a Bayesian filtering formulation. The EnKF is non-intrusive and is relatively simple to implement, even with complex nonlinear models, requiring only an observational operator that maps the state variables from the model space into the observation space. The standard EnKF approach for state-parameter estimation is based on the joint estimation technique which concurrently estimates the state and the parameters by simply augmenting the filter state vector with unknown parameters, assuming constant dynamics for the parameters [7]. This technique is very popular in groundwater flow and contamination data assimilation problems for estimating for instance the flow field,

© Springer International Publishing Switzerland 2015
S. Ravela and A. Sandu (Eds.): DyDESS 2014, LNCS 8964, pp. 207–214, 2015.
DOI: 10.1007/978-3-319-25138-7_19

hydraulic head, contaminant concentration and spatially variable permeability and porosity parameters [3,4,6].

In this study, we introduce a new EnKF-based state-parameter estimation scheme, the one-step-ahead Joint-EnKF (Joint-EnKF$_{\mathrm{OSA}}$), following the one-step-ahead smoothing formulation of the Bayesian filtering problem. This reverses the order of the measurement-update step that usually follows the model forecast step. More precisely, starting from an analysis ensemble of the state and parameters at a given time, the new algorithm uses the current observation to: (1) update the parameter ensemble, (2) compute a one step-ahead smoothed state ensemble, and (3) update the state distribution after integrating the smoothed ensemble and the updated parameters with the model. The proposed Joint-EnKF$_{\mathrm{OSA}}$ algorithm exploits the observations in both the state smoothing and analysis steps. This is shown to be beneficial in terms of estimation accuracy as compared to the standard Joint-EnKF using a subsurface contaminant transport model and estimating the contaminant concentration and the conductivity parameter fields.

2   Problem Formulation

Consider a discrete-time state-parameter dynamical system:

$$\begin{cases} \mathbf{x}_{n+1} = \mathcal{M}_n\left(\mathbf{x}_n, \theta\right) + \eta_n, \\ \mathbf{y}_n = \mathbf{H}_n\mathbf{x}_n + \varepsilon_n, \end{cases} \tag{1}$$

in which $\mathbf{x}_n \in \mathrm{I\!R}^{N_x}$ and $\mathbf{y}_n \in \mathrm{I\!R}^{N_y}$ respectively denote the system state and the observation at time t_n, and $\theta \in \mathrm{I\!R}^{N_\theta}$ is the parameter vector. $\mathcal{M}_n$ is a nonlinear operator integrating the state from time t_n to t_{n+1}, while $\mathbf{H}_n$ denotes a linear observational operator at time t_n. The model process noise, $\eta = \{\eta_n\}_{n\in\mathrm{I\!N}}$, and the observation process noise, $\varepsilon = \{\varepsilon_n\}_{n\in\mathrm{I\!N}}$, are assumed to be statistically independent, jointly independent and independent of $\mathbf{x}_0$ and θ, which, in turn, are assumed independent. Also let $\eta_n \sim \mathcal{N}\left(\mathbf{0}, \mathbf{Q}_n\right)$ and $\varepsilon_n \sim \mathcal{N}\left(\mathbf{0}, \mathbf{R}_n\right)$. Througouht this paper, $\mathbf{y}_{0:n} \overset{\mathrm{def}}{=} \{\mathbf{y}_0, \mathbf{y}_1, \cdots, \mathbf{y}_n\}$, and $p(\mathbf{x}_n)$ and $p(\mathbf{x}_n|\mathbf{y}_{0:l})$ respectively stand for probability density function (pdf) with respect to the Lebesgue measure of $\mathbf{x}_n$ and the pdf of $\mathbf{x}_n$ conditional on $\mathbf{y}_{0:l}$; the other pdfs are defined similarly.

We focus on the state-parameter *filtering* problem, say, the estimation, at each time, t_n, of the state, $\mathbf{x}_n$, and the parameters, θ, from the historic of the observations, $\mathbf{y}_{0:n}$. One solution to this problem is given by the *a posteriori* mean (AM),

$$\mathbb{E}_{p(\mathbf{x}_n|\mathbf{y}_{0:n})}[\mathbf{x}_n] = \int \mathbf{x}_n p(\mathbf{x}_n, \theta|\mathbf{y}_{0:n})d\mathbf{x}_n d\theta, \tag{2}$$

$$\mathbb{E}_{p(\theta|\mathbf{y}_{0:n})}[\theta] = \int \theta p(\mathbf{x}_n, \theta|\mathbf{y}_{0:n})d\mathbf{x}_n d\theta, \tag{3}$$

which minimizes the *a posteriori* mean squared error. However, in practice, analytical computation of (2) and (3) are very often not available owing to the nonlinear character of the model operator, $\mathcal{M}_n(\mathbf{x}_n, \theta)$, in addition to the very large state and parameter dimensions, N_x and N_θ, respectively. To overcome this problem, the Joint-EnKF, and latter the dual EnKF (Dual-EnKF) [7] have been proposed as efficient algorithms providing good approximations of (2) and (3) at reasonable computational cost. At each assimilation cycle, these algorithms involve a forecast step by the model followed by an update step with incoming observations.

3   Smoothing-Based Joint-EnKF

We start from the standard Joint-EnKF and consider the augmented state $\mathbf{z}_n = \left[\mathbf{x}_n^T \ \theta^T\right]^T$, but introduce a different structure to the algorithm. More specifically, when moving from the analysis pdf, $p(\mathbf{z}_{n-1}|\mathbf{y}_{0:n-1})$ to $p(\mathbf{z}_n|\mathbf{y}_{0:n})$, our algorithm involves the one-step-ahead smoothing pdf, $p(\mathbf{z}_{n-1}|\mathbf{y}_{0:n})$, instead of the forecast pdf, $p(\mathbf{z}_n|\mathbf{y}_{0:n-1})$, as in the Joint-EnKF. The idea of using the one-step-ahead smoothing pdf in the filtering algorithm is not entirely new (e.g. [8]), and was used to derive several particle filters (PFs) and Kalman filters (KFs) in low-dimensional state-space systems (see also [9] and references therein).

3.1   The One-Step-Ahead Smoothing-Based Filtering Algorithm

The analysis pdf, $p(\mathbf{x}_n, \theta|\mathbf{y}_{0:n})$, can be computed from $p(\mathbf{x}_{n-1}, \theta|\mathbf{y}_{0:n-1})$ in two steps as follows:

- *Smoothing step:* $p(\mathbf{x}_{n-1}, \theta|\mathbf{y}_{0:n})$ is first computed using the likelihood $p(\mathbf{y}_n|\mathbf{x}_{n-1}, \theta)$ as,

$$p(\mathbf{x}_{n-1}, \theta|\mathbf{y}_{0:n}) \propto p(\mathbf{y}_n|\mathbf{x}_{n-1}, \theta)p(\mathbf{x}_{n-1}, \theta|\mathbf{y}_{0:n-1}), \qquad (4)$$

with

$$p(\mathbf{y}_n|\mathbf{x}_{n-1}, \theta) = \int p(\mathbf{y}_n|\mathbf{x}_n)p(\mathbf{x}_n|\mathbf{x}_{n-1}, \theta)d\mathbf{x}_n. \qquad (5)$$

- *Analysis step:* Only the analysis pdf of $\mathbf{x}_n$, $p(\mathbf{x}_n|\mathbf{y}_{0:n})$, needs to be computed from $p(\mathbf{x}_{n-1}, \theta|\mathbf{y}_{0:n})$ as the analysis pdf of θ has already been computed in the smoothing step. Indeed, using the a *posteriori* transition pdf, $p(\mathbf{x}_n|\mathbf{x}_{n-1}, \theta, \mathbf{y}_n)$, we obtain:

$$p(\mathbf{x}_n|\mathbf{y}_{0:n}) = \int p(\mathbf{x}_n|\mathbf{x}_{n-1}, \theta, \mathbf{y}_n)p(\mathbf{x}_{n-1}, \theta|\mathbf{y}_{0:n})d\mathbf{x}_{n-1}d\theta, \qquad (6)$$

with

$$p(\mathbf{x}_n|\mathbf{x}_{n-1}, \theta, \mathbf{y}_n) \propto p(\mathbf{y}_n|\mathbf{x}_n)p(\mathbf{x}_n|\mathbf{x}_{n-1}, \theta). \qquad (7)$$

3.2   Practical Implementation

As the standard Joint-EnKF, the Joint-EnKF$_{OSA}$ is based on the transformation of the state-parameter system (1) into a classical state-space system with the augmented state, $\mathbf{z}_n$:

$$\begin{cases} \mathbf{z}_{n+1} = \widetilde{\mathcal{M}}_n\left(\mathbf{z}_n\right) + \widetilde{\eta}_n, \\ \mathbf{y}_n = \widetilde{\mathbf{H}}_n\mathbf{z}_n + \varepsilon_n, \end{cases} \tag{8}$$

in which $\widetilde{\mathcal{M}}_n\left(\mathbf{z}_n\right) = \begin{bmatrix} \mathcal{M}_n(\mathbf{z}_n) \\ \theta \end{bmatrix}$, $\widetilde{\eta}_n = \begin{bmatrix} \eta_n^T & \mathbf{0} \end{bmatrix}^T$, $\widetilde{\mathbf{H}}_n = [\mathbf{H}_n \ \mathbf{0}]$, with $\mathbf{0}$ the zero matrix with appropriate dimensions.

It is practically not possible to derive the analytical solution of (4)–(7) in system (8) because of the nonlinear character of the model $\mathcal{M}(.,.)$. We thus resort to a Monte Carlo ensemble-based approximation under the Gaussian assumption of $p(\mathbf{x}_{n-1}, \theta|\mathbf{y}_{0:n})$ and $p(\mathbf{x}_n|\mathbf{y}_{0:n})$ for all n. Let, from now on, for an ensemble $\{\mathbf{r}^{(m)}\}_{m=1}^{N_e}$, $\hat{\mathbf{r}}$ denote its empirical mean and $\mathbf{S_r}$ denote a matrix with N_e-columns whose m^{th} column is defined as $\left(\mathbf{r}^{(m)} - \hat{\mathbf{r}}\right)$.

Smoothing. Based on Eqs. (4) and (5), the smoothing ensemble at time t_{n-1}, $\{\mathbf{x}_{n-1}^{s,(m)}, \theta_{|n}^{(m)}\}_{m=1}^{N_e}$, can be computed from the analysis ensemble, $\{\mathbf{x}_{n-1}^{a,(m)}, \theta_{|n-1}^{(m)}\}_{m=1}^{N_e}$, as follows:

$$\mathbf{y}_n^{f,(m)} = \mathbf{H}_n\left(\mathcal{M}_{n-1}(\mathbf{x}_{n-1}^{a,(m)}, \theta_{|n-1}^{(m)}) + \mathbf{u}_{n-1}^{(m)}\right) + \mathbf{v}_n^{(m)}, \tag{9}$$

$$\mathbf{x}_{n-1}^{s,(m)} = \mathbf{x}_{n-1}^{a,(m)} + \mathbf{P}_{\mathbf{x}_{n-1}^a, \mathbf{y}_n^f} \underbrace{\mathbf{P}_{\mathbf{y}_n^f}^{-1}(\mathbf{y}_n - \mathbf{y}_n^{f,(m)})}_{\nu_n^{(m)}}, \tag{10}$$

$$\theta_{|n}^{(m)} = \theta_{|n-1}^{(m)} + \mathbf{P}_{\theta_{|n-1}, \mathbf{y}_n^f} \times \nu_n^{(m)}, \tag{11}$$

with $\mathbf{u}_{n-1}^{(m)} \sim \mathcal{N}(\mathbf{0}, \mathbf{Q}_{n-1})$, $\mathbf{v}_n^{(m)} \sim \mathcal{N}(\mathbf{0}, \mathbf{R}_n)$, $\mathbf{P}_{\mathbf{x}_{n-1}^a, \mathbf{y}_n^f} = \frac{1}{N_e-1}\mathbf{S}_{\mathbf{x}_{n-1}^a}\mathbf{S}_{\mathbf{y}_n^f}^T$, $\mathbf{P}_{\mathbf{y}_n^f} = \frac{1}{N_e-1}\mathbf{S}_{\mathbf{y}_n^f}\mathbf{S}_{\mathbf{y}_n^f}^T$ and $\mathbf{P}_{\theta_{|n-1}, \mathbf{y}_n^f} = \frac{1}{N_e-1}\mathbf{S}_{\theta_{|n-1}}\mathbf{S}_{\mathbf{y}_n^f}^T$.

Analysis. Following Eq. (6), the analysis ensemble, $\{\mathbf{x}_n^{a,(m)}\}_{m=1}^{N_e}$, can be obtained from the smoothing ensemble, $\{\mathbf{x}_{n-1}^{s,(m)}, \theta_{|n}^{(m)}\}_{m=1}^{N_e}$, once the *a posteriori* transition pdf, $p(\mathbf{x}_n|\mathbf{x}_{n-1}, \theta, \mathbf{y}_n)$, is computed. Furthermore, following (7), this pdf is Gaussian with a covariance $\tilde{\mathbf{Q}}_{n-1} = \mathbf{Q}_{n-1} - \tilde{\mathbf{K}}_n\mathbf{H}_n\mathbf{Q}_{n-1}$ with $\tilde{\mathbf{K}}_n = \mathbf{Q}_{n-1}\mathbf{H}_n^T[\mathbf{H}_n\mathbf{Q}_{n-1}\mathbf{H}_n^T + \mathbf{R}_n]^{-1}$. The computation cost of $\tilde{\mathbf{K}}_n$ and $\tilde{\mathbf{Q}}_{n-1}$ can be prohibitive for very large dimensions. One way to avoid the use of (7) is to assume that $\mathbf{x}_n$ and $\mathbf{y}_n$ are independent conditionally on $(\mathbf{x}_{n-1}, \theta)$, similarly to [11,12], *i.e.*,

$$p(\mathbf{x}_n|\mathbf{x}_{n-1}, \theta, \mathbf{y}_n) = p(\mathbf{x}_n|\mathbf{x}_{n-1}, \theta). \tag{12}$$

In our Gaussian framework, this means that the "gain", $\tilde{\mathbf{K}}_n$, associated with $\mathbf{y}_n$, vanishes ($= \mathbf{0}$), case in which, one can see that the covariance, $\tilde{\mathbf{Q}}_{n-1}$, reduces to that of $p(\mathbf{x}_n | \mathbf{x}_{n-1}, \theta)$, namely, $\mathbf{Q}_{n-1}$. Similarly, the mean of $p(\mathbf{x}_n | \mathbf{x}_{n-1}, \theta, \mathbf{y}_n)$ reduces to that of $p(\mathbf{x}_n | \mathbf{x}_{n-1}, \theta)$, namely, $\mathcal{M}_{n-1}(\mathbf{x}_{n-1}, \theta)$. Finally, using the assumption (12) in (6), on can easily verify that $\{\mathbf{x}_n^{a,(m)}\}_{m=1}^{N_e}$ can be obtained from $\{\mathbf{x}_{n-1}^{s,(m)}, \theta_{|n}^{(m)}\}_{m=1}^{N_e}$ as,

$$\mathbf{x}_n^{a,(m)} = \mathcal{M}_{n-1}(\mathbf{x}_{n-1}^{s,(m)}, \theta_{|n}^{(m)}) + \mathbf{u}_{n-1}^{(m)}; \quad \mathbf{u}_{n-1}^{(m)} \sim \mathcal{N}(\mathbf{0}, \mathbf{Q}_{n-1}). \quad (13)$$

The updated Joint-EnKF$_{\mathrm{OSA}}$ updates both the state ensemble members, $\mathbf{x}_{n-1}^{s,(m)}$, and the parameters ensemble members, $\theta_{|n}^{(m)}$ are then integrated forward in time by the model to obtain the analysis members of the state at time t_n, $\mathbf{x}_n^{a,(m)}$. This may explain the superior performance of the proposed scheme compared to the standard Joint-EnKF in our numerical experiments, which involves $\mathbf{x}_{n-1}^{a,(m)}$ rather than $\mathbf{x}_{n-1}^{s,(m)}$ in the computation of $\mathbf{x}_n^{a,(m)}$.

The Joint-EnKF$_{\mathrm{OSA}}$ exhibits some similarities with the Dual-EnKF [1,7] in the sense that it separately updates the state and the parameters, but using the future observation to update the state. The proposed filtering scheme can be (in theory) further generalized to a L-step-ahead smoothing based filtering scheme, with $L > 1$ is an arbitrary fixed lag, or in other words, to a fully fixed-lag smoothing algorithm (some literature on fixed-lag smoothing can be found for example in [13–15] and references theirein). This may however significantly increase the computational cost, since it requires L times additional computations of the forecast model and Kalman-type update.

4 Subsurface Contaminant Transport Experiments

4.1 Experimental Setup

We consider a steady-state groundwater flow system inside a rectangular domain of total aquifer area of $0.1125 \, \mathrm{km}^2$. North and south boundaries are assumed impermeable, whereas the east and west boundaries are assigned constant hydraulic heads equal to 18 and $12 \, \mathrm{m}$-water, respectively. Pure water conditions are assumed in the aquifer except for an elongated Cs-137 plume of concentration $10 \, \mathrm{mg/l}$ located near the west boundary. Cs-137 is a radioactive isotope of Caesium with a half-life of $30.17 \, \mathrm{years}$, and generally used in gauges for measuring liquid flows and the thickness of materials. We simulate the migration of the radioactive plume across the domain towards the east boundary for 50-years period. Figure 1 below shows three snapshots of the polluted domain in time. We assume linear sorption conditions in a medium textured soil type aquifer.

We conduct twin-experiments in which we perform a reference (or *truth*) contaminant transport simulation and use a perturbed forecast model to reproduce the reference solution while assimilating perturbed observations extracted from the reference run. We consider a monitoring network of 15 wells distributed

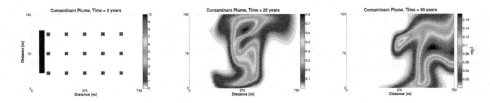

Fig. 1. Reference contaminant spatial maps of the domain after 0, 25 and 50 years. Blue squares shown on the left panel correspond to observation wells that are installed for measuring the concentration of the groundwater (Color figure online).

uniformly in the domain as shown in the left panel of Fig. 1. For updating the concentration and conductivity ensembles, we assume that concentration data is available every 6 month (i.e., total of 100 EnKF updates). We sample the initial state ensemble assuming Gaussian conditions by selecting the mean of the reference run and perturbing around it. The initial conductivity ensemble is generated using a sequential Gaussian simulation toolbox [5]. To perform data assimilation in a realistic settings, we perturb the model's porosity, radioactive decay and sorption.

4.2 Assimilation Results

In this section, we present assimilation results from the standard and the proposed smoothing-based joint-EnKFs. We set the ensemble size, N_e, in both filters to 100 and impose a 10 % measurement error on the pseudo concentration observations.

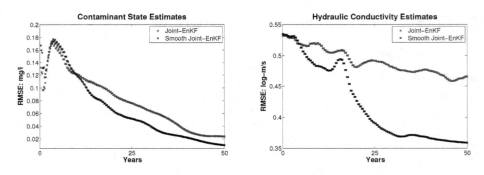

Fig. 2. Time evolution of the root-mean-square errors (RMSE) as they result from the joint-EnKF and the Joint-EnKF$_{OSA}$ over time. Shown in the left panel are estimates of the contaminant state, whereas the right panel plots the hydraulic conductivity estimates.

To assess the performance of the filters, we first examine the time evolution of the root-mean-squared-errors (RMSE) for both the contaminant concentration and the hydraulic conductivity. As shown in Fig. 2, the RMSE of the contaminant estimates decreases gradually in time for both filters. The average RMSE evaluated over the whole 50 years-period is 0.0812 and 0.0682 mg/l for the joint-EnKF and the proposed Joint-EnKF$_\text{OSA}$, respectively. This indicates that the proposed algorithm is more accurate, providing around 16 % improvement over the standard joint-EnKF. Concerning the estimates of the 2D conductivity field, the Joint-EnKF$_\text{OSA}$ algorithm significantly outperforms the standard joint-EnKF, recovering much more accurate parameter field by the end of the 50 years assimilation interval. Compared to the true conductivity field (Fig. 3, south-left panel), the Joint-EnKF$_\text{OSA}$ conductivity estimate is about 23 % more accurate than the standard Joint-EnKF.

We have also analyzed the spatial patterns of the estimated fields. As shown in Fig. 3, the standard Joint-EnKF provides poor estimates of the final contaminant concentration, exhibiting some overshooting in the right region of the domain. In contrast, the Joint-EnKF$_\text{OSA}$ better delineates these polluted areas and provides spatial patterns in better agreement with the reference solution, especially in the northeast part of the aquifer. With regard to the parameter field, the proposed filter exhibits better representation of the high conductivity and low conductivity areas in the western and central parts of the domain.

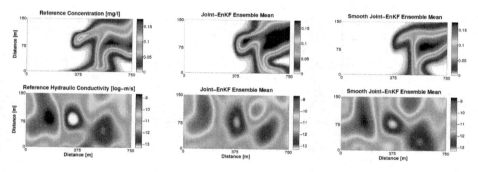

Fig. 3. Reference and analysis ensemble mean maps after 50 years. Shown in the top row of subplots are the contaminant concentration maps from the reference, joint-EnKF and Joint-EnKF$_\text{OSA}$ runs. The reference and recovered conductivity fields are shown in the subplots of the bottom row.

5   Conclusion

In this study, we presented a smoothing-based joint ensemble Kalman filter for state-parameter estimation problem. While sharing with the standard Joint-EnKF the idea of concatenating the state and parameters in the same vector, the new filter reverses the order of the time-update step (forecast by the model) and the measurement-update step (correction by the incoming observations). This enables more updates to the state by incoming observations, which should result in improved estimated without any significant increase in the computational cost. This is confirmed through numerical synthetic assimilation experiments based on a subsurface contaminant transport model, clearly demonstrating the efficiency of the proposed scheme. This indeed resulted in significant better state and parameters estimates compared to the standard Joint-EnKF.

References

1. Gharamti, M.E., Kadoura, A., Valstar, J., Sun, S., Hoteit, I.: Constraining a compositional flow model with flow-chemical data using an ensemble-based Kalman filter. Water Resour. Res. **50**, 2444–2467 (2014)
2. Gharamti, A., Valstar, J., Hoteit, I.: An adatpive hybrid EnKF-OI scheme for efficient state-parameter estimaton of reactive contaminant transport models. Adv. Water Resour. **71**, 1–15 (2014)
3. Gharamti, M.E., Hoteit, I.: Complex step-based low-rank extended Kalman filtering for state-parameter estimation of subsurface transport models. J. Hydrol. **509**, 588–600 (2013)
4. Hendricks-Franssen, H., Kinzelbach, W.: Real-time groundwater flow modeling with the ensemble kalman filter: Joint estimation of states and parameters and the filter inbreeding problem. Water Resour. Res. **44**, W09408 (2008)
5. Gómez-Hernández, J.J., Journel, A.G.: Joint sequential simulation of multigaussian fields. Geostatistics Troia. **92**, 85–94 (1993)
6. Li, L., Zhou, H., Gómez-Hernández, J.J., Hendricks-Franssen, H.-J.: Jointly mapping hydraulic conductivity and porosity by assimilating concentration data via ensemble kalman filter. J. Hydrol. **428**, 152–169 (2012)
7. Moradkhani, H., Sorooshian, S., Gupta, H.V., Houser, P.R.: Dual state-parameter estimation of hydrological models using ensemble Kalman filter. Adv. Water Resour. **28**(2), 135–147 (2005)
8. Desbouvries, F., Petetin, Y., Ait-El-Fquih, B.: Direct, prediction- and smoothing-based kalman and particle filter algorithms. Signal Process. **91**(8), 2064–2077 (2011)
9. Lee, W., Farmer, C.: Data assimilation by conditioning of driving noise on future observations. IEEE Trans. Signal Process. **62**(15), 3887–3896 (2014)
10. Reichle, R.H., McLaughlin, D.B., Entekhabi, D.: Hydrologic data assimilation with the ensemble Kalman filter. Mon. Weather Rev. **130**(1), 103–114 (2002)
11. Smidl, Y., Quinn, A.: Variational Bayesian filtering. IEEE Trans. Signal Process. **56**, 5020–5030 (2008)
12. Smidl, Y., Quinn, A.: The Variational Bayes Method in Signal Processing. Springer, Heidelberg (2006)
13. Cohn, S.E., Sivakumaran, N.S.: Ricardo todling.: a fixed-lag kalman smoother for retrospective data assimilation. Mon. Weather Rev. **122**, 2838–2867 (1994)
14. Polson, N.G., Stroud, J.R., Müller, P.: Practical filtering with sequential parameter learning. J. Roy. Stat. Soc. **70**(2), 413–428 (2008)
15. Cuzol, A., Mémin, E.: Monte Carlo fixed-lag smoothing in state-space models. Nonlin. Process. Geophys. **21**, 633–643 (2014)

A Sampling Approach for Four Dimensional Data Assimilation

Ahmed Attia$^{(\boxtimes)}$, Vishwas Rao, and Adrian Sandu

Computational Science Laboratory, Department of Computer Science,
Virginia Polytechnic Institute and State University, 2201 Knowledgeworks II,
2202 Kraft Drive, Blacksburg, VA 24060, USA
attia@vt.edu
http://csl.cs.vt.edu/

Abstract. This paper studies a direct approach to smoothing by sampling the posterior distribution in four dimensional data assimilation. The methodology is based on a hybrid Monte Carlo approach and can be applied to non-linear models, non-linear observation operators, and non-Gaussian probability distributions. The generated ensemble is used to construct both the analysis state (the minimum variance estimator) and the analysis error covariance matrix. Numerical tests performed with the Lorenz-96 model and with both linear and quadratic observation operators illustrate the usefulness and performance of the approach.

1 Introduction

Predicting the behavior of complex dynamical systems such as the atmosphere requires incorporating information from periodic observations to decrease the uncertainty in the forecast. Data assimilation (DA) combines information from a numerical model, prior knowledge, and observations, all with associated errors, in order to obtain an improved estimate of the true state of the system. Two approaches have gained widespread popularity in data assimilation: variational and ensemble-based methods. The variational approach requires the development of the adjoint of the tangent linear numerical model, which is an extremely challenging task for real applications. An estimate of the uncertainty in the analysis is not immediately available in variational schemes [3]. Ensemble-based schemes, like the Ensemble Kalman Filter (EnKF), use an ensemble of states to represent the probability density (PDF) of the state of the system. The computations performed in ensemble schemes are proportional to the size of the state space of the ensemble. The dimension of ensemble space is always much smaller than the dimension of the model state space, which is typically $10^6 - 10^9$ for atmospheric models, and this leads to considerable sampling errors. Hybrid data assimilation schemes couple the variational solution with an ensemble of states to estimate posterior uncertainty. Hybrid approaches are a promising new direction as they can, in principle, combine the advantages of both families of methods and alleviate their disadvantages [2, 5, 12].

© Springer International Publishing Switzerland 2015
S. Ravela and A. Sandu (Eds.): DyDESS 2014, LNCS 8964, pp. 215–226, 2015.
DOI: 10.1007/978-3-319-25138-7_20

This work presents a sampling approach to four-dimensional data assimilation. Specifically, the method samples directly from the posterior distribution associated with four dimensional variational (4D-Var) data assimilation. The posterior ensemble allows to generate an analysis state based on a minimum variance estimation, and to estimate consistently the statistics of the analysis error, e.g., the analysis error covariance matrix.

The paper is organized as follows. Section 2 reviews the Bayesian formulation of variational data assimilation. Numerical experiments and results are discussed in Sect. 3. Conclusions and future directions are given in Sect. 4.

2   Data Assimilation

Data assimilation is the process of combining the information contained in the prior knowledge, the model, and the observations, in order to produce an optimal (in some sense) estimate of the state of a complex, and usually high-dimensional, system such as the atmosphere. The variational approach to data assimilation, rooted in control theory, finds a maximum aposteriori (MAP) estimate of the true state [9]. We present the variational approach to data assimilation from the Bayesian point of view which will serve our goal of sampling from the posterior PDF. The numerical model is assumed to be perfect throughout this study.

2.1   Variational Data Assimilation

The background (prior) probability density $\mathcal{P}^b(\mathbf{x})$ encapsulates the knowledge of the system prior to taking any observations. It describes the uncertainty with which one knows the true state $\mathbf{x}^{\text{true}}$ at a specific time point prior to collecting any new observations. The conditional probability distribution of observations given the state of the system is referred to as the likelihood PDF and denoted by $\mathcal{P}(\mathbf{y}|\mathbf{x})$. From Bayes's theorem [9]:

$$\mathcal{P}^a(\mathbf{x}) = \mathcal{P}(\mathbf{x}|\mathbf{y}) = \frac{\mathcal{P}(\mathbf{y}|\mathbf{x})\mathcal{P}^b(\mathbf{x})}{\mathcal{P}(\mathbf{y})}, \tag{1}$$

where $\mathcal{P}(\mathbf{x}|\mathbf{y})$ refers to the probability distribution of the state of the system after incorporating the information from the observations. This simply refers to the analysis PDF or posterior. The denominator is the marginal density of the observations and acts as a scaling factor. Equation (1) can be rewritten as

$$\mathcal{P}^a(\mathbf{x}) = \mathcal{P}(\mathbf{x}|\mathbf{y}) \propto \mathcal{P}(\mathbf{y}|\mathbf{x})\mathcal{P}^b(\mathbf{x}). \tag{2}$$

Under the common assumptions that background and the observation errors are normally distributed, that is $\mathcal{P}^b(\mathbf{x}) = \mathcal{N}(\mathbf{x}^b, \mathbf{B})$, and $(\mathcal{H}(\mathbf{x}) - \mathbf{y}) \sim \mathcal{N}(0, \mathbf{R})$, the prior and the likelihood PDFs can be written as follows:

$$\mathcal{P}^b(\mathbf{x}) = (2\pi)^{-\frac{N_{\text{var}}}{2}}|\mathbf{B}|^{-\frac{1}{2}} \exp\left(-\frac{1}{2}(\mathbf{x} - \mathbf{x}^b)^T \mathbf{B}^{-1}(\mathbf{x} - \mathbf{x}^b)\right),$$

$$\propto \exp\left(-\frac{1}{2}(\mathbf{x} - \mathbf{x}^b)^T \mathbf{B}^{-1}(\mathbf{x} - \mathbf{x}^b)\right), \tag{3}$$

$$\mathcal{P}(\mathbf{y}|\mathbf{x}) = (2\pi)^{-\frac{m}{2}} |\mathbf{R}|^{-\frac{1}{2}} \exp\left(-\frac{1}{2}(\mathcal{H}(\mathbf{x}) - \mathbf{y})^T \mathbf{R}^{-1}(\mathcal{H}(\mathbf{x}) - \mathbf{y})\right),$$

$$\propto \exp\left(-\frac{1}{2}(\mathcal{H}(\mathbf{x}) - \mathbf{y})^T \mathbf{R}^{-1}(\mathcal{H}(\mathbf{x}) - \mathbf{y})\right). \tag{4}$$

Here $\mathcal{H}$ is the observation operator that maps the state space of the system to observation space, and N_{var} is the dimension of model state space. The normality assumptions are sometimes difficult to justify, especially with highly non-linear models, however they are widely used due to their convenience. In this case, we can use the continuous Bayes' rule to get the posterior as follows:

$$\mathcal{P}^a(\mathbf{x}) \propto \exp\left(-\frac{1}{2}(\mathbf{x} - \mathbf{x}^b)^T \mathbf{B}^{-1}(\mathbf{x} - \mathbf{x}^b)\right)$$

$$\times \exp\left(-\frac{1}{2}(\mathcal{H}(\mathbf{x}) - \mathbf{y})^T \mathbf{R}^{-1}(\mathcal{H}(\mathbf{x}) - \mathbf{y})\right),$$

$$= \exp\left(-\mathcal{J}(\mathbf{x})\right), \tag{5a}$$

$$\mathcal{J}(\mathbf{x}) = \frac{1}{2}(\mathbf{x} - \mathbf{x}^b)^T \mathbf{B}^{-1}(\mathbf{x} - \mathbf{x}^b) + \frac{1}{2}(\mathcal{H}(\mathbf{x}) - \mathbf{y})^T \mathbf{R}^{-1}(\mathcal{H}(\mathbf{x}) - \mathbf{y}). \tag{5b}$$

The posterior (5) is Gaussian only if the observation operator is linear. Usually the observations lie in a space of much lower dimension than the state space of the system, that is $m \ll N_{var}$.

In the four dimensional variational (4D-Var) formulation, several observations at different time instances are assimilated simultaneously. Given a background state $\mathbf{x}^b(t_0)$, and a set of observations $\mathbf{y}_k = \mathbf{y}(t_k)$; $k = 0, 1, \ldots, N_{obs}$, and assuming that observation errors are independent of each other and of the error in state of the system, the posterior is given by:

$$\mathcal{P}^a(\mathbf{x}(t_0)) = \mathcal{P}^a(\mathbf{x}_0) \propto \exp\left(-\mathcal{J}(\mathbf{x}_0)\right), \tag{6a}$$

$$\mathcal{J}(\mathbf{x}_0) = \frac{1}{2}(\mathbf{x}_0 - \mathbf{x}_0^b)^T \mathbf{B}_0^{-1}(\mathbf{x}_0 - \mathbf{x}_0^b) \tag{6b}$$

$$+ \frac{1}{2}\sum_{k=0}^{N_{obs}} (\mathcal{H}(\mathbf{x}_k) - \mathbf{y}_k)^T \mathbf{R}_k^{-1}(\mathcal{H}(\mathbf{x}_k) - \mathbf{y}_k),$$

where $\mathbf{B}_0$ represents the background error covariance matrix at the initial time t_0, and $\mathbf{x}_k = \mathcal{M}_{t_0 \to t_k}(\mathbf{x}_0)$ is the model state propagated forward in time by the forward model $\mathcal{M}$. The model solution operator $\mathcal{M}$ represents, for example, a discrete approximation of the partial differential equations that governs the evolution of the dynamical system (e.g. atmospheric or oceanic processes). While the forward model $\mathcal{M}$ propagates the state of the system to future times, perturbations (small errors $\delta\mathbf{x}$) of the state of the system evolve according to the tangent linear model

$$\delta\mathbf{x}_k = \mathbf{M}_{0,k}(\mathbf{x}_0) \cdot \delta\mathbf{x}_0, \quad k = 1, \ldots, N_{obs}, \tag{7}$$

where, $\mathbf{M}_{0,k} = (\mathcal{M}_{t_0 \to t_k}(\mathbf{x}))_\mathbf{x}$. This tangent linear model is useful in sensitivity analysis.

The 4D-Var formulation [9] computes the maximum a posteriori estimate, i.e., obtains the analysis $\mathbf{x}_0^a$ as the argument which minimizes the cost function $\mathcal{J}(\mathbf{x}_0)$. The gradient is:

$$\nabla_{\mathbf{x}_0} \mathcal{J}(\mathbf{x}_0) = \mathbf{B}^{-1}(\mathbf{x}_0 - \mathbf{x}_0^b) + \sum_{k=0}^{N_{obs}} \mathbf{M}_{0,k}^T \mathbf{H}_k^T \mathbf{R}^{-1}(\mathcal{H}(\mathbf{x}_k) - \mathbf{y}_k), \qquad (8)$$

where $\mathbf{M}_{0,k}^T$ is the adjoint of the tangent linear model and $\mathbf{H}_k^T$ is the adjoint of the observation operator. This strategy incorporates time by assimilating all observations available in the time window simultaneously. This method requires the development of both tangent linear model and adjoint which is in many cases a challenging task.

2.2   Sampling from the Posterior Distribution

The 4D-Var formulation does not automatically provide a statistically consistent description of the posterior uncertainty [3], e.g., it does not include a mechanism to estimate the analysis error covariance matrix. Different hybrid approaches [10, 11] are based on using an ensemble of simulations, to complement the variational approach and to provide analysis error estimates. These methods require additional work and may suffer from inconsistency since the analysis $\mathbf{x}_0^a$ and the analysis covariance matrix are obtained by different algorithms. Sandu et al. have considered approaches based on subspace error decompositions [3, 14]. These approaches also require additional computational effort.

Direct sampling from the posterior distribution can be a powerful and efficient strategy, that is capable of dealing with the high-dimensionality of the state space.

Implicit particle filter [4] is a sequential Monte Carlo sampling algorithm for data assimilation that samples from the posterior PDF by targeting the sampling procedure to the high density areas in the posterior to keep the number of particles manageable independently from the dimension of the state space. An optimization step per particle is required, to locate high density areas, followed by a solution of a set of algebraic equations to generate the target ensemble. Another sequential data assimilation scheme [15] that uses the Gaussian mixture models, was developed to account for non-Gaussian statistics. Ensemble Kalman smoother (EnKS) [7,8] is an extension to the ensemble Kalman filter that is capable of producing an analysis state of a weakly nonlinear system by taking the observations at a later time instance into account. However, most of the available strategies tend to fail in presence of high non-linearities or when the Gaussianity assumptions do not hold.

Our main goal is to produce an efficient, robust, and easy to implement sampling scheme for four dimensional data assimilation that is not limited to the Gaussian cases, and can deal efficiently with nonlinear observations as well as linear observations. A detailed comparison of these strategies with our sampling scheme will be given in a future work.

In our previous work [1] we proposed the use of Hybrid Monte Carlo (HMC) sampling strategy and employed it to build a nonlinear, non-Gaussian version of the ensemble Kalman filter. In this paper we extend this approach to the four dimensional data assimilation case, where several observations in a given assimilation window are used simultaneously, and the posterior is of the form (6). The resulting algorithm can be thought of as a sampling smoother in this case.

Consider a set of observations $\mathbf{y}_0, \mathbf{y}_1, \ldots, \mathbf{y}_{N_{obs}}$, over the assimilation window $[t_0, t_f]$, and an ensemble of N_{ens} states, $\{\mathbf{x}_0^b(e)\}_{e=1,2,\ldots,N_{ens}}$ sampled from the background PDF of the beginning of the assimilation window. The ensemble of states are obtained, in the forecast step of the smoother, by propagating the analysis ensemble obtained in the previous assimilation window forward in time to t_0, the beginning of the current window.

In the analysis step we apply a modified version of the HMC sampling strategy presented in [1] to obtain an ensembles of states $\{\mathbf{x}_0^a(e)\}_{e=1,2,\ldots,N_{ens}}$ sampled from the posterior PDF $\mathcal{P}^a(\mathbf{x}_0)$. This ensemble is used to calculate the best estimate of the initial condition of the system (e.g. the mean $(\overline{\mathbf{x}}_0^a)$ of the ensemble), and to estimate the analysis error covariance matrix $\mathbf{A}$,

$$\overline{\mathbf{x}}_0^a = \frac{1}{N_{ens}} \sum_{e=1}^{N_{ens}} \mathbf{x}_0^a(e) , \tag{9a}$$

$$\mathbf{X}^a = [\mathbf{x}_0^a(1) - \overline{\mathbf{x}}_0^a, \ldots, \mathbf{x}_0^a(N_{ens}) - \overline{\mathbf{x}}_0^a] , \tag{9b}$$

$$\mathbf{A}_0 = \frac{1}{N_{ens} - 1} \left(\mathbf{X}^a \ (\mathbf{X}^a)^T \right) \tag{9c}$$

The forecast and analysis steps are repeated sequentially as one cycles through subsequent assimilation windows.

Given $\mathcal{J}(\mathbf{x})$ as in (6b), the sampling procedure is summarized in Algorithm 1. The details of each step in the algorithm can be found in [1].

3   Numerical Experiments

In this study we test our sampling scheme using the 40-variables Lorenz-96 model [13]:

$$\frac{dx_i}{dt} = x_{i-1} (x_{i+1} - x_{i-2}) - x_i + F , \tag{10}$$

where $\mathbf{x} = (x_1, x_2, \ldots, x_{40})^T \in \mathbb{R}^{40}$ is the state vector, and the forcing $F = 8$.

We use two observation operators, one linear and one quadratic. Only each second component of the state vector is observed. For the linear operator, $\mathcal{H}(\mathbf{x}) = \mathbf{H}\mathbf{x} = (x_1, x_3, \ldots, x_{N_{var}})^T$, while in the case of a quadratic operator, $\mathcal{H}(\mathbf{x}) = (x_1^2, x_3^2, \ldots, x_{N_{var}}^2)^T$. The number of ensemble members is $N_{ens} = 100$. The synthetic observations used are created by perturbing the reference trajectory with normal noise at uncertainty level of 5 %. The level of background error is set to 8 %. Each assimilation window is of length 0.5, with $N_{obs} = 5$ equidistant observations time-points. For convenience, no observations are taken at the

Algorithm 1. Sampling smoother algorithm

1: set $e \leftarrow 1$
2: Draw a a normal synthetic momentum $\mathbf{p}_e$.
3: Solve the Hamiltonian system to generate a proposal state with $\mathcal{J}(\mathbf{x})$ as in (6b).
4: Accept/Reject the proposal.
5: **if** $e = \mathrm{N_{ens}}$ **then**
6:     Stop.
7: **else if** *Proposal state rejected* **then**
8:     Goto step (2)
9: **else**
10:     $e \leftarrow e + 1$
11:     Goto step (2)
12: **end if**

---

beginning of each window. The infinite dimensional integrator, as given in [1], with step-size set to 0.01 is used. The number of steps between successive selections in the generated chain is set to 10. Two versions of the background error covariance matrix $\mathbf{B}_0$ are used, a modelled (fixed) version and a hybrid version. The hybrid version we used is a simple linear combination (11) of the modelled and the ensemble-based (flow-dependent forecast error covariance matrix (obtained from the forecast ensemble)

$$\mathbf{B}_0^{\mathrm{hybrid}} = \gamma \times \mathbf{B}_0^{\mathrm{modelled}} + (1 - \gamma) \times \mathbf{B}_0^{\mathrm{ensemble}}. \tag{11}$$

Setting $\gamma = 1$, ignores the error-of-the day update to the background error covariances. Choosing $\gamma = 0$, simply means we use the flow-dependent background error covariance matrix obtained from the ensemble and ignore the modelled one. For $\gamma \in (0, 1)$, a hybrid version of the background error covariance matrix is obtained. For simplicity, and since we trust the modelled $\mathbf{B}_0$, we chose and empirical weight of $\gamma = 0.75$.

3.1 Numerical Results

In what follows, we compare the results of the proposed sampling scheme with the standard 4D-Var solution. The root-mean-square error (RMSE) is used to compare the sampling analysis and the 4D-Var solution, relative to the reference solution, on each window. The analysis error, and the hybrid background error, covariance matrices at the beginning of the four assimilation windows, are also viewed and discussed.

The RMSE is given by

$$\mathbf{RMSE} = \sqrt{\frac{1}{\mathrm{N_{var}}} \sum_{i=1}^{\mathrm{N_{var}}} (x_i - x_i^{\mathrm{true}})^2}, \tag{12}$$

where $\mathbf{x}^{\mathrm{true}}$ is the reference solution, and $\mathbf{x}$ is the DA analysis (both propagated forward in time over the window). RMSEs are calculated over each window by

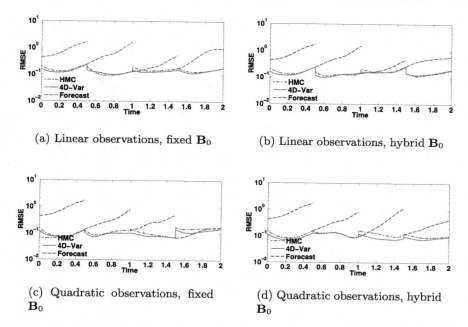

(a) Linear observations, fixed $\mathbf{B}_0$

(b) Linear observations, hybrid $\mathbf{B}_0$

(c) Quadratic observations, fixed $\mathbf{B}_0$

(d) Quadratic observations, hybrid $\mathbf{B}_0$

Fig. 1. Data assimilation results over four consecutive windows. RMSE results for HMC smoother, and 4D-Var, solutions are shown.

propagating the states, $\mathbf{x}$, and, $\mathbf{x}^{\mathrm{true}}$ using the full model and applying (12) along the trajectories. Figure 1 shows the RMSE (on a logarithmic scale) of the average of the ensemble generated by the HMC sampling scheme along with the conventional 4D-Var analysis and the forecast (*no assimilation*). The forecast trajectory here is generated by propagating the forecast state, generated by the HMC sampling algorithm, available at the beginning of each assimilation window along this window only. Using hybrid version of the background error covariance matrix, for linear observations (Fig. 1a,b), and quadratic observations (Fig. 1c,d), enhances the performance of both 4D-Var and the sampling algorithm. For example, the average RMSE for the HMC analysis on the last assimilation window reduces from 1.458×10^{-1} to 1.394×10^{-1} for linear observations, and reduces from 1.559×10^{-1} to 1.001×10^{-1} for quadratic observations. Also, the RMSE of the 4D-Var solution reduces from 1.363×10^{-1} to 1.249×10^{-1} for linear observations, and reduces from 1.239×10^{-1} to 8.492×10^{-2} for quadratic observations. Figures 2 and 3 show the contour plots of the hybrid (updated) background error covariance matrices throughout the four assimilation windows for both cases of the observation operator, the linear and the quadratic, consecutively.

As mentioned before, the analysis error covariance matrix is calculated from the analysis ensemble of the HMC sampling scheme and is not generally available in variational schemes. Figures 4, 5, 6 and 7 show contour plots of the analysis error covariance matrix obtained at the beginning of each of the four assimilation

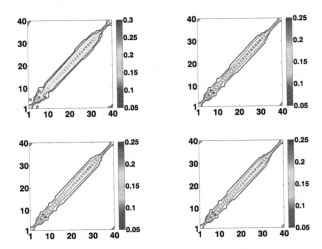

Fig. 2. Contour plots of the hybrid background error covariance matrix $\mathbf{B}_0$ for each of the four windows. Observations are Linear.

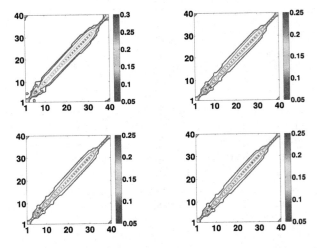

Fig. 3. Contour plots of the background error covariance matrix $\mathbf{B}_0$ for each of the four windows. Quadratic observations, and hybrid $\mathbf{B}_0$ are used.

windows. The results show that the developed sampling scheme is capable of generating analysis state that competes with the 4D-Var solution. Also, the forecast ensemble, generated by propagating the analysis ensemble members forward in time, yields a flow-dependent background error covariance matrix that enhances the performance of both 4D-Var and HMC sampling scheme.

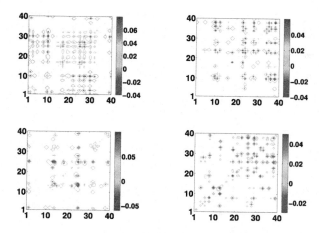

Fig. 4. Contour plots of the analysis error covariance matrices for each of the four windows. Linear observations, and fixed $\mathbf{B}_0$ are used.

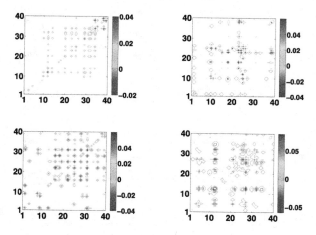

Fig. 5. Contour plots of the analysis error covariance matrices for each of the four windows. Linear observations, and hybrid $\mathbf{B}_0$ are used.

3.2   Computational Cost

We performed the 4D-Var optimization using Poblano toolbox [6]. The optimization required 54 gradient evaluations and 200 function evaluations in case of linear observations. Hundred gradient evaluations and 341 function evaluations with quadratic observations. Each function and gradient evaluation requires one forward model and one adjoint model run respectively. One adjoint model run costs approximately 2.5 times the cost of the forward model. The total cost of optimization for linear and quadratic observation operators are ≈ 335 and 600 forward model runs respectively. For the sampling scheme, 2 adjoint calls, per time-step, are needed by the Hamiltonian time integrator to generate a proposal

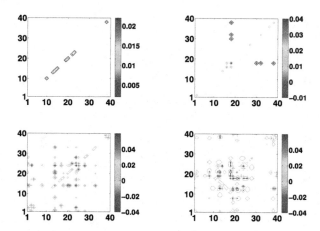

Fig. 6. Contour plots of the analysis error covariance matrices for each of the four windows. Quadratic observations, and fixed $\mathbf{B}_0$ are used.

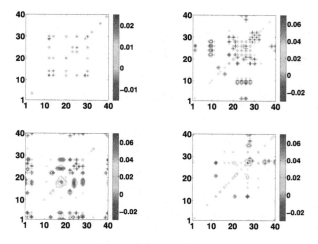

Fig. 7. Contour plots of the analysis error covariance matrices for each of the four windows. Quadratic observations, and hybrid $\mathbf{B}_0$ are used.

state. In this experiment, the number of time steps is 10. The total number of adjoint evaluations per proposal is 20. The cost to generate each ensemble member is ≈ 50 forward model runs for both linear and quadratic observations. An ensemble of 30 members, for example, would cost a total of ≈ 1500 (less than 3 times the cost of 4D-Var for quadratic observations).

4   Conclusion and Future Work

In this paper we have successfully applied hybrid Monte Carlo sampling to build a smoother for four-dimensional data assimilation. This methodology can be viewed as an alternative to 4D-Var data assimilation: while the variational app-roach provides a maximum a posteriori estimate, the sampling approach dis-cussed herein provides a minimum variance estimate. The results show that the minimum variance analysis obtained from the sampled states is at least as good as the conventional 4D-Var analysis. Propagating the analysis ensemble forward in time generates an ensemble of forecasts, that makes it easy to build a background error covariance matrix at the beginning of the next assimilation window. Unlike the hybrid approaches, the analysis covariance is consistent with the analysis state as they are produced by the same data assimilation procedure. The computational cost of the sampling scheme, compared to 4D-Var, suggests that it can be efficiently applied to practical models.

In future, we will apply this scheme to a large-scale imperfect model with non-Gaussianity assumptions.

Acknowledgements. This work was supported by AFOSR DDDAS program through the award AFOSR FA9550–12–1–0293–DEF managed by Dr. Frederica Darema.

References

1. Attia, A., Sandu, A.: A Sampling Filter for Non-Gaussian Data Assimilation. CoRR (2014). http://arxiv.org/abs/1403.7137.
2. Buehner, M., Houtekamer, P.L., Charette, C., Mitchell, H.L., He, B.: Intercom-parison of variational data assimilation and the ensemble Kalman Filter for global deterministic NWP. Part II: one-month experiments with real observations. Mon. Wea. Rev. **138**(5), 1567–1586 (2010)
3. Cheng, H., Jardak, M., Alexe, M., Sandu, A.: A hybrid approach to estimating error covariances in variational data assimilation. Tellus Ser. A - Dyn. Meteorol. Oceanogr. **62**(3), 288–297 (2010). Wiley Online Library
4. Chorin, A., Morzfeld, M., Tu, X.: Implicit particle filters for data assimilation. Commun. Appl. Math. Comput. Sci. **5**(2), 221–240 (2010)
5. Clayton, A.M., Lorenc, A.C., Barker, D.M.: Operational implementation of a hybrid ensemble/4d-var global data assimilation system at the met office. Q. J. R. Meteorol. Soc. **139**(675), 1445–1461 (2013)
6. Dunlavy, D.M., Kolda, T.G., Acar, E.: Poblano v1.0: a matlab toolbox for gradient-based optimization. Technical report - Sandia National Laboratories, Albuquerque, NM and Livermore, CA, March (2010)
7. Evensen, G., Van Leeuwen, P.J.: An ensemble Kalman smoother for nonlinear dynamics. Mon. Wea. Rev. **128**(6), 1852–1867 (2000)
8. Evensen, G.: The ensemble Kalman filter: theoretical formulation and practical implementation. Ocean Dyn. **53**(4), 343–367 (2003)
9. Evensen, G.: Data Assimilation: The Ensemble Kalman Filter. Springer, Heidelberg (2007)
10. Gustafsson, N., Bojarova, J.: Four-dimensional ensemble variational (4D-En-Var) data assimilation for the High Resolution Limited Area Model (HIRLAM). Nonlin. Process. Geophys. **21**(4), 745–762 (2014)
11. Hunt, B.R., Kalnay, E., Kostelich, E.J., Ott, E., Patil, D.J., Sauer, T., Szunyogh, I., Yorke, J.A., Zimin, A.V.: Four-dimensional ensemble Kalman filtering. Tellus A **56**(4), 273–277 (2004). Wiley Online Library

12. Liu, C., Xiao, Q., Wang, B.: An ensemble-based four-dimensional variational data assimilation scheme. Part II: observing system simulation experiments with advanced research WRF (ARW). Mon. Wea. Rev. **137**(5), 1687–1704 (2009)
13. Lorenz, E.N.: Predictability: a problem partly solved. In: Proceedings of Seminar on Predictability 1996, vol. 1 (1996)
14. Sandu, A., Cheng, H.: A Subspace Approach to Data Assimilation and New Opportunities for Hybridization (2014, submitted to)
15. Sondergaard, T., Lermusiaux, P.F.J.: Data assimilation with Gaussian mixture models using the dynamically orthogonal field equations. Part I. theory and scheme. Mon. Wea. Rev. **141**(6), 1737–1760 (2012)

Ensemble Learning in Non-Gaussian Data Assimilation

Hansjörg Seybold$^{(\boxtimes)}$, Sai Ravela$^{(\boxtimes)}$, and Piyush Tagade

Earth Signals and Systems Group, Earth, Atmospheric and Planetary Sciences
Massachusetts Institute of Technology, Cambridge, USA
{hseybold,ravela}@mit.edu

Abstract. The demand for tractable non-Gaussian Bayesian estimation has increased the popularity of kernel and mixture density representations. Here, using Gaussian Mixture Models (GMM), we posit that the reduction of total variance also remains an important objective in non-linear filtering, particularly in the presence of bias. We propose multi-objective estimation as an essential ingredient in data assimilation.

Using Ensemble Learning, two relatively weak estimators, namely the EnKF and Mixture Ensemble Filter (MEnF), are combined to produce a strong one. The Boosted-MEnF (B-MEnF) stacks MEnF and EnKF to mitigate bias and uses cascade generalization to reduce variance. In the Lorenz-63 model, it lowers mixture complexity without resampling and reduces posterior variance without increasing estimation error.

Our MEnF is a purely ensemble-based GMM filter with a reduced dimensionality burden and without ad-hoc ensemble-mixture member associations. It is expressed as a compact ensemble transform which enables efficient fixed-interval and fixed-lag smoothers (MEnS) as well as the B-MEnF/S.

Keywords: Data assimilation · Gaussian mixture models · Ensemble learning · Multi-objective assimilation · Non-linear filtering and smoothing · Non-Gaussian estimation

1 Introduction

Bayesian estimation is of interest to solve inference problems from models and data. In environmental state and parameter estimation, for example, fixed-point, fixed-interval or fixed lag problems are solved using sequential filters and smoothers. This includes classical schemes such as Kalman [10] filters and smoothers, and contemporary approaches including the Ensemble Kalman filter (EnKF) and smoother [7,16], Particle filter and smoother [2], and many popular variants [4] in between.

Sequential Bayesian state estimation can be viewed in three parts: (a) A *prediction* step which uses a model to propagate the state forward in time; (b) a *filtering* procedure where the current model state is updated recursively using

© Springer International Publishing Switzerland 2015
S. Ravela and A. Sandu (Eds.): DyDESS 2014, LNCS 8964, pp. 227–238, 2015.
DOI: 10.1007/978-3-319-25138-7_21

experimental observations up to the current time; and (c) a *smoothing* step which uses the current observations to update the model state at previous times.

However, many challenges to representation and reduction of uncertainty remain in sequential Bayesian estimation. One important issue is the tractability of inference in high-dimensional numerical models. Another is the emergence of non-Gaussian uncertainties in nonlinear processes, for example, as multimodal or heavy tailed distributions. To compound matters, grossly inadequate environmental observations decidedly complicate inference from data and models in many applications.

Current sequential Bayesian estimation practice offers two primary alternatives. On the one hand are rank-reduced, localized or multiscale ensemble Kalman filters and variants. These methods ease linearization issues and the use of Gaussian prior and likelihood yields direct state update equations. Recognizing the operational use of ensemble forecasts and the methods by which they are generated, the direct adjustment of individual ensemble members, often incorporating balance, appears to be beneficial. Nevertheless, the Gaussian assumption can be problematic, for example, for localized phenomena [15,17].

On the other hand, non-parametric Bayesian inference, notably the Particle Filter [2], can be attractive for non-Gaussian estimation but tractability in higher dimensions is challenging. The Environmental Systems Science community recognizes that efficient high-dimensional non-Gaussian estimation is essential in many applications. Emerging approaches to overcome these issues include kernel [11,14] and mixture density representations [1,8,18–20] in both information-theoretic [14] and classical estimation formulations.

The conceptual simplicity with which Gaussian Mixture Models (GMM) [13] apply to non-Gaussian estimation makes them potentially attractive for data assimilation [1]. In time dependent filtering, for example, it was proposed that propagated mixture element parameters be corrected with data [1]. However, identifying optimal mixture parameters and efficiently propagating and updating them remains problematic in high-dimensional systems. Recent approaches [19] dovetail efficient ensemble propagatation with mixture parameter updates to partially advance the methodology. Fully ensemble-based approaches [5,8,18] have the potential to advance further but remain hamstrung by ad-hoc ensemble-mixture association rules and ad-hoc balanced sampling rules. Clarity is lacking.

Another problem with GMM-based filtering is more insidious. Mixture modes are statistically estimated from ensemble members dispersed in the state space. The total variance includes the variance of the means which becomes significant as the number of mixture members increases. Current GMM-based filters have no representation for it. So, when model error manifests as a bias relative to the GMM modes, convergence can be extremely slow. Simple experiments show that beyond a very small bias, GMM performance is worse than the ensemble Kalman filter. In such a case, minimizing overall variance cannot be ignored, especially if estimating estimation uncertainty is also important. We posit that, in general, non-Gaussian estimation cannot lose sight of minimizing variance, particularly when our confidence in real-world models is low.

In this paper, we examine the role of mixture representations in the context of high-dimensional non-Gaussian Bayesian state estimation. We first present a Mixture Ensemble Filter (MEnF) which neither requires explicit moment representation nor relies on ad-hoc rules for association. Akin to the Ensemble Kalman Filter, MEnF is a compact ensemble transform which immediately enables a mixture ensemble smoother (MEnS).

We then formulate a Boosted Mixture Ensemble Filter (B-MEnF) that enables multi-objective, non-Gaussian Bayesian Estimation. Multiple weak estimators are combined to produce a strong one that simultaneously targets non-Gaussian estimation and overall variance reduction. In particular, we stack [21] a GMM with an EnKF estimator to overcome bias issues and use cascade generalization of the coupled estimator [9] to improve variance reduction. The posterior in B-MenF has lower complexity and smaller variance at the same level of estimation error than either GMM or EnKF, requiring no re-sampling in Lorenz 63 model experiments. B-MEnF is also expressible as a compact transform that enables efficient smoothing.

The remainder of this paper is organized as follows. The mixture ensemble filter and smoother results are discussed in Sect. 2. GMM is examined critically in Sect. 3, and the stacked-cascade ensemble filter is presented in Sect. 4. Finally, the paper is summarized and concluded in Sect. 5.

2   The Mixture Ensemble Framework

Consider a dynamical system $x_{t+\Delta t} = f(x_t, u_t)$, where $x_t, x_{t+\Delta t} \in \mathcal{R}^n$ is an n-dimensional discrete state vector and $f(\cdot, \cdot)$ is a possibly non-linear model with parameters u_t as inputs. For simplicity, the model is illustrated without "process noise", utilizing instead the epistemic uncertainties of the initial conditions as the primary source of uncertainty. Measurements $y_{t'} \in \mathcal{R}^m$ are assumed to be related by a linear or linearized observation equation $y_{t'} = H\hat{x}_{t'} + v_{t'}$ where $\hat{x}_{t'}$ is the *true* but unknown state vector, H is a measurement process, and $v_{t'} \sim \mathcal{N}(0, R)$ the (additive) Gaussian measurement uncertainty.

We are interested in both the filtering and smoothing problems, namely to quantify the distributions $p(x_t \mid y_{0:t})$ and $p(x_{0:t} \mid y_{0:t})$ respectively, and to seek to estimate their modes. For a Markov process, data can be assimilated sequentially, and the recursive nature of the estimation process allows us to consider the Bayesian "update" process at a single time instance, i.e.

$$p(x \mid y) \propto p(y \mid x)p(x). \tag{1}$$

Non-Gaussian priors are modeled as mixtures of Gaussians as defined by [13]

$$p(x; \theta) = \sum_{m=1}^{M} \alpha_m \ \mathcal{N}(x; \mu_m, P_m). \tag{2}$$

Here the parameter θ includes M, the number of mixture components, $\alpha_m = p(z_m)$ are the mixture weights representing the probability of a mixture element

z_m, and $\mathcal{N}(\boldsymbol{x}; \boldsymbol{\mu}_m, \boldsymbol{P}_m)$ are multivariate normal distributions with means $\boldsymbol{\mu}_m$ and covariances $\boldsymbol{P}_m$. The mixture weights are constrained by $\sum_{m=1}^{M} \alpha_m = 1$. Any ensemble member $\boldsymbol{x}_e$ has a finite probability of belonging to every other mixture element in a GMM. This fact is modeled through a weight vector,

$$\omega_{em} = \frac{\mathcal{N}(\boldsymbol{x}_e; \boldsymbol{\mu}_m, \boldsymbol{P}_m)\alpha_m}{\sum_{j=1}^{M} \mathcal{N}(\boldsymbol{x}_e; \boldsymbol{\mu}_j, \boldsymbol{P}_j)\alpha_j} \tag{3}$$

The GMM parameters are typically estimated using Maximum Likelihood Estimation (MLE)[1] via the Expectation Maximization (EM) [13]. The EM algorithm consists of two alternating steps: an expectation (E) step and a maximization (M) step. They are repeated until convergence for α_m, $\boldsymbol{\mu}_m$ and $\boldsymbol{P}_m$ is obtained. In the E-step, ω_{em} is computed while in the M-step, the optimal mixture parameters are estimated using ω_{em}. To calculate the mixture parameters, we first define $N_m = \sum_{e=1}^{N} \omega_{em}$ for an ensemble of size N, then write

$$\alpha_m = \frac{N_m}{N}; \quad \boldsymbol{\mu}_m = \frac{\sum_{e=1}^{N} \omega_{em}\boldsymbol{x}_e}{N_m}; \quad \boldsymbol{P}_m = \frac{\sum_{e=1}^{N} \omega_{em}\left(\boldsymbol{x}_e - \boldsymbol{\mu}_m\right)\left(\boldsymbol{x}_e - \boldsymbol{\mu}_m\right)^T}{N_m} \tag{4}$$

The EM algorithm assumes that the number of mixture components M is known which is seldom the case. Therefore, the number of mixture components M is estimated by using an information criterion. While several exist, the Bayesian Information Criterion (BIC) is used here. EM algorithm is run for different values of M, and the model with lowest best information criterion is chosen.

In time-dependent GMM-filtering, a measurement update follows density estimation. The mixture update can be synthesized by solving two inference problems. The first for "state" $p(\boldsymbol{x}|\boldsymbol{y})$ that yields the posterior means $\boldsymbol{\mu}_m^a$ and covariances P_m^a. Using $\mathcal{K}(\boldsymbol{P}_m^f)$ as a Kalman gain, we get:

$$\boldsymbol{\mu}_m^a = \boldsymbol{\mu}_m^f + \mathcal{K}(\boldsymbol{P}_m^f)\left(\boldsymbol{y} - \boldsymbol{H}\boldsymbol{\mu}_m^f\right); \qquad (\boldsymbol{P}_m^a)^{-1} = \left((\boldsymbol{P}_m^f)^{-1} + \boldsymbol{H}^T \boldsymbol{R}^{-1} \boldsymbol{H}\right) \tag{5}$$

The second step is parameter estimation $\alpha_m^a = p(z_m|\boldsymbol{y}) \propto \sum_e p(\boldsymbol{y}|\boldsymbol{x}_e)$ $p(\boldsymbol{x}_e|z_m)\alpha_m^f$ which yields the mixture weight update as a *convolution of two Gaussians*:

$$\alpha_m^a = \frac{\mathcal{N}\left(\boldsymbol{y}; \boldsymbol{H}\boldsymbol{\mu}_m^f, \boldsymbol{H}\boldsymbol{P}_j^f \boldsymbol{H}^T + \boldsymbol{R}\right)\alpha_m^f}{\sum_{j=1}^{M} \mathcal{N}\left(\boldsymbol{y}; \boldsymbol{H}\boldsymbol{\mu}_j^f, \boldsymbol{H}\boldsymbol{P}_j^f \boldsymbol{H}^T + \boldsymbol{R}\right)\alpha_j^f} \tag{6}$$

The parametric posterior distribution is sampled to produce a new ensemble and the filtering process repeats with a new density estimation step. This is the nominal approach which we call the GMM filter.

2.1   Application Example

We perform an identical twin experiment on a Lorenz-63 system [12]. The Lorenz model is a type of classic chaotic dynamical system consisting of three coupled,

---

[1] MAP problem can also be solved.

ordinary, differential equations in three dimensions. It is a simplified model for atmospheric convection [12].

$$\frac{\mathrm{d}x}{\mathrm{d}t} = \sigma(y - x), \quad \frac{\mathrm{d}y}{\mathrm{d}t} = x(\rho - z) - y, \quad \frac{\mathrm{d}z}{\mathrm{d}t} = xy - \beta z \qquad (7)$$

Here σ is the Prandl number, ρ the Raleigh number and β a geometric factor. Typical values for the parameters are $\sigma = 10$, $\rho = 28$ and $\beta = 8/3$. Equation 7 are integrated using an adaptive Runge Kutta 45 scheme with convergence error of 10^{-7}. The system is integrated forward for $T = 100$ time units from a random initial condition to remove transients. An ensemble is then initialized with 1000 members and a very small offset of 0.0001 and variance 0.01. Measurements are obtained over a long time interval of $\Delta T = 2.5$ time units. The typical model timestep is automatically determined but of O(0.01).

The Lorenz system exhibits two chaotic attractors causing the statistics of particle trajectories to be bimodal at very long timescales. Even at the integration time scale used here, the distribution of ensemble members is non-Gaussian (see Fig. 1). The measurement errors are constructed as being normally distributed with variance 2.0 in each dimension.

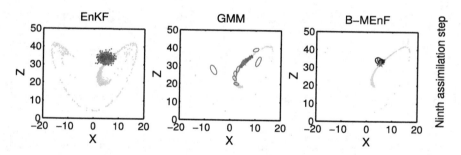

Fig. 1. A comparison of EnKF, GMM and stacked-cascade Mixture Ensemble filter(B-MEnF) shows that B-MEnF forecast ensemble is less dispersed, and its posterior variance is smaller as assimilation continues. BMenF identifies two closely spaced posterior modes and GMM returns multiple, of which only one has significant weight.

Figure 1 presents the filter results in a 2D X-Z projection for EnKF (left column), GMM (middle column) at the first assimilation (top) step and after nine assimilation cycles (bottom). The right column shows the result of B-MEnF that is developed later in Sect. 4. The predicted point cloud is shown in light gray and the posterior point cloud is depicted by dark points. The probability contours are indicated by solid lines. The truth is marked by a red star.

Initially, a Gaussian model works as well as the mixture model but, as the attractor structure becomes highly non-Gaussian, the EnKF forecast ensemble members are far more dispersed, suggesting that the GMM better constrains the uncertainty over time. Here, we regularize EM by a convex combination of the two smallest eigen values of the forecast error covariance; this provides reasonable GMM clusters. We note that there is a marked sensitivity to the regularization parameter. As the posterior ensemble point cluster depicts, filtering with Gaussian measurement noise leaves (see Eq. 4) one dominant posterior mode. Figure 2 quantitatively shows that the GMM is with lower variance and complexity even if the estimation error (using MAP estimate) is comparable to EnKF.

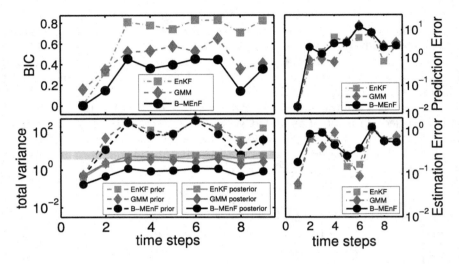

Fig. 2. BIC (top-left), total variance (bottom-left), estimation error (bottom-right), and prediction error (top-right) of all methods. Noise variance marked as gray stripe.

The GMM approach is promising and, if dimensionality issues are reduced, it will be a practical advance. This is possible using an ensemble approach. In so doing, other issues are also addressed. For example, as figure Fig. 1 shows, the posterior mixture can suffer from degeneracy; many posterior mixture elements reduce to negligible weight. This can get "cleaned up" at the next density estimation but is still an inappropriate analysis. The mixture ensemble reformulation presented in the next section easily solves such problems.

2.2   Compact Mixture Ensemble Transform: MEnF/S

Several attempts have been made at ensemble formulations. Bengtsson et al. [3] propose clustering and individual Kalman updates based on cluster membership. Smith [18] uses EM with BIC but projects the GMM onto an approximate posterior Gaussian distribution. Dovera and Rossa [5] sample an index according to the posterior mixture weight and update the corresponding ensemble member using EnKF. Frei and Kunsch [8] extend this scheme by using balanced sampling to determine the ensemble member for update. Although dimensionality issues could be reduced by these methods, the tussle for managing ensemble members' associations with mixture elements is evident.

The tussle is not necessary, as we show here. The mixture filter can be expressed as a compact ensemble transform that needs no ad hoc association rules, and the posterior ensemble can be resampled using effective sample size measures [2] akin to the particle filter.

In the density estimation step that preceds filtering, EM can be made tractable by noting that $\mathbf{S}_m = \frac{1}{\sqrt{N_m}} W_{\frac{1}{2}m} \circ \tilde{\mathbf{A}}_m$ is a reduced-rank square-root of $\mathbf{P}_m = \mathbf{S}_m \mathbf{S}_m^T$. Here $W_{\frac{1}{2}m}(i, e) = \sqrt{w}_{em}$, $\tilde{\mathbf{A}}_m$ is the matrix of ensemble perturbations from mixture m's mean, and $\circ$ denotes the Schur product. EM Gaussian evaluations and updates can be carried out in square-root form.

For the measurement update, there are two equations. The first is a solution to $p(\boldsymbol{x}|\boldsymbol{y})$ using the ensemble mean as a constraint, so that:

$$\boldsymbol{x}_e^a \equiv \boldsymbol{x}_e + \sum_{m=1}^{M} \{\mathcal{K}(\mathbf{P}_m)\,(\boldsymbol{d}_{em} - \boldsymbol{H}\omega_{em}\boldsymbol{x}_e)\} \tag{8}$$

Here $\boldsymbol{d}_{em} = \omega_{em}\boldsymbol{y}$ without perturbed observations and $\boldsymbol{d}_{em} = \alpha_m \boldsymbol{y}_e$ with perturbed observations. This is different from Tagade's earlier proposal [14]. It has not been shown before.

The second equation is for the posterior weights, obtained by solving for $w_{em}^a = p(z_m|\boldsymbol{x}_e, \boldsymbol{y}) \propto p(\boldsymbol{y}|\boldsymbol{x}_e)p(\boldsymbol{x}_e|z_m)p(z_m)$ analogously to Eq. 3. It can also be evaluated without explicitly constituting covariances. The posterior ensemble and weights can be evaluated for effective sample size [2] and resampled to avoid sample degeneracy.

Of course, posterior moments (via reduced-rank square-root forms) can also be occasionally sampled to avoid sample impoverishment and so can other practical approaches, e.g., breeding. Interestingly, however, no deviation in inference methodology ensues. After a forward numerical integration, the EM algorithm always identifies a new distribution from the ensemble pattern that emerges. In this way, the GMM-filter shares the advantages of a particle filter but exploiting the parametric GMM form enables direct ensemble adjustment without running into dimensionality issues. This is significant and in a form that has not hitherto been shown.

Even more interestingly, the ensemble update is a compact transform:

$$A^a = A^f \sum_{m=1}^{M} \varXi_m \circ (W_m^N)^T = A^f \varXi \tag{9}$$

A^f is the forecast ensemble, A^a is the estimated ensemble and $W_m^N(1 : N, e) = w_{em}$. The compact matrix $\varXi$ in ensemble size $N \times N$ in the sense of Evensen [7] is a nonlinear transformation of the prediction. We call this the Mixture Ensemble Filter (MEnF) that has not hitherto been shown in this form.

As a compact ensemble transform, MEnF immediately enables the derivation of a fast mixture ensemble smoother (MEnS) akin to EnKS [7]. The smoother

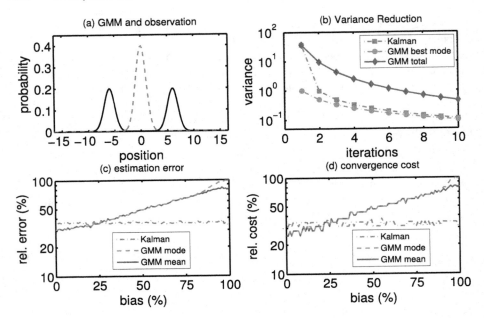

Fig. 3. Bi-modal example depicts worsening GMM estimation error with bias because it does not account for the variance of the means; see text.

analysis A_k^s at time step k, nominally expressed as $A_k^s = A_k^a \prod_{i=k+1}^{L} \Xi^{(i)}$ in a window L ahead of k. In fixed interval smoothing, L extends to the interval endpoint and in fixed-lag, up to some lead time ahead. We point out that, as Ravela and McLaughlin [16] showed, the smoothing equation can be reformulated via recursion so that fixed interval estimation is of order $O(L)$ for interval L via a forward-backward pass, and fixed-lag estimation is of order $O(1)$ via a first-in-first out queue. For limitations in space, the smoother form is not further explored. The compact transform form of MEnF/S has other advantages that subsequent sections will develop.

3   The Importance of Variance Reduction

Despite these advances in GMM filtering, there are fundamental unsolved issues. The Lorenz example was constructed with a very small bias where it was always reasonable to expect a dominant mixture mode in the vicinity of truth. However, if this identification is not possible, a fundamental problem of mixture models becomes obvious. When the observations are noisy, the dominant mixture mode estimated by filtering (see Eq. 4) can "chatter" between measurement intervals thus slowing convergence. Similarly, a misalignment between the mixture's modes and truth is a bias that can arise due to an imperfect model, an impoverished ensemble, incorrect EM regularization, sensitivity of GMM density estimation, or a large ensemble dispersion, among other factors. Although it is beyond the scope of this paper to probe each of these bias-inducing factors, it is easy to study bias' net effect on GMM estimation, described in the following synthetic experiment.

Consider a bimodal prior with mean at zero. The modes are positioned at $\mu_m = \pm 6\sigma$ with a variance of $\sigma_m^2 = 1$ each of weight $\alpha_m = 0.5$, see Fig. 3(a). Imagine now a measurement of truth somewhere in between (dotted line). When the truth is aligned with one of the modes, the bias is zero and when the measurement lies in between the two mixture modes, we define the bias as 100 %.

In this simple problem, consider the truth to be stationary and use a trivial forward model $\dot{x} = 0$, and a measurement with noise variance $\sigma_r^2 = 1$. For comparison, we also run a Kalman filter with a prior variance equal to the total variance of the GMM, $\sigma^2 = \sum_m \alpha_m((\mu_m - \mu)^2 + \sigma_m^2)$. Once a measurement is obtained, a posterior distribution is calculated. Because truth is stationary[2], we expect some convergence in the estimated mean and covariance for each filter. We track the estimation error over five filtering iterations in each trial and repeatedly conduct a large number of trials to acquire statistics.

With increasing bias, the GMM on average performs far worse than the EnKF. Figure 3(c) shows the average normalized RMS estimation error comparing the Kalman estimate's posterior mean, the GMM's dominant mode, and its mean, respectively, with truth. Figure 3(d) shows that the convergence to an 80 % reduction in error is also much slower.

The reason for this is quite simple. Even if the best posterior mode has slightly lower variance than the EnKF, the estimation error increases because the total variance, which includes the variance of the means, is not accounted for (see Fig. 3(b)). As a result, the filter converges slower under bias and with a larger estimation error. On the other hand, the EnKF has a larger initial Kalman gain and therefore rapidly reduces overall variance to the asymptotic estimation error. Thus, the total error is smaller. Clearly, as the modes fragment, GMM filter loses track of the total variance. This is particularly damning when model errors are present, a situation that is almost always the case in the real world. For a system with low bias, however, the GMM performance is impressive in the accuracy with which it tracks the non-Gaussian nature of the uncertainty, as seen in the Lorenz example.

Can non-Gaussian Bayesian estimation also minimize total variance? In the next section, we show how multiple objectives can be accomplished through Ensemble Learning.

4 Ensemble Learning with a Stacked Cascade

One way to incorporate global variance reduction in the GMM approach is to build a hierarchical mixture model where each GMM targets variance at a different scale. Finally, the outputs of the individual estimators are combined. Here,

---

[2] Note that this problem is not the same as a Wiener filtering problem.

we use a simple version of this general idea. Our approach starts with an ensemble propagated to the filtering step where density estimation is about to be performed.

We assume that the different estimators used during a measurement update are based on differences in prior probability density (mass) functions. Each such estimator is *weak* in some way, meaning that it performs poorly on the applied model. For example, EnKF cannot represent non-Gaussian predictions while the GMM does not account for the variance of the means. Ensemble Learning, here referring to an ensemble of estimators, offers a possible approach to produce better estimators by combining weaker ones.

A variety of methods including bagging, boosting, cascading, stacking and Bayesian model averaging, among others, are feasible in principle but cannot fully be discussed in this paper. Here, we select two techniques: stacking [21] or stacked generalization, and cascaded generalization [9]. The base estimators are the GMM and EnKF where the latter may trivially be thought of as a GMM with only one mixture. The resulting combined estimator B-MEnF, combining the two using the "stacked cascade", outperforms either one. We discuss this approach in the following section and illustrate it on a Lorenz-63 example.

4.1   Stacked Regression and Cascaded Generalization

From a machine learning perspective, estimators can be viewed as (possibly nonlinear) regression machines. This framework, though unusual within data assimilation, is nevertheless useful. Multiple regression machines form an ensemble of regression machines (ERM), each of which produces an estimate. The purpose of "Learning" is to combine them in a meaningful way. In this paper, we will only consider two such machines, $\mathcal{M}_g$ for the GMM and $\mathcal{M}_e$ for the EnKF respectively, each represented by a compact ensemble transform.

By interpreting the ensemble of numerical model predictions as training data, a bootstrap sample can typically be extracted along with measurements, perturbed if needed, to "train" the regression machines in the ERM (i.e., estimate their parameters). We then apply each machine to the full ensemble, the test data, and combine individual outputs to produce a composite posterior ensemble.

The architecture for combining the two machines used here is shown in Fig. 4. This is an iterative process where stacking is used at each stage [21] to combine the outputs followed by a cascaded generalization [9] on new machines trained from the outputs. During stacking, the "meta learner" combines the outputs by selecting the regression machine with the lower error with respect to perturbed measurements (the truth is unknown) [6]; a higher posterior can also be used. Cascading can be terminated when the model complexity of the estimated GMM on posterior ensemble no longer improves. Typically, two to three cascade iterations are needed. Note that each stacking stage can also be written as a compact ensemble transform. Cascading is, therefore, a product of ensemble transforms. Thus, smoother form B-MEnS is enabled akin to MEnS.

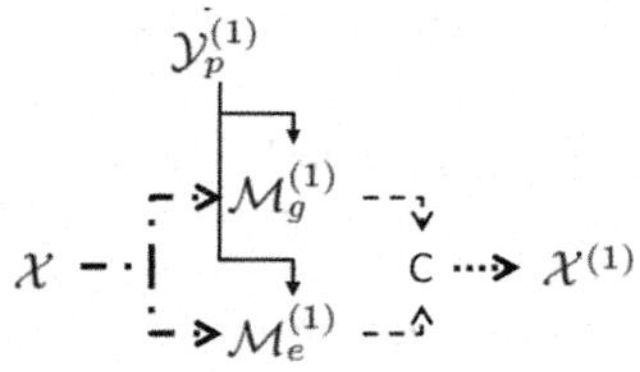

$$\mathcal{Y}_p^{(1)}$$

$$\mathcal{X} - \cdot \begin{array}{c} - \triangleright \boxed{\mathcal{M}_g^{(1)}} - - \smallsetminus \\ \qquad \qquad C \cdots \triangleright \mathcal{X}^{(1)} \\ - \triangleright \mathcal{M}_e^{(1)} - - \smallfrown \end{array}$$

Fig. 4. The Stacked-cascade approach is shown for a single iteration. Stacked generalization consists of $\mathcal{M}_e$ and $\mathcal{M}_g$ which are combined by picking the posterior ensemble member with lower error. A cascade of stacked machines are used with perturbed observations in training and testing, and with a bootstrap ensemble for training.

The motivation for stacked generalization and cascaded generalization stems from the fact that the former is a bias reducing approach (multiple probability-models to reduce overall estimation bias) and the cascade reduces variance. These ideas have been applied to a variety of problems though, to the best of our knowledge, their use in data assimilation application is new. It is argued that the combination of bootstrap sampling with perturbed measurements prevents overfitting; this is a common approach in many randomized learning problems. Neverthless, some caution must be exercised in this regard.

In Fig. 1, we compare the results of the three filters: EnKF, GMM and stacked cascade. All three estimators produce comparable estimates (when the most probable ensemble member is compared to truth), with the GMM tracking the attractor structure slightly better than EnKF.

Without any resampling whatsoever, B-MEnF produces posterior GMMs of lower complexity, lower variance, and lower dispersion than EnKF or GMM alone. The lower variance is the best so far and with explicit representation of non-Gaussianity. In the Lorenz-63 example (Fig. 1), the posterior GMM has two elements.

5   Conclusions

Whilst mixture approaches seem promising for non-Gaussian estimation, they actually perform worse than EnKF in the presence of bias. The absence of a total variance objective is the culprit. The proposed MEnF reduces dimensionality issues and mitigates sampling problems. The compact mixture ensemble transform directly enables smoothing, a new standard for nonlinear, non-Gaussian filtering and smoothing. Furthermore, it allows constructing B-MEnF/S. B-MenF, a stacked-cascade ensemble learner, reduces uncertainty better than either GMM or EnKF alone and, in experiments here, it needed no resampling. We posit that Ensemble Learning (analogous to multi-model ensembles) can be an efficient way to deal with model error and bias in non-Gaussian systems, even in high dimensions. In ongoing work, we study the generalization of data assimilation to model errors using ensemble learning.

References

1. Alspach, D.L., Sorenson, H.W.: Nonlinear bayesian estimation using Gaussian sum approximations. IEEE Trans. Autom. Control. **17**, 439–448 (1972)
2. Arulampalam, M.S., Maskell, S., Gordon, N., Clapp, T.: A tutorial on particle filters for online nonlinear/non-Gaussian bayesian tracking. IEEE Trans. Signal Proc. **50**(2), 174–188 (2002)
3. Bengtsson, T., Snyder, C., Nychka, D.: Toward a nonlinear ensemble filter for high-dimensional systems. J. Geophys. Res. **108**, 8775 (2003)
4. Choi, S.C., Wette, R.: Maximum likelihood estimation of the parameters of the gamma distribution and their bias. Technometrics **11**, 683–690 (1969)
5. Dovera, L., Rossa, E.D.: Multimodal ensemble kalman filtering using Gaussian mixture models. Comput. Geosci. **15**, 307–323 (2011)
6. Dzeroski, S., Zenko, B.: Is combining classifiers better than selecting the best one? Mach. Learni. **54**(3), 255–273 (2004). Morgan Kaufmann
7. Evensen, G.: The ensemble kalman filter: theoretical formulation and practical implementation. Ocean Dyn. **53**, 343–367 (2003)
8. Frei, M., Kunsch, H.R.: Mixture ensemble kalman filters. Comput. Stat. Data Anal. **58**, 127–138 (2013)
9. Gama, J., Brazdil, P.: Cascade generalization. Mach. Learn. **41**(3), 315–343 (2000)
10. Gelb, A.: Applied Optimal Estimation. The MIT Press, Cambridge (1974)
11. Hoteit, I., Pham, D.T., Triantafyllou, G., Korres, G.: A new approximate solution of the optimal nonlinear filter for data assimilation in meteorology and oceanography. Mon. Wea. Rev. **136**, 317–334 (2008)
12. Lorenz, E.N.: Deterministic nonperiodic flow. J. Atmos. Sci. **20**, 130–141 (1963)
13. McLachlan, G.J., Krishnan, T.: The EM Algorithm and Extensions. Wiley, Hoboken (2008)
14. Tagade, P.M., Ravela, S.: A quadratic information measure for data assimilation. In: American Control Conference 2014, Portland, USA (2014)
15. Ravela, S., Emanuel, K., McLaughlin, D.: Data assimilation by field alignment. Phys. D **230**, 127–145 (2007)
16. Ravela, S., McLaughlin, D.: Fast ensemble smoothing. Ocean Dyn. **57**, 123–134 (2007)
17. Ravela, S.: Spatial inference for coherent geophysical fluids by appearance and geometry. In: Winter Conference on Applications of Computer Vision (2014)
18. Smith, K.W.: Cluster ensemble kalman filter. Tellus **59**, 749–757 (2007)
19. Sondergaard, T., Lermusiaux, P.F.J.: Data assimilation with Gaussian mixture models using dynamically orthogonal field equations. Part 1. Theory and scheme. Mon. Wea. Rev. **141**, 1737–1760 (2013)
20. Tagade, P., Seybold, H., Ravela, S.: Mixture ensembles for data assimilation in dynamic data-driven environmental systems. In: Proceedings of the International Conference on Computational Science, ICCS 2014, Cairns, Queensland, Australia, pp. 1266–1276, 10–12 June 2014
21. David, H.W.: Stacked generalization. Neural Netw. **5**, 241–259 (1992)

Variational Data Assimilation Based on Derivative-Free Optimization

Elias D. Nino[1,2]([⊠]) and Adrian Sandu[1]

[1] Computational Science Laboratory, Computer Science Department,
Virginia Tech, Room 2201, KnowledgeWorks II Bldg. 2202 Kraft Dr,
Blacksburg, VA 24061, USA
enino@vt.edu, asandu@cs.vt.edu
http://csl.cs.vt.edu/
[2] Computer Science Department, Universidad del Norte, KM5 Via Puerto Colombia,
Barranquilla, ATL, Colombia
enino@uninorte.edu.co

Abstract. This study develops a hybrid ensemble-variational approach for solving data assimilation problems. The method, called TR-4D-EnKF, is based on a trust region framework and consists of three computational steps. First an ensemble of model runs is propagated forward in time and snapshots of the state are stored. Next, a sequence of basis vectors is built and a low-dimensional representation of the data assimilation system is obtained by projecting the model state onto the space spanned by the ensemble deviations from the mean. Finally, the low-dimensional optimization problem is solved in the reduced-space using a trust region approach; the size of the trust region is updated according to the relative decrease of the reduced order surrogate cost function. The analysis state is projected back onto the full space, and the process is repeated with the current analysis serving as a new background. A heuristic approach based on the trust region size is proposed in order to adjust the background error statistics from one iteration to the next. Experimental simulations are carried out using the Lorenz 96 model. The results show that TR-4D-EnKF is an efficient computational approach, and is more accurate than the current state of the art 4D-EnKF implementations such as the POD-4D-EnKF and the Iterative Subspace Minimization methods.

Keywords: Trust region · 4D-EnKF · Hybrid methods

1 Introduction

Data assimilation [SC11] is the process of estimating the true state $\mathbf{x}_M^{\text{true}} \in \mathbb{R}^n$ of a dynamical system at the current time t_M given a history of prior evolution and noisy observations of the state at times t_k

$$\mathbf{y}_k = \mathcal{H}_k\left(\mathbf{x}_k^{\text{true}}\right) + \boldsymbol{\epsilon}_k \in \mathbb{R}^{m \times 1}, \quad 0 \leq k \leq M. \tag{1}$$

Here n is the number of components in the model state, m is the number of observed components from $\mathbf{x}^{\text{true}}$, $\mathcal{H}_k : \mathbb{R}^n \to \mathbb{R}^m$ is the observation operator,

© Springer International Publishing Switzerland 2015
S. Ravela and A. Sandu (Eds.): DyDESS 2014, LNCS 8964, pp. 239–250, 2015.
DOI: 10.1007/978-3-319-25138-7_22

$\epsilon_k \in \mathbb{R}^{m \times 1}$ is the error associated to the k-th observation time, and M is the number of observation times. Typically, observational errors are assumed to be normal distributed $\epsilon_k \sim \mathcal{N}(\mathbf{0}_m, \mathbf{R}_k)$ where $\mathbf{0}_m$ is the m-th dimensional vector whose components are all zeros, and $\mathbf{R}_k \in \mathbb{R}^{m \times m}$ is the data error covariance matrix at the assimilation time t_k.

A dynamical model encapsulating our knowledge of the physical laws approximates the evolution of the dynamical system. The evolution of the model state $\mathbf{x}$ is given by

$$\mathbf{x}_{k+1} = \mathcal{M}_{t_k \to t_{k+1}}(\mathbf{x}_k), \quad 0 \le k \le M - 1, \tag{2}$$

where $\mathcal{M}$ represents a nonlinear model solution operator (e.g., which simulates the evolution of the ocean or the atmosphere).

Two families of methods, statistical filters and variational, are widely used to solve data assimilation problems. Representative methods of those classes are the Ensemble Kalman Filter (EnKF) and the Four-Dimensional Variational Method (4D-Var), respectively. In EnKF an ensemble of model runs is propagated in time; when data is available the filtering step generates an *analysis ensemble* whose empirical mean is an estimator for $\mathbf{x}^{\text{true}}$. Strong constraint 4D-Var seeks an *analysis initial state* such that the corresponding forecast best fits the observations within the assimilation window. It is well-accepted that both methods face specific challenges in practical applications where $n \sim 10^9$. For instance, ensemble-based filters suffer from statistical sampling errors, while variational methods require adjoint models which are labor-intensive to develop and computationally expensive to run.

Hybrid methods have been proposed in order to combine the strengths of EnKF and 4D-Var methods. The theoretical similarities between the two approaches have been used to construct look-ahead assimilation techniques [SH13]. Other hybrid approaches are based on model reduction and/or space reduction [CNF11]. In this paper, we focus on the reduced-space approach where a subspace of the state space is identified, the variational problem is solved in this subspace, then the analysis is projected back onto the model space. The new solution can be treated as a new background and the process is repeated.

In this work we formulate a hybrid data assimilation algorithm in the context of derivative-free optimization. A rigorous Trust Region (TR) framework is proposed where the TR radius in the model space is linked with the spread of the ensemble members and with the quality of the solutions found in the reduced-space. The new method is named TR-4D-EnKF. The remainder of the paper is organized as follows. Section 2 reviews the current state of the art ensemble-based approaches to data assimilation. Section 3 develops the novel derivative free TR-4D-EnKF method. Numerical results using the Lorenz-96 are reported in Sect. 4, and conclusions are presented in Sect. 5.

2   Four-Dimensional Ensemble-Based Approaches to Data Assimilation

EnKF [Eve09a] is one of the most widely used methods in data assimilation due to its simple formulation and ease of implementation. Normality assumptions are made on both the background and data errors [Eve09b]. The method contains two steps, the forecast and the analysis.

The *prior* (background) distribution is approximated by an ensemble of $N+1$ model state samples

$$\mathbf{X}_0 = \left[\mathbf{x}_0^{b(1)}, \mathbf{x}_0^{b(2)}, \ldots, \mathbf{x}_0^{b(N+1)} \right] \in \mathbb{R}^{n \times (N+1)}, \tag{3}$$

with the empirical moments

$$\overline{\mathbf{x}}_0 = \frac{1}{N+1} \cdot \sum_{i=1}^{N+1} \mathbf{x}_0^{b(i)} \in \mathbb{R}^{n \times 1}, \tag{4a}$$

$$\mathbf{S}_0 = \frac{1}{N} \cdot \boldsymbol{\delta} \mathbf{X}_0 \cdot \boldsymbol{\delta} \mathbf{X}_0^T \in \mathbb{R}^{n \times n}, \tag{4b}$$

where $\mathbf{x}_0^{b(i)}$ is the i-th ensemble member and the columns of matrix $\boldsymbol{\delta} \mathbf{X}_0 \in \mathbb{R}^{n \times (N+1)}$ are given by $\boldsymbol{\delta} \mathbf{x}_0^{(i)} = \mathbf{x}_0^{b(i)} - \overline{\mathbf{x}}_0$, for $1 \le i \le N+1$. Prior any measurement, the background state $\mathbf{x}_0^b \approx \overline{\mathbf{x}}_0$ provides the best estimation to $\mathbf{x}_0^{true}$.

In the forecast step the background ensemble (3) is obtained by an ensemble of model runs that propagate each model state to the current time t_k.

In the analysis step a *posterior* (analysis) ensemble is constructed by making use of the observation $\mathbf{y}_k$ and by applying the Kalman filter to each background ensemble member:

$$\mathbf{x}_k^{a(i)} = \mathbf{x}_k^{b(i)} + \mathbf{K} \left[\mathbf{y}_k^{s(i)} + \boldsymbol{\epsilon}_k^{s(i)} - \mathbf{H}_k \cdot \mathbf{x}_k^{b(i)} \right], \quad 1 \le i \le N+1, \tag{5}$$

where $\mathcal{H}_k' = \mathbf{H}_k \in \mathbb{R}^{m \times n}$ is a linearized observation operator at time t_k, $\mathbf{y}_k^{s(i)} \sim \mathcal{N}(\mathbf{y}_k, \mathbf{R}_k)$ are the observations $\mathbf{y}_k$ with added synthetic noise $\boldsymbol{\epsilon}_k^{s(i)} \sim \mathcal{N}(\mathbf{0}_m, \mathbf{R}_k)$, and the Kalman gain matrix is $\mathbf{K} = \mathbf{S}_k \cdot \mathbf{H}_k^T \left[\mathbf{H}_k \cdot \mathbf{S}_k \cdot \mathbf{H}_k^T + \mathbf{R}_k \right]^{-1} \in \mathbb{R}^{n \times m}$. The ensemble members are further propagated in time

$$\mathbf{x}_{k+1}^{b(i)} := \mathcal{M}_{t_k \to t_{k+1}} \left(\mathbf{x}_k^{a(i)} \right), \tag{6}$$

to obtain the background ensemble for the forecast step. EnKF can provide flow-dependent error estimates of the background errors using a Monte Carlo approach [NSA12,NRSA14], but it does not have the ability to assimilate the observation data available at distributed times.

4D-Var considers cost functions of the form

$$\mathcal{J}(\mathbf{x}_0) = \underbrace{\frac{1}{2} \left\| \mathbf{x}_0 - \mathbf{x}_0^b \right\|_{\mathbf{B}_0^{-1}}^2}_{\mathcal{J}^b(\mathbf{x})} + \underbrace{\frac{1}{2} \sum_{k=0}^{M} \left\| \mathbf{y}_k - \mathcal{H}(\mathbf{x}_k) \right\|_{\mathbf{R}_k^{-1}}^2}_{\mathcal{J}^o(\mathbf{x})}, \tag{7}$$

where $\mathcal{J}^b(\mathbf{x})$ and $\mathcal{J}^o(\mathbf{x})$ are known as the background and observation cost functions, respectively. The cost function (7) is the negative logarithms of the a posteriori probability density when all the data and background errors are normally distributed. The maximum likelihood estimate of the initial state is then obtained by minimizing the cost function, i.e., the analysis step is computed by solving the optimization problem

$$\mathbf{x}_0^{\text{a}} = \arg\min_{\mathbf{x}_0} \mathcal{J}(\mathbf{x}_0) \qquad \text{subject to (2).} \tag{8}$$

The formulation of (7) allows 4D-Var to assimilate data which appears at different observation times.

The computation of the gradient (7) with respect to the control variable $\mathbf{x}_0 \in \mathbb{R}^{n \times 1}$ requires one forward and one adjoint model integration. The construction of an adjoint model for real, large forecast models is an extremely labor-intensive process. In order to avoid the implementation of adjoint models four dimensional ensemble Kalman filter methods (4D-EnKF) [ZZ11] have been recently proposed. They naturally propagate flow dependent background covariance matrices via ensembles. Numerical experiments show robust performance with a small number of ensemble members [YMW+13, THL+13]. Moreover, the solution (8) can be treated as the new background state in (7), which provides a better solution [CCF+13].

4D-EnKF based methods are defined as follows. The initial ensemble (3) is propagated in time and $M + 1$ snapshots of each background ensemble member state at time moments $t_0, t_1, \ldots, t_M$ along the trajectory are stored

$$\mathbf{X}^s = \begin{bmatrix} \mathbf{x}_0^{b(1)} & \mathbf{x}_0^{b(2)} & \cdots & \mathbf{x}_0^{b(N+1)} \\ \mathbf{x}_1^{b(1)} & \mathbf{x}_1^{b(2)} & \cdots & \mathbf{x}_1^{b(N+1)} \\ \vdots & \vdots & \ddots & \vdots \\ \mathbf{x}_M^{b(1)} & \mathbf{x}_M^{b(2)} & \cdots & \mathbf{x}_M^{b(N+1)} \end{bmatrix} \in \mathbb{R}^{(n \cdot (M+1)) \times (N+1)}. \tag{9}$$

Each entry of the background ensemble matrix $\mathbf{X}^s$ is an n-dimensional vector $\mathbf{x}_k^{b(i)}$ which represents the state of ensemble member i at time t_k. The i-th column of $\mathbf{X}^s$ contains all the snapshots of the i-th ensemble member, and the k-th row of blocks corresponds to all ensemble member states at t_k.

Consider now a trajectory of the model. The state $\mathbf{x}_k$ at t_k is approximated by a linear combination of the anomalies (deviations from the mean)

$$\mathbf{x}_k = \overline{\mathbf{x}}_k + \sum_{i=1}^{N} \alpha_i \cdot \underbrace{\left(\mathbf{x}_k^{b(i)} - \overline{\mathbf{x}}_k \right)}_{\psi_k^{(i)}} = \overline{\mathbf{x}}_k + \boldsymbol{\Psi}_k \cdot \boldsymbol{\alpha}, \tag{10}$$

where $\overline{\mathbf{x}}_k = \frac{1}{N+1} \cdot \sum_{i=1}^{N+1} \mathbf{x}_k^{b(i)} \in \mathbb{R}^{n \times 1}$, $\boldsymbol{\Psi}_k = \left[\psi_k^{(1)}, \psi_k^{(2)}, \ldots, \psi_k^{(N)} \right] \in \mathbb{R}^{n \times N}$ and the time-independent weight vector $\boldsymbol{\alpha} = [\alpha_1, \alpha_2, \ldots, \alpha_N]^T \in \mathbb{R}^{N \times 1}$, contains the coordinates of $\mathbf{x}_k$ in the ensemble space.

By replacing (10) in (7) and linearizing the observation operator $\mathcal{H}_k \approx \mathbf{H}_k$, the 4D-Var cost function (7) can be written in the ensemble space as follows:

$$\mathcal{J}_{\mathrm{ens}}(\boldsymbol{\alpha}) = \frac{1}{2} \left\| \mathbf{d}^{\mathrm{b}} - \boldsymbol{\Psi}_0 \cdot \boldsymbol{\alpha} \right\|_{\mathbf{B}_0^{-1}}^2 + \frac{1}{2} \sum_{k=0}^{M} \left\| \mathbf{d}_k^{\mathrm{o}} - \mathbf{Q}_k \cdot \boldsymbol{\alpha} \right\|_{\mathbf{R}_k^{-1}}^2 \tag{11}$$

where $\mathbf{d}^{\mathrm{b}} = \mathbf{x}_0^{\mathrm{b}} - \overline{\mathbf{x}}_0 \in \mathbb{R}^{n \times 1}$ and $\mathbf{d}_k^{\mathrm{o}} = \mathbf{y}_k - \mathbf{H}_k \cdot \overline{\mathbf{x}}_k \in \mathbb{R}^{m \times 1}$ are the innovation vectors on the background and observations, respectively, and $\mathbf{Q}_k = \mathbf{H}_k \cdot \boldsymbol{\Psi}_k \in \mathbb{R}^{m \times N}$.

The optimal solution in the ensemble space

$$\boldsymbol{\alpha}^* = \arg\min_{\boldsymbol{\alpha}} \mathcal{J}_{\mathrm{ens}}(\boldsymbol{\alpha}) \in \mathbb{R}^{N \times 1}, \tag{12}$$

provides an approximation of the analysis trajectory started from (8) through the relation

$$\mathbf{x}_k^{\mathrm{a}} = \mathbf{x}_k^{\mathrm{b}} + \boldsymbol{\Psi}_k \cdot \boldsymbol{\alpha}^* \in \mathbb{R}^{n \times 1}. \tag{13}$$

The derivatives of (11) are

$$\nabla_{\boldsymbol{\alpha}} \mathcal{J}_{\mathrm{ens}}(\boldsymbol{\alpha}) = \left[\boldsymbol{\Psi}_0^T \cdot \mathbf{B}_0^{-1} \cdot \boldsymbol{\Psi}_0 + \sum_{k=0}^{M} \mathbf{Q}_k^T \cdot \mathbf{R}_k \cdot \mathbf{Q}_k \right] \cdot \boldsymbol{\alpha} \tag{14a}$$

$$- \left[\boldsymbol{\Psi}_0^T \cdot \mathbf{B}_0^{-1} \cdot \mathbf{d}^{\mathrm{b}} + \sum_{k=0}^{M} \mathbf{Q}_k^T \cdot \mathbf{R}_k^{-1} \cdot \mathbf{d}_k \right] \in \mathbb{R}^{N \times 1},$$

$$\nabla_{\boldsymbol{\alpha},\boldsymbol{\alpha}}^2 \mathcal{J}_{\mathrm{ens}}(\boldsymbol{\alpha}) = \boldsymbol{\Psi}_0^T \cdot \mathbf{B}_0^{-1} \cdot \boldsymbol{\Psi}_0 + \sum_{k=0}^{M} \mathbf{Q}_k^T \cdot \mathbf{R}_k \cdot \mathbf{Q}_k \in \mathbb{R}^{N \times N}, \tag{14b}$$

and the solution of the quadratic minimization problem (12) is

$$\boldsymbol{\alpha}^* = \nabla_{\boldsymbol{\alpha},\boldsymbol{\alpha}}^2 \mathcal{J}_{\mathrm{ens}}(\boldsymbol{\alpha})^{-1} \cdot \left[\boldsymbol{\Psi}_0^T \cdot \mathbf{B}_0^{-1} \cdot \mathbf{d}^{\mathrm{b}} + \sum_{k=0}^{M} \mathbf{Q}_k^T \cdot \mathbf{R}_k^{-1} \cdot \mathbf{d}_k \right]. \tag{15}$$

Since $\mathbf{x}_k^{\mathrm{a}}$ in (13) represents an approximated solution rather than an exact solution, the initial analysis $\mathbf{x}_0^{\mathrm{a}}$ is only recovered and propagated in time in order to obtain an approximation of the optimal trajectory of (7).

Equivalent bases for the range of $\boldsymbol{\Psi}_k$ can be utilized to formulate the subspace approximation (10). For instance, the proper orthogonal decomposition (POD) [TXD08] is widely used to obtain a basis that captures most of the variance of the snapshot (9). Consider the matrix of snapshots deviations

$$\delta \mathbf{X}^s = \frac{1}{\sqrt{N}} \left[\boldsymbol{\Psi}_0^T, \boldsymbol{\Psi}_1^T, \ldots, \boldsymbol{\Psi}_M^T \right]^T \in \mathbb{R}^{(n \cdot (M+1)) \times N},$$

and its singular value decomposition (SVD) $\delta \mathbf{X}^s = \mathbf{U} \cdot \boldsymbol{\Sigma} \cdot \mathbf{V} \in \mathbb{R}^{(n \cdot (M+1)) \times N}$, where $\mathbf{U} \in \mathbb{R}^{(n \cdot (M+1)) \times (n \cdot (M+1))}$ and $\mathbf{V} \in \mathbb{R}^{N \times N}$ are the right and left singular vectors, respectively, and $\Sigma = \mathrm{diag}\{\sigma_1, \sigma_2, \ldots, \sigma_N\} \in \mathbb{R}^{(n \cdot (M+1)) \times N}$ is a diagonal matrix whose diagonal entries are the singular values with $\sigma_1 \geq \sigma_2 \geq \ldots \geq \sigma_N$. Since $\delta \mathbf{X}^{sT} \cdot \delta \mathbf{X}^s = \mathbf{V} \cdot \mathbf{\Sigma}^2 \cdot \mathbf{V}^T \in \mathbb{R}^{N \times N}$, the POD basis vectors can be computed as $\mathbf{\Phi}_k = \mathbf{\Psi}_k \cdot \mathbf{V} \cdot \Sigma^{-1/2} \in \mathbb{R}^{n \times N}$ and therefore, equivalent to (12), $\mathbf{x}_k$ can be expressed as follows:

$$\mathbf{x}_k = \overline{\mathbf{x}}_k + \sum_{i=1}^{r} \beta_i \cdot \left(\frac{\mathbf{\Psi}_k \cdot \mathbf{v}_i}{\sqrt{\sigma_i}} \right) = \overline{\mathbf{x}}_k + \mathbf{\Phi}_k^r \cdot \boldsymbol{\beta} , \tag{16}$$

where we have chosen the columns of $\mathbf{\Sigma}$ to be orthonormal, $\mathbf{\Phi}_k^r$ holds the first r basis vectors, $\boldsymbol{\beta} = [\beta_1, \beta_2, \ldots, \beta_r]^T \in \mathbb{R}^{r \times 1}$ is the vector of weights to be determined, and r can be computed as follows

$$r = \arg \min_p \left\{ p, I(p) : \frac{\sum_{i=1}^{p} \sigma_i}{\sum_{i=1}^{N} \sigma_i} > \gamma : \gamma \in (0, 1) \right\} . \tag{17}$$

Note that, the parameter γ provides how much variance we want to retain in the POD bases. POD bases reduce the Eq. (11) to

$$\mathcal{J}_{\mathrm{ens}}^{\mathrm{POD}} (\boldsymbol{\beta}) = \frac{1}{2} \cdot N \cdot \|\boldsymbol{\beta}\|^2 + \frac{1}{2} \cdot \sum_{k=0}^{M} \|\mathbf{d}_k - \mathbf{Z}_k \cdot \boldsymbol{\beta}\|_{\mathbf{R}_k^{-1}}^2 , \tag{18}$$

whose first and second derivatives are

$$\nabla_{\boldsymbol{\beta}} \mathcal{J}_{\mathrm{ens}}^{\mathrm{POD}} (\boldsymbol{\beta}) = \left[N \cdot \mathbf{I}_{r \times r} + \sum_{k=0}^{M} \mathbf{Z}_k^T \cdot \mathbf{R}_k^{-1} \cdot \mathbf{Z}_k \right] \cdot \boldsymbol{\beta}$$
$$- \sum_{k=0}^{M} \mathbf{Z}_k^T \cdot \mathbf{R}_k^{-1} \cdot \mathbf{d}_k \in \mathbb{R}^{r \times 1} , \tag{19a}$$

$$\nabla_{\boldsymbol{\beta}, \boldsymbol{\beta}}^2 \mathcal{J}_{\mathrm{ens}}^{\mathrm{POD}} (\boldsymbol{\beta}) = N \cdot \mathbf{I}_{r \times r} + \sum_{k=0}^{M} \mathbf{Z}_k^T \cdot \mathbf{R}_k^{-1} \cdot \mathbf{Z}_k \in \mathbb{R}^{r \times r} , \tag{19b}$$

where $\mathbf{Z}_k = \mathbf{H}_k \cdot \mathbf{\Phi}_k$ and $\mathbf{I}_{r \times r}$ is the identity matrix of dimension $r \times r$. Thus, an equivalent problem to (12) is

$$\boldsymbol{\beta}^* = \arg \min_{\boldsymbol{\beta}} \mathcal{J}_{\mathrm{ens}}^{\mathrm{POD}}(\boldsymbol{\beta}) \in \mathbb{R}^{r \times 1} , \tag{20}$$

whose solution reads:

$$\boldsymbol{\beta}^* = \nabla_{\boldsymbol{\beta}, \boldsymbol{\beta}}^2 \mathcal{J}_{\mathrm{ens}}^{\mathrm{POD}} (\boldsymbol{\beta})^{-1} \cdot \left[\sum_{k=0}^{M} \mathbf{Z}^{(k)T} \cdot \mathbf{R}_k^{-1} \cdot \mathbf{d}_k \right] . \tag{21}$$

The optimal solution of the POD-4D-EnKF provides an approximation of the analysis (8). The process can be continued in an iterative fashion in order to improve the analysis; the solution of one iteration becomes the new background state for the next iteration. The idea of using a sequence of minimizations of the surrogates (11) or (18) in order to approach the minimum of (7) has been explored in the derivative-free optimization literature [CSV09]. For instance, the *Iterative Subspace Minimization* (ISM) method makes use of this strategy [GLS13].

The Trust Region (TR) framework can be employed in order to exploit the information brought by the derivatives of the ensemble cost functions (11) and (18) and to provide descent directions. One of the most attractive features of TR methods is that they are provably globally convergent under general assumptions [CGT00a, CGT00b, CGT00c]. This work develops a TR-based approach which performs a sequence of optimizations in ensemble spaces. The ensemble based partial solutions are linked to the full space solutions at each iteration. The background error statistics of the estimates obtained at each iteration are linked to the TR radius size and the spread of the underlying ensemble. The new method enjoys all these properties and is presented in the next section.

3   The TR-4D-EnKF Method

In this section we develop a Trust Region 4D-EnKF (TR-4D-EnKF) approach to data assimilation. The method uses two nested loops. Outer iterations are related to forming and running an ensemble of full-size models and generating a basis. Inner iterations are related to computing search directions in the low dimensional space and minimizing the reduced cost function (7). For simplicity of notation we avoid the use of indices that denote outer iteration numbers and refer to the current and next iterations only.

The initial solution in the model space is given by the initial approximation of the background $\mathbf{x}_0^{[\text{current}]} = \mathbf{x}_0^b$, from which the initial ensemble (3) is built. We initialize the vector of weights to $\boldsymbol{\alpha} = \mathbf{0}_N$.

In order to solve the numerical optimization problem (8) we build a quadratic model for the cost function (7) optimization process. The standard approach makes use of the full space gradient, and possibly Hessian, of (7). We seek to avoid the implementation of a full adjoint model to compute exact derivatives. The idea is to approximate the derivatives of $\mathcal{J}(\mathbf{x})$ by the ensemble space derivatives (14a) and Hessian (14b). The resulting quadratic model is:

$$\mathcal{Q}(\mathbf{s}_{\boldsymbol{\alpha}}) = \mathcal{J}_{\text{ens}}(\boldsymbol{\alpha}) + \mathbf{s}_{\boldsymbol{\alpha}}^T \nabla_{\boldsymbol{\alpha}} \mathcal{J}_{\text{ens}}(\boldsymbol{\alpha}) + \frac{1}{2} \mathbf{s}_{\boldsymbol{\alpha}}^T \nabla_{\boldsymbol{\alpha},\boldsymbol{\alpha}}^2 \mathcal{J}_{\text{ens}}(\boldsymbol{\alpha}) \mathbf{s}_{\boldsymbol{\alpha}} . \tag{22}$$

The optimal step $\mathbf{s}_{\boldsymbol{\alpha}}^*$ in the ensemble space is given by the solution of the constrained optimization sub-problem

$$\mathbf{s}_{\boldsymbol{\alpha}}^* = \arg\min_{\mathbf{s}_{\boldsymbol{\alpha}}} \mathcal{Q}(\mathbf{s}_{\boldsymbol{\alpha}}), \tag{23a}$$

$$\text{subject to } \|\boldsymbol{\Psi}_0 \cdot (\boldsymbol{\alpha} + \mathbf{s}_{\boldsymbol{\alpha}})\| \leq \Delta . \tag{23b}$$

The trust region constraint (23b) is formulated such as to use the trust region radius Δ from the full model space.

The solution of (23a) and (23b) provide the following trial point in the ensemble space $\boldsymbol{\alpha}^{\text{trial}} = \boldsymbol{\alpha} + \mathbf{s}_{\alpha}{}^*$ which corresponds to the following state in the model space

$$\mathbf{x}_0^{\text{trial}} = \mathbf{x}_0^{\text{current}} + \underbrace{\boldsymbol{\Psi}_0 \cdot \overbrace{(\boldsymbol{\alpha} + \mathbf{s}_{\alpha}{}^*)}^{\boldsymbol{\alpha}^{\text{trial}}}}_{\delta \mathbf{x}^*} . \tag{24}$$

Then, $M + 1$ snapshots of the full model solution started from $\mathbf{x}_0^{\text{trial}}$ (24) are stored. The following ratio is computed:

$$\rho = \frac{\mathcal{J}\left(\mathbf{x}^{\text{current}}\right) - \mathcal{J}\left(\mathbf{x}^{\text{trial}}\right)}{\mathcal{Q}\left(\mathbf{0}_N\right) - \mathcal{Q}\left(\mathbf{s}_{\alpha}{}^*\right)} = \frac{\mathcal{J}\left(\mathbf{x}^{\text{current}}\right) - \mathcal{J}\left(\mathbf{x}^{\text{trial}}\right)}{\mathcal{J}_{\text{ens}}\left(\boldsymbol{\alpha}\right) - \mathcal{J}_{\text{ens}}\left(\boldsymbol{\alpha}^{\text{trial}}\right)} . \tag{25}$$

Based on the ρ value, the next updates are made for the solution

$$\left(\mathbf{x}^{\text{current}}, \boldsymbol{\alpha}\right) := \begin{cases} \left(\mathbf{x}^{\text{current}}, \boldsymbol{\alpha}\right) & \text{for } \rho \le \eta, \\ \left(\mathbf{x}^{\text{trial}}, \boldsymbol{\alpha}^{\text{trial}}\right) & \text{otherwise}, \end{cases} \tag{26}$$

and for the TR radius size

$$\Delta := \begin{cases} \Delta \cdot \gamma_{\text{dec}} & \text{for } \rho < \theta_1, \\ \Delta & \text{for } \theta_1 \le \rho < \theta_2 \text{or } \rho > 1, \\ \min\left(\Delta \cdot \gamma_{\text{inc}}, \Delta_{\max}\right) & \text{for } \theta_2 \le \rho \le 1. \end{cases} \tag{27}$$

The new solutions in the model and ensemble space are utilized and a new optimization problem in (23a) is solved. This process is repeated until a maximum number of inner iterations is reached or a full step is taken. Next, the current solution becomes the new background $\mathbf{x}_0^{\text{b}} := \mathbf{x}_0^{\text{current}}$, a new ensemble of full model solutions is generated, snapshots are taken, a new set of basis vectors is built, and the overall process is repeated.

The uncertainty associated with the new background is changed after the inner iterations since a partial assimilation of observations has been carried out. As an analogy, in the EnKF the spread of the ensemble members around the background is decreased after the analysis step. Consequently, before generating a new ensemble, we want to adjust the spread of the background errors. This is done according to the heuristic formula

$$\mathbf{B}_0 := \lambda_{\mathbf{B}}(\Delta) \cdot \mathbf{B}_0 , \tag{28}$$

where $\lambda_{\mathbf{B}}(\Delta)$ is a function of the current TR radius size. Note that the TR radius is large when the decrease of the current (quadratic) model is a good predictor of the full model function decrease. In our context, if the dynamics of the full (nonlinear) model is well represented by the ensemble, the prediction done using the quadratic model $\mathcal{Q}(\mathbf{s}_{\alpha})$ is close to the actual reduction of the cost function $\mathcal{J}(\mathbf{x})$ and the TR radius is increased. In this case, we want the $\lambda_{\mathbf{B}}(\Delta)$ value to be small in order to decrease the uncertainty of the new ensemble around $\mathbf{x}_0^{\text{b}}$.

Vice-versa, a small TR radius indicates that the current set of basis vectors does not represent well the dynamics of the model. The current assimilation step is not expected to decrease uncertainty; to keep the same uncertainty level for the next ensemble generation we need $\lambda_{\mathbf{B}}(\Delta) \approx 1$. Both cases are captured by the following heuristic function

$$\lambda_{\mathbf{B}}(\Delta) = \frac{\Delta_{\max}}{\Delta_{\max} + \Delta}, \tag{29}$$

which provides an inverse relation between the TR radius and the spread of the ensemble members. Other functions can be considered as well.

Now we are ready to test our implementation and compare it with other 4D-EnKF implementations discussed in Sect. 2.

4   Numerical Experiments

In this section we study the accuracy and performance of the TR-4D-EnKF approach. The proposed implementation is compared with the 4D-EnKF implementations discussed in Sect. 2 (POD, SVD and ISM), using the Lorenz-96 model [CSV13]:

$$\frac{dx_i}{dt} = \begin{cases} (x_2 - x_n) \cdot x_n - x_1 + \varphi & \text{for } i = 1, \\ (x_{i+1} - x_{i-2}) \cdot x_{i-1} - x_i + \varphi & \text{for } 2 \leq i \leq n - 1, \\ (x_1 - x_{n-2}) \cdot x_{n-1} - x_n + \varphi & \text{for } i = n, \end{cases} \tag{30}$$

All the methods are coded in MATLAB. The metrics used in the tests are the CPU time (which is reported per iteration), the cost function value (7), and the root mean square error. The experimental setting is described below.

- One time unit of the Lorenz-96 model corresponds to 1.5 days of the atmosphere.
- Snapshots are taken every 1.5 days over 150 days.
- The true (reference) initial solution $\mathbf{x}_0^{\text{true}}$ is computed numerically.
- Errors in the initial background follow the distribution $\mathcal{N}(\mathbf{0}, 0.05 \cdot \mathbf{I})$, where $\mathbf{I} \in \mathbb{R}^{n \times n}$ is the identity matrix in the model space.
- The number of ensemble members is equal to $N = 40$.
- Three model resolutions n are considered: small ($n = 10^3$), medium ($n = 10^4$), and large ($n = 10^5$). In all the cases, the full model space is observed.
- Observations are taken every day over 100 days (100 time units) At each observation time, the error on the measurements is 1 %.
- The number of outer loops for the ISM and TR-4D-EnKF is equal to 100.
- The initial parameters for the TR-4D-EnKF are $\gamma_{\text{inc}} = 1.01$, $\gamma_{\text{dec}} = 0.99$, $\Delta_{\max} = 20$, $\Delta_0 = 0.1$, $\eta = 0.1$, $\theta_1 = 0.25$ and $\theta_2 = 0.75$.

Table 1 the accuracy and the computational effort for several 4D-EnKF implementations applied to the Lorenz-96 model are shown in. All data assimilation methods provide improvements over the background case. POD-4D-EnKF

Table 1. Cost function values, RMSE, and CPU times for different 4D-EnKF implementations applied to the Lorenz-96 model. After 100 of outer iterations, the proposed TR implementation provides the most accurate results within a reasonable computational time per iteration.

n	4D-EnKF method	$\mathcal{J}(\mathbf{x})$	RMSE	CPU time/iter.
10^3	Background	2.2250×10^7	6.6623	N/A
	POD	4.2737×10^6	2.9072	21.97 s
	ISM	2.7937×10^5	0.6782	15.83 s
	TR	6.6009×10^4	0.1860	16.33 s
10^4	Background	1.8497×10^8	19.2080	N/A
	POD	5.4845×10^7	10.4290	29.17 s
	ISM	1.3560×10^7	5.1129	22.20 s
	TR	1.5994×10^6	1.4928	32.48 s
10^5	Background	1.7709×10^9	59.4288	N/A
	POD	3.3592×10^8	25.7407	127.74 s
	ISM	1.4964×10^8	17.0213	133.46 s
	TR	3.5433×10^7	7.8282	206.46 s

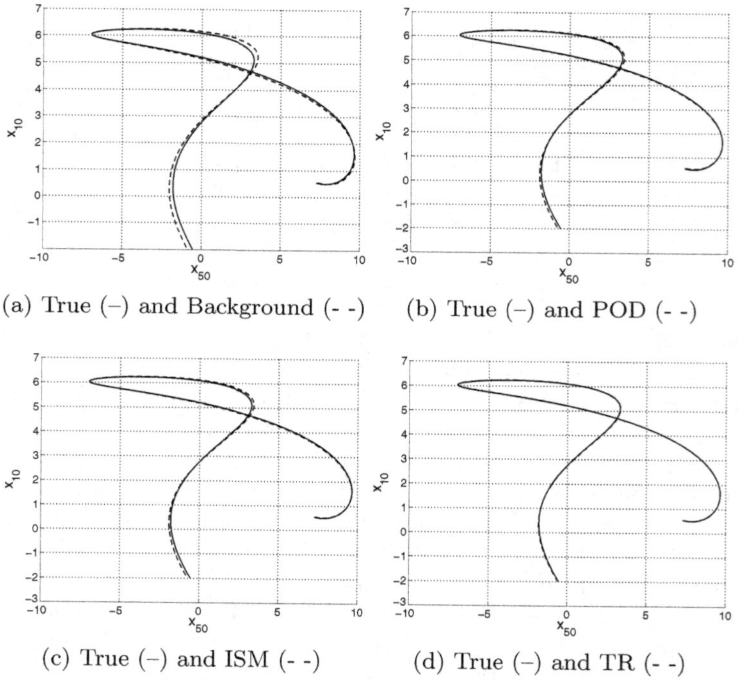

(a) True (–) and Background (- -)

(b) True (–) and POD (- -)

(c) True (–) and ISM (- -)

(d) True (–) and TR (- -)

Fig. 1. Snapshots of the 4D-EnKF implementations POD, SVD, ISM, and TR for the model resolution $n = 10^5$. The x_{50} and x_{10} components are plot for each method (- -) and the true solution (–).

performs a single outer iteration and its analysis improves the RMSE over the background by ~56 %. The ISM method takes a more complex approach and adjusts the set of POD-basis vectors at each outer iteration. On average the ISM analyses after 100 of iterations improve the RMSE by ~80 % over the background. The TR-4D-EnKF implementation provides a more accurate solution with the same number of outer iterations. On average, the proposed implementation improves the RMSE over the background trajectory by 92 %. The TR-4D-EnKF analysis provides the best fit to the reference solution as can been in Fig. 1 for $n = 10^5$. The TR-4D-EnKF compute solutions within a reasonable computational time; it is about as expensive as ISM for the small case and about 50 % more expensive than ISM for the largest case. This is acceptable in view of the higher accuracy allowed by the method.

5 Conclusions

This paper develops TR-4D-EnKF, an ensemble-based 4D-Var data assimilation method based on the trust region framework. The proposed implementation projects the model space onto the space spanned by the deviations of the ensemble members from the mean, as is typically done in 4D-EnKF implementations. Small optimization problems are solved in the ensemble space. At each outer iteration a new ensemble-based surrogate model of the 4D-Var cost function is constructed, and the convergence is controlled by the trust region method. The trust region radius connects the optimal solution found in the ensemble space with the corresponding solution in the full model space. Moreover, the evolution of error statistics throughout iterations are captured by an empirical relation that uses the changes in trust region radius as a proxy for uncertainty decrease. Experimental results shows that the proposed implementation provides more accurate results than some of the best 4D-EnKF implementations available in the literature within a reasonable computational effort.

Acknowledgments. This work was supported in part by awards NSF CCF–1218454, AFOSR FA9550–12–1–0293–DEF, AFOSR 12-2640-06, and by the Computational Science Laboratory at Virginia Tech.

References

[CCF+13] Candiani, G., Carnevale, C., Finzi, G., Pisoni, E., Volta, M.: A comparison of reanalysis techniques: applying optimal interpolation and ensemble Kalman filtering to improve air quality monitoring at mesoscale. Sci. Total Environ. **458**, 7–14 (2013)

[CGT00a] Conn, A.R., Gould, I.M., Toint, P.L.: Global convergence of the basic algorithm, chapter 6. In: Trust Region Methods. MOS-SIAM Series on Optimization, pp. 115–168 (2000)

[CGT00b] Conn, A.R., Gould, I.M., Toint, P.L.: The Trust-region subproblem, chapter 7. In: Trust Region Methods. MOS-SIAM Series on Optimization, pp. 169–248 (2000)

[CGT00c] Conn, A.R., Gould, I.M., Toint, P.L.: Further convergence theory issues, chapter 8. In: Trust Region Methods. MOS-SIAM Series on Optimization, pp. 249–306 (2000)

[CNF11] Chen, X., Navon, I.M., Fang, F.: A dual-weighted trust-region adaptive POD 4D-Var applied to a finite-element shallow-water equations model. Int. J. Numer. Methods Fluids **65**(5), 520–541 (2011)

[CSV09] Conn, A.R., Scheinberg, K., Vicente, L.N.: Introduction to Derivative-Free Optimization. MPS-SIAM Book Series on Optimization. Society for Industrial Mathematics, Philadelphia (2009)

[CSV13] Conn, A.R., Scheinberg, K., Vicente, L.N.: The Lorenz Equations: Bifurcations, Chaos, and Strange Attractors. Springer, New York (2013)

[Eve09a] Evensen, G.: Rank issues. In: Evensen, G. (ed.) Data Assimilation: The Ensemble Kalman Filter, Chapter 14, pp. 210–237. Springer, Heidelberg (2009)

[Eve09b] Evensen, G.: The ensemble Kalman filter for combined state and parameter estimation. IEEE Control Syst. **29**(3), 83–104 (2009)

[GLS13] Gratton, S., Laloyaux, P., Sartenaer, A.: Derivative-free optimization for large-scale nonlinear data assimilation problems. Q. J. Roy. Meteorol. Soc. **140**, 943–957 (2013)

[NRSA14] Nino-Ruiz, E.D., Sandu, A., Anderson, J.: An efficient implementation of the ensemble Kalman filter based on an iterative Sherman-Morrison formula. Stat. Comput. **25**, 561–577 (2014)

[NSA12] Niño, E., Sandu, A., Anderson, J.L.: An Effcient implementation of the ensemble Kalman filter based on iterative Sherman Morrison formula. Procedia Comput. Sci. **9**, 1064–1072 (2012)

[SC11] Sandu, A., Chai, T.F.: Chemical data assimilation–an overview. Atmosphere **2**(3), 426–463 (2011)

[SH13] Sandu, A., Cheng, H.A.: Subspace approach to data assimilation and new opportunities for hybridization. Int. J. Uncertainty Quantification (2013, submitted)

[THL+13] Triantafyllou, G., Hoteit, I., Luo, X., Tsiaras, K., Petihakis, G.: Assessing a robust ensemble-based Kalman filter for efficient ecosystem data assimilation of the Cretan sea. J. Mar. Syst. **125**(SI), 90–100 (2013)

[TXD08] Tian, X., Xie, Z., Dai, A.: An ensemble-based explicit four-dimensional variational assimilation method. J. Geophys. Res. Atmos. **113**(D21), 1984–2012 (2008)

[YMW+13] Yussouf, N., Mansell, E., Wicker, L., Wheatley, D., Stensrud, D.: The ensemble Kalman filter analyses and forecasts of the 8 May 2003 Oklahoma City Tornadic supercell storm using single- and double-moment microphysics schemes. Mon. Weather Rev. **141**(10), 3388–3412 (2013)

[ZZ11] Zhang, M., Zhang, F.: E4DVar: coupling an ensemble Kalman filter with four-dimensional variational data assimilation in a limited-area weather prediction model. Mon. Weather Rev. **140**(2), 587–600 (2011)

Aspects of Particle Filtering
in High-Dimensional Spaces

Peter Jan van Leeuwen[✉]

Data Assimilation Research Centre (DARC), University of Reading, Reading, UK
p.j.vanleeuwen@reading.ac.uk

Abstract. Nonlinear data assimilation is high on the agenda in all fields of the geosciences as with ever increasing model resolution and inclusion of more physical (biological etc.) processes, and more complex observation operators the data-assimilation problem becomes more and more nonlinear. The suitability of particle filters to solve the nonlinear data assimilation problem in high-dimensional geophysical problems will be discussed. Several existing and new schemes will be presented and it is shown that at least one of them, the Equivalent-Weights Particle Filter, does indeed beat the curse of dimensionality and provides a way forward to solve the problem of nonlinear data assimilation in high-dimensional systems.

1 Introduction

There is a growing need for nonlinear data-assimilation methods for high dimensional systems. This is evidenced by the inclusion of more and more nonlinear processes in the systems at hand. Also more and more indirect observations are being utilised, leading quite often to highly nonlinear relations between model space and observation space.

Several nonlinear data-assimilation methods based on Metropolis-Hastings have been generated, including Langevin-sampling, Hybrid Monte-Carlo, and more efficient extensions, but all have in common that they are extremely inefficient: one first has to generate large numbers of samples to converge to the correct posterior probability density function (pdf), and then several samples have to be generated for each independent sample of the posterior. The former problem can be eliminated by using techniques from inverse modelling, like the commonly used variational schemes, e.g. 4Dvar, but the latter remains an unresolved issue.

Particle filters are another branch of nonlinear data assimilation methods, but have long been though of as very inefficient too because of the so-called curse of dimensionality, in which it is claimed that the number of particles needed to generate a few samples from the high-probability areas of the posterior grows exponentially with the dimension of the state vector (Snyder et al. 2008; Van Leeuwen 2009). This is due to the highly peaked likelihood in high-dimensions, leading to particle weights varying widely, with a few particles having much

© Springer International Publishing Switzerland 2015
S. Ravela and A. Sandu (Eds.): DyDESS 2014, LNCS 8964, pp. 251–262, 2015.
DOI: 10.1007/978-3-319-25138-7_23

higher weight than all the others. Even the so-called 'optimal proposal density' particle filters suffer from this problem. It should be noticed that it is not the dimension of the state space that is the problem, but the dimension of the observation space. The higher this last dimension, the more peeked the likelihood is, and the more unlikely it is for the majority of particles to end up close to all of them (see Ades and Van Leeuwen 2013).

However, it has recently been shown that this problem can easily be avoided by construction by leading the particles towards the observations and at the same time forcing them into position in state space such that they have weights very close to each other (Van Leeuwen 2009; 2010, Ades and Van Leeuwen 2013; 2015a; 2015b).

In this short paper we will discuss several existing and new particle filter variants and discuss their relative merits and problems. A very simple numerical example will be used to show that at least one particle filter exists that does beat the curse of dimensionality, the so-called Equivalent-Weights Particle Filter. The paper is closed with a summary and discussion of possible future directions in nonlinear filtering.

2   The Standard Particle Filter

Starting from Bayes Theorem:

$$p(x|y) = \frac{p(y|x)}{p(y)}p(x) \tag{1}$$

in which $x \in \Re^d$ is the state vector and $y \in \Re^M$ is the observation vector, we introduce a representation of the prior $p(x)$ as a sum of particles:

$$p(x) = \frac{1}{N}\sum_{i=1}^{N}\delta(x - x_i) \tag{2}$$

to find for the posterior:

$$p(x|y) = \sum_{i=1}^{N}w_i\delta(x - x_i) \tag{3}$$

in which we introduced the likelihood weights

$$w_i = \frac{1}{N}\frac{p(y|x_i)}{\sum_{j=1}^{N}p(y|x_j)} \tag{4}$$

To derive this we used the expansion

$$p(y) = \int p(y|x)p(x)\,dx \tag{5}$$

These weights measure how close each particle is to all observations. The issue in high-dimensional systems, or rather high-dimensional observation spaces, is that independent observations lead to very highly peaked likelihoods. A simple example will illustrate this nicely. Suppose we have two particles, and both are very close to all observations. We assume that the observation errors are independent Gaussian distributed and that the first particle is 0.1 standard deviations away from *all* observations, and the other particle is 0.2 standard deviations from all observations. This is of course highly artificial, but it will illustrate the point. The weight of particle one will be

$$w_1 \propto \exp\left[-\frac{1}{2}(y - H(x_1))R^{-1}(y - H(x_1))\right] = \exp(-0.005M) \qquad (6)$$

in which M is the number of independent observations, and we explored the independence of the observations. Similarly, the weight of particle two will be

$$w_2 \propto \exp\left[-\frac{1}{2}(y - H(x_2))R^{-1}(y - H(x_2))\right] = \exp(-0.02M) \qquad (7)$$

The ratio of these two weights is

$$\frac{w_2}{w_1} = \exp(-0.015M) \qquad (8)$$

Assuming the number of independent observations to be 1000, a moderate number for the geosciences, we find that this ratio is about 10^{-7}! Hence we see that even though the two particles are both doing extremely well, the likelihood is so strongly peaked that one particle has negligible weight compared to the other. Clearly something is needed to save the particle filter, and that is the so-called proposal density. This is explained in detail in e.g. Doucet et al. (2001), see also Van Leeuwen (2009) and will not be repeated here. The basic idea is that instead of drawing samples directly from the prior $p(x)$, we draw the samples from another density $q(x|y)$ where we explicitly include a dependence on the observations. We can always do this as long as we adapt the weights, as follows:

$$p(x|y) = \frac{p(y|x)}{p(y)}p(x) = \frac{p(y|x)}{p(y)}\frac{p(x)}{q(x|y)}q(x|y) \qquad (9)$$

Using a particle representation for $q(x|y)$, so drawing particles from q instead of from the prior, we find:

$$p(x|y) = \sum_{i=1}^{N} \frac{p(y|x_i)}{Np(y)}\frac{p(x_i)}{q(x_i|y)}\delta(x - x_i) = \sum_{i=1}^{N} w_i\delta(x - x_i) \qquad (10)$$

in which the weights now become:

$$w_i = \frac{p(y|x_i)}{N\sum_j p(y|x_j)}\frac{p(x_i)}{q(x_i|y)} \qquad (11)$$

These weights consist of a likelihood part, as before, and a part related to the use of the proposal density. The usefulness of the proposal is that we can choose q such that the particles are closer to the observations, so that the likelihood part of the weights are more equal, while at the same time ensuring that p/q does not spoil this gain in efficiency. The different particle filter variants differ in the proposal density used. In the following we will discuss a few recent developments in generating efficient proposal densities.

3   The Implicit Particle Filter

The implicit particle filter was introduced by Chorin and Tu (2009) and has been further detailed in Chorin et al. (2010). It works as follows. Define a function $F(x)$ as minus the logarithm of the posterior pdf:

$$F(x) = -\log(p(x|y, x_i^m)) \tag{12}$$

in which x can be either a state vector at a certain time, or an evolution of the system over a time window $x = (x^1, \ldots, x^n)^T$. x_i^m is the starting point of the particle i at the start of the time window starting at time m, and m can be equal to $n-1$. Define the minimum of $F(x)$ as

$$\phi_F = \min(F(x)) \tag{13}$$

The basic idea in the implicit particle filter is to draw samples from a pdf $g(\xi)$ from which it is easy to draw, e.g. a multivariate Gaussian. Define $G(\xi)$ as

$$p(\xi) \propto \exp(-G(\xi)) \tag{14}$$

and denote

$$\phi_G = \min(G(\xi)) \tag{15}$$

The relation between the samples ξ_i and the samples of the posterior pdf x_i is *defined* by the solution of

$$F_i(x) - \phi_{F_i} = G(\xi_i) - \phi_{G_i} \tag{16}$$

where we emphasise that ϕ_F and ϕ_G can depend on the particle index i.

The weight of the particle i using proposal density $g(\xi)$ is given by:

$$w_i = \frac{p(x_i|y)}{q(x_i|y)} = \frac{p(x_i|y)}{g(\xi_i|y)} |J(\xi_i)| \tag{17}$$

in which

$$J(\xi) = \det\left(\frac{\partial x}{\partial \xi}\right) \tag{18}$$

Using the expression for the posterior and the relation between x and ξ we find for the weights:

$$w_i = \frac{p(x_i|y)}{q(x_i|y)} \propto \frac{\exp(-F_i(x)))}{\exp(-F_i(x) + \phi_{F_i} - \phi_{G_i})} |J(\xi_i)| = \exp(-\phi_{F_i} + \phi_{G_i}) |J(\xi_i)| \tag{19}$$

Several proposal densities have been explored in the literature. Here we focus on the so-called random map method (Morzfelt et al. 2012) which takes ξ to be Gaussian distributed $N(0, I)$, so $\phi_G = 0$, and writing

$$x_i = argmin(F_i(x)) + \lambda(\xi_i)\xi_i \tag{20}$$

in which $\lambda(x_i)$ a scalar function of ξ_i. In case $F_i(x)$ is quadratic in x λ is scalar constant and the Jacobian $|J(\xi)|$ is constant over the particles, so can be dropped, leading to:

$$w_i = \exp(-\phi_{F_i}) \tag{21}$$

This is typically the case when observations and model errors are Gaussian distributed and H is linear for a filter, and for a smoother with the additional constraint that the model is linear.

To summarise the procedure is, for each particle:

(1) Calculate $argmin(F_i(x))$ (not necessary, but typically done for efficiency)
(2) Draw ξ_i from $g(\xi)$
(3) Solve for the corresponding x_i, from $F_i(x) - \phi_{F_i} = G(\xi_i) - \phi_{G_i}$
(4) Evaluate the weight w_i.

In can be shown that this method is very similar to the so-called optimal proposal density when observations are present every time step (see e.g. Ades and Van Leeuwen 2013). Assuming Gaussian observation errors and a linear observation operator $H(x)$ it is easy to show that the weights are equal to:

$$w_i \propto \exp\left[-\frac{1}{2}(y^n - Hf(x_i^{n-1}))^T (HQH^T + R)^T (y^n - Hf(x_i^{n-1}))\right] \tag{22}$$

in which n is the time index. Ades and Van Leeuwen (2013) show that these minus the logarithm of these weights are non-central χ^2 distributed with variance proportional to the number of independent observations M. Hence, for high-dimensional observation systems the implicit particle filter is expected to be degenerate, which is confirmed by our experiments presented later.

Another potential issue is that the Jacobian $|J(\xi)|$ has to be nonzero, which means that $F_i(x)$ has to be unimodal, at last close to the position of the state that produces the maximum weight for each particle.

4   The Equivalent-Weights Particle Filter

The Equivalent-Weights Particle filter introduced in Van Leeuwen (2010) and investigated in detail in Ades and Van Leeuwen (2013; 2015a; 2015b) works as follows.

First, we calculate the state for which $F_i(x)$ is minimal, in which $F_i(x)$ is defined as before as:

$$F_i(x) = -\log(p(x|y, x_i^m) \tag{23}$$

in which x_i^m is the starting point of the particle i at the start of the time window starting at time m, and m can be equal to $n-1$.

After we have done this for each particle we rank the particles in acceding order of $min(F_i(x))$. We choose the number of particles we'd like to keep in the ensemble, let's say 80 %. We then set a target weight as the value of $w_{target} = \exp[-min(F_i(x))]$ for that particle that ranks as the 80 % particle in the ranking. For instance, if we have 100 particles we rank them and set the target weight as the value of $\exp[-min(F_i(x))]$ for the 80th particle in the ranking.

The next step is to solve for each particle x_i for which its weight $\exp[-min(F_i(x))$ is larger than the target weight (or $min(F_i(x))$ is smaller than $-\log(w_{target})$) as:

$$F_i(x) = -\log(w_{target}) \qquad (24)$$

This is the case for 80 % of the particles by this construction. The other 20 % of the particles cannot reach this target weight: no matter how we move them in state space their weight will be smaller than the target weight. These particles will come back via a resampling step later.

Then we add to each particle a small random perturbation and recalculate the weight for each particle. Since the perturbation is small the weights will not change much, meaning that 80 % of the particles will all have very similar, or equivalent, weights. For details see Ades and Van Leeuwen (2015a).

Finally a resampling step is performed in which N particles are drawn from the weighted ensemble of 80 % of the particles. This is the whole scheme, which can be summarised as:

(1) Calculate $argmin(F_i(x))$
(2) Determine w_{target}
(3) Solve for x_i^* from $F_i(x) = -\log(w_{target})$
(4) Draw η_i from mixture density with small amplitude and write $x_i = x_i^* + \eta_i$.
(5) Evaluate final weight.

This scheme is not degenerate by construction, as has been shown in e.g. Ades and Van Leeuwen (2015a) who used this scheme in a 65,000 dimensional barotropic vorticity model.

5   Another Non-degenerate Scheme

Using the scheme above we can easily derive new variants of the EWPF that are not degenerate by construction. We present one example here. The comparison of the two methods discussed above shows that the number of calculations is identical. The implicit particle filter (IPF) first draws the random vector ξ before solving an equation for x_i, while the EWPF first solves for x^* and than adds η. The advantage of the IPF is that the draw is simply done for a Gaussian, but the disadvantage is that the weights are degenerate.

Would it be possible in the EWPF to draw η from a Gaussian before solving for x^* ($= x_i^n$ in that case)? This would mean to replace the procedure above with:

(1) Calculate $argmin(F_i(x))$
(2) Determine w_{target}
(3) Draw ξ_i from $g(\xi) \propto \exp(-G(\xi))$
(4) Solve for x_i^* from $F_i(x) = -\log(w_{target}) + G(\xi_i)$
(5) Evaluate weight.

(Note that step 4 is easily done with the existing software for the Equivalent-Weights Particle Filter by simply replacing $-\log(w_{target})$ with $-\log(w_{target}) + G(\xi_i)$.) The weights will become:

$$
\begin{aligned}
w_i &= \frac{p(x_i|y)}{q(x_i|y)} \\
&\propto \frac{\exp(-F_i(x_i)))}{\exp(-G(\xi_i))} |J(\xi_i)| \\
&= \frac{\exp(-F_i(x_i)))}{\exp(-F_i(x_i) + \log(w_{target}))} |J(\xi_i)| \\
&= \exp(-w_{target}) |J(\xi_i)|
\end{aligned}
\tag{25}
$$

If $F_i(x)$ is a quadratic function of x_i, as we usually assume via Gaussian errors in observations, H linear, and Gaussian model errors, the Jacobian is constant and drops out, and the weights are all equal again!

Finally, the difference between this scheme and the IPF is that we have a small extra step to calculate w_{target} that ensures that all ϕ_{F_i} are equal to avoid degeneracy.

This is one of the ways to avoid degeneracy in particle filtering, and no doubt many more will be developed over the coming years.

6   A Simple Numerical Example

To test the ideas the standard particle filter, Equivalent-Weights Particle Filter and the Implicit Particle Filter are comparer on a simple model given by:

$$
x^1 = x^0 + \eta
\tag{26}
$$

The distribution of x^0 is taken as independent Gaussian for simplicity. The state vector is d-dimensional and we will investigate the performance of the filters when d increases. Finally, the model errors are also independent Gaussian. The state x^1 is observed as

$$
y = x^1 + \epsilon
\tag{27}
$$

in which the observation errors are also taken independent and Gaussian.

While this system is completely Gaussian, so linear, so the traditional linear data-assimilation methods can be used, we will explore the particle filter performance here. The idea is that if the particle filters fail in this simple linear case it is unlikely they will perform better in a nonlinear setting.

Several experiments were performed with different values for initial, model, and observational errors. Here we report on the following experimental settings, mentioning that other settings give similar results: the initial mean is 0 for each variable, the initial variance is 1 for each variable, the model variance is 0.01, and the observation error variance is 0.16. The number of ensemble members or particles is 10 in all experiments. We set the number of particles kept in the equivalent-weights procedure equal to 80 %.

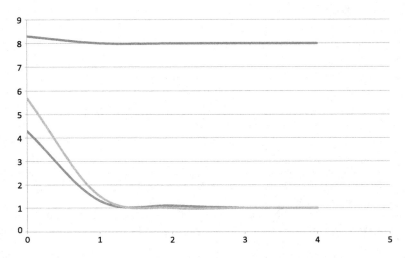

Fig. 1. Effective ensemble size for SIR (blue), EWPF (red), and IPF (green) as function of the power of the state dimension, so 10^0 to 10^4 (Color figure online).

Figure 1 shows the effective ensemble size, defined as

$$N_{eft} = \frac{1}{\sum w_i^2} \tag{28}$$

for the standard particle filter with proposal density equal to the prior, the Equivalent-Weights Particle Filter (EWPF) and the Implicit Particle Filter (IPF), which is equal to a particle filter using the so-called Optimal Proposal density. The results shown are averages over 1000 experiments. We can clearly see that apart from a state dimension of 1, all filters are degenerate, except for the EWPF, in which we find constant effective ensemble sizes of 8 out of 10, identical to the percentage of particles kept in the equivalent-weights procedure.

Figure 2 shows the root-mean-square error (RMSE) of the ensemble mean from the truth for each method, averaged over state space. The results shown are again averages over 1000 experiments. One would expect that the RMSE is slightly smaller that the observation error, which is 0.4 in this case. Only the EWPF is able to do this, all other methods fail and return a RMSE close to that of the prior. This is consistent with the effective ensemble size results above.

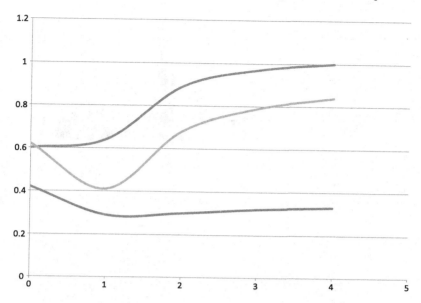

Fig. 2. State-space averaged root-mean-square error of ensemble mean for SIR (blue), EWPF (red), and IPF (green) as function of the power of the state dimension, so 10^0 to 10^4 (Color figure online).

One might wonder why the IPF does not do much better than the standard particle filter. The reason is simply More realistic high-dimensional that the members are moved to better positions but the filter is degenerate, so the mean only consist of the best particle, which does depend on the initial particle position, so the RMSE will converge to that of the prior. Note that, for this specific case in which the prior at time zero is a Gaussian one could take the drawing from that Gaussian into the sampling via the proposal q, in which case all samples would have equal weight as this system is linear. In that case the IPF reduces to the Ensemble Kalman Smoother (Evensen and Van Leeuwen 2000). The point here is that, in general, the prior at time zero is non-Gaussian as it arises from a sequential application of the algorithm so the starting point at time zero is a number of particles with unknown distribution.

7 More Realistic High-Dimensional Applications

We have applied the EWPF to several high-dimensional problems. Ades and Van Leeuwen (2015a) applied the method to a 65,000 dimensional barotropic vorticity model and found that the particle filter is indeed not degenerate, and quite robust. For instance, Fig. 3 shows how the histogram from 32 particles captures the main features of the histogram generated using 512 particles.

In this experiment only half of the state was observed, and of the observed part only every other point. The pdfs shown in Fig. 3 are for a point in the

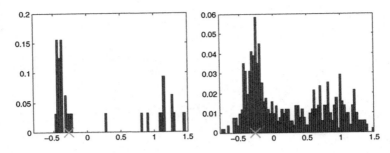

Fig. 3. Marginal posterior pdf of an unobserved point using 32 and 512 particles. The green cross denotes the truth value for the vorticity at this point. Note the similarity between the main features of the pdf (Color figure online).

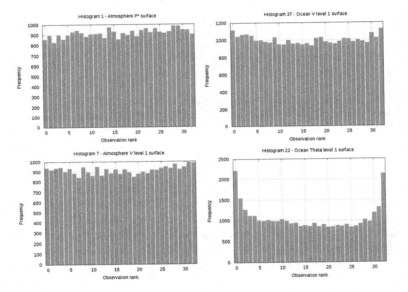

Fig. 4. Rank histogram showing how the truth ranks in the ensemble. For a proper ensemble the rank histogram should be flat. This is indeed the case for the atmospheric surface pressure and the oceanic and atmospheric surface meridional velocity fields, but the ocean temperature in the first ocean layer shows signs of an under-dispersive ensemble.

middle of the unobserved half, where nonlinearities can grow and non-Gaussian pdfs are common.

Finally we show first results from an application of the EWPF to the climate model HadCM3, with about 2 million state variables. In this experiment only the Sea-Surface Temperature (SST) was observed every day. The initial results are encouraging, although not all problems have been solved. Figure 4 shows rank histograms of atmospheric surface pressure, the oceanic and atmospheric velocity fields, and the ocean temperature in the first layer (which is different from the SST). Is shows that for several of the model variables the rank histograms are flat, indicating a proper ensemble, for others the rank histograms are U-shaped, indicating an under-dispersive ensemble. Ideally all marginal histograms would be flat, but it will be clear that this is hard to achieve in general. The main point here is, however, that, again, the EWPF is not degenerate and can be fine-tuned further.

8   Conclusions

High-dimensional spaces poses a few counter intuitive features. One of those directly related to nonlinear filtering in these spaces is that the likelihood is extremely narrow when the number of independent observations is large. A simple example with only 1000 independent observations showed catastrophic filter collapse when the proposal density is taken equal to the prior. New developments like the implicit particle filter try to avoid that problem by exploring the so-called optimal proposal density. It has been shown theoretically that this filter and its variants also suffer from ensemble collapse in Ades and Van Leeuwen (2013), and that finding is confirmed in an very simple experiment in this paper. The only particle filter that is insensitive to the dimension of the state or, rather, of the observation space is the Equivalent-Weights Particle Filter, which avoids ensemble collapse by construction. The simple experiment has confirmed this, as have more realistic systems, such as the barotropic vorticity equation model and the climate model HadCM3.

We have also shown that it is easy to combine the EWPF scheme with other schemes like the IPF and formulate other non-degenerate schemes. One undesirable feature of the EWPF is that one has to set the percentage of particles kept in the equivalent weight step, and the results do depend on this (see e.g. Ades and Van Leeuwen 2013). Ideally one would get rid of this step and manages to find non-degenerate particles without resampling. There is room for good ideas to explore these methods further.

References

Ades, M., Van Leeuwen, P.J.: An exploration of the equivalent weights particle filter. Q. J. Meteorol. **139**, 820–840 (2013)

Ades, M., Van Leeuwen, P.J.: The equivalent weights particle flter in a high dimensional system. Q. J. Meteorol. **141**, 484–503 (2015a). doi:10.1002/qj.2370

Ades, M., Van Leeuwen, P.J.: The effect of the equivalent-weights particle flter on dynamical balance in a primitive equation model. Mon. Weather Rev. **143**, 581–596 (2015b). doi:10.1175/MWR-D-14-00050.1

Chorin, A.J., Morzfeld, M., Tu, X.: Interpolation and iteration for nonlinear filters. Commun. Appl. Math. Comput. Sci. **5**(221), 240 (2010)

Chorin, A.J., Tu, X.: Implicit sampling for particle filters. Proc. Nat. Acad. Sci. **106**(41), 17249–17254 (2009)

Doucet, A., de Freitas, N., Gordon, N.: Sequential Monte-Carlo Methods in Practice, vol. 686. Springer, New York (2001)

Evensen, G., van Leeuwen, P.J.: An ensemble Kalman smoother for nonlinear dynamics. Mon. Weather Rev. **129**, 709–728 (2000)

Morzfeld, M., Tu, X., Atkins, E., Chorin, A.J.: A random map implementation of implicit filters. J. Comput. Phys. **231**, 2049–2066 (2012)

Snyder, C., Bengtsson, T., Bickel, P., Anderson, J.: Obstacles to high-dimensional particle filtering. Mon. Weather Rev. **136**, 4629–4640 (2008)

Van Leeuwen, P.J.: Particle filtering in geophysical systems. Mon. Weather Rev. **137**, 4089–4114 (2009)

Van Leeuwen, P.J.: Nonlinear data assimilation in geosciences: an extremely efficient particle filter. Q. J. Roy. Meteorol. Soc. **136**, 1991–1999 (2010)

A Hybrid Particle-Ensemble Kalman Filter for High Dimensional Lagrangian Data Assimilation

Laura Slivinski[1], Elaine Spiller[2]([✉]), and Amit Apte[3]

[1] Woods Hole Oceanographic Institution, Woods Hole, USA
[2] Marquette University, Milwaukee, USA
elaine.spiller@marquette.edu
[3] International Centre for Theoretical Sciences -TIFR, Bangalore, India

Abstract. We apply the recently proposed hybrid particle-ensemble Kalman filter to assimilate Lagrangian data into a non-linear, high-dimensional quasi-geostrophic ocean model. Effectively the hybrid filter applies a particle filter to the highly nonlinear, low-dimensional Lagrangian instrument variables while applying an ensemble Kalman type update to the high-dimensional Eulerian flow field. We present some initial results from this hybrid filter and compare those to results from a standard ensemble Kalman filter and an ensemble run without assimilation.

1 Introduction

Monitoring the behavior of oceans relies heavily on Lagrangian instruments – drifters, gliders, and floats – because they not only provide the most effective source of subsurface information, but also provide vast spatio-temporal coverage both on- and sub-surface. Drifters and floats are passive instruments and thus their trajectories are purely Lagrangian. Data from drifters[1] comes in the form of a time series of locations sampled from these trajectories. Drifters' Lagrangian paths can exhibit very nonlinear behavior even if the dynamics governing the underlying flow are linear [1]. Furthermore, realistic ocean models are high-dimensional and this poses a great challenge to nonlinear filters [19]. Recently the authors developed a hybrid particle-ensemble Kalman filter designed to assimilate nonlinear Lagrangian data into (potentially) high-dimensional Eulerian flow models [18]. In this paper, we describe the first application of this hybrid filter to a high-dimensional flow field.

Much progress has been made over the last dozen years in assimilating Lagrangian data into ocean models. There are two prevailing approaches: converting the path data into local velocity data [9,10], or appending the dynamics of drifter advection to the state and assimilating trajectory data directly [6,8]. The latter approach is typically referred to as the *augmented state space approach*

---

[1] We will use the term *drifter* going forward to refer to any Lagrangian instrument.

© Springer International Publishing Switzerland 2015
S. Ravela and A. Sandu (Eds.): DyDESS 2014, LNCS 8964, pp. 263–273, 2015.
DOI: 10.1007/978-3-319-25138-7_24

to Lagrangian data assimilation (LaDA) and the hybrid filter we will describe is designed for this strategy. Both particle filters (PF) and ensemble Kalman filters (EnKF) have been used for LaDA. Particle filters have successfully assimilated data from Lagrangian paths which travel near unstable fixed points [20], but only in a low-dimensional setting. The ensemble Kalman filter has been applied to a high-dimensional flow setting [16], but has only proved effective with relatively frequent (near linear) observations. A hybrid grid-particle filter designed for LaDA in [14,15] inspired the strategy we followed by applying different filtering approaches to different parts of the state space.

The hybrid particle-ensemble Kalman filter begins with a relatively small ensemble of flow members. Each flow member is assigned a large ensemble of drifters (as opposed to one member per flow in a typical EnKF). This particular set up is motivated by two reasons: (i) flow evolution is computationally expensive relative to drifter evolution but the nonlinearities are less prominent compared with drifter dynamics, and (ii) a cloud of drifters can naturally explore possible nonlinear paths whereas a single drifter member will only explore a single path that may diverge from the true path due to nonlinearity.

An essential step in any particle filtering algorithm is the *resampling* needed when the weights of many particles become too small, which happens very frequently in high-dimensional systems – this is the well-known curse of dimensionality. In the hybrid filter when resampling is needed, we apply an ensemble Kalman type update to the flow variables and a particle filter type update to the drifter variables. Furthermore, strategies developed for the EnKF, like localization, can readily be applied in the hybrid PF-EnKF filter. Details of the hybrid filter will be described in the next section. Then we will present an application of the hybrid filter to the quasi-geostrophic model and follow it with a discussion.

2 Hybrid Filter

In this section, we will give an overview of the hybrid filter. Since the main focus of this work is on application of this filter to a nonlinear high-dimensional quasi-geostrophic model, we refer the reader to [18] where we introduced and discussed it in much greater detail. We will also outline some refinements to the approach that we foresee as being needed to make it sufficiently robust for operational applications.

We begin by combining the drifter location (Lagrangian components) $\mathbf{x}^D$ and flow field (typically the solution of a PDE defined over a grid – Eulerian components) $\mathbf{x}^F$ by writing the whole state as $\mathbf{x} = [\mathbf{x}^F, \mathbf{x}^D]^T$. The evolution of the state is then described by

$$\frac{d\mathbf{x}^F}{dt} = f^E(\mathbf{x}^F), \qquad \frac{d\mathbf{x}^D}{dt} = f^L(\mathbf{x}^F, \mathbf{x}^D), \qquad (1)$$

with f^L and f^E being the forward time operators in the models describing the Lagrangian and Eulerian components, respectively. We will assimilate observations of the drifter position, so taking observation noise to be Gaussian, we write the observation $\mathbf{y}$ at time t as

$$\mathbf{y} = \mathbf{H}\mathbf{x}(t) + \epsilon = \mathbf{x}^D(t) + \epsilon, \qquad \epsilon \sim \mathcal{N}(0, \mathbf{R}) \tag{2}$$

where $\mathbf{H} = [0 \ \mathbf{I}]$ is the observation operator and $\mathbf{R}$ is the noise covariance.

At any given time, the filtering distribution is described by a set of states and weights $\{\mathbf{x}_i^{F,f}, \mathbf{x}_{i,j}^{D,f}, w_{i,j}^f\}_{i=1,...,N_e}^{j=1,...,M}$ where N_e is the number of flow ensemble members and M is the number of drifter members for each flow member yielding a total number of $M \cdot N_e$ particles. A pictorial representation of this decomposition is given in Fig. 1. A description of just the flow distribution can be obtained by marginalizing over the drifter variables. That is, we define $\tilde{w}_i^f = \sum_j w_{i,j}^f$ and we have flow the distribution represented by a weighted ensemble, $\{\mathbf{x}_i^{F,f}, \tilde{w}_i^f\}$. The superscript f refers to states/weights from the *forecast*/prior distribution (likewise the superscript a will represent *analysis*/posterior).

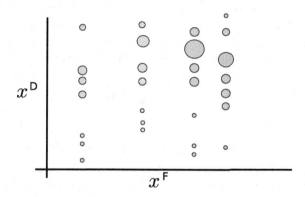

Fig. 1. Above is a visualization of the partition of ensemble members. In this example, there are four flow members and each flow member has seven drifter members. The size of each dot represents the relative weight of that particle.

To begin the process, samples are chosen empirically from the initial prior distribution and weights are set to $w_{i,j}^f = 1/(MN_e)$. In the case that the effective sample size N_{eff} of the ensemble, approximated by $N_{eff} = \sum_{i,j} 1/w_{i,j}^2$, remains above a user-defined threshold, $N_{eff} > N_{eff}^{thresh}$, our filter proceeds similar in fashion to a Rao-Blackwellized PF [5]. That is, all states evolve forward in time to the next observation instance according to Eq. 1 and retain their old weights to form the prior $\{\mathbf{x}_i^{F,f}, \mathbf{x}_{i,j}^{D,f}, w_{i,j}^f\}$. Then the observation is compared to each particle under the likelihood $p(\mathbf{y}|\mathbf{x})$ to update the weights as

$$w_{i,j}^a = \frac{p(\mathbf{y}|\mathbf{x}_{i,j}^{D,f})w_{i,j}^f}{\sum_{i,j} p(\mathbf{y}|\mathbf{x}_{i,j}^{D,f})w_{i,j}^f} . \tag{3}$$

Next we set $\mathbf{x}^a = \mathbf{x}^f$, yielding a drifter analysis/posterior distribution $\{\mathbf{x}_{i,j}^{D,a}, w_{i,j}^a\}$, and after marginalizing, a flow analysis/posterior $\{\mathbf{x}_i^{F,a}, \tilde{w}_i^a\}$.

The states in the analysis are then pushed forward to the next observation instance and the process just described is repeated.

At an observation instance where N_{eff} falls beneath N_{eff}^{thresh}, we proceed with an update/resampling step and this is where our algorithm differs from a typical PF – it treats the drifter and flow ensemble updates separately. The drifter variables are updated/resampled by using the current observation to update the weights to $w_{i,j}^a$. Then drifter states are resampled via a bootstrap and noise consistent with the observation covariance is added to spread out the samples. The current observation is used in a different manner to update the flow ensemble. First, we take the weighted flow prior (recall the state has been evolved to the current time, but each particle retains its prior weight) $\{\mathbf{x}_j^{F,f}, \tilde{w}_j^f\}$. At this point we apply a perturbed-observation EnKF update on the flow variables. To describe this, we let $\mathbf{A}^{F,f}$ be an $N_F \times N_e$ matrix (where N_F is the number of flow variables) with the ith column comprised of $\mathbf{x}_i^{F,f}$. We also let $\tilde{\mathbf{A}}^{D,f}$ be a $2 \times N_e$ matrix comprised of averaged drifter states $\bar{\mathbf{x}}_i^{D,f}$ corresponding to the respective $\mathbf{x}_i^{F,f}$ flow member, e.g. from the "averaged" distribution $\{\mathbf{x}_i^{F,f}, \bar{\mathbf{x}}_i^{D,f}, \tilde{w}_i\}$. We use this to calculate the sample covariance matrix $\mathbf{P}$ which for LaDA is typically decomposed as

$$\mathbf{P} = \begin{bmatrix} \mathbf{P}_{FF} & \mathbf{P}_{FD} \\ \mathbf{P}_{FD}^T & \mathbf{P}_{DD} \end{bmatrix}. \tag{4}$$

Now the flow variables are updated by

$$\mathbf{A}^{F,a} = \mathbf{A}^{F,f} + \mathbf{P}_{FD}^f (\mathbf{P}_{DD}^f + \mathbf{R})^{-1} (\mathbf{Y} - \tilde{\mathbf{A}}^{D,f}) \tag{5}$$

where $\mathbf{Y}$ is a $2 \times N_e$ matrix of perturbed observations. (Note that details of obtaining perturbed observations for weighted samples can be found in [18].) Then we have weighted posterior flow members $\{\mathbf{x}_i^{F,a}, \tilde{w}_i^f\}$ and we resample these with a Metropolis-Hastings implementation of a bootstrapping algorithm and set $\tilde{w}_i^a = 1/N_e$. Now we have $\{\mathbf{x}_i^{F,a}, \mathbf{x}_{i,j}^{D,a}, 1/(MN_e)\}$ and the algorithm moves forward employing either a PF weight update or EnKF resampling step as needed.

Note that the update/resampling step effectively culls low weight flow ensemble members and retains multiple copies of high weight flow ensemble members. Also note that these replicate flow members will only remain the same until the next EnKF update. At that point, each will get a different correction according to Eq. 5 as each has its own ensemble of drifters and its own perturbed observation. In Sect. 3.2, we present some encouraging results that this approach is adequate as a first implementation of the hybrid PF-EnKF to a high dimensional problem. That said, we suspect this approach underestimates the covariance in the flow variables. Thus we are currently investigating function space sampling techniques to perturb the bootstrapped ensemble flow members.

3   Application to a High Dimensional Model

In this section, we will discuss the application of the hybrid filter, introduced above, to the Lagrangian data assimilation problem in a high dimensional fluid flow problem. In particular, we will consider a nonlinear quasi-geostrophic model (QG) with a constant wind forcing in a rectangular basin over a flat bottom. The observations are that of a passive Lagrangian drifter in this flow. We perform identical twin type numerical experiments with the hybrid PF-EnKF filter, and also the usual perturbed observation ensemble Kalman filter. We compare the outcomes of these filters to that of a free run of the QG model without assimilation of these observations.

3.1 QG Model and Observational Setup

The quasi-geostrophic model we consider describes the dynamics of the changes in surface height $\eta(x, y, t)$ of a shallow layer of water over a flat bottom. The time evolution of η is given by the following equation, [11] for $(x, y) \in [0, 2L] \times [0, L]$, with $L = 2000$ km in our numerical results:

$$\left[\frac{\partial}{\partial t} - \frac{\partial \eta}{\partial y} \frac{\partial}{\partial x} + \frac{\partial \eta}{\partial x} \frac{\partial}{\partial y} \right] \Delta \eta = F(x, y, t). \tag{6}$$

Here the right hand side is the wind forcing which we choose to be $F(x, y, t) = \alpha \cos(\pi y / L)$, Δ is the two-dimensional Laplacian, and we use no-slip boundary conditions. The velocity components (u, v) and the vorticity ω are given by following:

$$u(x, y, t) = -\frac{\partial \eta}{\partial y}, \qquad v(x, y, t) = \frac{\partial \eta}{\partial x}, \qquad \omega = \Delta \eta. \tag{7}$$

The quasi-geostrophic Eq. (6) can be thought of as the equation for conservation of vorticity in the case when the forcing is absent: $F = 0$. Thus, instead of considering the surface height η as the dynamical variable, we can consider the vorticity ω as the dynamical variable, obtaining the height by inverting the Laplacian: $\eta = \Delta^{-1}\omega$ and then obtaining the velocity using Eq. (7).

We solve the above Eq. (6) using a 3rd order upwind advection scheme along with a predictor-corrector (Heun) method for time-stepping, with variable step size that is fixed by using a CFL condition[2]. The basic parameters of the model and the forcing are chosen so that the basic flow consists of a classic double gyre solution of the QG equations, as illustrated in Fig. 2. As we can see, the Lagrangian trajectories are quite chaotic, a fact that will be of importance later when discussing the results of the filtering estimates.

The Lagrangian dynamics is given by the following equations for the position (x_d, y_d) of the drifter:

$$\frac{dx_d}{dt} = u(x_d, y_d, t) = -\frac{\partial \eta}{\partial y}(x_d, y_d, t), \qquad \frac{dy_d}{dt} = v(x_d, y_d, t) = \frac{\partial \eta}{\partial x}(x_d, y_d, t). \tag{8}$$

The observations are that of the position of the drifter (x_d, y_d). We will use the augmented state consisting of the flow variables (vorticity ω) and the drifter

---

[2] We use a modified version of the codes due to Guillaume Roullet. [13].

A few drifter trajectories and snapshot of height (shading) and velocity fields

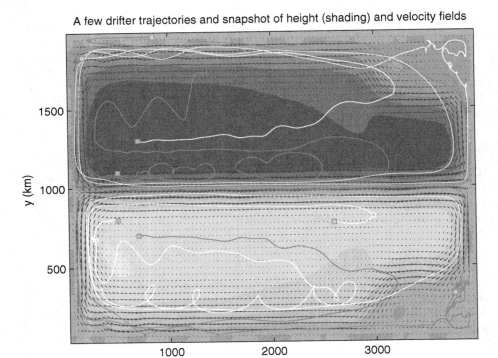

Fig. 2. The basic double gyre solution used in this work. A few typical Lagrangian trajectories are shown as well.

position (x_d, y_d). Thus the observation operator is just a projection onto the drifter variables.

We use a regular rectangular grid for solving Eq. (6), with grid spacing of $\delta = 40$ km in both x- and y-directions, whereas the basin size is set to be 4000×2000 km. Thus numerically, the dimension of the flow state space $\mathbf{x}^F$ is 5000 but since we assimilate data from only a single drifter trajectory, the drifter state space $\mathbf{x}^D$ is two-dimensional. In the next section, we now describe the comparative results of the hybrid and ensemble Kalman filters with free run of the above model.

3.2 Numerical Results

The identical twin experiments we perform consist of the following setup. We first choose a "random" initial condition for the vorticity field and the drifter location and generate a solution of the QG equations along with a drifter trajectory. We call this the "truth" or the "true trajectory."

For assimilation, we generate an ensemble of vorticity fields along with an ensemble of drifter initial conditions by choosing states of the system at various times in its evolution. This is done mainly to ensure that each of the ensemble members has a smooth vorticity field, which can be inverted without numerical instabilities to get the height field. For the hybrid filter, the flow ensemble consists of $N_e = 50$ members whereas the drifter ensemble consists of $M = 50$ members for each flow member. For the EnKF, we choose an ensemble size of $N_e = 50$. We also run this same ensemble forward in time without assimilation and this is called a "free run." The specific results we present are for the case in which the time between observations is chosen to be $T_{\text{obs}} = 0.25$ days, with a total of 50 observations assimilated.

We note that for the flow resampling step of the hybrid filter, currently we are using bootstrap resampling scheme that involves reproducing the particles with probabilities proportional to their weights. [12] This effectively reproduces most of the high weight particles multiple times while effectively discarding the low weight particles. As mentioned at the end of previous section, a careful examination of effects of different sampling schemes for the flow resampling, in particular those suited to high or infinite dimensional sampling, [2–4, 7, 17] is certainly an area of future work, and we feel that it will lead to further improvements of the hybrid filter.

In Fig. 3, we show the mean of the three ensembles obtained from the free run (top right), from EnKF (bottom left), and from hybrid method (bottom right), as compared to the truth (top left), at the end of the assimilation window, i.e., at $t = 12.5$ days. We see that even the fairly short drifter trajectory (shown in the inset) contains useful information about the velocity field. This can be seen from the following observation: the mean of the free run ensemble does not have the vortices near the middle left of the domain while the EnKF and hybrid ensembles show the presence of these vortices. We also see that indeed the assimilation has improved the estimation of the velocity and height fields quite substantially.

We also quantify these conclusions by plotting the root mean square error between the truth and the means of these three ensembles – Fig. 4 shows these errors. We see that there is a gradual decrease in the error as more observations are assimilated and the hybrid filter performs well in estimating the velocity field. The free run is certainly very inefficient in estimating the drifter position, clearly because of highly chaotic nature of the drifter trajectories even in this simple flow field.

4   Discussion

Continuing the work in [18], we have presented the application of a hybrid particle-ensemble Kalman filter for assimilating Lagrangian data into ocean models. Note that the hybrid filter developed in [18] was only applied to a low-dimensional flow in that work so that resulting distributions could be compared to a bench mark very-large-sample particle filter.

Lagrangian data assimilation is a challenging problem because of the following two reasons, each of which creates difficulties for some of the possible assimilation methods: (1) Lagrangian data are obtained from highly nonlinear

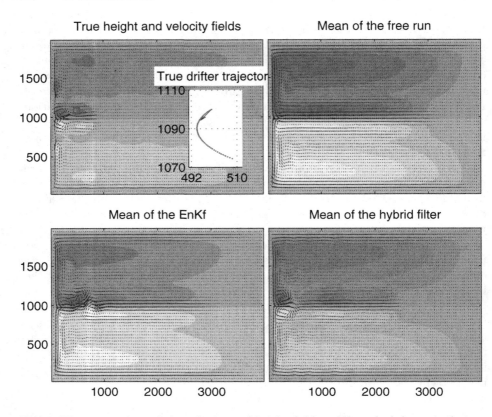

Fig. 3. The comparison of the velocity and height fields at the end of the assimilation window, i.e., after 12.5 days, as given by the free run, the EnKF, and the hybrid filter

drifter trajectories, and Kalman filter based techniques such as the ensemble Kalman filter may fail because of this reason; (2) The fluid flow models into which this data are assimilated are high dimensional, creating difficulties for the use of particle filter based methods.

We presented the hybrid method which applies the EnKF to the high dimensional part of the phase space consisting of the fluid flow variables (e.g. the vorticity field in the quasi-geostrophic model we used), while it applies the particle filter to the low dimensional but highly nonlinear drifter dynamics. We illustrated the application of this method in a moderately high-dimensional quasi-geostrophic model consisting of 5000 variables.

The results, even though preliminary in nature, are promising as can be seen from Figs. 3 and 4. With a judicious choice of parameters, the hybrid filter can outperform the EnKF and certainly does well in comparison to a free run of the model without assimilation. We also pointed out the questions that need to be investigated further, including the role of high-dimensional function space sampling methods and the effect of choice of various parameters in the hybrid

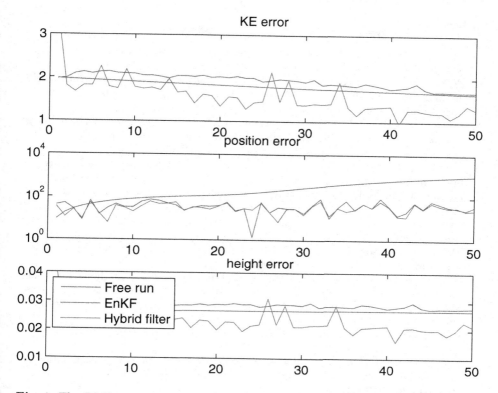

Fig. 4. The RMS errors in the velocity field, drifter position, and vorticity field, as compared to the truth, for the free run, EnKF, and the hybrid filter. Notice the log scale for the position errors, which are essentially exponential for the free run.

filter. Furthermore, although this approach was developed for purely Lagrangian instruments, we think it could prove effective for assimilating data from semi-Lagrangian instruments such as gliders. We envision that uncertainty reflected by variance in the Eulerian field could be used as on-the-fly guidance for choosing future way points during a glider assimilation/control study.

Acknowledgments. The authors would like to acknowledge the use of the numerical implementation of the QG model by Guillaume Roullet (see http://stockage.univ-brest.fr/~roullet/codes.html). The authors would like to thank Chris Jones for initially suggesting this collaboration and the Mathematics and Climate Research Network (NSF grant DMS-0940363) for enabling this collaboration. Apte would like to thank the EADS/Airbus Chair in 'Mathematics of Complex Systems' at TIFR for partial support for this work. Spiller would like to acknowledge support by NSF grant DMS-1228265 and ONR grant N00014-11-1-0087.

References

1. Apte, A., Jones, C.: The effect of nonlinearity on Lagrangian data assimilation. Nonlin. Process. Geophys. **20**, 329–341 (2013)
2. Beskos, A., Crisan, D., Jasra, A.: On the stability of sequential Monte Carlo methods in high dimensions. Ann. Appl. Probab. **24**(4), 1396–1445 (2014). http://arxiv.org/abs/1103.3965
3. Beskos, A., Crisan., D., Jasra., A., Whiteley., N.: Error bounds and normalizing constants for sequential Monte Carlo in high dimensions. Adv. Appl. Probab. (To appear). http://arxiv.org/abs/1112.1544
4. Cotter, S., Dashti, M., Robinson, J., Stuart, A.: Bayesian inverse problems for functions and applications to fluid mechanics. Inverse Prob. **25**, 115008 (2009)
5. Doucet, A., De Freitas, N., Murphy, K., Russell, S.: Rao-blackwellised particle filtering for dynamic bayesian networks. In: Proceedings of the Sixteenth Conference on Uncertainty in Artificial Intelligence, Morgan Kaufmann Publishers Inc., pp. 176–183 (2000)
6. Ide, K., Kuznetsov, L., Jones, C.K.R.T.: Lagrangian data assimilation for point vortex systems. J. Turbul. **3**, 053 (2002)
7. Kantas, N., Beskos, A., Jasra, A.: Sequential Monte Carlo methods for high-dimensional inverse problems: a case study for the Navier-Stokes equations. SIAM/ASA J. Uncertain. Quantif. **2**(1), 464–489 (2014). http://arxiv.org/abs/1307.6127
8. Kuznetsov, L., Ide, K., Jones, C.K.R.T.: A method for assimilation of Lagrangian data. Mon. Wea. Rev. **131**, 2247–2260 (2003)
9. Molcard, A., Piterbarg, L., Griffa, A., Özgökmen, T., Mariano, A.: Assimilation of drifter positions for the reconstruction of the Eulerian circulation field. J. Geophys. Res. **108**, 3056 (2003)
10. Özgökmen, T., Molcard, A., Chin, T., Piterbarg, L., Griffa, A.: Assimilation of drifter positions in primitive equation models of midlatitude ocean circulation. J. Geophys. Res. **108**, 3238 (2003)
11. Pedlosky, J.: Geophysical Fluid Dynamics. Springer, New York (1986)
12. Robert, C., Casella, G.: Monte Carlo Statistical Methods. Springer, New York (1999)
13. Roullet, G.: 2d versatile model - multimod (2013). http://stockage.univ-brest.fr/roullet/codes.html
14. Salman, H.: A hybrid grid/particle filter for lagrangian data assimilation. i: formulating the passive scalar approximation. Q. J. Roy. Meteor. Soc. **134**, 1539–1550 (2008a)
15. Salman, H.: A hybrid grid/particle filter for lagrangian data assimilation. ii: application to a model vortex flow. Q. J. Roy. Meteor. Soc. **134**, 1539–1550 (2008b)
16. Salman, H., Kuznetsov, L., Jones, C.K.R.T., Ide, K.: A method for assimilating Lagrangian data into a shallow-water equation ocean model. Mon. Wea. Rev. **134**, 1081–1101 (2006)
17. Cotter, S.L., Roberts, G.O., Stuart, A., White, D.: MCMC methods for functions: modifying old algorithms to make them faster. Stat. Sci. **28**, 424–446 (2013)
18. Slivinski, L., Spiller, E., Apte, A., Sandstede, B.: A hybrid particle-ensemble Kalman filter for Lagrangian data assimilation. Mon. Wea. Rev. **143**, 195–211 (2014). http://www.whoi.edu/cms/files/hybrid_MWR_2col_194185.pdf

19. Snyder, C., Bengtsson, T., Bickel, P., Anderson, J.: Obstacles to high-dimensional particle filtering. Mon. Wea. Rev. **136**, 4629–4640 (2008)
20. Spiller, E., Budhiraja, A., Ide, K., Jones, C.: Modified particle filter methods for assimilating Lagrangian data into a point-vortex model. Physica D **237**, 1498–1506 (2008)

Specification of the Ionosphere-Thermosphere Using the Ensemble Kalman Filter

Humberto C. Godinez[1]([✉]), Earl Lawrence[1], David Higdon[1], Aaron Ridley[2],
Josef Koller[1], and Alexei Klimenko[1]

[1] Applied Mathematics and Plasma Physics, Los Alamos National Laboratory,
Los Alamos, NM 87544, USA
hgodinez@lanl.gov
[2] University of Michigan, Ann Arbor, USA

Abstract. The Ionosphere-Thermosphere environment undergoes constant and sometimes dramatic changes due to solar and geomagnetic activity. Furthermore, given that this environment has a significant effect on space infrastructure, such as satellites, it is important to understand the potential changes caused by space weather events.

This work presents the implementation of the ensemble Kalman filter assimilation technique to improve the nowcast and forecast of the thermosphere environment. Specifically, the assimilation tries to adjust F10.7, a solar radio flux parameter at 10.7 cm wavelength that acts as a proxy for solar activity.

The results show that during high solar activity, the measured F10.7 index is able to account for the variability in the ionosphere-thermosphere, hence the correction provided by the assimilation is small. On the other hand, during low solar activity, F10.7 is unable to account for variability in the ionosphere-thermosphere, and the correction provided by the assimilation drastically improves the nowcast/forecast.

1 Introduction

The Ionosphere-Thermosphere environment is host to vast majority of space infrastructure, and is the dominant effect on drag exerted by a number of satellites. Hence understand and correctly specifying this upper atmospheric environment is critical for the safekeeping of the space infrastructure.

There are a number of model that simulate the ionosphere-thermosphere. These include the Mass-Spectrometer-Incoherent-Scatter (MSIS) [7], and empirical based model, the NCAR Thermosphere-Ionosphere-Electrodynamics General Circulation Model (TIE-GCM) [2,18], and the Global Ionosphere-Thermosphere Model (GITM) [19] to name a few. Although these models include most of the relevant physics, their forecast error can be significant without proper prior calibration and/or initial conditions.

Data assimilation are methods that combine information from a model, observational data, and corresponding error statistics, to provide an enhanced approximation of the true state of the system [1,11]. Assimilation methods are widely

© Springer International Publishing Switzerland 2015
S. Ravela and A. Sandu (Eds.): DyDESS 2014, LNCS 8964, pp. 274–283, 2015.
DOI: 10.1007/978-3-319-25138-7_25

used in geophysical sciences, including atmospheric sciences, space weather, and climate and ocean sciences to name a few. Additionally, assimilation methods are increasingly being implemented in heliophysical and upper atmospheric sciences. The TIE-GCM has been used to assimilate electron density profiles [12], and to derive neutral mass density from CHAMP and GRACE satellites [13] More recently Morozov et al., [14] used GITM to assimilate CHAMP and GRACE data for the estimation of model state variables and parameters.

In this work, we present the implementation of the ensemble Kalman filter to the GITM model in order to better approximate the ionosphere-thermosphere density. One of the main drivers for the variability within the ionosphere-thermosphere is the Sun, whose influence is included in the form of the $F_{10.7}$ solar radio flux parameter. In order to improve the forecast in GITM, the assimilation is performed by correcting the model variables as well as estimating an appropriate $F_{10.7}$ parameter value. Given that $F_{10.7}$ is a time-varying index, the estimation is meant to involve a correction to the parameter that can change from one time period to another. The assimilation is performed using derived neutral density from CHAMP and GRACE, where a data denial experiment is performed to validate the results. A couple of experiments are performed, one during solar maximum and the other during solar minimum. Although a couple of studies have also tuned the $F_{10.7}$ parameter value in TIE-GCM [13] as well as GITM [14], both studies concentrate on Solar maximum time periods, where the Sun exerts a dominant influence upon the ionosphere-thermosphere. The main objective is to understand how the assimilation performs during different solar activity, that is, during solar maximum and solar minimum. The main difference is that in solar maximum, the Sun is the main driver for the variability within the ionosphere-thermosphere, while during solar minimum, internal processes within Earth ionosphere-thermosphere are responsible for their variability. The following sections describe the GITM model, assimilation algorithm, observations, experiment setup and results, and finally conclusions and future work.

2   Ionosphere-Thermosphere Model and Assimilation Method

2.1   Ionosphere-Thermosphere Model

The Global Ionosphere-Thermosphere Model (GITM) [19] is a physics based model that solves the full Navier-Stokes equations for density, velocity, and temperature for a number of neutral and charged components. The model explicitly solves for the neutral densities of O, O_2, $N(^2D)$, $N(^2T)$, $N(^4S)$, N_2, NO, H, and He; and the ion species $O^+(^4S)$, $O^+(^2D)$, $O^+(^2P)$, O_2^+, N^+, N_2^+, NO^+, H^+, and He^+. It also contains chemistry between species of ions and neutrals, ions and electrons, and neutral and neutrals. In addition, GITM self-consistently solves for the neutral, ion, and electron temperature; the bulk horizontal neutral winds; the vertical velocity of the individual species; and the ion and electron velocities. To account for solar activity GITM can use $F_{10.7}$ as a proxy or direct EUV spectrum measurements.

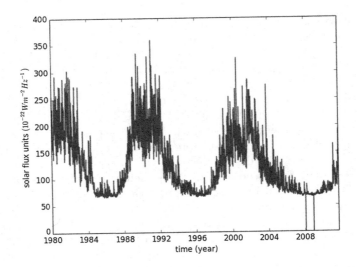

Fig. 1. $F_{10.7}$

Some of the more important features of GITM are: adjustable resolution; non-uniform grid in the altitude and latitude coordinates; the dynamics equations are solved without the assumption of hydrostatic equilibrium; the advection is solved for explicitly, so the time-step in GITM is approximately 2–4 s; the chemistry is solved for explicitly, so there are no approximations of local chemical equilibrium; the ability to choose different models of electric fields and particle precipitation patterns; the ability to start from MSIS [6,15] and IRI [16] solutions; and the ability to use a realistic (or ideal) magnetic field determined at the time of the model run.

The main parameter of interest is $F_{10.7}$, which solar radio flux at 10.7 cm wavelength measuring the noise level generated by the Sun at the Earth's orbit, used as a proxy in GITM for solar activity. Figure 1 shows the $F_{10.7}$ solar radio flux index from 1980 up to approximately 2011, where the 11-year solar cycle is clearly visible in the high and low activity peaks.

2.2   Ensemble Kalman Filter

The ensemble Kalman Filter (EnKF) [3,4] is a Monte Carlo approximation to Kalman filtering [10] for non-linear models, and has gained wide acceptance in data assimilation applications. The EnKF uses an ensemble of model simulations or forecasts to calculate the model mean and error covariance matrix. The ensemble is updated using the Kalman filter equations to reflect information provided by the observations, and is evolved using the forecast model between assimilation cycles. For more details on the EnKF algorithm see [4,8].

For a vector of m measurements $\mathbf{y}^o$ and an ensemble of N forecasts $\mathbf{x}_i^f, i = 1, \ldots, N$ the EnKF analysis equations are given by:

$$\mathbf{x}_i^a = \mathbf{x}_i^f + \mathbf{K}\left(\mathbf{y}_i^o - \mathbf{H}\mathbf{x}_i^f\right), \quad i = 1, \ldots, N, \tag{1}$$

$$\mathbf{K} = \mathbf{P}^f\mathbf{H}^T\left(\mathbf{H}\mathbf{P}^f\mathbf{H}^T + \mathbf{R}\right)^{-1}. \tag{2}$$

where $\mathbf{K} \in \mathbb{R}^{n \times m}$ is referred to as the Kalman gain matrix; $\mathbf{x}_i^a \in \mathbb{R}^n$ is the analysis; $\mathbf{P}^f \in \mathbb{R}^{n \times n}$ is the forecast covariance matrix; $\mathbf{R} \in \mathbb{R}^{m \times m}$ is the observations covariance matrix; $\mathbf{H} \in \mathbb{R}^{m \times n}$ is the linear observation operator that maps from state space to observations space; and $\mathbf{y}_i^o \in \mathbb{R}^m$ is a perturbed observations vector. For more details on the EnKF algorithm see [4,8].

For our particular problem, the GITM state variables and $F_{10.7}$ are both estimated using the EnKF. So the state vector $\mathbf{x}_i^f$ is composed of the GITM state variables and the $F_{10.7}$ parameter appended at the end. Specifically, since $F_{10.7}$ is a measured quantity, the EnKF assimilation will estimate a correction to the parameter. The correction of $F_{10.7}$ is to estimate the appropriate coupling between the observed $F_{10.7}$ and the model. For a given observed $F_{10.7}$ index $p_{F10.7}^o$, the model $F_{10.7}$ parameter is given by

$$p_{F10.7}^m = p_{F10.7}^o + \delta p_{F10.7}$$

where $\delta p_{F10.7}$ is the "correction" provided by the EnKF data assimilation.

Given that the EnKF uses an ensemble of model forecast to estimate the model covariance matrix, artificial cross-correlation terms will be present in this matrix. These spurious cross-correlations terms can introduce significant noise into the analysis, ultimately leading to an incorrect analysis [5]. To address this problem, the estimation of the GITM variables and $F_{10.7}$ parameter are done using a local variant of the EnKF, specifically the Local Ensemble Transform Kalman Filter (LETKF) [9]. The LETKF uses the same basic equations as the EnKF but it assimilates each model grid-point by defining an appropriate spatial local region. The localization is regularizing the model covariance matrix to reduce the introduction of noise into the updated model state and parameters. More details refer to the article by Hunt et al. [9]. For our problem, a small local grid-point state vector is formed, composed of the corresponding GITM variables, as well as the $F_{10.7}$ parameter. In the end, each model grid-point will have estimated a correction to the $F_{10.7}$ parameter, and a global correction is obtained by averaging all of the grid-point corrections. Additionally, we implement an inflation technique for the $F_{10.7}$ parameter equal to 45 % of the initial parameter spread used to generate the ensemble. That is, the parameters are inflated by

$$\hat{p}_{F10.7,i} = \bar{p}_{F10.7} + \lambda\left(p_{F10.7,i} - \bar{p}_{F10.7}\right),$$

where $p_{F10.7,i}$ is the $F_{10.7}$ parameter value for ensemble i, $\bar{p}_{F10.7}$ is the ensemble average parameter value, $\hat{p}_{F10.7,i}$ is the inflated parameter value for ensemble i, and λ is the inflation factor equal to 45 % of the standard deviation of the initial parameter spread used in the ensemble.

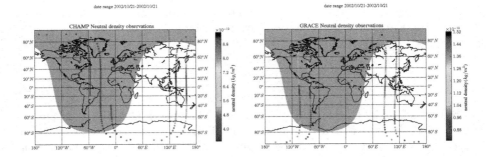

Fig. 2. Derived total neutral density from CHAMP (left plot) and GRACE (right plot) satellites for October 21 2010 from 00:00 to 03:00 UTC. The shading shows the day/night state of the globe at the time of observations.

3   Assimilation Experiments

3.1   Total Neutral Density Observations

The observational data used the assimilation in GITM is derived total neutral density measurements from Challenging Minisatellite Payload (CHAMP) [17] and Gravity Recovery and Climate Experiment (GRACE) satellites [22]. The satellites of both missions contain very accurate accelerometers, which can be used to infer drag and therefore provide an estimate of the total neutral density along the satellite track [20,21]. Both CHAMP are GRACE are polar-orbiting satellites with an orbital period of about 90 min, slowly precessing through different solar local times over the course of 133 days. Figure 2 shows the CHAMP and GRACE derived total neutral density for October 21, 2002 from 00:00–03:00 UTC. The neutral density is highest during the dayside of the globe, and lowest during the nightside of the globe. All CHAMP and GRACE data is available at www.impact.lanl.gov.

3.2   Model and Assimilation Setup

There are two GITM data assimilation experiments (DAE):

- DAE1: valid for October 21–24, 2002, during solar maximum (see Fig. 1)
- DAE2: valid for August 28–31, 2009, during solar minimum

In order to get a realistic simulation of the ionosphere-thermosphere, GITM is provided with Hemispheric Power index, obtained from the NOAA Space Weather Prediction Center website, http://www.swpc.noaa.gov, and the Solar conditions from NASA OMNI website, http://omniweb.gsfc.nasa.gov/, valid for the corresponding time periods. All GITM simulations are done on a $5° \times 5°$ grid, with 50 vertical levels on a stretched grid that goes from 100 km to approximately 600 km for solar maximum and 500 km for solar minimum. Additionally, all simulations use MSIS model solution as their initial condition, and are spunned up for two days to establish the correct dynamics and a consistent solution for the Navier-Stokes equations.

The ensemble for each assimilation experiment is generated by perturbing both the initial condition and the $F_{10.7}$ parameter. The $F_{10.7}$ is perturbed using a Latin Hypercube sampling strategy with a normal distribution, where the average and standard deviation used is the time average and standard deviation for each corresponding time period. For DAE1 the average is 163.62 and standard deviation of 15.0, while for DAE2 the average is 97.7 and standard deviation 3.0. Each EnKF assimilation experiment uses an ensemble of 20 members. The assimilation is performed every 30 min, for the whole time period.

An important aspect of the localized EnKF assimilation scheme is the size of the local region around each model grid-point. After some testing, it was determined that a local region in the shape of a three dimensional ellipsoid was most appropriate, with a longitude axis of ~ 1000 km, a latitudinal axis of ~ 750 km and altitudinal axis of ~ 50 km.

To validate the results of the assimilation experiments, a data denial setup is used, where observations from GRACE are assimilated and the analysis compared with observations from CHAMP. In this way, the analysis is not unfairly compared with observations that have been already been assimilated, and provides a more valid comparison with a set of independent unassimilated set of observations.

3.3   Assimilation Results

For DAE1, the time period is during solar maximum, which means that the Sun is the main driving force for the variability observed in the ionosphere-thermosphere. During these time periods, the GITM model includes a good representation of the effects of the Sun, and provides an accurate estimate for the ionosphere-thermosphere. The results show that simulated GITM, without any data assimilation, provides a good approximation to CHAMP neutral density data. The right plot of Fig. 3 shows the comparison of neutral density from CHAMP (green line) with GITM (red line) and assimilated GITM (blue line) for October 21–24, 2002. As seen in Fig. 3, the improvement provided by the assimilation is not significant, indicating that the physics within the model for this time period are well represented. Evidence of the performance of GITM is further seen in the left plot of Fig. 3, where the measured $F_{10.7}$ (red line) is compared against assimilated $F_{10.7}$ (blue line). The assimilated $F_{10.7}$ is seen oscillating very closely to the measured $F_{10.7}$, indicating that not much correction is needed for this parameter to have GITM match the observed density from GRACE.

For DAE2, the time period is during solar minimum when the Sun does not have a significant influence in the variability of the ionosphere-thermosphere. During solar minimum, more complex internal processes dominate how the ionosphere-thermosphere changes, and are more difficult to model since they are not completely well understood. In these cases, the assimilation can make a dramatic improvement to GITM through the correction of the $F_{10.7}$ parameter.

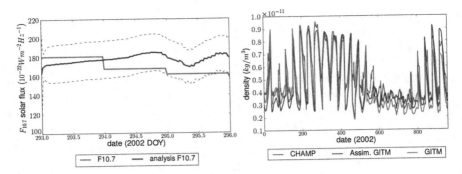

Fig. 3. Left plot: observed $F_{10.7}$ (red line) for October 21–24, 2002, used in the unassimilated GITM simulation, compared with analysis $F_{10.7}$ from the assimilation experiment (blue line) using GRACE total neutral density for the same time period. Right plot: total neutral density for CHAMP (green line) for October 21–24, 2002, compared with corresponding density from unassimilated GITM (read line) and assimilated GITM (blue line) using GRACE total neutral density observations for the same time period (Color figure online).

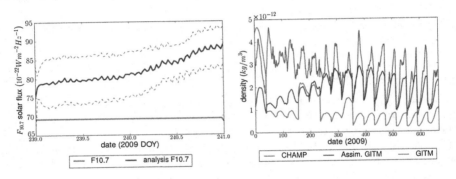

Fig. 4. Left plot: observed $F_{10.7}$ (red line) for August 28–30, 2009, used in the unassimilated GITM simulation, compared with analysis $F_{10.7}$ from the assimilation experiment (blue line) using GRACE total neutral density for the same time period. Right plot: total neutral density for CHAMP (green line) for August 28–30, 2009, compared with corresponding density from unassimilated GITM (read line) and assimilated GITM (blue line) using GRACE total neutral density observations for the same time period (Color figure online).

The improvement is shown in the right plot of Fig. 4, where the total neutral density from CHAMP (green line) is compared with GITM (red line) and assimilated GITM (blue line) for August 21–24, 2009. Recall that the assimilation is performed using GRACE observations, and is validated using CHAMP observations. From Fig. 4, it can be seen how the assimilation provides a solution that converges towards the observed density as time progresses. This time lag, or assimilation spin up, is mainly caused by the convergence rate for the correction of $F_{10.7}$, as seen in the left plot of Fig. 4.

4 Conclusions

In this work the implementation of the ensemble Kalman filter data assimilation method to the Global Ionosphere-Thermosphere model to improve the nowcast/forecast. One of the main drivers responsible for most of the variability in the Ionosphere-thermosphere is the Sun, whose contribution is included in the model through $F_{10.7}$ solar radio flux index. Hence, in order to get the correct thermosphere environment, the assimilation corrects the model variables, as well as estimate an appropriate $F_{10.7}$ parameter value to reduce the forecast error. The assimilation is done using derived total neutral density measurements from Challenging Minisatellite Payload (CHAMP) and Gravity Recovery and Climate Experiment (GRACE) satellites. A data denial experiment is utilized, where observational data from GRACE is used in the assimilation, and the resulting analysis is compared with observational data from CHAMP. Two separate data assimilation experiments are performed, one for October 21–24, 2002 and another for August 28–30, 2009. The first data assimilation experiment takes place during solar maximum, which is when there is significant solar activity during a solar 11-year cycle. The second experiment takes place during solar minimum, which is a time period of low solar activity in the solar cycle.

For the first assimilation experiment, the results show that during solar maximum the GITM model provides a reasonable estimate of the ionosphere-thermosphere. Given that the physics during solar maximum are fairly understood and well represented in the GITM model, the assimilation can only provide a small correction to the model. Additionally, during solar maximum, the Sun dominates most of the relevant physics and variations within the ionosphere-thermosphere. On the other hand, for the second assimilation experiment, the results show that during solar minimum the GITM model is unable to give a reasonable estimate of the ionosphere-thermosphere. This is due to the fact that during solar minimum, internal processes dominate the variability within the ionosphere-thermosphere. These are complex processes that are yet not well understood, hence their influence is not well represented in the GITM model. Hence, for this time period, the assimilation makes a significant improvement in the GITM model through the $F_{10.7}$ parameter, even though the parameter is a proxy for solar activity.

The assimilation has proven to be an important tool to improve the forecast of the ionosphere-thermosphere. Future work will include expanding the data sources to include observational data from other satellites and ground stations. Additionally, other model parameter within GITM will be explored for correction, such as EUV spectrum parameter, cooling and heating rate coefficients, and solar absorption rate parameters.

Acknowledgments. This research was conducted as part of the Integrated Modeling of Perturbations in Atmospheres for Conjunction Tracking (IMPACT) project, funded by the Laboratory Directed Research and Development program within Los Alamos National Laboratory. More information on www.impact.lanl.gov.

References

1. Daley, R.: Atmospheric Data Analysis. Cambridge University Press, Cambridge (1991)
2. Dickinson, R., Ridley, E., Roble, R.: A three-dimensional general circulation model of the thermosphere. J. Geophys. Res. **86**, 1499–1512 (1981)
3. Evensen, G.: Sequential data assimilation with a nonlinear quasi-geostrophic model using Monte Carlo methods to forecast error statistics. J. Geophys. Res. **99**(C5), 10143–10162 (1994)
4. Evensen, G.: The ensemble Kalman filter: Theoretical formulation and practical implementation. Ocean Dyn. **53**, 343–367 (2003)
5. Hamill, T., Whitaker, J., Snyder, C.: Distance-dependent filtering of background error covariance estimates in an ensemble Kalman filter. Mon. Wea. Rev. **129**, 2776–2790 (2001)
6. Hedin, A.: A revised thermospheric model based on mass spectrometer and incoherent scatter data: Msis-83. J. Geophys. Res. **88**, 10170–10188 (1983)
7. Hedin, A., Fleming, E., Manson, A., Schmidlin, F., Avery, S., Clark, R., Franke, S., Fraser, G., Tsuda, T., Vial, F., Vincent, R.: Empirical wind model for the upper, middle and lower atmosphere. J. Atmos. Terr. Phys. **58**, 1421–1447 (1996)
8. Houtekamer, P., Mitchell, H.: Data assimilation using an ensemble Kalman filter technique. Mon. Wea. Rev. **126**, 796–811 (1998)
9. Hunt, B., Kostelich, E., Szunyogh, I.: Efficient Data Assimilation for Spatiotemporal Chaos: a Local Ensemble Transform Kalman Filter. Arxiv preprint physics/0511236 (2005)
10. Kalman, R.: A new approach to linear filtering and prediction problems. Trans. ASME Ser. D J. Basic Eng. **82**, 35–45 (1960)
11. Kalnay, E.: Atmospheric Modeling, Data Assimilation, and Predictability. Cambridge University Press, Cambridge (2003)
12. Lee, I., Matsuo, T., Richmond, A., Liu, J., Wang, W., Lin, C., Anderson, J., Chen, M.: Assimilation of formosat-3/cosmic electron density profiles into a coupled thermosphere/ionosphere model using ensemble kalman filtering. J. Geophys. Res. **117**, A10318 (2012)
13. Matsuo, T., Lee, I.T., Anderson, J.: Thermospheric mass density specification using an ensemble kalman filter. J. Geophys. Res. Space Phys. **118**, 1339–1350 (2013)
14. Morozov, A., Ridley, A., Bernstein, D., Collins, N., Hoar, T., Anderson, J.: Data assimilation and driver estimation for the global ionosphere-thermosphere model using the ensemble adjustment kalman filter. J. Atmos. Sol.-Terr. Phy. **104**, 126–136 (2013)
15. Picone, J., Hedin, A., Drob, D., Aikin, A.: Nrlmsise-00 empirical model of the atmosphere: Statistical comparisons and scientific issues. J. Geophys. Res. **107**, 1468 (2002)
16. Rawer, K., Bilitza, D., Ramakrishnan, S.: Goals and status of the international reference ionosphere. Rev. Geophys. **16**, 177 (1978)
17. Reigber, C., Luhr, H., Schwintzer, P.: Champ mission status. Adv. Space Res. **30**, 129–134 (2002)
18. Richmond, A., Ridley, E., Roble, R.: A thermosphere/ionosphere general circulation model with coupled electrodynamics. Geophys. Res. Lett. **19**(6), 601–604 (1992)
19. Ridley, A.J., Deng, Y., Toth, G.: The global ionosphere-thermosphere model. J. Atmos. Sol.-Terr. Phys. **68**, 839–864 (2006)

20. Sutton, E.: Normalized force coefficients for satellites with elongated shapes. J. Spacecraft Rockets **46**, 112–116 (2009)
21. Sutton, E., Nerem, R., Forbes, J.: Density and winds in the thermosphere deduced from accelerometer data. J. Spacecraft Rockets **44**, 1210–1219 (2007)
22. Tapley, B., Bettadpur, S., Watkins, M., Reigber, C.: The gravity recovery and climate experiment: mission overview and early results. Geophys. Res. Lett. **31**, L09607 (2004)

Ensemble Adjustment Kalman Filter Data Assimilation for a Global Atmospheric Model

Tarkeshwar Singh[1(✉)], Rashmi Mittal[2], and H.C. Upadhyaya[1]

[1] Indian Institute of Technology (IIT) Delhi, New Delhi, India
tarkphysics87@gmail.com, hcdhyaya@cas.iitd.ac.in
[2] IBM Research, New Delhi, India
rashmitt@in.ibm.com

Abstract. This work describes the implementation and evaluation of an Ensemble Adjustment Kalman Filter (EAKF) with a global atmospheric zoom model (version 5) of the Laboratoire de Météorologie Dynamique (LMDZ5, Z stands for zoom). An interface has been developed to use Data Assimilation Research Testbed (DART), a community EAKF system, with LMDZ5 model. The NCEP PREBUFR real observation data have been assimilated to evaluate the performance of newly developed LMDZ5-DART system. It has been demonstrated with the help of a numerical experiment that LMDZ5-DART system successfully assimilates real observations. A one month LMDZ5-DART analysis has been created using assimilation of NCEP PREBUFR observation data, and the assimilated fields are compared with NCEP CDAS reanalysis. Results show that LMDZ5-DART produces remarkably similar reanalysis to NCEP products. This is therefore a very encouraging result towards a long-term goal of creating a high quality analysis over the Indian subcontinent from the assimilation of local satellite products.

Keywords: Data assimilation · Ensemble Kalman filter · LMDZ5 · DART · Global reanalysis

1 Introduction

Data assimilation is a necessary prerequisite for current day numerical weather prediction system. A typical weather forecast is subjected to various uncertainties in the specification of the initial conditions. Modern methods of determining the model initial conditions use data assimilation techniques to optimize observational data with a short-range model forecast to produce an analysis. Data assimilation also is an important tool to evaluate the forecast model by identifying quantities that are poorly predicted and by estimating values for a model parameter that are consistent with the local observations [1]. In global perspective, it is used to generate reanalysis products or a best estimate of the atmospheric state by cycling the assimilation of observations in global model over a given time period. A recent study of Raeder et al. [2] demonstrated that data assimilation has the ability to improve the climate model development and should thus become an integral part of that process as well. They used data assimilation in detection of noise associated with polar filter and latitudes/longitudes, correction of

© Springer International Publishing Switzerland 2015
S. Ravela and A. Sandu (Eds.): DyDESS 2014, LNCS 8964, pp. 284–298, 2015.
DOI: 10.1007/978-3-319-25138-7_26

short-term bias in model prognostic fields and in parameter estimation in a climate model.

The EAKF is a variant of Ensemble Square Root Kalman Filter. Unlike 3D or 4D variational methods; the ensemble kalman filter (EnKF) technique has advantage of estimating flow dependent background error covariance, which enables advanced data assimilation with a prediction model. Moreover, the EnKF methods are potentially attractive for many reasons. They are very simple to code without any need of an adjoint of the forecast model. In addition to ensemble of analyses, they also provide an estimate of analysis error distribution. For geophysical data assimilation, recent results have suggested that this method is competitive to variational system [3, 4].

In this work, description of an interface developed for using EAKF [5] with a global atmospheric model LMDZ5 atmospheric has been presented. Now days, along with in-situ measurements, data from many satellites e.g. INSAT 3D, KALPANA, Megha-Tropique are available over India and the surrounding domain. The primary goal of development of LMDZ5-DART system is to improve and understand various features of ASM through assimilation of these observations. This requires one to generate a high quality gridded atmospheric data for the Indian region. As a first step towards this long-term goal, the main objectives of the current work are as follows.

To present the platform LMDZ5-DART that has been developed for studying ASM using high quality data
To test both consistency and accuracy of this system by assimilating real observations in numerical experiments

The remaining text in the papers has been organized as follows; Sect. 2 describes LMDZ5-DART system and interface development. In Sect. 3, a detailed description of numerical experiments is provided. Section 4 presents the result of numerical experiments with the real observations and finally the findings of this work are summarized in Sect. 5 along with the scope for future work.

2   The LMDZ5-DART Atmospheric Data Assimilation System

2.1   LMDZ5

The LMDZ5 is a grid point atmospheric general circulation model initially described by Sadourny and Laval [6] and its physical parameterizations have been evaluated by Le Treut and Li [7]. It is an atmospheric component in the earth system model of the Institut Pierre Simon Laplace (IPSL), which participated in 4th and 5th assessment report of IPCC [8]. The details of physical package and model performance on the global scale are provided in Hourdin et al. [9]. This model has capability of archiving stretched horizontal grid [10], which can be used to run this model at finer regional scale as well [11]. The dynamical core uses a finite difference formulation of the hydrostatic primitive equations in hybrid vertical coordinate system (sigma-pressure).

The variables of the governing equations are staggered on longitude-latitude Arakawa C grid as shown in Fig. 1.

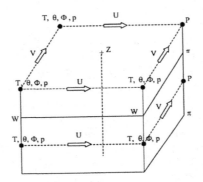

Fig. 1. The representation of model variables on Arakawa C grid.

2.2   Data Assimilation Research Test Bed (DART)

DART routines have been incorporated in LMDZ5 through an interface to implement EAKF. The DART is an open-source community facility employing different (deterministic and stochastic) EnKF for data assimilation [12]. It has been developed and maintained at National Center for Atmospheric Research (NCAR) and it is widely used for different weather and climate applications [2, 13, 14]. The modular structure of DART facilitates the interfacing of new models with minimal code changes. The EnKF data assimilation (also called 'filter') computes the sample covariance between model state variables and prior estimate of the observation by using a set of model forecasts. The ensemble of model state analyses is computed from covarinces using Bayes's theorem [15]. The basic ensemble assimilation algorithm is though useful for theoretical studies with low order models; but for large geophysical models, use of algorithms is necessary for archiving a high quality performance of ensemble data assimilation system. DART includes the latest advanced algorithms; two of the most useful algorithms are describe below.

Covariance Inflation. Numerical models are associated with significant errors due to their inability to resolve complex physical process that are involved in geophysical phenomena. The model errors are shared with data assimilation along with many others sources of error, e.g. sampling error from smaller ensembles, systematic observational error, miss-specification of observational error covariance and error of observation representativeness. These error sources result in a prior estimate with insufficient variance and persistent loss of variance during assimilation of observation. A damped adaptive inflation algorithm in DART is used to resolve this issue by inflating the spread of ensemble periodically [16].

Localization. In large models, use of finite number of ensemble members to compute sample covariance results in a non-negligible spurious correlation between widely separated variables. Localization is a mechanism to ignore such spurious correlations.

DART can employ a user specified localization distance or modify this value based on the local density of observations [17].

In the sequel, usefulness of the above-mentioned methods is discussed with real data experiments.

2.3   Interface Development of LMDZ5 with DART

Implementation of DART in the LMDZ5 model requires developing and including a set of interface routines in the latter to archive exchange of information with the former. For the interface, a state vector is composed of subset of LMDZ5 prognostic variables namely surface pressure (ps), temperature (T), wind component (U, V), specific humidity (Q) and cloud liquid water (CLDLIQ). The other variables could also be added in state vector by minor code modifications. The key sections of interface routines are static model initialization, input/output (I/O) read-write, model interpolation, vector to field & field to vector translation of model variables, find nearest state variables to a given location and some other utility routines.

The static initialization of the model is the first call made to the model by any DART compliant assimilation routine for runtime initialization of the model. It reads a specified parameter for LMDZ5 model, sets the calendar type (the Gregorian calendar is used with the LMDZ5 model), determines the state vector length and retrieves model information (e.g. grid dimensions, vertical hybrid coefficients, time step etc.).

The I/O section has many sets of routines written using netCDF library to perform read-write task of several netCDF files. It reads meta-data information and prognostic state variables from LMDZ5 I/O files for each ensemble member and overwrites the same files with updated prognostic state variables that are generated after assimilation. The updated input files are used by LMDZ5 to advance each of the ensemble members for next assimilation cycle. It also writes ensemble members, ensemble mean and spread, adaptive inflation values and several other variables in netCDF files periodically.

Reformation of state vector is one of the key elements of this interface to exchange information between 1D states vector in assimilation model and 2D and 3D fields vectors of LMDZ5. Vector to field and field to vector translation routines are used to carryout this task. This is done by two interfaces routine "dart_to_lmdz" and "lmdz_to_dart" (Fig. 2), which allow interface of DART with LMDZ5 without modification of codes.

The model interpolation section applies the forward operator H (2D & 3D scalar interpolation) to the model states to create an expected or prior observation at the desired location. It supports interpolation in pressure, height and hybrid pressure vertical coordinates. Interpolation at a given location is done directly to Arakawa C grids at hybrid pressure levels where the model variables are distributed. The LMDZ5 grids (Arakawa C) have no staggered latitude grids points of meridional wind component V at both poles but there can be observation of V in the proximity of pole. Here maximum latitudes for V observations to be assimilated are defined as user specified input. Similarly some observations are taken at the surface near to topography of LMDZ5 model, which are approximations of the real topography. In the current version, no interpolation is performed from model grid to observations that are below the lowest model levels or at surface.

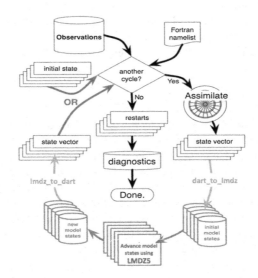

Fig. 2. A schematic description of the LMDZ5-DART assimilation system [18].

Localization of observation impact requires some interface routines that compute the distances both in horizontal and vertical state variables to the observation location and find the state variables that are close to nearest given observation location. For vertical distance computations all vertical coordinates are converted to a common pressure coordinate. At higher vertical levels, the observation assimilation needs special treatment. Strongly damping is used at top vertical levels of LMDZ5 where the model variables are not free to adjust with assimilation of observations. This makes the ensemble spread too small for the assimilation algorithm to work in the model top levels. There are two mechanism adopted from DART/CAM interface [2] to sidestep this problem. In the first mechanism, influence of observations on model points is reduced as a function of distance above the user specified pressure level. Similar to CAM interface [2], this pressure is usually set to 150 hPa, which turns the observation influence falling to 0 by about 60 hPa. In 29-level vertical resolution of LMDZ5, these correspond to model levels 19 and 23, counted from bottom. In second mechanism, which is essentially a simplification of first mechanism, all the observations are removed above a user specified pressure level.

A schematic representing the data flow in LMDZ5-DART system has been shown in Fig. 2. Starting from given observations and ensemble of initial states, "filter" assimilates the observation, updates the states variables and determines the model advance time for next assimilation cycle. The analyses of the prognostic state variables are done on their native model grid (Arakawa C-grid), which affects the successive forecast. The LMDZ5 model is then used to forecast all ensemble members to next available observation time. This update-forecast cycle continues until there are observations to assimilate or the specified observation time is reached. The cycling of LMDZ5-DART is run in a restart mode. For a single analysis time, there are multiple analysis files. Since LMDZ5-DART is run in restart mode, each member should keep its own LMDZ5 restart file from the previous cycle. At the end of assimilation a set of restart files for each ensemble member and diagnostics files are written.

3 Experimental Design

The aim of the numerical experiments is to evaluate the performance of LMDZ5-DART system with assimilation of real observations. For the numerical experiments presented here, the global resolution of LMDZ5 is setup at 2.5 × 2.5 degree in horizontal and 29 levels in vertical with model top level at 3 hPa. The lower boundary conditions in the model are specified from AMIP (Atmospheric Model Intercomparison Project), viz., sea surface temperature (SST), albedo, soil moisture, snow cover. All experiments have been done using a 60-ensemble member of model for one-month assimilation period (May 2009). The same lower boundary data are used to realize all ensemble members throughout this study. Further details on the design of experiments are given in what follows.

3.1 Observations

LMDZ5-DART system is tested with real observations from the NCEP PREBUFR database, (http://rda.ucar.edu/datasets/ds090.0/) which constitute of data from radiosondes, dropsondes, pibals, ship, buoy and satellite processed at National Environmental Satellite, Data and Information Service (NESDIS). These datasets serve as primary input to the climate data assimilation (CDAS) to produce the reanalysis data at National Centre for Environmental Prediction (NCEP). For this study, a subset of these data is included which comprises of observations of temperature and horizontal wind velocity (U, V) with a view to simplify evaluation of performance of LMDZ-DART system. However, the other model state variables such as surface pressure are also undoubtedly influenced by the use of such observations in the system.

3.2 Assimilation Cycle and Quality Control of Observations

NCEP CDAS assimilate observations at every 6 h; hence, PREPBUFR data exist every 6 h for making available the analysis at 0000, 0600, 1200, 1800 UTC which include observation data in the 6 h window centered at the respective analysis times. Here, in this study the LMDZ5-DART forecast/assimilation cycle is chosen 6 h with assimilation length of one month between 0000 UTC 1 May 2009 and 0000 UTC 1 June 2009. Appropriate limited quality controls have been performed for these observations. The observations, more precisely, which have standard deviation of three from model-derived expected observations, have been rejected. Also the observations are limited above the level 150 hPa and below the top of the model.

3.3   Generation of Initial Background Ensemble

The ensemble of initial conditions for data assimilation cycle experiments has been generated by adding Gaussian noise to a single state taken from NCEP reanalysis at 0000 UTC 23 April 2009. Starting from each perturbed states, LMDZ5 has been integrated up to 0000 UTC 1 May 2009 for spin-up to balance all model fields. This choice of generating initial ensemble has a disadvantage in the sense that the initial ensemble members may not be independent as perturbing a single state generates them. On the other hand, it has the advantage because it is easier to create perturbed model initial conditions in comparison to finding ensemble of initial conditions from climatological archive. Figure 3 represents the ensemble mean and spread of LMDZ5 temperature and horizontal wind velocity states variables, which are calculated from 60-ensemble member. Here, the large spread in state variables represents the gross estimate of variability of the LMDZ5 initial states. It can be seen that the LMDZ5 forecast is more uncertain in extra tropical region compare to tropics for all three state variables (Fig. 3).

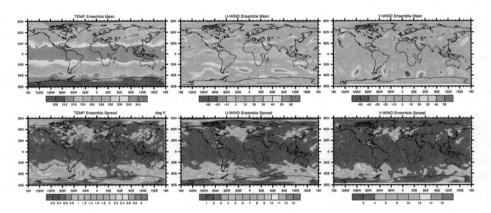

Fig. 3. Ensemble mean (first row) and ensemble spread (second row) at 500 hPa of initial conditions for LMDZ5 temperature (first column) in K, horizontal wind components U (second column) and V (Last column) in m/s.

3.4   Verification Methods

The main challenge in verifying the performance of any data assimilation system by ingesting real observations is that the true value of a verified variable is not known, which further makes it difficult to obtain reliable estimates of statistics for analysis error. The best method of determining the performance of experiments with real data is to compare in the 'observation-space'. Here we use observations as a proxy for true states because we always have the observations, though far from perfect yet they are the best. We compare the real observations with model-estimated ensemble mean at the observation locations. This is generated by first applying forward operators to the ensemble members in model space and then computing the mean over all the members of model-estimated observations. Following criteria has been used with LMDZ5-DART to test the stable performance of assimilation system.

Spread. The spread of ensemble should not collapse. Insufficient spread leads to large observation rejection ratio and filter divergence.

RMSE. RMSE (root-mean-square error) of ensemble should be relatively stable with time. A low RMSE is desirable and is a much stronger result if most/all of the observations are being assimilated successfully without rejection.

Bias. Bias of forecast and analysis ensemble means relative to observations should be close to zero.

4 Results and Discussion

In this section the results on the LMDZ5-DART performance have been presented. First the outcome of various sensitivity experiments done to tune this system is given. The tuned system is verified with the radiosonde data and the findings are demonstrated. Further in order to evaluate the potential of this system for generating reanalysis relative to CDAS reanalysis data, comparison between the analysis generated by LMDZ5-DART and CDAS is done.

4.1 Adjustment of LMDZ5-DART Parameters

One of the most significant exercises in model set up is to assess its sensitivity to various tunable parameters. A number of experiments with LMDZ5-DART were first performed to find an optimal value of localization radius for delineating observation impact, both in horizontal and vertical directions. Also the experiments have been performed to evaluate the assimilation system performance with and without covariance inflation.

For horizontal localization, three experiments were carried out respectively with different localization radius of 2400 km (HLOC2400), 1800 km (HLOC1800) and 1200 km (HLOC1200). These experiments have been evaluated in terms RMSE of 6 h forecasts (prior) relative to observed radiosondes temperature. Figure 4 shows that the HLOC1200 experiment has lower RMSE for entire period of assimilation compared to HLOC1800 and HLOC2400 experiments. A lower value of RMSE was also observed at all vertical levels for HLOC1200 experiment as shown in Fig. 5. Similar experiments were carried out to determine the optimum value of vertical localization distance (in hPa). It was found that 1000 hPa in vertical produced better LMDZ5-DART results. (Results not shown).

To test the performance of most advanced damped adaptive covariance inflation, two experiments were performed with and without covariance inflation. The inflation experiment was carried out with initial inflation factor 1 and standard deviation 0.6. In this experiment the RMSE of the ensemble mean forecast relative to radiosonde temperature has lower value in compare to the experiment without inflation as shown in

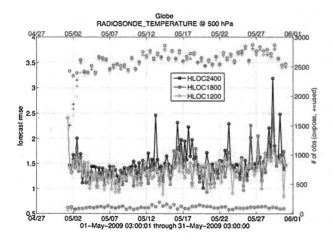

Fig. 4. Global RMSE of ensemble mean 6 h forecast relative to radiosonde temperature for May 2009 at 500 hPa. Circles represent the number of available observations and pluses represent used observations at each assimilation time (Right Axis).

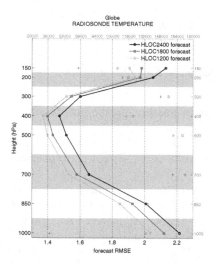

Fig. 5. Global RMSE of ensemble mean 6 h forecasts relative to radiosonde temperature averaged over different vertical bands indicated by shading.

Fig. 6. It can be seen that adaptive covariance inflation improve the 6 h forecast skills by up to 13.5 % throughout the period. Without inflation, one can notice that the ensemble spread gets reduced quickly due to rejecting of a large number of observations (Fig. 7). Clearly this leads to a bad performance of data assimilation system. These results emphasize the advantage of using adaptive covariance inflation.

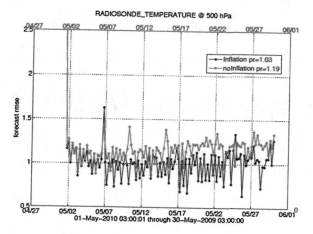

Fig. 6. Global RMSE of ensemble mean 6 h forecasts with inflation (black lines) and without inflation (red lines) relative to radiosonde temperature (Color figure online).

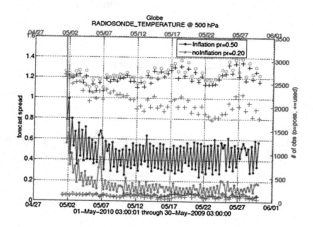

Fig. 7. Global SPREAD of ensemble mean forecasts with inflation (black lines) and without inflation (red lines). Circles represent the number of available observations and pluses represent used observations at each assimilation period (Right Axis) (Color figure online).

In accordance to the results of above discussed experiment, all the simulations of LMDZ5-DART have been set with damped adaptive covariance inflation, 1200 km in horizontal localization and 1000 hPa in vertical localization.

4.2 Verification Using Radiosonde Observations

A 6 h forecast and analysis (posterior) of LMDZ5-DART have been compared with radiosonde temperatures represented as ensemble mean of forecast and analysis. Figure 8 shows the ensemble spreads or standard deviations (both prior and posterior) of expected

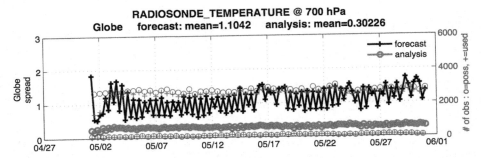

Fig. 8. Global prior (black) and posterior (red) ensemble spread (Left Axis) of expected radiosonde temperature for entire assimilation period (May 2009). Blue symbols show the number of observations available (o) and used (+) at each assimilation time (Right Axis) (Color figure online).

radiosonde temperatures across the 60 ensemble members. It shows that the spreads of ensemble is stable and does not collapse. Also it can be seen that the number of rejected observations is small and the ratio of rejected observations with respect to all observation varies marginally in time. This demonstrates sufficient spread of ensemble to cover

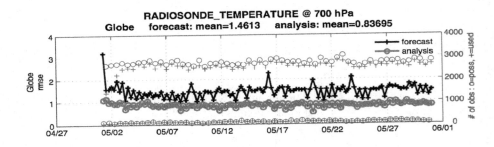

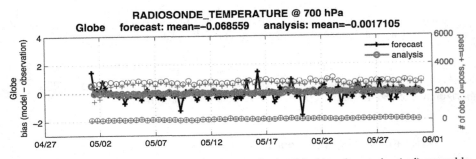

Fig. 9. Global RMSE (upper) and BIAS (lower) of prior (black) and posterior (red) ensemble mean relative to radiosonde temperature for entire assimilation period (May 2009). Blue symbols show the number of observations available (o) and used (+) at each assimilation time (Right Axis) (Color figure online).

(a)

(b)

(c)

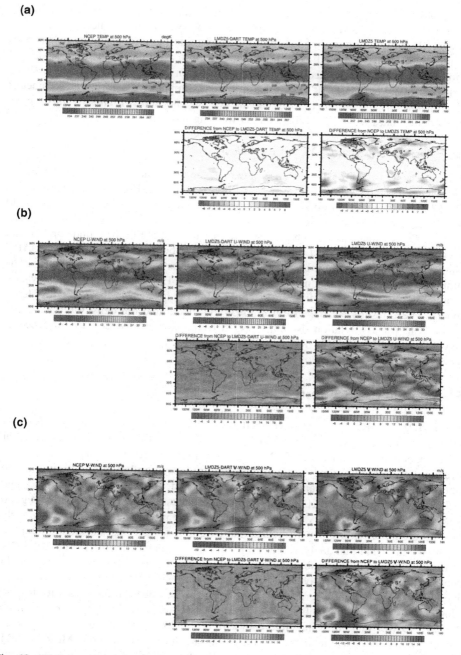

Fig. 10. Global comparison of May 2009 mean (a) Temperature (b) wind component U and (c) wind component V from LMDZ5-DART (middle, upper panel) assimilation system and from LMDZ5 forecast (right, upper panel) with NCEP Reanalysis (left, upper panel) at 500 hPa. Left, lower panels are difference from NCEP to LMDZ5-DART and right lower panels are difference from NCEP to LMDZ5.

observations. In Fig. 9 it is demonstrated that the predicted temperature is significantly improved in terms of RMSE and BIAS relative to observation used in the assimilation. In fact the RMSE of analysis (0.83) is reasonably close to the error range of radiosondes temperature (on average 0.80) pointing to a low error in assimilation. Also the RMSE of prior and posterior has limited variability as a function of time demonstrating a stable performance of LMDZ5-DART assimilation system. Similar results have been obtained at all vertical levels and for other model variables (figures not shown). These results furnish the evidence that LMDZ5-DART system is working properly.

4.3   Verification Against NCEP Reanalysis

A comparison of LMDZ5-DART ensemble mean analysis and simple LMDZ5 forecast with NCEP reanalysis averaged over May 2009 is shown in Fig. 10. One can see that LMDZ5-DART temperature and wind component analysis is remarkably similar to NCEP reanalysis whereas simple LMDZ5 forecast has poor performance. The LMDZ5-DART analysis has a high degree of similarity both in magnitude and spatial structure with NCEP product demonstrating a decent performance of LMDZ5-DART system even though only a subset of NCEP observations were used in assimilation. The similarity of analysis is distinctly visible in Northern Hemisphere where observation data are dense, but notable differences could however be seen in the Southern Hemisphere. These results are dependent both on the model and the density of the observation data for assimilation. Nonetheless, this comparison provides a confidence in newly designed LMDZ5-DART system to create high quality reanalysis data comparable to that from an operational center.

5   Summary and Future Plans

The LMDZ5-DART has been developed and successfully tested for analysis/forecast cycle in assimilating the NCEP PREBUFR observations for an extended period. For experimental setup with LMDZ5-DART, some tuning experiment were necessary to evaluate advantage of using damped adaptive covariance inflation and determine the optimums localization distance both in vertical and horizontal. It was found that 1200 km in horizontal and 1000 hPa in vertical localization distance resulted in a good performance of LMDZ5-DART system. The adaptive inflation scheme was obviously advantageous, providing better forecast and ensemble spread than no inflation experiment. We also find that analysis created by this system is remarkably similar to NCEP reanalysis although only subset of observations was used. LMDZ5 can now benefit directly from many tools available in Data Assimilation Research Test bed. These include detection of short-term model biases and some code errors, the ability to start single as well as ensemble LMDZ5 forecast from analyses generated from LMDZ5-DART that are compatible with LMDZ5 and have no foreign model biases.

Our future work will mainly focus on testing the different feature of LMDZ5-DART data assimilation system, adding support of GPS RO and INSAT 3D data assimilation. The current development adds to our efforts of improving forecast skills to accurately predict different features of Indian summer monsoon in the medium range and extended range.

Acknowledgment. The authors are grateful to the Space Application Centre (SAC) of the Indian Space Research Organization (ISRO) for providing valuable funds in the form of a Research Scholarship to one of us (T. Singh) to carry out this work at the Indian Institute of Technology Delhi (IITD), New Delhi (India).

References

1. Aksoy, A., Zhang, F., Nielsen-Gammon, J.W.: Ensemble-based simultaneous state and parameter estimation with MM5. Geophys. Res. Lett. **33**, L12801 (2006)
2. Raeder, K., Anderson, J.L., Collins, N., Hoar, T.J., Kay, J.E., Lauritzen, P.H., Pincus, R.: DART/CAM: an ensemble data assimilation system for CESM atmospheric models. J. Clim. **25**, 6304–6317 (2012)
3. Buehner, M., Houtekamer, P.L., Charette, C., Mitchell, H.L., He, B.: Intercomparison of variational data assimilation and the ensemble Kalman filter for global deterministic NWP. Part II: One-month experiments with real observations. Mon. Weather Rev. **138**, 1902–1921 (2010)
4. Miyoshi, T., Sato, Y., Kadowaki, T.: Ensemble Kalman filter and 4D-Var intercomparison with the Japanese operational global analysis and prediction system. Mon. Weather Rev. **138**, 2846–2866 (2010)
5. Anderson, J.L.: An ensemble adjustment kalman filter for data assimilation. Mon. Weather Rev. **129**, 2884–2903 (2001)
6. Sadourny, R.A., Laval, K.: January and July performances of LMD general circulation model. In: Berger, A., Nicolis, C. (eds.) New Perspectives in Climate Modelling, pp. 173–198. Elsevier, Amsterdam (1984)
7. Le Treut, H., Li, Z.X.: Sensitivity of an atmospheric general circulation model to prescribed SST changes: feedback effects associated with the simulation of cloud optical properties. Clim. Dyn. **5**, 175–187 (1991)
8. Dufresne, J.-L., et al.: Climate change projections using the IPSL-CM5 Earth System Model: from CMIP3 to CMIP5. Clim. Dyn. **40**(9–10), 2123–2165 (2013)
9. Hourdin, F., Musat, L., Bony, S., Codron, F., Dufresne, J.-L., Fairhead, L., Filiberti, M.-A., Friedlingstein, P., Grandpeix, J.Y., Krinner, G., LeVan, P., Li, Z.X., Lott, F.: The LMDZ4 general circulation model: climate performance and sensitivity to parametrized physics with emphasis on tropical convection. Clim. Dyn. **27**, 787–813 (2006)
10. Sharma, O.P., Upadhyaya, H.C., Braine-Bonnaire, T., Sadourny, R.: Experiments on regional forecasting using stretched coordinate general circulation model. J. Meteorol. Soc. Jpn., Special NWP Symposium, 263–271 (1987)
11. Sabin, T.P., Krishnan, R., Ghattas, J., Denvil, S., Dufresne, J.L., Hourdin, F., Pascal, T.: High resolution simulation of the South Asian monsoon using a variable resolution global climate model. Clim. Dyn. **41**, 173–194 (2013)
12. Anderson, J., Hoar, T., Raeder, K., Liu, H., Collins, N., Torn, R., Avellano, A.: The data assimilation research testbed: a community facility. Bull. Am. Meteorol. Soc. **90**, 1283–1296 (2009)
13. Zubrow, A., Chen, L., Kotamarthi, V.: Introduction and evaluation of a data assimilation for cmaq based on the ensemble adjustment Kalman filter. J. Geophys. Res. **113**, D09302 (2008)
14. Dowell, D.C., Wicker, L.: Additive noise for storm-scale ensemble data assimilation. J. Atmos. Oceanic Technol. **26**, 911–927 (2009)

15. Anderson, J.: A local least squares framework for ensemble filtering. Mon. Weather Rev. **131**, 634–642 (2003)
16. Anderson, J.L.: Spatially and temporally varying adaptive covariance inflation for ensemble filters. Tellus A **61**, 72–83 (2009)
17. Torn, R.D.: Performance of a mesoscale ensemble Kalman filter (EnKF) during the NOAA High-Resolution Hurricane test. Mon. Weather Rev. **138**, 4375–4392 (2010)
18. DART Website. http://www.image.ucar.edu/DAReS/DART/

Planning and Adaptive Observation

A Greedy Approach for Placement of Subsurface Aquifer Wells in an Ensemble Filtering Framework

Mohamad E. Gharamti[1,4]([✉]), Youssef M. Marzouk[2], Xun Huan[2], and Ibrahim Hoteit[1,3]

[1] Earth Sciences and Engineering, King Abdullah University of Science and Technology, Thuwal 23955, Saudi Arabia
mohamad.gharamti@nersc.no
[2] Department of Aeronautics and Astronautics, Massachusetts Institute of Technology, Cambridge, MA 02139, USA
[3] Applied Mathematics and Computational Sciences, King Abdullah University of Science and Technology, Thuwal 23955, Saudi Arabia
[4] Mohn-Sverdrup Center, Nansen Environmental and Remote Sensing Center, 5006 Bergen, Norway

Abstract. Optimizing wells placement may help in better understanding subsurface solute transport and detecting contaminant plumes. In this work, we use the ensemble Kalman filter (EnKF) as a data assimilation tool and propose a greedy observational design algorithm to optimally select aquifer wells locations for updating the prior contaminant ensemble. The algorithm is greedy in the sense that it operates sequentially, without taking into account expected future gains. The selection criteria is based on maximizing the information gain that the EnKF carries during the update of the prior uncertainties. We test the efficiency of this algorithm in a synthetic aquifer system where a contaminant plume is set to migrate over a 30 years period across a heterogenous domain.

1 Introduction

In subsurface hydrology, field measurements of groundwater flow and contaminant transport play an essential role in constraining numerical prediction models. These models are indeed highly uncertain and data may be used to improve our knowledge of various modeling parameters such as permeability, biodegradation factors, and porosity. However, collecting such measurements (e.g. pressure, concentration) from deep or shallow hydraulic wells is difficult and an expensive process. It is therefore important to minimize extra costs of monitoring networks by limiting the number of wells to some few "optimal" locations.

Optimal monitoring design can be divided into two categories; open and closed loops. The first category (a.k.a batch design), involves evaluating all possible network designs concurrently without accounting for any result or feedback from any other design. Such approach, although optimal, could be prohibitive in large scale hydrologic systems where the dimension of the state can be of the

© Springer International Publishing Switzerland 2015
S. Ravela and A. Sandu (Eds.): DyDESS 2014, LNCS 8964, pp. 301–309, 2015.
DOI: 10.1007/978-3-319-25138-7_27

order $10^8 - 10^{10}$ variables. The other category (a.k.a sequential design), evaluates the networks in sequence, allowing a feedback from new data to be used to plan for the upcoming designs [6,7]. With this formulation, a sub-optimal greedy approach would take into account information from previous designs and optimize the next observational network without paying attention to any expected future gain as a consequence of the decision at hand [1,10]. This greedy approach can be coupled with an ensemble Kalman filtering framework where observations are used to constrain subsurface models as they become available [4].

The ensemble Kalman filter (EnKF) is a sequential Monte Carlo technique that aims at estimating the probability distribution of the state of a dynamical system following a Bayesian filtering formulation in a Gaussian framework. The EnKF represents the first two moments of the state distribution by means of an ensemble of state vectors, which are then approximated as the sample mean and covariance of the ensemble [5]. The ensemble is first integrated forward in time with the model for forecasting. A Kalman update, derived from the Bayes' rule under the Gaussian assumption, is then applied to update the forecast ensemble with incoming observations. One way to optimize the wells placement would be to select those that are most informative for the EnKF update steps.

To evaluate the contribution of an observation, we use the Kullback-Leibler (KL) divergence criterion [8]. The KL divergence provides an intuitive indicator of the information gain by reflecting the difference between two distributions [11]. Consequently, in an EnKF setting, the KL criterion can be computed from both the posterior and prior distributions of the state ensemble, and hence decisions on more informative observations are properly analyzed. Most of the Bayesian approaches, arising from information theory, that discriminate between posterior and prior statistics involve computing the expectation of the Fisher information matrix [6,7,11].

Several previous studies considered the observations placement or "targeted observations" as for instance in meteorology and signal processing. These studies considered similar information-based criteria in order to achieve a reduction in the ensemble forecast variance. For instance, Mujadmar *et al.* (2000) [9] discussed the ability of the ensemble transform Kalman filter (ETKF) to provide quantitative estimates of the reduction of operational analysis and forecast error variance when deploying dropwindsondes. Choi *et al.* [2,3] presented an efficient backward formulation of the sensor targeting problem using ensemble-based filtering. The backward approach which was tested on a Lorenz-95 model is equivalent and never slower than the forward approach.

In this study, we present a greedy algorithm to smartly select well locations, which are meant to improve the prior distribution of the hydrologic contaminant state. This algorithm is utilized in an ensemble assimilation framework before updating model forecast ensemble. Well locations are selected by solving a discrete optimization problem that maximizes the expected information gain from the forecast ensemble statistics. The proposed approach make use of the Fisher's information gain not only at the analysis/update step of EnKF but rather over long prediction periods. This procedure is novel because it reflects on the most informative well locations ahead of time thus making rapid placement decisions and maximizing the economic benefit. We conduct numerical experiments following a contaminant detection problem and simulate the migration of a plume in a heterogeneous two-dimensional aquifer domain. We look for the observation wells that yield the minimum posterior uncertainties over a 3 years forecast period. We analyze the experimental results based on the time evolution of the analysis ensemble variance at every point of the domain.

2   Greedy Approach for Well Placement

2.1   The Ensemble Kalman Filter (EnKF)

The EnKF simplifies the standard Bayesian filtering problem making use of samples or ensemble members to approximate the Gaussian parts of the state's distribution [4]. Starting from an analysis ensemble $\mathbf{x}_{k-1}^{a,i}$ at a given time t_{k-1}, the forecast ensemble is obtained by integrating these members forward in time with the dynamical model as:

$$\mathbf{x}_k^{f,i} = \mathcal{M}_k \left(\theta, \mathbf{x}_{k-1}^{a,i}, \mathbf{w}_k \right), \qquad i = 1, 2, ..., N_e \tag{1}$$

where $\mathcal{M}_k$ is the nonlinear subsurface model, θ is the vector of model parameters and $\mathbf{w}_k$ is the source term at time t_k. Once new data, $\mathbf{y}_k$, becomes available, the EnKF updates every ensemble member of Eq. (1) as follows:

$$\mathbf{x}_k^{a,i} = \mathbf{x}_k^{f,i} + \mathbf{P}_k^f \mathbf{H}_k^T \left(\mathbf{H}_k \mathbf{P}_k^f \mathbf{H}_k^T + \mathbf{R}_k \right)^{-1} \left(\mathbf{y}_k^i - \mathbf{H}_k \mathbf{x}_k^{f,i} \right). \tag{2}$$

The matrices $\mathbf{H}_k$ and $\mathbf{R}_k$ denote the observational operator and the observation error covariance at time t_k, respectively. $\mathbf{y}_k^i$ is the perturbed observation ensemble. The mean forecast state and the sample error covariance matrix are denoted by $\overline{\mathbf{x}}_k^f$ and $\mathbf{P}_k^f$, respectively.

We consider here the operator $\mathbf{H}_k$ of size $[N_\mathbf{y}, N_\mathbf{x}]$ consisting of ones and zeros. Every row vector of this matrix has zeros in all entries except for one observed variable location where the value is set to 1. The matrix $\mathbf{R}_k$, on the other hand, is of size $[N_\mathbf{y}, N_\mathbf{y}]$ and is assumed diagonal. Each diagonal entry carries the variance of the error for that specific observation.

The analysis error covariance matrix, $\mathbf{P}_k^a$, which is not explicitly needed for implementing the EnKF, matches that of the Kalman filter based on the forecast ensemble covariance, i.e.,

$$\mathbf{P}_k^a = \mathbf{P}_k^f - \mathbf{P}_k^f \mathbf{H}_k^T \left(\mathbf{H}_k \mathbf{P}_k^f \mathbf{H}_k^T + \mathbf{R}_k \right)^{-1} \mathbf{H}_k \mathbf{P}_k^f. \tag{3}$$

2.2   Greedy Algorithm and Optimization

Assume at time t_{k-1}, $N_\mathbf{y}$ wells have been placed and that we intend to place one new well. Then, the question would be: *Where to place this well?*

In practical terms, this question implies that a new row of zeros and 1 at one location will be added to the observation operator $\mathbf{H}_k$ (so that its size becomes $[N_\mathbf{y} + 1, N_\mathbf{x}]$) and the goal is to find the position, s, in that row that is equal 1. The new position, s, should satisfy the following conditions:

$$(1)\ s \in \mathbb{N}, \qquad (2)\ 0 < s \leq N_\mathbf{x}, \qquad (3)\ s \neq \{\ell_1, \ell_2, ..., \ell_{N_\mathbf{y}}\}.$$

The third condition means that the well should not be placed at an existing well position. Ideally, after assimilating the observations, one would expect the uncertainties in the prior estimates to shrink. Thus, using the Kullback-Leibler (KL) divergence, one can choose s that maximizes the information gain, $\mathcal{F}(s)$, at time t_k as follows:

$$\max_s \mathcal{F}(s) \quad = \quad \max_s tr\left[\mathbf{P}_k^f - \mathbf{P}_k^a\right], \tag{4}$$

$$\stackrel{\text{using}(3)}{=} \max_s tr\left[\mathbf{P}_k^f \mathbf{H}_k^T \left(\mathbf{H}_k \mathbf{P}_k^f \mathbf{H}_k^T + \mathbf{R}_k\right)^{-1} \mathbf{H}_k \mathbf{P}_k^f\right], \tag{5}$$

where $tr[\cdot]$ denotes the trace of a matrix. This maximization problem is a 1D problem retaining s which yields the largest reduction in the forecast variance after the EnKF update. One should note here that at any specific time t_k the maximization problem in (4) is also equivalent to minimizing the trace of $\mathbf{P}_k^a$.

A more challenging, yet more appropriate, objective would be to find the location s at time t_k so that we maximize the *expected* information gain not only at time t_k but also at subsequent future updates, i.e., at times t_{k+1}, t_{k+2}, etc. The problem can then be written as:

$$\min_s\ \mathcal{U}(s) = \min_s\ \left\{tr\left[\mathbf{P}_k^a\right] + tr\left[\mathbf{P}_{k+1}^a\right] + tr\left[\mathbf{P}_{k+2}^a\right] + \cdots\right\}. \tag{6}$$

One substantial difference between Eqs. (4) and (6) is that the latter does not only depend on s but rather on s, $\mathbf{y}_k$, and $\mathbf{y}_{k+1}$. This is because the analysis covariance at time t_{k+1}, $\mathbf{P}_{k+1}^a$, can only be obtained after assimilating $\mathbf{y}_k$ at time t_k and then integrating the members $\mathbf{x}_k^{a,i}$ to time t_{k+1}. The same applies for the analysis covariance $\mathbf{P}_{k+2}^a$. Hence, evaluating $\mathcal{U}(s)$, referred to as expected utility hereafter, requires Monte Carlo sampling of future observations as follows:

$$\mathcal{U}(s) = \mathbb{E}_{(\mathbf{y}_k, \mathbf{y}_{k+1}, \cdots)} \left\{tr\left[\mathbf{P}_k^a\right] + tr\left[\mathbf{P}_{k+1}^a\right] + tr\left[\mathbf{P}_{k+2}^a\right] + \cdots\right\}, \tag{7}$$

$$\approx \frac{1}{N_m} \sum_{m=1}^{N_m} \left\{tr\left[\mathbf{P}_k^a(s)\right] + tr\left[\mathbf{P}_{k+1}^a\left(s, \mathbf{y}_k^m\right)\right] + tr\left[\mathbf{P}_{k+2}^a\left(s, \mathbf{y}_k^m, \mathbf{y}_{k+1}^m\right)\right]\right\},$$

where N_m is the number of Monte Carlo samples. Here we sample the observations from a Gaussian distribution of the forecast ensemble statistics. It is important to note here that these Monte Carlo runs are independent and thus, one could easily implement them in parallel.

Once the expected utility, $\mathcal{U}(s)$, is computed, optimization is then performed taking into account the three constraints introduced before. To avoid solving a discrete optimization problem, we propose to relax the first constraint such that the observation operator would be a function of $g(s)$ rather than simply s. Such function is the nearest integer function (or the round function), commonly denoted as:

$$g(s) \equiv \lfloor s \rceil. \tag{8}$$

The second constraint that deals with bounds is easy to handle, however, the third non-equality constraint is tricky. One simple way to tackle this constraint is to introduce a penalty term in the objective as follows:

$$\min_{s} \ \mathcal{U}(s) + \log(s - \ell_j). \qquad j = 1, 2, ..., N_{\mathbf{y}} \tag{9}$$

Since our objective is a single-variable function and given that the variable is bounded within a bracket, i.e., $s \in (0, N_{\mathbf{x}}]$, we use a hybrid optimization algorithm that utilizes a golden section search (*Bisection*-like method) with successive parabolic interpolation (*Secant*-like method). Other stochastic optimization techniques such as Simultaneous Perturbations Stochastic Approximation (SPSA), can be also used. These techniques can be however less efficient and involve tuning a number of parameters which is not an easy task for complicated objectives. Gradient-based algorithms are not very appropriate for the current objective as they require solving a complex adjoint system.

3   Subsurface Contaminant Transport Experiments

3.1   Experimental Setup

We consider a steady-state groundwater flow system inside a rectangular domain of total aquifer area of 0.84 km^2. North and south boundaries are assumed impermeable, whereas the the east and west boundaries are assigned constant hydraulic heads equal to 10 and 20 m-water, respectively. Pure water conditions are assumed in the aquifer except for an elongated plume of concentration 100 mg/l located near the west boundary. We simulate the migration of the plume across the domain towards the east boundary for 30-years period. Figure 1 below shows three snapshots of the polluted domain in time. For simplification, we ignore the reactive effects such as radioactive decay, biodegradation and use a linear sorption instead.

We conduct twin-experiments in which we perform a reference (or *truth*) contaminant transport simulation and use a perturbed forecast model to reproduce the reference solution while assimilating perturbed observations. We consider a monitoring network of 3 wells distributed uniformly in the domain as shown in the left panel of Fig. 1. For updating the prior contaminant ensembles, we assume the concentration data is available on a yearly basis (i.e., total of 30 EnKF updates). In addition, we propose to install a new well every 3 years starting from the fourth year. Thus by the end of the simulation, we will have a total of 12 wells after adding additional 9. An illustration sketch for this scenario is shown in Fig. 2.

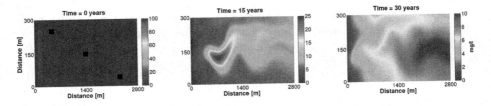

Fig. 1. Reference contaminant spatial maps of the domain after 0, 15 and 30 years. Black squares shown on the left panel correspond to the fixed wells initially installed for measuring the groundwater concentration.

For installing the wells, we present three different approaches. In the first approach, we simply select some random locations in the domain. In the second approach, we choose to maximize the information gain at the time of installation only, i.e., by solving the optimization problem of Eq. (4). For the most general approach, we focus on maximizing the expected information gain at the installation time plus two years in advance. In other words, we try to find the well location that is most informative over a 3 years-period right before installing the next well.

Fig. 2. A sketch illustrating the scenario considered in the study for data assimilation. 9 wells are added every 3 years on top of the initially installed 3 (shown in Fig. 1).

We sample the initial ensemble assuming Gaussian conditions by selecting the mean of the reference run and perturbing around it. To perform data assimilation in a realistic settings, we perturb the model's porosity, hydraulic conductivity and sorption. We also introduce uncertainties to the contaminant source term.

3.2 Assimilation Results

In this section, we present assimilation results from the proposed greedy algorithm. The observational error variance is assumed to be known, which we set as follows. We use the yearly snapshots of the reference run and evaluate the total variance at each spatial point in the domain. We then take each diagonal element of $\mathbf{R}_k$ to be equal to 10 % of the calculated variance.

We first perform a convergence test and run the assimilation scenario described in Fig. 2 using the second approach in which optimizing the well location is carried only at the time of installation. As mentioned, we use for optimization a hybrid Bisection-Secant algorithm and compare the output results with a

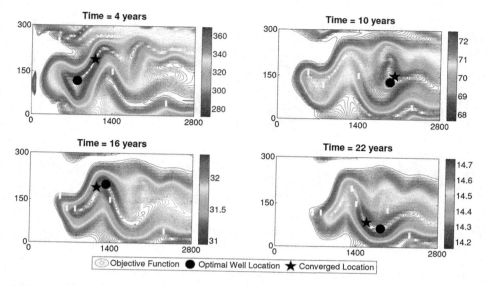

Fig. 3. A contour plot for the objective function of Eq. (4). Optimal and converged well locations at 4 different installation times are shown by circles and pentagrams, respectively. The small white rectangles shown on the contour maps represent existing well locations.

full enumeration run. In the enumeration run, we do not carry any optimization but instead we evaluate the objective function at every cell in the domain. This would help us visualize the objective function and find the global minimum; i.e., the optimal location of the well. In this run, we use an ensemble of 100 contaminant realizations. In Fig. 3, we plot the contour maps of the objective function after 4, 10, 16 and 22 years. The contour maps exhibit spatial patterns similar to the snapshots of the migrating contaminant plume from the reference run (Fig. 1) suggesting that the wells located closer to the plume are more informative than others. In terms of convergence, we see that the hybrid algorithm works very well and retains reliable solutions that are close to the optimal ones. On average, convergence occurs in less than 20 iterations.

Next, we run the third approach and use the greedy algorithm over a 3 years-window, as in Eq. (6), to find the optimal well locations that maximize the expected information gain over this time interval. We plot the analysis ensemble variance at every point in the domain after 7, 13, 19 and 25 years. We compare the results of the proposed greedy scheme to the output of two other optimization-free runs. In the first run, we randomly place 9 observation wells in the domain and in the other, we consider a fixed network of 12 wells (distributed uniformly in the aquifer). We set $N_e = 50$ and utilize 30 Monte Carlo samples.

Constraining the model outputs with data reduces the uncertainties over time. This is nicely observed in all 3 runs as shown in Fig. 4. The proposed greedy algorithm yields the largest improvements. This is indeed due to the

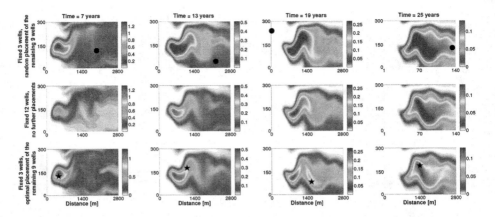

Fig. 4. Analysis ensemble variance shown from left to right after 7, 13, 19 and 25 years. The top row of subplots are results from a run where a random placement of the 9 wells is performed. Maps of the middle row are obtained from an assimilation run where the number of wells is fixed and equal to 12. The bottom row maps are outputs of the proposed greedy algorithm where the 9 wells are placed by solving the optimization problem of Eq. (6). Random and converged well locations are shown by circles and pentagrams, respectively.

optimal selection of the well locations that are more or less aligned around the center of the migrating plume. The run with 12 fixed wells shows smaller ensemble variance during the early assimilation period. This is expected because initially the uncertainties are larger and more information is available for guiding the system. Nevertheless, after around 15 years (mid simulation period), the proposed algorithm is more accurate. When we randomly select the 9 wells, the uncertainties in the ensemble statistics are the largest.

4   Conclusion

In this study, we tackled the optimal observational design problem in subsurface hydrology in a Bayesian filtering context. We proposed a greedy optimization approach to optimally select the observation wells. The approach is based on maximizing the expected information gain over a given time interval. We presented this approach in a Bayesian framework using the well-known ensemble Kalman filter (EnKF). We evaluated the expected information gain by discriminating between the EnKF-based prior and posterior error covariances based on the Kullback-Leibler divergence.

The numerical experiments were based on a synthetic subsurface contaminant transport system. The experimental results clearly demonstrated the efficiency of the proposed greedy approach resulting in a significant uncertainty reduction as compared to random selection techniques.

For future work, one could improve on the inference method by evaluating the KL divergence using non-Gaussian information, and turning to a full dynamic programming formulation to tackle the problem in a non-greedy fashion. The proposed approach is a practical compromise that appears to work quite well, on a relatively realistic and large-scale hydrological model. It is also well suited to how filtering problems are tackled on dynamical systems of this size. Potential further research will aim at incorporating more sophisticated optimal experimental design methodologies, keeping in mind the computational burden and the feasibility of implementation with realistic subsurface models.

References

1. Cavagnaro, D.R., Myung, J.I., Pitt, M.A., Kujala, J.V.: Adaptive design optimization: a mutual information-based approach to model discrimination in cognitive science. Neural Comput. **22**, 887–905 (2012)
2. Choi, H.-L., How, J.P.: Efficient targeting of sensor networks for large-scale systems. IEEE Trans. Control Syst. Technol. **19**, 1569–1577 (2011)
3. Choi, H-L., How, J.P., Hansen, J.A.: Ensemble-based adaptive targeting of mobile ensor networks. In: Proceedings of the 2007 American Control Conference. ThA09.3, pp. 2393–2398 (2007)
4. Gharamti, M.E., Valstar, J., Hoteit, I.: Dual states estimation of a subsurface flow-transport coupled model using ensemble Kalman filtering. Adv. Water Resour. **60**, 75–88 (2013)
5. Gharamti, M.E., Kadoura, A., Valstar, J., Sun, S., Hoteit, I.: Constraining a compositional flow model with flow-chemical data using an ensemble-based Kalman filter. Water Resour. Res. **50**, 2444–2467 (2014)
6. Huan, X., Marzouk, Y.M.: Simulation-based optimal Bayesian experimental design for nonlinear systems. J. Comput. Phys. **232**(1), 288–317 (2013)
7. Huan, X., Marzouk, Y.M.: Gradient-based stochastic optimization methods in Bayesian experimental design. Int. J. Uncertainty Quantification **4**(6), 479–510 (2014). doi:10.1615/Int.J.UncertaintQuantification.2014006730
8. Kullback, S., Leibler, R.A.: On information and sufficiency. Ann. Math. Stat. **22**, 79–86 (1951)
9. Majumdar, S.J., Bishop, C.H., Etherton, B.J., Szunyogh, I., Toth, Z.: Can an ensemble transform Kalman filter predict the reduction in forecast error variance produced by targeted observations? Q. J. Roy. Meteorol. Soc. **126**, 1–999 (2000)
10. Solonen, A., Haario, H., Laine, M.: Simulation-based optimal design using a response variance criterion. J. Comput. Graph. Stat. **21**, 234–252 (2012)
11. Yakirevich, A., Pachepsky, Y.A., Gish, T.J., Guber, A.K., Kuznetsov, M.Y., Cady, R.E., Nicholson, T.J.: Augmenting of groundwater monitoring networks using information theory and ensemble modeling with pedotransfer functions. J. Hydrol. **501**, 13–24 (2013)

Parameter Estimation of Atmospheric Release Incidents Using Maximal Information Collection

Reza Madankan[(✉)], Puneet Singla, and Tarunraj Singh

Mechanical and Aerospace Engineering Department,
University at Buffalo, Buffalo, NY 14228, USA
{rm93,psingla,tsingh}@buffalo.edu

Abstract. The effects of data measurement on source parameter estimation are studied. The concept of mutual information is applied to find the optimal location for each sensor to improve accuracy of the overall estimation process. For validation purposes, an advection - diffusion simulation code, called SCIPUFF, is used as a modeling testbed to study the effects of using dynamic data measurement. Bayesian inference framework is utilized for model-data fusion using stationary and mobile sensor networks, where in mobile sensors, the proposed approach is used to locate data observation sensors. As our numerical simulations show, using the proposed approach leads to a *considerably* better estimate of parameters comparing with stationary sensors.

1 Introduction

With increasing number of instances of toxic material release, there is tremendous interest in precise source characterization and generating accurate hazard maps of toxic material dispersion for appropriate disaster management. There is no doubt that proper sensor placement is intimately tied to the performance of the source estimation and model uncertainty characterization.

Different strategies have been suggested to determine the optimal path of the mobile sensors for source parameters characterization. Earlier works in this area can be categorized as Chemotaxis [1], Anemotaxis [2], and Fluxotaxis [3].

In chemotaxis approach [1], mobile sensors follow the concentration gradient. Therefore, the motion toward the largest concentration is the goal direction for the chemotaxis. In anemotaxis strategy [2], mobile sensors always move upstream while they locate inside the plume, hence the upstream is the goal direction for mobile sensors. With fluxotaxis approach [3], the mobile sensors compute the amount of dispersal material flux passing through virtual surfaces formed by neighboring sensors. Where, each individual sensor independently calculates the amount of local material flux relative to the current position of its neighbors.

Even though, each of the above approaches has its own advantage and application, but the major drawback of aforementioned approaches lies in the possibility of being trapped in local maxima and plateaus of the concentration field.

Recently, there have been numerous works focusing on application of information theoretic concepts in optimal sensor placement [4–10]. For instance, an

© Springer International Publishing Switzerland 2015
S. Ravela and A. Sandu (Eds.): DyDESS 2014, LNCS 8964, pp. 310–321, 2015.
DOI: 10.1007/978-3-319-25138-7_28

information theoretic framework was developed in [4] for distributive control of a set of mobile robots, where the key idea was to move mobile robots along gradient of mutual information map to maximize information collection. The major drawback of this work is that applied robots are susceptible to being trapped in local optima, due to tracking gradient of mutual information. In another research by Hoffmann et al. [7], a control approach for mobile sensor networks was proposed to maximize the mutual information, where an iterative approach was used at each time step to find optimal control signal. Applied particle filter framework in this method makes it possible to use the proposed method in presence of nonlinear and non-Gaussian target state and sensor models. However, using Monte Carlo integration for evaluation of mutual information could reduce its computational performance.

The key idea of this paper is to determine the location of data monitoring sensors over the spatial domain of interest such that the uncertainty involved in parameter estimates is minimized. This has been achieved by maximizing the mutual information between the model output and data measurements. As it will be shown, proposed approach expedites the convergence of estimation process and avoids possible local optimalities while finding mobile sensor locations by maximizing the mutual information, rather than moving along its gradient. Along proposed approach for optimal sensor placement, a Bayesian inference based method is used for data assimilation process that allows us to apply our method in presence of nonlinear dynamics and sensor model and non-Gaussian uncertainties, without using any Monte Carlo sampling. As well, a set of recently developed quadrature points, named as Conjugate Unscented Transform points [11,12], are used to alleviate the computational complexities associated with evaluation of mutual information, uncertainty propagation, and estimation process.

Outline of this article is as follows: First, the proposed dynamic data monitoring (DDM) method for optimal sensor placement is explained in Sect. 2. Mathematical framework for uncertainty quantification and data assimilation are then briefly described in Sects. 3 and 4, respectively. Finally, numerical simulations and conclusion are presented in Sects. 5 and 6.

2   Dynamic Data Monitoring: Methodology

The major role of dynamic data monitoring is to determine the locations of a set of mobile sensors such that measurements with *more information content* are sought at each time step. Location of each mobile sensor at a given time can be achieved by maximizing the *mutual information* between model predictions and observed data. In the following, we first explain the concept of mutual information and utilized mobile sensor models. Then, mathematical details for optimal allocation of mobile sensors are presented.

Mutual Information as a Measure for Sensor Performance. According to information theory, the mutual information between parameter Θ and measurement $\mathbf{z}$ can be written as, [13],

$$I(\Theta; \mathbf{z}) = \int_{\mathbf{z}} \int_{\Theta} p(\Theta, \mathbf{z}) \ln \left(\frac{p(\Theta, \mathbf{z})}{p(\Theta) p(\mathbf{z})} \right) d\Theta d\mathbf{z} \tag{1}$$

Using Bayes' rule, $I \equiv I(\Theta; \mathbf{z})$ can be written as:

$$I = \int_{\mathbf{z}} \underbrace{\int_{\Theta} p(\Theta|\mathbf{z}) ln \left(\frac{p(\Theta|\mathbf{z}) p(\mathbf{z})}{p(\Theta) p(\mathbf{z})} \right) d\Theta}_{D_{KL}(p(\Theta|\mathbf{z}))\|p(\Theta)} p(\mathbf{z}) d\mathbf{z} = \mathcal{E}_z[D_{KL}(p(\Theta|\mathbf{z})\|p(\Theta))] \tag{2}$$

Hence, mutual information can be interpreted as the average Kullback-Leiber distance between prior pdf $p(\Theta)$ and posterior pdf $p(\Theta|\mathbf{z})$. In other words, by maximizing mutual information one inherently maximizes the difference between entropies of prior and posterior distributions of Θ.

UAV Model. We consider a set of Unmanned Aerial Vehicles (UAV) for data observation, where each of the UAVs is equipped with a chemical sensor to measure the concentration of pollutant material. The dynamic model of each of the UAVs is given as:

$$\mathbf{s}_{k+1}^v = F(\mathbf{s}_k^v, u_k^v), \quad v = 1, 2, \cdots, N_u \tag{3}$$

where, N_u is total number of UAVs and k denotes k^{th} time step. Initial condition of vth UAV is assumed to be given as $\mathbf{s}_0^v$. $\mathbf{s}_k^v$, consists of (x, y) components of position and heading angle. In detail, UAVs are modeled as:

$$\begin{bmatrix} s_1 \\ s_2 \\ \lambda \end{bmatrix}_{k+1} = \begin{bmatrix} s_1 \\ s_2 \\ \lambda \end{bmatrix}_k + \begin{bmatrix} u_k^h \cos(\lambda_k + \frac{\pi u_k^\lambda}{2}) \\ u_k^h \sin(\lambda_k + \frac{\pi u_k^\lambda}{2}) \\ \frac{\pi u_k^\lambda}{2} \end{bmatrix}, \quad u_k = [u_k^h, u_k^\lambda]^T \tag{4}$$

where $(s_1, s_2)_k$ is (lon, lat) coordinate of each UAV on spatial domain and λ_k represents the heading angle of UAV at time t_k. In this manuscript, it is always assumed that control signals u_k^h and u_k^λ take discrete values. In detail, u_k^λ is assumed to take one of the following discrete values:

$$u_k^\lambda = \begin{cases} -1, & move\ toward\ south \\ 0, & move\ toward\ east \\ 1, & move\ toward\ north \\ 2, & move\ toward\ west \\ 3, & s_{s+1} = s_k \end{cases} \tag{5}$$

2.1 Optimal Sensor Placement

Our objective is to find a sequence of control inputs $U^{1:N_u} = \{u_0^{1:N_u}, \cdots, u_{N_t-1}^{1:N_u}\}$ such that it maximizes the mutual information between sequence of expected observational data and parameters Θ over the time $t \in [t_1, t_{N_t}]$. This can be mathematically formulated as:

$$\min_{U^{1:N_u}} J = \min_{U^{1:N_u}} \sum_{v=1}^{N_u} \left\{ -I(\Theta^1, \cdots, \Theta^{N_t}; \mathbf{z}^1, \cdots, \mathbf{z}^{N_t} | \mathbf{s}_1^{1:N_u}, \cdots, \mathbf{s}_{N_t}^{1:N_u}) \right\} \quad (6)$$

$$\text{constrained to } \begin{cases} \mathbf{s}_{k+1}^v = F(\mathbf{s}_k^v, u_k^v), & \mathbf{s}_0^v \quad v = 1, 2, \cdots, N_u \\ s_k^a \neq s_k^b, & a, b = 1, 2, \cdots, N_u, \quad a \neq b \end{cases} \quad (7)$$

where, $\mathbf{z}^k$ and Θ^k are measurement data and uncertain parameter at time step t_k, respectively. N_t is the total number of time steps during the estimation process. $\mathbf{s}_0^v$ represents the initial condition and u_k^v denotes the applied control signal at time t_k for v^{th} UAV.

Unfortunately, performing this optimization requires finding optimal control signals for all the N_u UAVs over the time $t \in [t_1, t_{N_t}]$ which is computationally intractable. Hence, one needs to simplify the original problem and find the approximate solution for optimal control signals of each UAV. To alleviate the computational cost, one can *approximate* the original optimization problem as the following:

$$\min_{U^{1:N_u}} J(\mathbf{s}_0^{1:N_u}) = \min_{U^{1:N_u}} \sum_{k=0}^{N_t-1} \left(\sum_{v=1}^{N_u} \left\{ -I(\Theta^k; \mathbf{z}^k | \mathbf{s}_k^v) \right\} \right) \quad (8)$$

$$\text{constrained to } \begin{cases} \mathbf{s}_{k+1}^v = F(\mathbf{s}_k^v, u_k^v), & \mathbf{s}_0^v \quad v = 1, 2, \cdots, N_u \\ s_k^a \neq s_k^b, & a, b = 1, 2, \cdots, N_u, \quad a \neq b \end{cases} \quad (9)$$

One should notice that Eq. (8) is a function of a sequence of control signals $U^{1:N_u} = \{u_0^{1:N_u}, u_1^{1:N_u}, \cdots, u_{N_t-1}^{1:N_u}\}$ which are enforced on a set of N_u UAVs during the time. Also, the cost function J is a function of initial position of UAVs, i.e. $J = J(\mathbf{s}_0^{1:N_u})$. Hence, above optimization shall be performed for every possible combination of initial positions of N_u UAVs.

2.2 Dynamic Programming

Dynamic programming [14] is used to find the optimal policy $U^{1:N_u}$ that minimizes Eq. (8). Optimal policy $U^{1:N_u}$ is computed by backward optimization in time, i.e. first finding the optimal control input $u_{N_t-1}^{1:N_u}$, and then using $u_{N_t-1}^{1:N_u}$ to find optimal control signal $u_{N_t-2}^{1:N_u}$. This procedure will be repeated recursively to find the rest of control signals u_k^vs.

Unfortunately, computational complexity of the dynamic programming method grows exponentially with the number of UAVs. Hence, an enormous computational effort is required to perform such minimization. A simpler alternative approach to overcome this drawback in minimizing Eq. (8) is to recursively find *sub-optimal* policies for each one of the UAVs with slight modifications in original cost function. The idea is to first find optimal position for the first UAV during the time. Then, *sub-optimal* policies for all other UAVs can be found by minimizing the following modified cost function:

$$\min_{U=\{u_0^v, u_1^v, \cdots, u_{N_t-1}^v\}} J(\mathbf{s}_0^v), \quad \text{constrained to} = \begin{cases} \mathbf{s}_{k+1}^v = F(\mathbf{s}_k^v, u_k^v) \\ \mathbf{s}_0^v \end{cases} \tag{10}$$

where,

$$J(\mathbf{s}_0^v) = \sum_{k=0}^{N_t-1} \left\{ -I(\Theta_k, \mathbf{z}_k | \mathbf{s}_k^v) + \alpha \sum_{j=1}^{v-1} e^{-[\mathbf{s}_k^v - \mathbf{s}_k^j]^T W [\mathbf{s}_k^v - \mathbf{s}_k^j]} \right\} \tag{11}$$

where, $v = 2, 3, \cdots, N_u$ and $\alpha > 0$ and the positive definite diagonal matrix W are penalty factors that determine the separation between neighboring UAVs. Hence, the UAVs are forced to *spread out* over the spatial domain of interest, thus avoiding redundancy in measurements.

2.3   Limited Lookahead Policy

Depending on the nature of phenomenon under study, evaluation of mutual information map for all the future time steps can be computationally expensive. This will result in computational complexity while finding optimal control policies for the UAVs over the whole time period. Hence, using Eq. (11) restricts real time applications of proposed algorithm. One way to avoid these computational complexities is to approximate the true cost-to-go function J_{k+1} in Eq. (11) with some function that is a *limited lookahead* approximation of true cost-to-go function J_{k+1}. For instance, J_{k+1} in Eq. (11) can be approximated as:

$$J_{k+1} \simeq \sum_{i=k+1}^{k+1+l} \left\{ -I(\Theta_i, \mathbf{z}_i | F(\mathbf{s}_{i-1}^v, u_{i-1}^v)) + \alpha \sum_{j=1}^{v-1} e^{-[\mathbf{s}_i^v - \mathbf{s}_i^j]^T W [\mathbf{s}_i^v - \mathbf{s}_i^j]} \right\} \tag{12}$$

where, $v = 2, 3, \cdots, N_u$ and l is the number of future time steps which are used for approximation of true cost-to-go function J_{k+1}. As one can see, evaluation of Eq. (11) requires knowledge of mutual information for all the time steps between $k+1$ and N_t-1. While in *limited lookahead* method, J_{k+1} is approximated by a limited number of future time steps.

Limited lookahead policy has two major benefits with respect to original dynamic programming algorithm. First, limited lookahead policy could result in considerably less computational cost involved in finding *sub-optimal* control policies. The second, benefit of limited lookahead policy is that due to dependence of optimal policies on future wind data, the optimal policies obtained using the original cost function may be erroneous for distant future time steps. Hence, using limited lookahead policy avoids erroneous optimal policies by approximating the true cost-to-go function with limited number of future time steps.

The only drawback of using limited lookahead policy is that it may result in slower convergence of estimation process, especially if the UAVs are located far away from the mutual information map. To illustrate this more clearly, consider the situation shown in Fig. 1. If initial position of UAV is far from the mutual information map, given maximum speed of UAV and lookahead time step $l = 3$, there will not be any information inside the range of UAV. Hence, UAV does not move and proposed algorithm suggests that UAV should stay at the same position. This deficiency can be overcome by minimizing the distance between the UAV position and mutual information map, whenever the mutual information inside the range of UAV is zero. This can be mathematically described as:

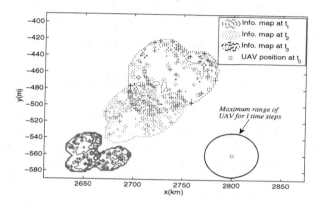

Fig. 1. Schematic layout of applied UAV sensor and mutual information maps at three consecutive times. Red square shows initial position of UAV and black circle shows its maximum range, given maximum speed of UAV and $l = 3$.

If $\sum_{i=k+1}^{k+1+l} I(\Theta_i, \mathbf{z}_i | F(\mathbf{s}_{i-1}^v, u_{i-1}^v)) = 0$, then

$$\tilde{J}_{k+1}(\mathbf{s}_k^v, u_k^v) = \sum_{i=k+1}^{k+1+l} d(\mathbf{s}_{I_{max}}^i, F(\mathbf{s}_{i-1}^v, u_{i-1}^v)) + \alpha \sum_{j=1}^{v-1} e^{-[\mathbf{s}_i^v - \mathbf{s}_i^j]^T W[\mathbf{s}_i^v - \mathbf{s}_i^j]} \quad (13)$$

where, $d(\mathbf{s}_{I_{max}}^i, F(\mathbf{s}_{i-1}^v, u_{i-1}^v))$ is the Euclidean distance between the spatial location where mutual information obtains its maximum (denoted by $\mathbf{s}_{I_{max}}^i$) and location of the UAV. Using above algorithm, utilized UAVs always move toward the mutual information map, independent of their initial location or lookahead time step l. Note that this property of proposed approach ensures faster detection of the plume and consequently faster convergence of estimation process.

3   Uncertainty Quantification

Method of quadrature points is utilized to perform the task of uncertainty quantification. In this method, a set of *intelligently* selected points will be propagated through the dynamical model and statistics of the output are then determined by weighted average of model outputs.

To describe this in more detail, let $x(lat, lon, z, \Theta, t) \in \mathbb{R}^n$ represent the concentration of pollutant material at a given spatial point (lat, lon, z) and time t. Note that x is a function of uncertain model parameter vector $\Theta \in \mathbb{R}^m$. The parameter Θ contains parameters like source location, total mass of pollutant material, etc. Θ is assumed to be time invariant and function of a random vector $\boldsymbol{\xi} = [\xi_1, \xi_2, \cdots, \xi_m]^T \in \mathbb{R}^m$ defined by a pdf $p(\boldsymbol{\xi})$ over the support Ω.

Now, k^{th} order moment of model output $\mathbf{x}$, at a given point (lat, lon, z) on the domain and a specific time t can be written as

$$\mathcal{E}[x^k] = \int_{\boldsymbol{\xi}} x^k(\Theta)p(\boldsymbol{\xi})d\boldsymbol{\xi} \simeq \sum_q^M w_q x^k(\Theta(\boldsymbol{\xi}^q)), \quad k = 1, 2, \cdots \qquad (14)$$

where, M denotes total number of quadrature points and $\Theta(\boldsymbol{\xi}^q) \in \mathbb{R}^{m \times 1}$ represents q^{th} quadrature point, generated based on the applied quadrature scheme. Similarly, k^{th} order central moments of concentration can be evaluated by shifting the quadrature points by the computed mean and then using Eq. (14).

Different types of quadrature rules like classical Gaussian quadrature rule can be used to evaluate the integral in Eq. (14). The classic method of Gaussian quadrature exactly integrates polynomials of 1-Dimension up to degree $2M + 1$ with $M + 1$ quadrature points. Generally, in an n-dimensional parameter space, the tensor product of 1-dimension quadrature points is used to generate quadrature points. As a consequence of this, the number of quadrature points increases exponentially as the number of input parameters increases.

Herein, we have utilized Conjugate Unscented Transform (CUT) recently developed by Nagavenkat *et al.* [11,12], to overcome this drawback of regular quadrature points. CUT approach can be considered as an extension to the conventional Unscented Transformation method, by satisfying higher order moment constraint equations. CUT points are efficient in terms of accuracy while integrating polynomials and yet just employ a small fraction of the number of points used by Gaussian quadrature scheme. Figure 2 represents the number of 8th order quadrature points required by different quadrature schemes for a uniformly distributed random vector versus the dimensionality of the random vector. From this figure, it is clear that the CUT methodology requires less number of quadrature points comparing with other quadrature schemes.

4   Data Assimilation

Data assimilation can be described as finding posterior statistics of the parameter vector $\Theta \in \mathbb{R}^m$, given a set of measurement data $\mathcal{Z} = \{\mathbf{z}^1, \mathbf{z}^2, \cdots, \mathbf{z}^N\}$, where N denotes the total number of time steps where measurement data is available. Using Bayes' theorem, posterior distribution of Θ can be written as:

$$p(\Theta|\mathcal{Z}) = \frac{p(\Theta)p(\mathcal{Z}|\Theta)}{p(\mathcal{Z})}, \quad p(\mathcal{Z}) = \int_{\Theta} p(\mathcal{Z}|\Theta)p(\Theta)d\Theta = \mathcal{E}_\Theta\{p(\mathcal{Z}|\Theta)\} \qquad (15)$$

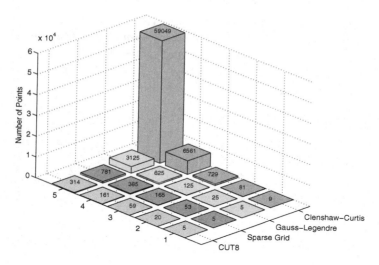

Fig. 2. Comparison of number of 8th order quadrature points required according to different quadrature scheme versus dimension of random variable.

where, $p(\Theta)$ is the prior distribution of parameter Θ, $p(\mathcal{Z}|\Theta)$ is the likelihood of measurements given the parameter.

Now, one can compute the posterior statistics of Θ by multiplication of appropriate functions of Θ in Eq. (15) and integrating with respect to Θ [15]. For instance, posterior mean of Θ, denoted by $\hat{\Theta}^+$, can be computed as:

$$\hat{\Theta}^+ = \mathcal{E}_\Theta\{\Theta\} = \frac{\int_\Theta \Theta p(\Theta)p(\mathcal{Z}|\Theta)d\Theta}{\mathcal{E}_\Theta\{p(\mathcal{Z}|\Theta)\}} = \frac{\mathcal{E}_\Theta\{\Theta p(\mathcal{Z}|\Theta)\}}{\mathcal{E}_\Theta\{p(\mathcal{Z}|\Theta)\}} \quad (16)$$

Posterior second order moment of Θ, denoted by Σ^+, can also be computed as:

$$\Sigma^+ = \int_\Theta \Theta\Theta^T p(\Theta|\mathcal{Z})d\Theta = \frac{\mathcal{E}_\Theta\{\Theta\Theta^T p(\mathcal{Z}|\Theta)\}}{\mathcal{E}_\Theta\{p(\mathcal{Z}|\Theta)\}} \quad (17)$$

CUT quadrature points are used to compute the integrals in Eqs. (16) and (17).

5   Numerical Simulations

For numerical simulations, dispersion/advection of propane is simulated over New York area. Domain of interest and corresponding wind field (at one specific time) are shown in Fig. 3(a). Simulation time is considered to be 24 $hrs.$, starting from $00:00$ of September 1st, 2013. North American Regional Reanalysis wind data at pressure level 100 kpa (height $\simeq 100$ $m.$) is used for simulation. Three instantaneous mass releases are considered where their location is known and the only uncertain parameters are their amount of mass release. It is assumed that releases happen at the same time, i.e. all source releases happen at $00:00$ of

September 1st. All mass releases are assumed to be uniformly distributed between 100 kg and 300 kg. Figure 3(a) illustrates source locations and the wind-field (at $t = 0$ $hrs.$) over the two dimensional spatial domain.

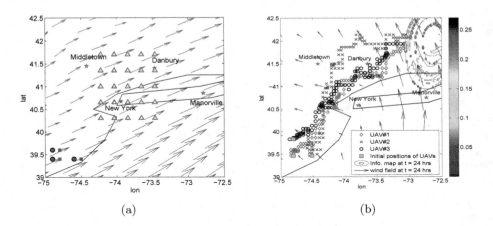

(a)   (b)

Fig. 3. a) Schematic layout of Propane release over New York region, source locations are shown with purple circles, the wind-field (at $t = 0$ hr and pressure level = 100 kPa) is shown over the two dimensional domain with blue vector field. Square markers show applied 3 stationary sensors, while triangles represent 25 stationary sensors. b) Optimal way-points for mobile sensors at different time steps obtained based on DDM approach. Contour map represents the information map at the final time (Color figure online).

Second-order Closure Integrated PUFF (SCIPUFF) [16] model is being used for numerical simulation of dispersion/advection phenomenon.

The sensor used for the measurements is a bar sensor similar to the one used in [17], with slight differences. The number of bars ranges from zero to fifteen. These bar readings indicate the concentration magnitude at the sensor location at the instant; the sensor displays $z = 0, \cdots , 15$, bars when the internal continuous-valued concentration magnitude $\mathbf{x}_{int}$ is between thresholds T_z and T_{z+1}, where $0 \leq T_z < T_{z+1}$. The thresholds T_z's are defined on a logarithmic scale, i.e. $T_z \in \{0, 5 \times 10^{-14}, 10^{-13}, 5 \times 10^{-13}, 10^{-12}, \cdots , 5 \times 10^{-7}\}$.

Probability density function of x_{int} given the corresponding concentration x is assumed to be Gaussian, i.e.

$$p(x_{int}|x) = \mathcal{N}(x_{int}; x, R) = \frac{1}{\sqrt{2\pi R}} e^{-\frac{(x_{int}-x)^2}{2R}} \tag{18}$$

where, $R(\tilde{x}) = \sigma^2(\tilde{x}) = (a\tilde{x} + b)^2$, $a = 1$ and $b = 10^{-15}$ in our simulations. Also, it is assumed that $\tilde{x} = T_z$, where T_z is the sensor bar corresponding to x_{int}. Following Eq. (18), likelihood function, or simply probability of $\mathbf{z}$ conditioned on $\mathbf{x}$, is determined by the following integral

$$P(\mathbf{z}|x) \propto \int_{T_z}^{T_{z+1}} p(\mathbf{x}_{int}|x)dx_{int}, \quad \sum_z P(\mathbf{z}|x) = 1 \tag{19}$$

Consequently, the mutual information in Eq. (2) will be written as:

$$I(\Theta; \mathbf{z}) = \sum_{z=0}^{N_z} \sum_{q=1}^{M} w_q \Gamma \ln (\Gamma) - \sum_{z=0}^{N_z} \left(\sum_{q=1}^{M} w_q \Gamma \right) \ln \left(\sum_{q=1}^{M} w_q \Gamma \right). \qquad (20)$$

where, $N_z = 15$ and

$$\Gamma \equiv \Gamma(T_{z+1}, T_z, \Theta(\boldsymbol{\xi}^q), R) = \frac{1}{2} \left\{ \mathrm{erf} \left(\frac{T_{z+1} - x(\Theta)}{\sqrt{2R}} \right) - \mathrm{erf} \left(\frac{T_z - x(\Theta)}{\sqrt{2R}} \right) \right\}$$

A set of 59 CUT8 quadrature points are used to quantify the uncertainty involved in concentration of dispersal material. Also, a 6th order gPC expansion is used to reconstruct distribution of parameters after each update. Simulation of dispersion/advection has been performed using SCIPUFF numerical model, where concentration of propane is recorded every 10 $mins$.

Performance of DDM approach is verified by comparing data assimilation results obtained by mobile and stationary sensors. Three sensors are used for data observation and a limited lookahead policy with $l = 6$ is used for finding location of each mobile sensor during the time. We considered $\alpha = 5$ and $W = diag([1,1])$ in our simulation. Figure 3(b) illustrates positions of UAVs during the time over the spatial domain. It can be observed from Fig. 3(b) that UAVs end up to the locations where the mutual information map obtains its maximum.

Convergence behavior for mean estimate of parameter m_3 using stationary and mobile sensors, along with the minimum and maximum range of the estimate are shown in Fig. 4. Figure 4(a) illustrates that using stationary sensors results in poor estimates of the parameters. This is due to the inefficient placement of sensors during data assimilation process. On the other hand, as Fig. 4(b) represents, DDM approach results in significantly better convergence and confidence for estimate of m_3.

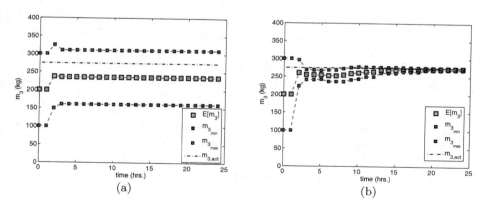

Fig. 4. m_3 estimate during the time obtained using a) stationary, and b) mobile sensors

Table 1. Root Mean Square Error (RMSE) between mean estimate of source parameters and their actual values while using different sensor networks/methods.

Sensor network/method	RMSE		
	m_1	m_2	m_3
3 *stationary* sensors	46.27	21.18	38.67
25 *stationary* sensors	14.49	19.42	33.86
3 *mobile* sensors / chemotaxis	16.11	11.97	14.32
3 *mobile* sensors / DDM	1.93	5.74	12.19

To summarize, Root Mean Square Error (RMSE) between mean estimate of source parameters and their actual values while using different sensor networks and different methods is shown in Table 1. RMSE of estimation results by using Chemotaxis approach is also shown in Table 1. It is clear from Table 1 that the proposed DDM algorithm outperforms all the other alternative methods or sensor networks, including Chemotaxis method. In other words, DDM approach results in least amount of RMSE comparing to other sensor networks and chemotaxis algorithm. To highlight performance of proposed DDM approach, we have also compared RMSE in parameter estimates obtained by DDM approach with RMSE of source parameter estimates using 25 stationary sensors (shown with triangle markers in Fig. 3(a)). As Table 1 represents, using DDM approach with just 3 sensors results in lower value of RMSE in parameter estimates, comparing with 25 stationary sensors. Hence, proposed DDM method provides more accurate estimates while using less number of data observation sensors.

6   Conclusion

In this research, a new approach for optimal allocation of data monitoring sensors is provided. The key idea of the presented method is to determine location of data monitoring sensors such that the mutual information between model predictions and measurement data is maximized, thereby giving a better reduction in uncertainty. The main advantage of this approach is that it *significantly increases* the accuracy of the estimation, while using *fewer* number of data observation sensors. Further, a new set of quadrature points, known as CUT, are used to alleviate the computational complexities involved in propagation of uncertainty in dynamical systems. Numerical simulations demonstrate performance of the proposed methodology, where the mobile sensors, when located based on DDM approach, provide better estimates and significantly outperform the estimates from stationary sensors or alternative methods like Chemotaxis approach.

Acknowledgement. This material is based upon work supported by the National Science Foundation under award number CMMI- 1054759 and AFOSR grant number FA9550-11-1-0012.

References

1. Sandini, G., Lucarini, G., Varoli, M.: Gradient driven self-organizing systems. In: Proceedings of the 1993 IEEE/RSJ International Conference on Intelligent Robots and Systems 1993, IROS'93, Vol. 1, pp. 429–432. IEEE (1993)
2. Hayes, A.T., Martinoli, A., Goodman, R.M.: Swarm robotic odor localization. In: 2001 Proceedings of IEEE/RSJ International Conference on Intelligent Robots and Systems, vol. 2, pp. 1073–1078. IEEE (2001)
3. Zarzhitsky, D., Spears, D.F., Spears, W.M.: Distributed robotics approach to chemical plume tracing. In: 2005 IEEE/RSJ International Conference on Intelligent Robots and Systems, (IROS 2005), pp. 4034–4039. IEEE (2005)
4. Julian, B.J., Angermann, M., Schwager, M., Rus, D.: Distributed robotic sensor networks: an information-theoretic approach. Int. J. Robot. Res. 31(10), 1134–1154 (2012)
5. MartíNez, S., Bullo, F.: Optimal sensor placement and motion coordination for target tracking. Automatica 42(4), 661–668 (2006)
6. Tharmarasa, R., Kirubarajan, T., Hernandez, M.L.: Large-scale optimal sensor array management for multitarget tracking. IEEE Trans. Syst. Man Cybern. Part C Appl. Rev. 37(5), 803–814 (2007)
7. Hoffmann, G.M., Tomlin, C.J.: Mobile sensor network control using mutual information methods and particle filters. IEEE Trans. Autom. Control 55(1), 32–47 (2010)
8. Choi, H.-L., How, J.P.: Continuous trajectory planning of mobile sensors for informative forecasting. Automatica 46(8), 1266–1275 (2010)
9. Williams, J.L., Fisher, J.W., Willsky, A.S.: Approximate dynamic programming for communication-constrained sensor network management. IEEE Trans. Sig. Process. 55(8), 4300–4311 (2007)
10. Krause, A., Guestrin, C., Gupta, A., Kleinberg, J.: Near-optimal sensor placements: maximizing information while minimizing communication cost. In: Proceedings of the 5th International Conference on Information Processing in Sensor Networks, pp. 2–10. ACM (2006)
11. Nagavenkat, A., Singla, P., Singh, T.: The conjugate unscented transform-an approach to evaluate multi-dimensional expectation integrals. In: Proceedings of the American Control Conference (2012)
12. Nagavenkat, A., Singla, P., Singh, T.: Conjugate unscented transform rules for uniform probability density functions. In: Proceedings of the American Control Conference (2013)
13. Cover, T.M., Thomas, J.A.: Elements of Information Theory (Wiley Series in Telecommunications and Signal Processing). Wiley-Interscience, Hoboken (2006)
14. Bertsekas, D.P.: Dynamic Programming and Optimal Control, vols. I and II, Cambridge (2000)
15. Madankan, R., Singla, P., Singh, T., Scott, P.D.: Polynomial-chaos-based Bayesian approach for state and parameter estimations. J. Guidance Control Dyn. 36(4), 1058–1074 (2013)
16. Sykes, R.I., Parker, S.F., Henn, D.S.: SCIPUFF Version 2.2 Technical Documentation (729)
17. Robins, P., Rapley, V., Thomas, P.: A probabilistic chemical sensor model for data fusion. In: 2005 8th International Conference on Information Fusion, vol. 2, p. 7. IEEE (2005)

Centralized Ensemble-Based Trajectory Planning of Cooperating Sensors for Estimating Atmospheric Dispersion Processes

Juliane Euler[1,2]([✉]), Tobias Ritter[1,2], Stefan Ulbrich[1,3],
and Oskar von Stryk[1,2]

[1] Graduate School Computational Engineering, Technische Universität Darmstadt,
Darmstadt, Germany
{euler,ritter,stryk}@sim.tu-darmstadt.de
[2] Department of Computer Science, Technische Universität Darmstadt,
Darmstadt, Germany
[3] Department of Mathematics, Technische Universität Darmstadt,
Darmstadt, Germany
ulbrich@mathematik.tu-darmstadt.de

Abstract. Optimal coordination of multiple sensors is crucial for efficient atmospheric dispersion estimation. The proposed approach adaptively provides optimized trajectories with respect to sensor cooperation and uncertainty reduction of the process estimate. To avoid the time-consuming solution of a complex optimal control problem, estimation and vehicle control are considered separate problems linked in a sequential procedure. Based on a partial differential equation model, the Ensemble Transform Kalman Filter is applied for data assimilation and generation of observation targets offering maximum information gain. A centralized model-predictive vehicle controller simultaneously provides optimal target allocation and collision-free path planning. Extending previous work, continuous measuring is assumed, which attaches more significance to the course of the trajectories. Local attraction points are introduced to draw the sensors to regions of high uncertainty. Moreover, improved target updates increase the sampling efficiency. A simulated test case illustrates the approach in comparison to non-attracted trajectories.

Keywords: Adaptive observation · ETKF · State estimation · Mobile sensors · Cooperative control

1 Introduction

Depending on the weather conditions, the dispersion of gaseous material in the atmosphere easily turns into a large-scale highly dynamic process. In order to

---

This work has been supported by the 'Excellence Initiative' of the German Federal and State Governments and the Graduate School of Computational Engineering at Technische Universität Darmstadt as well as the German Research Foundation (DFG) within the GRK 1362 "Cooperative, Adaptive and Responsive Monitoring of Mixed Mode Environments" (http://www.gkmm.tu-darmstadt.de).

S. Ravela and A. Sandu (Eds.): DyDESS 2014, LNCS 8964, pp. 322–333, 2015.
DOI: 10.1007/978-3-319-25138-7_29

understand its characteristics and predict future impacts, fast and accurate state estimation is required. The use of robotic systems for autonomous data gathering has been increasingly considered in this context [8]. Sensor-equipped autonomous vehicles are able to adapt their movement to a changing environment, which is particularly beneficial when dealing with atmospheric dispersion. Employing multiple mobile sensors permits to cover larger domains and optimal cooperation among them increases the efficiency of the estimation procedure.

As the dispersion dimensions, in general, prohibit pattern-based sampling or global exploration, immediate processing of the gathered data and adaptive sensor motion planning is essential. Information obtained from the sensors and the predictions of an underlying process model can be combined by a data assimilation method to estimate the current process state. In this way, uncertainties stemming from observation noise and model errors are reduced. Using a partial differential equation (PDE) model, more accurate forecasts can be obtained since the physics and the dynamic behavior of the dispersion process are considered.

Related approaches often avoid detailed PDE models and instead use simple models, such as Gaussian processes [15] or qualitative models [7]. They can provide results in a very short time and are frequently used in distributed systems. However, as important characteristics of the process dynamics are not considered, only inaccurate approximations can be obtained.

Adaptive observation strategies based on PDE models are commonly used in large-scale systems, e.g. for numerical weather prediction. Examples are the singular vector technique [3], the gradient method [5] or the Ensemble Transform Kalman Filter (ETKF) [2,12]. Due to the huge system dimensions, though, vehicle dynamics are not considered in these applications.

Only few publications focus on adaptive observation strategies combining PDE models and vehicle dynamics. While [14,16] deal with parameter estimation, [11,17] consider state estimation problems in conjunction with data assimilation. All these approaches involve a sophisticated optimal control problem subject to the process model, the covariance evolution, and the vehicle dynamics. Solving such complex problems is hard and time-consuming, especially regarding the real-time requirements of the application.

This is why [4,6] utilize computationally efficient suboptimal sensor guidance schemes based on the gradient of the mutual information rate and Lyapunov stability arguments, respectively. Although multiple sensor vehicles are employed, the cooperation among them is either not explicitly addressed or cannot be considered optimal.

In previous work [13], a centralized adaptive observation strategy was proposed that combines PDE-based process models and optimally cooperating mobile sensors for online state estimation. Instead of solving a sophisticated optimal control problem, state estimation and vehicle control are considered separate problems that are linked in a repeating sequential procedure: The process estimate, based on a PDE model, is improved by assimilation of new sensor data using an ETKF approach. Based on the estimate's error covariance matrix, measurement locations providing maximum information gain are determined and are used by a model-predictive controller to guide the sensor vehicles based on a discrete-continuous linear optimization program. This results in a significant gain of computational efficiency compared to solving a (nonlinear) optimal control problem incorporating process and vehicle dynamics. The focus was set on application scenarios where measurements are expensive so that they are only performed if one of the specified locations is reached by a sensor vehicle.

In contrast, this work adapts the strategy presented in [13] to exploit the advantages of a sensor system able to measure at every time step. Now that information is gathered en route, more importance is attached to the course of the trajectories leading to the target locations. Introducing additional local attraction points draws the sensor vehicles to regions afflicted with high uncertainty. Furthermore, a revised handling of target points accounts for the permanently changing error covariance.

The rest of the paper is organized as follows. Sections 2 and 3 give a short overview of the basic methodologies employed for state estimation and vehicle control, respectively. In Sect. 4, the adaptive motion planning approach is summarized. Testcases and evaluation results are presented in Sect. 5 followed by concluding remarks in Sect. 6.

2   Model and State Estimation

2.1   Process Model

The aim of the proposed approach is to estimate the state of a dynamic transport process that can be described by a PDE of the form

$$\frac{\partial \chi}{\partial t} = f(\chi(t), \nabla \chi(t), \Delta \chi(t), \mathbf{w}(t), \nabla \mathbf{w}(t)), \tag{1}$$

with the dispersing entity χ to be estimated and the underlying velocity field $\mathbf{w}$. Applying a spatial and temporal discretization scheme, an approximate solution of the PDE can be found by solving an equation of the form

$$\chi_{i+1}^{f} = M_i[\chi_i^{f}] \tag{2}$$

where M_i is the model operator obtained by the discretization scheme and χ is the state vector, which contains values of χ at certain, discrete spatial positions. With this formulation, the state vector at time t_{i+1} can be calculated from a model forecast (superscript $(\cdot)^{f}$) of the state vector at time t_i. However, the problem might be high-dimensional so that the solution of (2) becomes computationally intractable especially regarding the real-time requirements of the considered applications. Use of reduced order models [9] might be a possible remedy in this context but is not investigated in this paper.

It is assumed that compared to the true process state, a Gaussian and unbiased model error with known error covariance is made, introducing uncertainty into the calculations.

2.2   Observation Model and Data Assimilation

To alleviate the effects stemming from model uncertainty, the process is also measured by a network of sensors. At every time step t_i, all sensors take a measurement. The resulting observation vector ψ_i^o can be described by the relation

$$\psi_i^o = H_i[\chi_i^t] + \epsilon_i, \tag{3}$$

with the true state χ_i^t and the unbiased and Gaussian observation error ϵ_i. The observation operator H_i maps vectors from the state space onto the observation space and depends on the measurement positions of the sensors.

To combine results obtained from simulation and from observations, a data assimilation method has to be applied. Most of these methods rely on the formulation that the updated or analysis state vector χ_i^a results from a linear combination of the forecasted state vector and a weighted innovation due to the observation:

$$\chi_i^a = \chi_i^f + \mathbf{K}_i(\psi_i^o - H_i[\chi_i^f]). \tag{4}$$

The weight matrix $\mathbf{K}_i$ can depend on the model and the observation error covariance matrix as well as on the current estimate's error covariance $\mathbf{P}_i^f$ which is often calculated alongside with the mean estimate. As the estimate's error covariance matrix describes the quality of the state vector, it is especially important for adaptive observations. In this work, the Ensemble Transform Kalman Filter (ETKF) [2] is chosen as data assimilation scheme as it is especially suitable for high-dimensional problems. Furthermore, it is able to calculate the analysis error covariance matrix before the actual measurements are taken.

3   Cooperative Vehicle Control

The model-predictive control (MPC) approach employed in the proposed adaptive observation strategy simultaneously determines collision-free vehicle trajectories as well as optimal target allocation respecting the vehicles' physical characteristics. It can be adapted to various multi-vehicle constellations and task scenarios. Here, it is applied to guide a homogeneous team of sensor platforms to a number of specified target locations while minimizing the distances to attraction points in each vehicle's local environment. Attraction points are updated in every time step, whereas targets are recalculated at greater time intervals, but may shift slowly in the meantime.

Core of the control approach is a discrete-time mixed-integer linear program (MILP) formulation comprising the vehicles' motion dynamics, distance constraints, and several logical expressions. For details on the modeling, the reader is referred to [13]. An optimal control problem of the following form is set up and is solved in a receding horizon fashion to compute optimal control inputs for each vehicle:

$$\min_{U_N} |\mathbf{F}\boldsymbol{x}^N| + \sum_{k=0}^{N-1} |\mathbf{G}_1 \boldsymbol{u}^k| + |\mathbf{G}_2 \boldsymbol{\delta}^k| + |\mathbf{G}_3 \boldsymbol{z}^k| + |\mathbf{G}_4 \boldsymbol{x}^k| \tag{5a}$$

$$\text{s.t.} \quad \boldsymbol{x}^{k+1} = \mathbf{A}\boldsymbol{x}^k + \mathbf{B}_1 \boldsymbol{u}^k + \mathbf{B}_2 \boldsymbol{\delta}^k + \mathbf{B}_3 \boldsymbol{z}^k \tag{5b}$$

$$\mathbf{E}_2 \boldsymbol{\delta}^k + \mathbf{E}_3 \boldsymbol{z}^k \leq \mathbf{E}_1 \boldsymbol{u}^k + \mathbf{E}_4 \boldsymbol{x}^k + \mathbf{E}_5 \ . \tag{5c}$$

In this problem formulation, $\boldsymbol{x} = [\boldsymbol{x}_c \ \boldsymbol{x}_b]^T, \boldsymbol{x}_c \in \mathbb{R}^{n_c}, \boldsymbol{x}_b \in \{0,1\}^{n_b}$, is the system state comprising the vehicle states, the target locations, and each vehicle's local attraction point. $\boldsymbol{u} = [\boldsymbol{u}_c \ \boldsymbol{u}_b]^T, \boldsymbol{u}_c \in \mathbb{R}^{m_c}, \boldsymbol{u}_b \in \{0,1\}^{m_b}$, comprises the vehicle control inputs. $\boldsymbol{\delta} \in \{0,1\}^{r_b}$ and $\boldsymbol{z} \in \mathbb{R}^{r_c}$ represent auxiliary binary and continuous vectors, respectively, e.g. containing distances. The prediction time step $k = 0, \ldots, N-1$ relates to the global equidistant time steps $t_i \in \mathbb{N}$ according to $\boldsymbol{x}^k = \boldsymbol{x}(t_{i+k})$. As solution of problem (5), the sequence $U_N := \{\boldsymbol{u}^k\}_{k=0}^{N-1}$ of control inputs is obtained. The first element of U_N is applied to the real system, then its new state is measured for computing updated control inputs at the next time step t_{i+1}. In this manner, the prediction horizon N is shifted over time.

The constraints (5b)–(5c) form a so called mixed logical dynamical (MLD) system, which was proposed in [1] for modeling and controlling constrained linear systems containing interacting physical laws and logical rules. The objective function (5a) can reflect a prioritization of different problem aspects. For the proposed motion planning approach, these are the minimization of each vehicle's distance to its local attraction point, the minimization of distances to still unprocessed target locations, a reward for visiting target locations as well as the minimization of the required control effort. Problem (5) is a mixed-integer linear constrained finite time optimal control (CFTOC) problem. It can easily be transformed into a MILP at each time step of the MPC procedure. Therefore, a numerically robust, efficient computation of control inputs can be performed.

The described control scheme is applied in a centralized manner for the global system of vehicles and targets. Hence, globally optimal cooperative behavior within the scope of the system model and the chosen prediction horizon N is obtained. However, the efficiency of the centralized MPC approach strongly depends on the size of the system model, i.e. the number of vehicles.

4 Adaptive Sensor Motion Strategy

In contrast to related approaches [4,6,11,14,16,17], the proposed adaptive observation strategy, in principle, treats state estimation and vehicle control as two separate problems. However, to obtain a working and closed-loop solution, both parts are coupled by information exchange. In short, target and attraction points are calculated based on the error covariance matrix associated with the current state estimate. They serve as input for the vehicle controller responsible for the sensor trajectories. The measurement data obtained from the sensors is then refed to update the state estimate and error covariance, and so on.

In detail, the following steps, which are also schematically depicted in Fig. 1, are repeatedly processed:

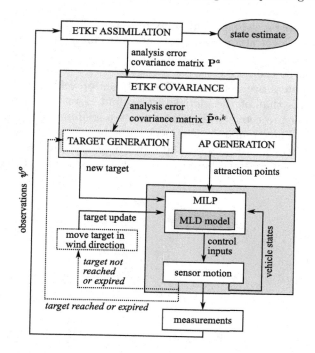

Fig. 1. Overview of the proposed adaptive observation strategy.

Determine Target Points. The error covariance matrix provided by the ETKF is a suitable measure of the quality of a state estimate. Large entries indicate high uncertainties, i.e. high deviations between true state and estimate. The objective is to iteratively reduce the entries in the covariance matrix by taking measurements at positions where the uncertainty is largest and, thus, the most valuable information can be obtained.

In order to determine such a target point, the location corresponding to the maximum value of the diagonal of the current error covariance matrix $\mathbf{P}_i^a$ is chosen. Further target points are calculated iteratively as described above, but considering the analysis error covariance matrix $\tilde{\mathbf{P}}_i^a$. The latter is obtained by applying the ETKF pretending that observations are available at all previously calculated target points, i.e. the observation matrix $\hat{\mathbf{H}}_i^k$ has to be determined in every iteration k. Hereby, clusterization of target points in regions with high uncertainty is avoided. The procedure is repeated until the number of target points corresponds to the number of sensor vehicles.

The target points then serve as input for the model-predictive controller guiding the sensor vehicles to obtain the corresponding measurement. A measurement at the target point can be considered globally optimum in terms of information gain at that very moment in time.

Determine Local Attraction Points. As the sensors are assumed to measure at every time step, the vehicle trajectories leading to the global measurement targets are of importance and should maximize the information gain on the way. For this purpose, local attraction points are introduced that intend to deviate the trajectories into regions of high uncertainty without changing their general orientation towards the target.

Attraction points are determined for each sensor vehicle individually. The calculation equals that of the global targets, but is restricted to the sensor's local environment projected to the next time step assuming the vehicle keeps its current velocity. The circular environment is further reduced to its front half as shown in Fig. 2 in order to preserve the forward motion. In every time step, the attraction points are updated based on the current error covariance matrix.

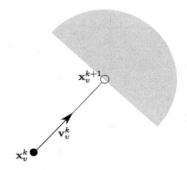

Fig. 2. Local region (gray) for the selection of attraction points based on a projection of the vehicle's position $\mathbf{x}_v^k$ along its current velocity vector $\mathbf{v}_v^k$.

Control Vehicles and Process Measurements. The model-predictive controller provides control inputs for the vehicles, such that each vehicle approaches one of the global targets taking slight detours to stay close to their individual attraction points. In every time step, the obtained measurement data is assimilated to improve the process state estimate and update the error covariance matrix.

Update Target Points. When dealing with dynamic processes, target points might have already lost their optimality by the time their calculation is completed. The information gain of a measurement there more and more decreases over time. That is why different expiration criteria for target points were implemented. Obviously, a target point is replaced as soon as a sensor vehicle has been on the spot to take a measurement. Moreover, a target is discarded if it has not been reached within a certain number of time steps or if the associated uncertainty value is lower than 20 % of the current global uncertainty maximum. In all three cases, a new target is generated applying the ETKF-based approach described above. If a target point does not have to be recalculated because of the above criteria, it is moved with the background wind velocity to account for the advective nature of the dynamic process.

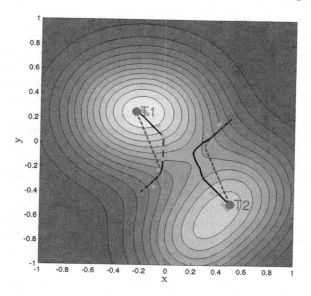

Fig. 3. Unattracted trajectory (blue dashed line) vs. trajectory (black solid line) influenced by attractor points (light blue, every third point is shown).

5   Results

5.1   Influence of Local Attraction Points

A simplified static test scenario is considered to illustrate the influence of local attraction points on the vehicle trajectories. Two sensor vehicles modeled as point masses with a maximum velocity of 0.015 and a maximum acceleration of 0.01 located on a two-dimensional domain at (-0.2,-0.4) and (0.5,0.2) are supposed to reach two target points at (-0.25,0.25) and (0.5,-0.5). To avoid collisions and redundant measurements, the minimum distance between two sensors is set to 0.1. An MPC prediction horizon of $N = 20$ time steps is used, while $\Delta t = 2$. The problem is solved twice - with and without the use of local attraction points. In the scenario with attraction points, those are determined based on a steady background function representing the error variance of the dynamic case.

The results obtained with the two approaches are depicted in Fig. 3. At first, the sensor vehicles mainly try to minimize the distance to both target points until they are close enough to head for the target points. The local attraction points influence the trajectory as the sensors are pulled towards locations with higher values of the background function. If the background function is supposed to represent locations with high uncertainty, the use of the attracted trajectories should produce a higher information gain.

5.2   Dynamic Test Case

The proposed observation strategy is now applied for state estimation of a two-dimensional dispersion process governed by the source-free linear advection-diffusion equation

$$\frac{\partial c}{\partial t} + \nabla \cdot (c\mathbf{w}) - \nabla \cdot (\mathbf{D}\nabla c) = 0, \tag{6}$$

where c represents the concentration to be estimated, $\mathbf{D}$ is the diffusion matrix, which is assumed to be homogeneous and constant, and the velocity field $\mathbf{w}$ is uniform with $w_1 = 0.005$ in x-direction and a vanishing component in y-direction. A finite element method with a characteristic Galerkin approach is applied to discretize and solve (6). The number of grid nodes amounts to about 1000. Note that although the considered problem is kept simple for reasons of clarity, the proposed approach can easily be extended to more sophisticated scenarios, e.g. involving complex velocity fields including eddies.

Observations are obtained by the use of a so-called twin experiment, i.e. the true solution is assumed to be known and it is simulated along with the estimated solution. With this approach, observations can be easily obtained using (3), where the measurement errors are assumed to be uncorrelated and to have a constant variance of 0.01. The difference between the true solution and the estimated solution resides amongst others in their initial condition. A combination of four Gaussian pulses is considered as initial condition. However, for the true initial state and the ensemble generation, the parameters (width, height and position of the pulses) are perturbed by adding numbers drawn from a Gaussian distribution. In total, the ensemble consists of 40 state vectors and localization is used to avoid spurious oscillations [10].

Again, two sensor vehicles with the same configuration as in the static scenario, now starting at (0,0.5) and (0,-0.5), respectively, are considered. For comparison, first, the adaptive observation approach presented in [13] is applied, but slightly modified assuming that the sensors measure at every time step. Then the problem is tackled applying the new motion planning approach involving local attraction points and improved target updates. After 60 time steps, the results depicted in Fig. 4 are obtained.

While using the first approach the vehicles are heading to the middle of the domain to minimize the distance to both target points, the vehicles are attracted more to the boundaries using the proposed extended strategy. The reason for this behavior is a higher uncertainty in the top and bottom area as the uncertainty distribution initially is horseshoe-shaped. Instead of driving through regions where only marginal information can be found, the trajectory is planned to also reduce a high amount of local uncertainty on the way to the target point. This leads to better quality estimates in shorter time.

Having a look on the error confirms this impression. As the true solution is assumed to be known, the quality of the resulting state estimates can be quantified considering their deviation from the true state. Thus, the error can be calculated by forming the norm of the deviation vector. The mean error over time is depicted in Fig. 5(a). Applying the new method with attraction points reduces the error much faster than without attraction points. While the error obtained from the simple strategy is around 0.05 at the final time $t = 120$, the proposed strategy in the same time reduces the error to 0.032. The same applies for the norm of the diagonal of the error covariance matrix, which is for the proposed strategy one third less than for the compared strategy (cf. Fig. 5(b)).

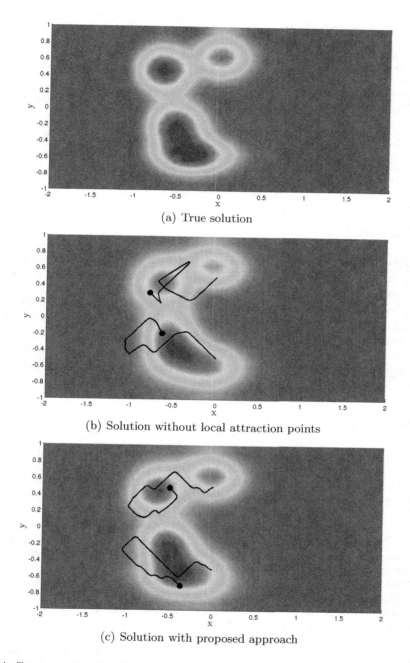

(a) True solution

(b) Solution without local attraction points

(c) Solution with proposed approach

Fig. 4. Concentration distribution at $t = 120$ and related sensor vehicle trajectories

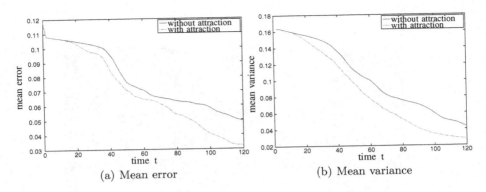

(a) Mean error   (b) Mean variance

Fig. 5. Mean error and variance over time.

6   Conclusion

A new centralized adaptive observation strategy was presented that relies on a PDE process model, adaptive ETKF-based generation of observation points, and the cooperation of mobile sensors controlled by a MILP-based model-predictive controller. The strategy is especially designed for sensor systems able to measure at high repetition rates as it aims to maximize the uncertainty reduction along the sensor trajectories. Furthermore, a flexible recalculation of target points accounts for the fast evolution of the error covariance. Compared to sensor motion planning without these new features, the proposed method provides estimates of increased quality in shorter time.

References

1. Bemporad, A., Morari, M.: Control of systems integrating logic, dynamics, and constraints. Automatica **35**, 407–427 (1999)
2. Bishop, C.H., Etherton, B.J., Majumdar, S.J.: Adaptive sampling with the ensemble transform Kalman filter. Part I: theoretical aspects. Mon. Weather Rev. **129**(3), 420–436 (2001)
3. Buizza, R., Montani, A.: Targeting observations using singular vectors. J. Atmos. Sci. **56**(17), 2965–2985 (1999)
4. Choi, H.L., How, J.P.: Continuous trajectory planning of mobile sensors for informative forecasting. Automatica **46**, 1266–1275 (2010)
5. Daescu, D.N., Navon, I.M.: Adaptive observations in the context of 4D-Var data assimilation. Meteorol. Atmos. Phys. **85**(4), 205–226 (2003)
6. Demetriou, M.A., Uciński, D.: State estimation of spatially distributed processes using mobile sensing agents. In: American Control Conference (ACC), pp. 1770–1776. IEEE (2011)
7. Duckham, M., Nittel, S., Worboys, M.: Monitoring dynamic spatial fields using responsive geosensor networks. In: 13th Annual ACM International Workshop on Geographic Information Systems, pp. 51–60 (2005)

8. Dunbabin, M., Marques, L.: Robotics for environmental monitoring: significant advancements and applications. IEEE Robotics & Automation Magazine **19**(1), 24–39 (2012)
9. Hinze, M., Volkwein, S.: Proper orthogonal decomposition surrogate models for nonlinear dynamical systems: error estimates and suboptimal control. In: Benner, P., Sorensen, D.C., Mehrmann, V. (eds.) Dimension Reduction of Large-Scale Systems, pp. 261–306. Springer, Heidelberg (2005)
10. Houtekamer, P.L., Mitchell, H.L.: A sequential ensemble Kalman filter for atmospheric data assimilation. Mon. Weather Rev. **129**(1), 123–137 (2001)
11. Hover, F.S.: Path planning for data assimilation in mobile environmental monitoring systems. In: IEEE/RSJ International Conference on Intelligent Robots and Systems, pp. 213–218 (2009)
12. Majumdar, S.J., Bishop, C.H., Etherton, B.J., Toth, Z.: Adaptive sampling with the ensemble transform kalman filter. Part II: field program implementation. Mon. Weather Rev. **130**, 1356–1369 (2002)
13. Ritter, T., Euler, J., Ulbrich, S., von Stryk, O.: Adaptive observation strategy for dispersion process estimation using cooperating mobile sensors. In: 19th IFAC World Congress, pp. 5302–5308 (2014)
14. Song, Z., Chen, Y., Liang, J., Uciński, D.: Optimal mobile sensor motion planning under nonholonomic constraints for parameter estimation of distributed systems. Int. J. Intell. Syst. Technol. Appl. **3**(3/4), 277–295 (2007)
15. Stranders, R., Farinelli, A., Rogers, A., Jennings, N.R.: Decentralised coordination of mobile sensors using the max-sum algorithm. In: 21st International Joint Conference on Artificial Intelligence, pp. 299–304 (2009)
16. Uciński, D.: Optimal Measurement Methods for Distributed Parameter System Identification. CRC Press, Boca Raton (2005)
17. Zhang, D., Colburn, C., Bewley, T.: Estimation and adaptive observation of environmental plumes. In: American Control Conference (ACC), pp. 4281–4286 (2011)

Active Singularities for Multivehicle Motion Planning in an N-Vortex System

Francis D. Lagor and Derek A. Paley[(✉)]

Department of Aerospace Engineering and Institute for Systems Research,
University of Maryland, College Park, MD, USA
dpaley@umd.edu

Abstract. This paper presents a path-planning paradigm for distributed control of multiple sensor platforms in a geophysical flow well-approximated by a point-vortex model. We utilize Hamiltonian dynamics to generate control vector fields for vehicle motion in N-vortex flows using the concept of an active singularity whose strength is a tunable control input. We introduce active singularities that are virtual point vortices possibly collocated with virtual point sources or sinks. We provide a principled method to stabilize relative equilibria of these virtual vortices in the presence of the actual point vortices, which represent the underlying geophysical flow. We illustrate how these relative equilibria may be useful for vehicle path planning and sampling in a geophysical flow. Preliminary results presented here are based on an adaptive control design.

Keywords: Path planning · Vortex dynamics · Environmental sampling · Cooperative control

1 Introduction

Distributed environmental sampling is an active field of research [2,14] due to its many applications, including contaminant plume localization [23], biological monitoring [18], and data assimilation in atmospheric and ocean sciences [5, 13]. Significant hardware and sensor improvements [19] as well as algorithmic performance guarantees [9,10] have further encouraged interest. However, there are open challenges about how mobile sensor platforms can most effectively sample and interact with strong, circulating flows [3,10,11].

Coherent vortices (eddies) in the ocean persist on mesoscales (10 to 500 km) and submesoscales (1 to 10 km) for weeks or even months and play an important role in global transport and mixing processes [8]. For example, small-scale (15 km) eddies appeared at the mouth of Monterey Bay during field experiments of the second Autonomous Ocean Sampling Network (AOSN-II) and contributed to the overall transport of cold water away from the southern part of the bay [18]. However, the movement of these eddies could not be correlated with local wind shear stress [18]. Understanding transport within these flow structures

© Springer International Publishing Switzerland 2015
S. Ravela and A. Sandu (Eds.): DyDESS 2014, LNCS 8964, pp. 334–346, 2015.
DOI: 10.1007/978-3-319-25138-7_30

is possible but requires in situ observations over a large spatiotemporal volume collected by fleets of autonomous vehicles [3,6,8,17]. Underwater gliders, which are steered, buoyancy-driven, long-endurance vehicles, and drifters, which are depth-controlled underwater platforms that passively drift, are deployed to reduce uncertainties in estimates of ocean processes [14,16,20] and to sample and track oceanographic features [2,18]. A steered sampling platform such as a glider that travels within the flowfield of an eddy taking targeted observations may be even more beneficial than passive drifter, even if the drifter has longer endurance.

Difficulties in accessing platforms during relatively long ocean-sampling missions has encouraged research in distributed algorithms that can maximize vehicle endurance, enhance vehicle autonomy, and reduce process uncertainty during sampling. Hsieh et al. [6] show that steering vehicles to flow patterns such as (almost) invariant sets can help maximize vehicle endurance. Frew et al. [4] construct Lyapunov-based guidance vector fields for specifying sampling trajectories that can be tracked by the onboard controller of an autonomous (aerial) vehicle. Further, focusing measurements on targeted areas [6] and stabilizing multivehicle formations have been shown to help maximize information collection [3] when sampling geophysical flows that can be modeled using reduced-order methods such as a point-vortex model.

This paper provides a theoretically-justified motion-planning framework that accounts for environmental flow effects and vehicle-to-vehicle interactions through the use of flow singularities. Flow singularities (point vortices, sources, and sinks) are standard elements of a reduced-order potential flow model that induce nearby fluid flow but are undefined (singular) at their centers. Distributed algorithms within this framework are designed to enhance autonomy and to allow sampling platforms to exploit, whenever possible, the underlying motion of their environment to maximize endurance in geophysical flows.

The study of vortex dynamics in this paper is an extension of the fundamental point-vortex work of Chen et al. [1], who show that augmenting a point-vortex system with dissipation stabilizes relative equilibria (regular patterns that are fixed points in a reduced configuration space) of the unmodified point-vortex dynamics [1]. The modification of the point-vortex dynamics to include dissipation is suggestive of control action being applied to the point-vortex system. Further, we observe that the modified vortex dynamics in [1] represent spiral vortices (vortices collocated with a sources or sinks) in the presence of a sink at the origin. These observations lead us to consider spiral vortices as basic modeling elements of a virtual singularity system in which virtual vortices are used to guide vehicle sampling trajectories. By manipulating the virtual vortex strengths, we create active singularities to generate artificial vector fields for vehicle guidance. The actual vortex dynamics (representing the geophysical flow) and the virtual vortex dynamics are connected via a one-way influence of actual vortices on the virtual ones.

A point-vortex system possesses Hamiltonian dynamics and exhibits conservation of certain physical properties that we exploit in Lyapunov analysis to obtain analytical guarantees for this motion-planning paradigm. We provide

Lyapunov stability analysis for the vortex dynamics of Chen et al. [1] based on conserved quantities of the Hamiltonian system. We extend the dynamics of Chen et al. [1] by showing how the location of the center of the relative equilibrium can be prescribed. We derive the total Hamiltonian, which is conserved by the virtual vortices in the actual-plus-virtual vortex dynamics, and use it to provide Lyapunov analysis demonstrating asymptotic convergence of virtual vortices to a relative equilibrium. The use of Lyapunov analysis to inform the selection of a parameter update law is a common theme in adaptive control [22]. As a preliminary example of the efficacy of this motion planning framework, we employ adaptive control to regulate the value of the total Hamiltonian.

The specific contributions of this paper are (1) Lyapunov analysis of the nonlinear stability of a relative equilibrium in the dissipative point-vortex system introduced by Chen et al. [1]; (2) a novel method for multivehicle motion planning in the presence of point vortices based on distributed control of active singularities; and (3) an adaptive control law for stabilizing lattice-shaped formations of sampling platforms around the actual center of vorticity in a point vortex flow. This work represents a framework in which multivehicle motion planning is achieved in the presence of idealized flow field dynamics.

The outline of the paper is as follows. Section 2 explains point vortex dynamics, summarizes the work of Chen et al. [1] on relative equilibrium configurations, and provides Lyapunov analysis of their model. Section 3 introduces active singularities for multivehicle motion planning and provides a Lyapunov analysis of relative-equilibrium stabilization for virtual vortices. Section 4 presents a Lyapunov-based, distributed control strategy for formations of virtual vortices based on adaptive control of the singularity strength, including numerical simulation of motion planning in the presence of an actual vortex pair. Section 5 summarizes the paper and ongoing research.

2   Point-Vortex Dynamics and Relative Equilibria

In potential flow theory, an irrotational or point vortex is an idealized flow element that models circulating flow [15]. Since the flow at the center of a point vortex is undefined, it is called a flow singularity, much like a source or sink. Let $z_\alpha = x_\alpha + iy_\alpha$ represent the position of vortex $\alpha \in \{1, \ldots, N\}$ in the complex plane and $\gamma_\alpha > 0$ be its strength, which determines the magnitude of the surrounding velocity field. The N-vortex system is Hamiltonian with [15]

$$\gamma_\alpha \dot{x}_\alpha = \frac{\partial \mathcal{H}}{\partial y_\alpha} = -\frac{1}{2\pi} \sum_{\beta \neq \alpha}^{N} \gamma_\alpha \gamma_\beta \frac{y_\alpha - y_\beta}{|z_\alpha - z_\beta|^2} \tag{1}$$

$$\gamma_\alpha \dot{y}_\alpha = -\frac{\partial \mathcal{H}}{\partial x_\alpha} = \frac{1}{2\pi} \sum_{\beta \neq \alpha}^{N} \gamma_\alpha \gamma_\beta \frac{x_\alpha - x_\beta}{|z_\alpha - z_\beta|^2}, \tag{2}$$

where the Hamiltonian $\mathcal{H}$ is

$$\mathcal{H} = -\frac{1}{4\pi} \sum_{\alpha=1}^{N} \sum_{\substack{\beta=1 \\ \beta \neq \alpha}}^{N} \gamma_\alpha \gamma_\beta \log |z_\alpha - z_\beta|. \tag{3}$$

We elect to use complex variables for compactness and the overbar $\overline{(\cdot)}$ to denote complex conjugation. The selection of $\gamma_k > 0$ ensures all vortices have the same signed circulation strength, preventing the possibility of vortex collapse. The Hamiltonian dynamics (1) and (2) are equivalent to [12,15]

$$\gamma_\alpha \dot{z}_\alpha = -2i \frac{\partial \mathcal{H}}{\partial \overline{z}_\alpha} = \frac{i}{2\pi} \sum_{\substack{\beta \neq \alpha}}^{N} \gamma_\alpha \gamma_\beta \frac{z_\alpha - z_\beta}{|z_\alpha - z_\beta|^2}, \tag{4}$$

where the partial derivative operators are [21]

$$\frac{\partial}{\partial z_\alpha} \triangleq \frac{1}{2}\left(\frac{\partial}{\partial x_\alpha} - i\frac{\partial}{\partial y_\alpha}\right) \quad \text{and} \quad \frac{\partial}{\partial \overline{z}_\alpha} \triangleq \frac{1}{2}\left(\frac{\partial}{\partial x_\alpha} + i\frac{\partial}{\partial y_\alpha}\right).$$

Let $\Gamma = \sum_{\alpha=1}^{N} \gamma_\alpha$ denote the total vorticity. In addition to $\mathcal{H}$, the N-vortex system conserves the center of vorticity $\mathcal{C} = \Gamma^{-1} \sum_{\alpha=1}^{N} \gamma_\alpha z_\alpha$ and the angular impulse $\mathcal{S} = \sum_{\alpha=1}^{N} \gamma_\alpha |z_\alpha|^2$ [15]. Note, these quantities are analogous to the center of mass and moment of inertia, respectively, in a point-mass system. Point vortices have the following relations to other flow singularities: replacing real circulation strength γ_α with an imaginary circulation strength $i\gamma_\alpha$ with $\gamma_\alpha > 0$ (resp. $\gamma_\alpha < 0$) produces a sink (resp. source); a complex circulation strength γ_α yields a spiral vortex [15].

Although the Hamiltonian dynamics of N vortices in the plane yield chaotic trajectories [1], Chen et al. [1] show that adding dissipation stabilizes relative equilibria, which are geometrical configurations of vortices not fixed in an inertial frame [15]. Here we provide a Lyapunov analysis of the N-vortex dynamics with dissipation, making use of the conservation of angular impulse $\mathcal{S} = \sum_{\alpha=1}^{N} \gamma_\alpha |z_\alpha|^2$ in the construction of a Lyapunov function. We utilize the dissipative vortex dynamics for controlling the trajectories of actuated vortices in Sect. 4.

Chen et al. [1] show that relative-equilibrium configurations of the vortex dynamics (4) are identical to the relative equilibria of the augmented system

$$\dot{z}_\alpha = \frac{i}{2\pi} \sum_{\substack{\beta \neq \alpha}}^{N} \gamma_\beta \frac{z_\alpha - z_\beta}{|z_\alpha - z_\beta|^2} + \mu\left(\frac{1}{2\pi} \sum_{\substack{\beta \neq \alpha}}^{N} \gamma_\beta \frac{z_\alpha - z_\beta}{|z_\alpha - z_\beta|^2} - \omega z_\alpha\right), \tag{5}$$

where $\mu > 0$ repesents a gain that governs the rate of convergence to the equilibrium configuration. Setting $\mu = 0$ in (5) yields the standard Hamiltonian vortex dynamics [1]; the significance of including $\mu > 0$ is that the solutions of (5) converge asymptotically to stable relative equilibria of (4), which are rotating vortex configurations. Chen et al. refer to (5) as a phenomenological model; it represents dynamics that aggregate the particles into crystalline patterns [1]. Note that when a relative equilibrium is attained, the dissipative term is zero and the unmodified vortex dynamics are restored [1].

Let $\mathcal{R}$ be a rotating reference frame with angular rate ω relative to inertial frame $\mathcal{I}$, and consider the coordinate change $z_\alpha = \xi_\alpha \exp(i\omega t)$. By the chain rule, $\frac{\partial \mathcal{H}}{\partial \bar{z}_\alpha} = \frac{\partial \mathcal{H}}{\partial \bar{\xi}_\alpha} \exp(i\omega t)$ and (4) becomes

$$\gamma_\alpha \dot{\xi}_\alpha = -2i \frac{\partial \mathcal{H}}{\partial \bar{\xi}_\alpha} - i\omega \gamma_\alpha \xi_\alpha. \tag{6}$$

The equilibria in $\mathcal{R}$ yield the following conditions for relative equilibria in $\mathcal{I}$:

$$\frac{\partial \mathcal{H}}{\partial \bar{\xi}_\alpha} + \frac{\omega}{2} \gamma_\alpha \xi_\alpha = 0, \quad \alpha = 1, \ldots, N. \tag{7}$$

Note, these conditions are invariant under transformation back to z_α, i.e.,

$$\frac{\partial \mathcal{H}}{\partial \bar{z}_\alpha} + \frac{\omega}{2} \gamma_\alpha z_\alpha = \frac{\partial \mathcal{H}}{\partial \bar{z}_\alpha} + \frac{\omega}{2} \frac{\partial \mathcal{S}}{\partial \bar{z}_\alpha} = 0. \tag{8}$$

The key observation is that (5) may be written in terms of the angular impulse $\mathcal{S}$, which is conserved by the unmodified dynamics, i.e.,

$$\gamma_\alpha \dot{z}_\alpha = -2i \frac{\partial \mathcal{H}}{\partial \bar{z}_\alpha} - 2\mu \left(\frac{\partial \mathcal{H}}{\partial \bar{z}_\alpha} + \frac{\omega}{2} \frac{\partial \mathcal{S}}{\partial \bar{z}_\alpha} \right). \tag{9}$$

The dynamics (9) consist of a Hamiltonian term and a gradient term. The gradient term suggests a Lyapunov function for asymptotic stability arguments, provided collisions between vortices do not occur. Consider the candidate Lyapunov function

$$V = \mathcal{H} + \frac{\omega}{2} \mathcal{S}, \tag{10}$$

whose dynamics along solutions of (9) are

$$\dot{V} = \sum_\alpha \frac{\partial V}{\partial z_\alpha} \dot{z}_\alpha + \frac{\partial V}{\partial \bar{z}_\alpha} \dot{\bar{z}}_\alpha$$

$$= \sum_\alpha \frac{2\omega}{\gamma_\alpha} \mathrm{Re} \left(-i \frac{\partial \mathcal{H}}{\partial \bar{z}_\alpha} \frac{\partial \mathcal{S}}{\partial z_\alpha} \right) - \frac{4\mu}{\gamma_\alpha} \left| \frac{\partial \mathcal{H}}{\partial \bar{z}_\alpha} + \frac{\omega}{2} \frac{\partial \mathcal{S}}{\partial \bar{z}_\alpha} \right|^2.$$

By plugging in for $\mathcal{H}$ and $\mathcal{S}$ and making use of $\mathrm{Im} \left(\sum_\alpha \sum_{\beta \neq \alpha} z_\beta \bar{z}_\alpha \right) = 0$, the first term vanishes, leaving

$$\dot{V} = -\sum_\alpha \frac{4\mu}{\gamma_\alpha} \left| \frac{\partial \mathcal{H}}{\partial \bar{z}_\alpha} + \frac{\omega}{2} \frac{\partial \mathcal{S}}{\partial \bar{z}_\alpha} \right|^2 \leq 0.$$

This observation leads to the following proposition.

Proposition 1. *Suppose $\gamma_\alpha > 0$ and $z_\alpha(t)$ is a collision-free, bounded trajectory of (9) for all $\alpha = 1, \ldots, N$. Then $z_\alpha(t)$ asymptotically converges to a relative equilibrium of the vortex dynamics given by (4).*

Proof. By assumption, $z_\alpha(t)$ is collision-free and bounded. Hence, V is well-defined for all time and there exists a compact set within which the trajectories reside for all time. $\dot{V}$ is negative semi-definite and zero only when (8) is satisfied $\forall\ \alpha = 1, \ldots, N$. The invariance principle [7] stipulates that the trajectories asymptotically converge to the largest invariant set for which condition (8) holds; this set contains the rotating relative equilibria of (4).   □

3   Active Singularities for Motion Planning

The vortex dynamics with dissipation (5) are useful for stabilizing relative equilibria. We now exploit this property to create a novel motion-planning paradigm based on virtual spiral vortices, which are singularities that add dissipation to a point vortex system. Spiral vortices have complex circulation strength because of the collocation of a vortex and a source or sink [15]. In this framework, virtual vortices generate control vector fields that are added to the drift vector field associated with the fluid flow. The control inputs to the system are the singularity strengths.

Suppose the trajectories of P vehicles are generated by integrating their dynamic interactions with N actual vortices and M virtual (spiral) vortices. Let the actual vortices be located at z_α for $\alpha \in \{1, \ldots, N\}$. Append the virtual vortex locations z_α for $\alpha \in \{N+1, \ldots, N+M\}$ and vehicle locations z_α for $\alpha \in \{N+M+1, \ldots, N+M+P\}$ to form the state vector $z_\alpha \in \mathbb{C}^{N+M+P}$. Let Γ_β be the (possibly complex) circulation of vortex $\beta = 1, \ldots, N+M$. The dynamics of the actual and virtual vortices in the active singularity system are

$$\dot{z}_\alpha = \frac{i}{2\pi} \sum_{\substack{\beta \neq \alpha}}^{N+M} \Gamma_\beta a_{\alpha,\beta} \frac{z_\alpha - z_\beta}{|z_\alpha - z_\beta|^2}, \quad \alpha = 1, \ldots, N+M, \tag{11}$$

where the sum is taken over $N+M$ to account for all singularities in the system. The interaction topology

$$a_{\alpha,\beta} = \begin{cases} 0, & \text{if } \alpha = \beta \text{ or } (\alpha \leq N \text{ and } \beta > N) \\ 1, & \text{otherwise} \end{cases}, \tag{12}$$

enforces the natural dynamics between actual vortices, whereas each virtual vortex evolves under the combined influence of the actual vortices and the other virtual vortices. The vehicle dynamics $\dot{z}_\alpha$ for $\alpha = N+M+1, \ldots, N+M+P$ depend on the association between virtual vortices and vehicles. The association may be one-to-one, multiple-to-one, involve a fixed virtual vortex, or be a mixed variant of these strategies. In the remainder of this paper, we assume that virtual vortices are collocated with vehicles under a one-to-one association.

View the complex circulations $\{\Gamma_{N+1}, \ldots, \Gamma_{N+M}\}$ associated with the virtual (spiral) vortices as control inputs; the problem is to characterize and stabilize the desired solutions of (11). Note that because it is necessary to have more than a single virtual vortex for controllability, the circulation strength Γ_β of virtual vortex β only influences virtual vortex β indirectly. When $\mathrm{Re}\{\Gamma_\beta\}=0$ and $\mathrm{Im}\{\Gamma_\beta\}\neq 0$, the active singularity β has radial flow only [15] (i.e., it is a source for $\mathrm{Im}\{\Gamma_\beta\}<0$ or a sink for $\mathrm{Im}\{\Gamma_\beta\}>0$). When $\mathrm{Re}\{\Gamma_\beta\}\neq 0$ and $\mathrm{Im}\{\Gamma_\beta\}=0$, the active singularity β represents an irrotational vortex. When $\Gamma_\beta=0$, β behaves as a passive (drifting) particle. Observe that if each vehicle is assigned to a virtual vortex, (11) is identical to (5) with $\Gamma_\beta=\gamma_\beta-i\mu\gamma_\beta$ for spiral vortices and a fixed sink of strength $2\pi\mu\omega|z_\alpha|^2$ at the origin. The sink at the origin serves only to center the relative equilibrium at the origin.

In fact, one may control the center of vorticity $\mathcal{C}$ (correspondingly, the center of the relative equilibrium) to be at a point $\mathcal{C}_0\in\mathbb{C}$ away from the origin. Define the shifted angular impulse

$$S' = \sum_{\alpha=1}^{N}\gamma_\alpha|z_\alpha - \mathcal{C}_0|^2, \tag{13}$$

and the modified Lyapunov function

$$V'=\mathcal{H}+\frac{\omega}{2}S'. \tag{14}$$

The following corollary to Proposition 1 represents a preliminary design consideration for virtual vortex control.

Corollary 1. *Suppose $\gamma_\alpha>0$ and $z_\alpha(t)$ is a collision-free, bounded trajectory of (9) with S replaced by S' for all $\alpha=1,\dots,N$. Then $z_\alpha(t)$ asymptotically converges to a relative equilibrium of the vortex dynamics given by (4) and centered at $\mathcal{C}_0$.*

Proof. Substituting S' into (9) in place of S, using the Lyapunov function (14), and following the approach of Proposition 1 shows that solutions converge to the largest invariant set in which (8) is satisfied with S replaced by S'. This implies $\mathcal{C}=\mathcal{C}_0$ because (after summing the invariance condition over all α), $\sum_{\alpha=1}^{N}\gamma_\alpha(z_\alpha-\mathcal{C}_0)=\Gamma(\mathcal{C}-\mathcal{C}_0)=0$. $\qquad\square$

Figure 1 illustrates the time evolution of virtual vortices from a random initial arrangement to a rotating relative equilibrium centered at $\mathcal{C}_0=200+200i$.

We now consider the actual-plus-virtual vortex system. Suppose the actual vortices interact according to their own natural dynamics (4) and the virtual vortices have dynamics

$$\gamma_\alpha\dot{z}_\alpha = -2i\frac{\partial\mathcal{H}_c}{\partial\bar{z}_\alpha} - 2\mu\left(\frac{\partial\mathcal{H}_c}{\partial\bar{z}_\alpha} + \frac{w}{2}\gamma_\alpha z_\alpha\right), \tag{15}$$

for $\alpha = N+1,\dots,N+M$, where

$$\mathcal{H}_c = -\frac{1}{2\pi}\sum_{\alpha}^{N}\sum_{\substack{N+1\\\beta\neq\alpha}}^{N+M}\gamma_\alpha\gamma_\beta\log|z_\alpha-z_\beta| - \frac{1}{4\pi}\sum_{N+1}^{N+M}\sum_{\substack{N+1\\\beta\neq\alpha}}^{N+M}\gamma_\alpha\gamma_\beta\log|z_\alpha-z_\beta|.$$

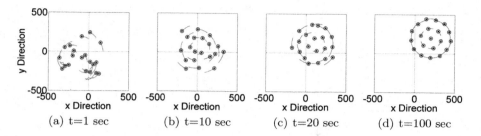

Fig. 1. Simulating convergence to a relative equilibrium centered at $\mathcal{C}_0 = 200 + 200i$

For $\mu = 0$, it can be shown that the virtual vortices conserve $\mathcal{H}_c$ even when interacting with the actual vortices (omitted for brevity). In the active singularity system, the dynamics (15) asymptotically stabilize relative equilibrium configurations of the virtual vortices in the presence of actual vortices, which are themselves in relative equilibrium. The formulation (15) of the path-planning problem gives rise to a Lyapunov-based control design in which one selects the dissipative terms to asymptotically stabilize a desired vehicle configuration for environmental sampling. In the following result, we make use of the conserved quantity $\mathcal{H}_c$ to suggest a candidate Lyapunov function.

Define the candidate Lyapunov function

$$V_c = \mathcal{H}_c + \frac{\omega}{2}\mathcal{S}_c, \tag{16}$$

where the angular impulse of the virtual vortices $\mathcal{S}_c$ is

$$\mathcal{S}_c = \sum_{\alpha=N+1}^{N+M} \gamma_\alpha |z_\alpha|^2. \tag{17}$$

The actual vortices contribute time-varying terms to the virtual vortex dynamics. However, in the rotating frame $\mathcal{R}$, the actual vortices appear fixed. Hence, changing coordinates yields

$$\dot{V}_c = \sum_{\alpha=N+1}^{N+M} \frac{-4\mu}{\gamma_\alpha} \left| \frac{\partial \mathcal{H}_c}{\partial \xi_\alpha} + \frac{\omega}{2}\frac{\partial \mathcal{S}_c}{\partial \xi_\alpha} \right|^2 \leq 0,$$

leading to the following proposition.

Proposition 2. *Suppose $\gamma_\alpha > 0$ and $z_\alpha(t)$ is a collision-free, bounded trajectory of the virtual vortex dynamics (15) for all $\alpha = N+1, \ldots, N+M$, in the presence of actual point-vortices in relative equilibrium. Then $z_\alpha(t)$ asymptotically converges to a relative equilibrium configuration of the actual-plus-virtual vortex system.*

Proof. Proceeding in the same manner as Proposition 1 and applying LaSalle's invariance principle [7] shows the virtual vortices converge to the largest invariant set that satisfies condition (7) with $\mathcal{H}$ replaced by $\mathcal{H}_c$, which is a relative equilibrium configuration fixed in rotating frame $\mathcal{R}$. □

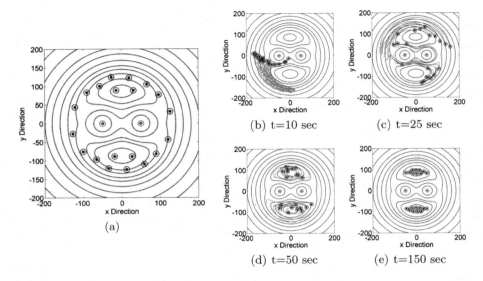

Fig. 2. (a) Actual-plus-virtual vortex system in relative equilibrium in frame $\mathcal{R}$; (b)–(e) Simulation of weaker virtual vortices undergoing relative equilibrium stabilization in the presence of an actual vortex pair (Color figure online)

Figure 2(a) illustrates the stabilization of relative equilibrium for $M = 20$ virtual vortices (blue) under the dynamics (15) in the presence of an actual vortex pair (green). Observe that the virtual vortices surround the origin and naturally separate into a rotating formation. The size and shape of the formation depend on the virtual and actual vortex strengths γ_α and the initial conditions. Figure 2(b), (c), (d) and (e) display simulation results of a set of weaker virtual vortices achieving a different configuration. Note that during convergence to the relative equilibrium, virtual vortices move along the flow streamlines while also interacting with each other. This choice of circulation strength yields two separate sampling groups located within the invariant regions of the flow generated by the actual vortex pair.

4   Adaptive Control Design

The use of Lyapunov analysis to inform the selection of a parameter update law is a common theme in adaptive control [22]. We employ this technique for the selection of a circulation-strength update law in the following example application of the path-planning methodology. Preliminary results show convergence to a desired level set $\mathcal{H}_c^d$ of the controlled Hamiltonian $\mathcal{H}_c$.

Consider the candidate Lyapunov function

$$V_c^d = \frac{1}{2} \left(\mathcal{H}_c - \mathcal{H}_c^d \right)^2. \tag{18}$$

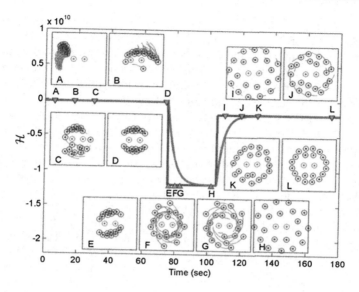

Fig. 3. Formations of virtual vortices under adaptive circulation control (Color figure online)

For simplicity of exposition and also to avoid virtual vortices having opposite signed circulation strengths, we restrict $\gamma_k = \gamma > 0$ for this example. Along trajectories of (15), the Lyapunov function (18) yields

$$
\dot{V}_c^d = \left(\mathcal{H}_c - \mathcal{H}_c^d\right)\left[\sum_{\alpha=N+1}^{N+M} \frac{\partial \mathcal{H}_c}{\partial \xi_\alpha}\dot{\xi}_\alpha + \frac{\partial \mathcal{H}_c}{\partial \bar{\xi}_\alpha}\dot{\bar{\xi}}_\alpha + \frac{\partial \mathcal{H}_c}{\partial \gamma}\dot{\gamma}\right]
$$

$$
= \left(\mathcal{H}_c - \mathcal{H}_c^d\right)\left[\sum_{\alpha=N+1}^{N+M} \frac{-4\mu}{\gamma}\left|\frac{\partial \mathcal{H}_c}{\partial \bar{\xi}_\alpha}\right|^2 - \frac{2\omega}{\gamma}\left(\mu\mathrm{Re}\left\{\frac{\partial \mathcal{H}_c}{\partial \bar{\xi}_\alpha}\frac{\partial \mathcal{S}_c}{\partial \xi_\alpha}\right\} + \mathrm{Im}\left\{\frac{\partial \mathcal{H}_c}{\partial \bar{\xi}_\alpha}\frac{\partial \mathcal{S}_c}{\partial \xi_\alpha}\right\}\right) + \frac{\partial \mathcal{H}_c}{\partial \gamma}\dot{\gamma}\right].
$$

The following choice of adaptation rate $\dot{\gamma}$ provides negative semi-definiteness of $\dot{V}_c^d$. In particular, choosing

$$
\dot{\gamma} = \left(\frac{\partial \mathcal{H}_c}{\partial \gamma}\right)^{-1}\left[-\sum_{\alpha=N+1}^{N+M}\left(\frac{-4\mu}{\gamma}\left|\frac{\partial \mathcal{H}_c}{\partial \bar{\xi}_\alpha}\right|^2 - \right.\right.
$$
$$
\left.\left.\frac{2\omega}{\gamma}\left(\mu\mathrm{Re}\left\{\frac{\partial \mathcal{H}_c}{\partial \bar{\xi}_\alpha}\frac{\partial \mathcal{S}_c}{\partial \xi_\alpha}\right\}+\mathrm{Im}\left\{\frac{\partial \mathcal{H}_c}{\partial \bar{\xi}_\alpha}\frac{\partial \mathcal{S}_c}{\partial \xi_\alpha}\right\}\right)\right) - K\left(\mathcal{H}_c - \mathcal{H}_c^d\right)\right] \qquad (19)
$$

results in $\dot{V}_c^d \leq -K\left(\mathcal{H}_c - \mathcal{H}_c^d\right)^2$, where $\dot{V}_c^d = 0$ only when the invariance condition $\mathcal{H}_c - \mathcal{H}_c^d \equiv 0$ holds.

Choosing the circulation of the virtual vortices to have the same sign as the actual vortices prevents the $(\partial \mathcal{H}_c/\partial \gamma)^{-1}$ term in (19) from becoming singular as long as $|z_\alpha - z_\beta| > 1$ for all pairs α, β due to the $\log(\cdot)$ terms in $\partial \mathcal{H}_c/\partial \gamma$. If is γ bounded, which remains to be shown, the invariance condition implies that $\mathcal{H}_c$

converges to $\mathcal{H}_c^d$, but it enforces nothing else about the configuration. The virtual vortices interact according to (15) in a rotating frame. A sufficient condition for maintaining a constant $\mathcal{H}_c$ value is for the second term in (15) to vanish, since the virtual vortices conserve $\mathcal{H}_c$ when $\mu = 0$. Although $\mu \neq 0$, the second term can still vanish if the rotating equilibrium condition is satisfied. In fact, virtual vortices converge to relative equilibrium configurations rotating at angular rate ω, as illustrated in the following numerical experiment.

Figure 3 displays a numerical simulation of the adaptive control algorithm for $M = 20$ virtual vortices in the presence of two actual vortices. Figure 3 shows the desired $\mathcal{H}_c^d$ signal (blue) and actual $\mathcal{H}_c$ signal (red). Inset plots are snapshots of the virtual vortices (blue) in the presence of the actual vortices (green) in frame $\mathcal{R}$. Virtual vortices interact with each other and the actual vortices during movement to the relative equilibrium. Additionally, the vortices form concentric disk formations influenced by the physical flow environment. For the $\mathcal{H}_c^d$ values chosen, the virtual vortex disk-like formations enclose the actual vortices, with disk size controlled by the specified $\mathcal{H}_c^d$ value. The locations of the virtual vortices in each configuration do not necessarily have exact symmetry, because the configuration in $\mathcal{H}_c^d$ is not unique.

5   Conclusion

This paper describes a distributed motion-planning paradigm for sampling applications in vortical flow environments. This paradigm enables theoretically justified control laws whose stability properties are ensured by virtue of a Lyapunov-based design that leverages the underlying Hamiltonian structure of the vortex dynamics. The approach employs fluid-like interactions between physical and virtual vortices based on the Hamiltonian dynamics. Gradient dynamics cause the virtual vortices to converge to relative equilibria configurations. We provide an adaptive control to regulate a collection of virtual vortices. Refinement and extension of this methodology to account for vehicle-specific constraints, time-varying and uncertain flows, track feasibility, and communication delays are all subjects of ongoing work.

Acknowledgments. The authors of this work acknowledge valuable discussions with Kayo Ide, Levi DeVries, Nitin Sydney and Daigo Shishika, and support by the National Science Foundation under Award No. CMMI-1362837.

References

1. Chen, Y., Kolokolnikov, T., Zhirov, D.: Collective behaviour of large number of vortices in the plane. Proc. R. Soc. A **469**, 1–12 (2013)
2. Das, J., Py, F., Maughan, T., O'Reilly, T., Messié, M., Ryan, J., Sukhatme, G.S., Rajan, K.: Coordinated sampling of dynamic oceanographic features with underwater vehicles and drifters. Int. J. Robotics Res. **31**(5), 626–646 (2012)

3. DeVries, L., Paley, D.A.: Multivehicle control in a strong flowfield with application to hurricane sampling. J. Guidance Control Dyn. **35**(3), 794–806 (2012)
4. Frew, E.W., Lawrence, D.A., Morris, S.: Coordinated standoff tracking of moving targets using Lyapunov guidance vector fields. J. Guidance Control Dyn. **31**(2), 290–306 (2008)
5. Hoffman, M.J., Miyoshi, T., Haine, T.W.N., Ide, K., Brown, C.W., Murtugudde, R.: An advanced data assimilation system for the Chesapeake Bay: Performance evaluation. J. Atmos. Ocean. Technol. **29**(10), 1542–1557 (2012)
6. Hsieh, M.A., Forgoston, E., Mather, T.W., Schwartz, I.B.: Robotic manifold tracking of coherent structures in flows. In: IEEE International Conference on Robotics and Automation (ICRA), pp. 4242–4247 (2012)
7. Khalil, H.: Nonlinear systems, 3rd edn. Prentice Hall, Upper Saddle River (2002)
8. Koszalka, I.: Mesoscale vortices, Lagrangian transport and marine ecosystem dynamics. Ph.D. thesis, Politecnico Di Torino (2008)
9. Lermusiaux, P.F.J., Lolla, T., Haley Jr., P.J., Yigit, K., Ueckermann, M.P., Sondergaard, T., Leslie, W.G.: Science of autonomy: Time-optimal path planning and adaptive sampling for swarms of ocean vehicles. In: Curtin, T. (ed.) Springer Handbook Ocean Eng. Auton. Ocean Veh. Subsystems Control. Springer (2013)
10. Lolla, T., Ueckermann, M.P., Yigit, K., Haley Jr., P.J., Lermusiaux, P.F.J.: Path planning in time dependent flow fields using level set methods. In: IEEE International Conference Robotics and Automation (ICRA), pp. 166–173 (2012)
11. Mallory, K., Hsieh, M.A., Forgoston, E., Schwartz, I.B.: Distributed allocation of mobile sensing swarms in gyre flows. Nonlinear Proces. Geophys. **20**(5), 657–668 (2013)
12. Marsden, J.E., Ratiu, T.S.: Introduction to mechanics and symmetry, vol. 48. Amer. Inst. of Physics, New York (1995)
13. Melet, A., Verron, J., Brankart, J.M.: Potential outcomes of glider data assimilation in the Solomon Sea: Control of the water mass properties and parameter estimation. J. Marine Sys. **94**, 232–246 (2012)
14. Mourre, B., Alvarez, A.: Benefit assessment of glider adaptive sampling in the Ligurian Sea. Deep Sea Res. Part I Ocean. Res. Papers **68**, 68–78 (2012)
15. Newton, P.: The N-vortex problem: Analytical techniques. Springer, New York (2001)
16. Paley, D., Zhang, F., Leonard, N.: Cooperative control for ocean sampling: The Glider Coordinated Control System. IEEE Trans. Control Sys. Tech. **1063–6536**, 1–10 (2008)
17. Pazos, M.: The GDP drifter data assembly center (DAC): Hurricane drifter array, NOAA AOML. http://www.aoml.noaa.gov/phod/dac/dacdata.php
18. Ramp, S., Davis, R., Leonard, N., Shulman, I., Chao, Y., Robinson, A., Marsden, J., Lermusiaux, P., Fratantoni, D., Paduan, J., Chavez, F., Bahr, F., Liang, S., Leslie, W., Li, Z.: Preparing to predict: The second Autonomous Ocean Sampling Network (AOSN-II) experiment in the Monterey Bay. Deep Sea Res. Part II: Topical Studies Ocean. **56**(3–5), 68–86 (2009)
19. Rudnick, D.L., Cole, S.T.: On sampling the ocean using underwater gliders. J. Geophys. Res. **116**(C08010), 1–12 (2011)
20. Smith, R.N., Schwager, M., Smith, S.L., Jones, B.H., Rus, D., Sukhatme, G.S.: Persistent ocean monitoring with underwater gliders: Adapting sampling resolution. J. Field Robotics **28**(5), 714–741 (2011)
21. Sorber, L., Barel, M., Lathauwer, L.: Unconstrained optimization of real functions in complex variables. SIAM J. Optim. **22**(3), 879–898 (2012)

22. Spong, M., Hutchinson, S., Vidyasagar, M.: Robot modeling and control. Wiley, Hoboken (2006)
23. Zhang, D., Colburn, C., Bewley, T.: Estimation and adaptive observation of environmental plumes. In: Amer. Control Conference, San Francisco, CA, pp. 4281–4286 (2011)

A Stochastic Optimization Method
for Energy-Based Path Planning

Deepak N. Subramani$^{(\boxtimes)}$, Tapovan Lolla, Patrick J. Haley Jr.,
and Pierre F.J. Lermusiaux

Massachusetts Institute of Technology, Cambridge, MA 02139, USA
{deepakns,ltapovan,phaley,pierrel}@mit.edu

Abstract. We present a novel stochastic optimization method to compute energy–optimal paths, among all time–optimal paths, for vehicles traveling in dynamic unsteady currents. The method defines a stochastic class of instantaneous nominal vehicle speeds and then obtains the energy–optimal paths within the class by minimizing the total time–integrated energy usage while still satisfying the strong–constraint time–optimal level set equation. This resulting stochastic level set equation is solved using a dynamically orthogonal decomposition and the energy–optimal paths are then selected for each arrival time, among all stochastic time–optimal paths. The first application computes energy–optimal paths for crossing a steady front. Results are validated using a semi-analytical solution obtained by solving a dual nonlinear energy–time optimization problem. The second application computes energy–optimal paths for a realistic mission in the Middle Atlantic Bight and New Jersey Shelf/Hudson Canyon region, using dynamic data–driven ocean field estimates.

Keywords: Energy–optimal · Time–optimal · Dynamically orthogonal equations · Level–set method · Autonomy · AUV · Dynamic data–driven

1 Introduction

Path planning refers to the navigation rules provided to autonomous mobile agents operating in a dynamic environment while optimizing an objective criterion. This criterion could be the travel time, energy utilized, quantity/quality of data collected, safety or a combination of these [12,16]. In the recent years, the growing usage of Autonomous Underwater Vehicles (AUVs) such as propelled vehicles and gliders in diverse applications (e.g. ocean exploration, security, conservation, and research) has led to increased research in path planning for underwater robotics [3,4,9,17,25,30]. As AUVs undertake complex tasks (e.g. cooperative exploration and sampling [19]), they are required to operate for long periods of time at sea by utilizing energy efficiently [4]. The dynamic environment in which these vehicles (and also other mobile agents such as land robots, drones, airplanes etc.) navigate can be utilized to reduce their energy consumption. In the case of AUVs, ocean currents can be comparable in magnitude to the

© Springer International Publishing Switzerland 2015
S. Ravela and A. Sandu (Eds.): DyDESS 2014, LNCS 8964, pp. 347–358, 2015.
DOI: 10.1007/978-3-319-25138-7_31

average operational speed of propelled vehicles, and up to 2–3 times the typical speed of gliders [26,28,29]. As such, there is an opportunity to reduce the energy consumption by intelligently utilizing favorable currents while avoiding adverse currents. The availability of numerical ocean prediction systems enables agents to plan their motion using a forecast of the ocean currents (within predictability limits). Dynamic data–driven re–planning of these trajectories may be performed by utilizing open–loop planning algorithms which have short run–times. Using this as a motivation, our goal here is to develop a computationally efficient and rigorous path planning algorithm that computes energy–optimal paths, among all time–optimal paths, of a vehicle navigating between two points in a dynamic flow field. We show that this computation can be posed as a stochastic PDE–based design/optimization problem. In this paper, we focus on addressing the question of how to evaluate such a solution, and whether an analytical (or semi–analytical) benchmark exists for validation. We also illustrate the applicability of such an algorithm for path planning utilizing real ocean forecasts.

Most path planning algorithms for AUVs find their roots in robotics, e.g. [2,5]. The A^* search algorithm, quite popular in robotic motion planning, has been applied to AUVs [6] to find near–optimal paths. These paths have been shown to utilize substantially lower energy compared to straight line paths when ocean currents are comparable to vehicle speeds [10]. Rapidly Exploring Random Trees (RRTs) [16], also popular in robotic path planning have been used for AUVs to obtain minimum work [14] and minimum energy (linear nominal relative speed) [24] paths. However, A^* and RRTs do not work well for strong flows [24]. First, they are not well suited to computing exact solutions in strong dynamic flows [21,22]. Second, the heuristics reported are for a linear energy cost function and do not readily extend to nonlinear cost functions. [1] discusses a genetic algorithm to optimize the paths parameterized in space and time. They minimize an energy cost function which is a path integral of the cube of vehicle speed. In [15], the paths are computed using nonlinear optimization, where a weighted cost function accounts for the energy to overcome drag (proportional to square of nominal relative speed) and provide acceleration (proportional to rate of change of nominal relative speed). As the success of this optimization depends heavily on the parameterization, it cannot be easily generalized to all types of flows and domains. [32] discusses potential field techniques for obstacle avoidance and [34] reports a swarm optimization approach to minimize an energy cost function on the parameterized paths. Other algorithms utilize Lagrangian Coherent Structures (LCS) of the flow to design near–optimal navigation paths [13,35]. They illustrate that the optimal energy (quadratic nominal speed)-time-weighted paths computed using a heuristic receding–horizon nonlinear programming method are close to the ridges of the LCS. Other nonlinear optimization methods and evolutionary algorithms have also been used to obtain near–optimal paths by approximately solving the governing optimal control problem. We encourage the reader to refer to [23,31] for an in–depth literature survey.

The present work is inspired from [21,22], where a modified level set methodology for *rigorous* time–optimal path planning is described. We extend this methodology to develop a novel energy optimal path planning algorithm, based on stochastic dynamically orthogonal level set equations [27]. In what follows, we state the problem and describe the new path planning method. We then consider a test case of a vehicle crossing a canonical steady front for a range of arrival times. We validate our results for a range of arrival times by comparing them to those of a dual energy and time optimization albeit for a single chosen arrival time. The latter is a semi–analytical solution for that front crossing problem, providing the energy and time optimal path(s) for a single arrival time. Finally, we apply our methodology to plan the time–dependent headings and energy usages of a vehicle undertaking a mission in the Middle Atlantic Bight region.

2   Problem Statement

Let $\Omega \subseteq \mathbb{R}^n$ be an open set. Consider a vehicle navigating from a start point $(\mathbf{x_s})$ to an end point $(\mathbf{x_f})$ with a specified instantaneous nominal speed $F(t) \geq 0$. The environmental flow is denoted by $\mathbf{v}(\mathbf{x}, t) : \Omega \times (0, \infty) \to \mathbb{R}^n$. The heading function is chosen such that when navigated at a relative *time–dependent* non–negative speed of $F(t)$, the vehicle reaches $\mathbf{x_f}$ in optimal time $T(\mathbf{x_f}; F(\bullet))$. Among all of these, we seek the $F(\bullet)$ that minimizes the energy cost function E, i.e.,

$$\min_{F(\bullet)} \quad E(\bullet) = \int_0^{T(\mathbf{x_f}; F(\bullet))} p(t)\, dt \tag{1a}$$

$$\text{s. t.} \quad \frac{\partial \phi(\mathbf{x}, t)}{\partial t} = -F(t) |\nabla \phi(\mathbf{x}, t)| - \mathbf{v}(\mathbf{x}, t) \cdot \nabla \phi(\mathbf{x}, t)$$

$$\text{in } (\mathbf{x}, t) \in \Omega \times (0, \infty) \tag{1b}$$

$$T(\mathbf{x_f}; F(\bullet)) = \min_t \{ t : \phi(\mathbf{x_f}, t) \leq 0 \}, \tag{1c}$$

$$\phi(\mathbf{x}, 0) = |\mathbf{x} - \mathbf{x_s}|, \tag{1d}$$

$$p(t) = F(t)^n, \quad \text{where } n \geq 1. \tag{1e}$$

Here, the scalar field $\phi(\mathbf{x}, t)$ is a reachability–front tracking level–set function [31]. For a given $F(\bullet)$, the viscosity solution of the level set Hamilton–Jacobi equation (1b) with initial conditions (1d) and the subsequent solution to the backtracking Eq. (2),

$$\frac{d\mathbf{x}^*}{dt} = -\mathbf{v}(\mathbf{x}^*, t) - F(t) \frac{\nabla \phi(\mathbf{x}^*, t)}{|\nabla \phi(\mathbf{x}^*, t)|}, \quad 0 \leq t \leq T(\mathbf{x_f}; F(\bullet)) \tag{2}$$

yield a continuous–time history of the time–optimal vehicle heading angles, $\theta^*(t)$ [21]. These headings guarantee time–optimality for the particular choice of the speed function $F(t)$ [31]. Then, among all such time–optimal paths which reach the target at relative speed $F(t)$, we seek to find the $F(t)$ that minimizes the energy required (1a). We reiterate that all of our paths are time–optimal: the optimization is on the total energy usage (1a). In contrast to multi–objective optimization formulations [1,15,34], in our method, the time–optimality is a strong constraint.

3   New Stochastic Dynamically Orthogonal Level Set Equations for Energy-Based Path Planning

Considering the nominal speed $F(t)$ as a random variable belonging to a stochastic class, i.e., $F(t) \to F(t; \omega)$, and a deterministic flow field $\mathbf{v}(\mathbf{x}, t)$, we obtain a stochastic Langevin form of the level set equation (1b):

$$\frac{\partial \phi(\mathbf{x}, t; \omega)}{\partial t} = -F(t; \omega) |\nabla \phi(\mathbf{x}, t; \omega)| - \mathbf{v}(\mathbf{x}, t) \cdot \nabla \phi(\mathbf{x}, t; \omega), \qquad (3)$$

where $(\mathbf{x}, t) \in \Omega \times (0, \infty)$ and ω denotes a random event. For $F(t; \omega) \geq 0$, we solve the SPDE (3) until the first time instant t such that $\phi(\mathbf{x_f}, t; \omega) \leq 0$, starting from deterministic initial conditions $\phi(\mathbf{x}, 0; \omega) = |\mathbf{x} - \mathbf{x_s}|$ with boundary condition $\frac{\partial^2 \phi(\mathbf{x}, t; \omega)}{\partial \mathbf{n}^2} |_{\delta \Omega} = 0$, where $\mathbf{n}$ denotes the outward normal to $\partial \Omega$. Such a stochastic simulation yields the distribution of the minimum time–to–reach $T(\mathbf{x_f}; F(\bullet; \omega))$ for an externally forced distribution of $F(\bullet; \omega)$. Then, the distribution of energy utilized is computed from $F(\bullet; \omega)$ and $T(\mathbf{x_f}; F(\bullet; \omega))$ as $E(\omega) = \int\limits_0^{T(\mathbf{x_f}; F(\bullet; \omega))} p(t) \, dt$. The function $p(t)$ can assume any power law dependence on $F(t)$. The power function $p(t)$ that has a linear dependence on $F(t)$ results in a constant drag optimal path (also known as fuel–optimal, e.g. [2]). It yields a linear drag optimal path when $p(t) \propto F(t)^2$, and a quadratic drag energy optimal path when $p(t) \propto F(t)^3$. Finally, for any choice of the time–to–reach (a particular time or a range of time), the speed function $F(\bullet; \omega)$ which minimizes the energy cost, $E(\omega)$, can be obtained by a search procedure. As we will see, the approach can operate on classes of stochastic functionals $F(\bullet; \omega)$ if these functionals can be efficiently represented by a reduced basis.

The most straightforward method to solve the SPDE (3) is through a Monte Carlo (MC) approach. The deterministic level set PDE (1b) can be solved for different realizations of $F(t; \omega)$ to yield a distribution of $T(\mathbf{x_f}; F(\bullet; \omega))$. Unfortunately, the MC solution is expensive and the computational cost increases with number of realizations used. Since in (3), $\mathbf{v}(\mathbf{x}, t)$ is the flow field velocity, and we consider ocean applications, an efficient solution method for solving (3) would be a methodology that exploits the nonlinearities of the flow, which tend to concentrate the scalar level set field, ϕ, responses into specific dynamic patterns. Such a methodology is offered by the Dynamically Orthogonal (DO) decomposition [27]. To the best of our knowledge, this approach has never been utilized to determine the stochastic viscosity solution of (3). A numerical challenge in obtaining the DO level set equations is the presence of the non–polynomial nonlinearity, $\gamma \equiv |\nabla \phi|$. We have considered several approaches for handling this term. One such approach [31] does not invoke a specific DO decomposition for γ, but evaluates it using an explicit Monte Carlo computation. This is the method we present in this paper. In what follows, the arguments $(\mathbf{x}, t)$ are dropped for the brevity of notation. The decompositions $F = \bar{F} + z\tilde{F}$, $\phi = \bar{\phi} + Y_i\tilde{\phi}_i$ are first substituted in (3). Enforcing the DO condition [27] then yields the following new equations for the mean $\bar{\phi}$, stochastic coefficients Y_i and modes $\tilde{\phi}_i$, in terms of the mean $(\bar{F})$, stochastic coefficients (z) and modes $(\tilde{F})$ of the nominal relative speed:

$$\frac{\partial \bar{\phi}}{\partial t} = -(\bar{F}\mathbb{E}[\gamma] + \mathbb{E}[z\gamma]\tilde{F}) - \mathbf{v} \cdot \nabla \bar{\phi}, \tag{4}$$

$$\frac{dY_i}{dt} = -\Big\langle \bar{F}(\gamma - \mathbb{E}[\gamma]) + \tilde{F}(z\gamma - \mathbb{E}[z\gamma]) + Y_k\mathbf{v} \cdot \nabla\tilde{\phi}_k, \tilde{\phi}_i \Big\rangle, \tag{5}$$

$$\frac{\partial \tilde{\phi}_i}{\partial t} = -C_{Y_iY_j}^{-1}(\bar{F}\mathbb{E}[Y_j\gamma] + \tilde{F}\mathbb{E}[zY_j\gamma]) + \mathbf{v} \cdot \nabla\tilde{\phi}_i$$
$$- \Big\langle -C_{Y_iY_j}^{-1}(\bar{F}\mathbb{E}[Y_j\gamma] + \tilde{F}\mathbb{E}[zY_j\gamma]) + \mathbf{v} \cdot \nabla\tilde{\phi}_i, \tilde{\phi}_n \Big\rangle \tilde{\phi}_n, \tag{6}$$

where $\langle \bullet, \bullet \rangle$ denotes the inner product. We have also developed methods where a DO decomposition is considered for the non–polynomial nonlinearity γ. These methods along with their derivations are provided in [31]. We note that an equivalent formulation is possible through bi–orthogonal methods [8].

Algorithm. Our algorithm for energy optimal path planning has 5 main steps. (i) The first step is to obtain a comprehensive sampling of the stochastic class $F(t; \omega)$. In the DO sense, we obtain a comprehensive sample of $F_{\mathrm{DO}}(t; r)$, where r denotes realizations. (ii) Next, the new stochastic DO level set Eqs. (4)–(6) are solved using the chosen samples of $F_{\mathrm{DO}}(t; r)$. (iii) The energy utilized by each sample is computed as $E(r) = \int_0^{T(\mathbf{x_f}; F_{\mathrm{DO}}(t;r))} p(t)\, dt$. ($iv$) For a given time–to–reach, the sample $F_{\mathrm{DO}}^*(t; r)$ that leads to the minimum energy usage is identified using a sorting algorithm. This $F_{\mathrm{DO}}^*(t; r)$ is energy optimal within the class of $F_{\mathrm{DO}}(t; r)$ that reach $\mathbf{x_f}$ at a given time. (v) Finally, the sample class can be enriched and the algorithm iterated until no further refinement is required. The computational cost for direct Monte Carlo solution of the SPDE is $O(MN)$, where M is the number of samples and N is the total size of discrete computational domain utilized. Our DO algorithm has a computational cost of $O(SN)$, where S is the size of the DO–subspace, where S is often such that $S \ll M$.

4   Applications

We first consider a simulated steady front test case and use it as a benchmark to test and validate our approach. Specifically, we compare our results to that of a nonlinear dual optimization approach that seeks a minimum energy path among time optimal paths for a fixed arrival time. We solve this problem using the iterated constrained nonlinear optimization toolbox of MATLAB. Next, we employ our methodology for path planning of a glider released from Buzzard's Bay (offshore from WHOI) to reach a target in the region of the Autonomous Wide Aperture Cluster for Surveillance (AWACS) experiment just south of the Hudson Canyon.

4.1   Energy Optimal Crossing of an Idealized Steady Front

Considering the test case of crossing a steady front, we first solve the energy optimal problem using a semi–analytical approach. This serves as a benchmark to test our new methodology. The schematic of the flow and the relevant notation is depicted in Fig. 1. The goal is to determine the optimal speed function $F(t)$, varying within limits F_{min} and F_{max} ($F_{min} \leq F(t) \leq F_{max}$ for all t), that minimizes the energy utilized while still reaching the end point in optimal time. In what follows, we provide arguments that allow us to formulate a dual minimization problem whose solution gives the energy–optimal trajectory in the sense defined in Sect. 2, but only for a specific arrival time.

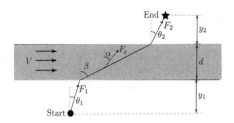

Fig. 1. Parameters involved in optimal crossing of a simulated steady front: steady front speed V and width d; start (circle), end (star), distances, vehicle nominal speed and headings are marked. Adapted from [23].

To start the arguments, we first consider the motion from the start point to the steady front. During this time, the vehicle remains unaffected by the environment and the corresponding zero–level–set expands radially outward at a rate equal to $F(t)$, the nominal instantaneous relative speed. The motion (e.g. the total displacement) achieved by any choice of the time series $F(t)$ over this period can be synthesized as the motion achieved by the mean nominal speed $\bar{F}(t)$ over the same time window. However, the energy consumed by the vehicle varies as a power function of $F(t)$, with $n \geq 1$ (see Sect. 3). As a result, that energy consumption will be different for each time series $F(t)$.

It can then be shown that the energy consumption is minimum when the mean speed is used over a given time interval. For instance, let us suppose that a vehicle (say v) travels at speed F_{min} for a total time of t_1 and at speed F_{max} for time t_2. The final position of this vehicle coincides with that of a different vehicle (say m), traveling at a uniform speed $\bar{F} = (F_{min}t_1 + F_{max}t_2)/(t_1 + t_2)$ for time $t_1 + t_2$. The energy expended by v is $E_v = F_{min}^n t_1 + F_{max}^n t_2$. On the other hand, m utilizes a total energy equal to $E_m = \bar{F}^n(t_1 + t_2)$. Hölder's inequality can now be used to show that $E_m \leq E_v$ [31]. In fact, it can be shown that the above result holds for any number of engine speed switches (≥ 2) and any $n \geq 1$. We also note that similar arguments can be made for the vehicle motion beyond the steady front to the end point.

To continue the arguments, we now consider the motion of the vehicle within the uniform and steady front proper. Inside this region, only the motion of vehicle in the x–direction is affected. Even here, it can be shown that using a single speed results in lower energy consumption, and that any time series $F(t)$ has an equivalent single time–mean speed [31]. Therefore, for a given travel time, the energy optimal path is executed by a vehicle that moves at a constant speed from the start point to the steady front at some to–be–determined point, then another speed (same or different) for the time optimal motion in the steady front and finally another speed from the steady front to the target. This completes the arguments that allow us to setup our dual minimization problem, 'energy–optimality subject to time–optimality'.

Using the above arguments, we set the time–variation of the unknown optimal relative speed to be the uniform speeds of F_1, F_d, and F_2 from start to the steady front, within the steady front, and from the exit of the steady front to the end point, respectively.

Let $\mathbf{U}$ denote the total effective velocity of the vehicle in the flow, as seen by a ground observer. Within the steady front, the component of $\mathbf{U}$ in the x–direction is $U_x = F_d \sin \alpha + V$ and in the y–direction, $U_y = F_d \cos \alpha$. The direction of resultant velocity and heading angle are related through the relation, $\tan \beta = \frac{U_x}{U_y} = \tan \alpha + \frac{V}{F_d} \sec \alpha$. Outside the steady front, the relations are the same, but with $V = 0$. Now, let X be the total downstream displacement of the vehicle, i.e. in the x direction. We have, from simple trigonometry, $X = y_1 \tan \theta_1 + d \tan \beta + y_2 \tan \theta_2$. Finally, the total travel time T can be written as the sum of travel times in each individual region, $T = \frac{y_1}{F_1 \cos \theta_1} + \frac{d}{F_d \cos \alpha} + \frac{y_2}{F_2 \cos \theta_2}$. Now, we want to determine the energy optimal path, for each arrival time such that they are also time–optimal. Hence, assuming for now, a general energy cost over dt, $dE = p(t)\,dt = F(t)^n\,dt$ where $n \geq 1$, we obtain the total energy expended from the start point to the end point: $E = F_1^{n-1} \frac{y_1}{\cos \theta_1} + F_d^{n-1} \frac{d}{\cos \alpha} + F_2^{n-1} \frac{y_2}{\cos \theta_2}$. For a fixed time–to–reach the target, the double optimal energy–time problem is

$$\min_{F_1, F_d, F_2} E = F_1^{n-1} \frac{y_1}{\cos \theta_1} + F_d^{n-1} \frac{d}{\cos \alpha} + F_2^{n-1} \frac{y_2}{\cos \theta_2} \tag{7}$$

$$\text{s.t.} \quad X = y_1 \tan \theta_1 + d \left(\tan \alpha + \frac{V}{F_d} \sec \alpha \right) + y_2 \tan \theta_2 \tag{8}$$

$$T = \min_{\theta_1, \alpha, \theta_2} \frac{y_1}{F_1 \cos \theta_1} + \frac{d}{F_d \cos \alpha} + \frac{y_2}{F_2 \cos \theta_2} \tag{9}$$

$$\theta_1, \theta_2, \alpha \geq 0, \quad F_{\min} \leq F_1, F_d, F_2 \leq F_{\max}, \quad n \geq 1 \tag{10}$$

where X, T, $F_{\min}$, and $F_{\max}$ are inputs to the optimization problem. We note that the time constraint for the outer energy optimization is another inner optimization. This completes the derivation of a dual minimization problem whose solution provides the energy-optimal path in the sense defined in Sect. 2, but again, only for a fixed single arrival time at a time. For $y_1 = 0.2167$, $d = 0.2$, $y_2 = 0.2167$, $V = 3$, $F_{\min} = 2$, $F_{\max} = 3$, $X = 0.6334$, and fixing the single target T to be $T = 0.26$, we obtain the numerical solution of our dual optimization problem as presented in Table 1. The results shown in column 1 are computed using the iterative nonlinear optimization toolbox of MATLAB.

Now, we compare this 'semi–analytical' solution to that obtained by our new stochastic DO level–set optimization scheme. To do so, we need to select an

Table 1. Parameters of the energy optimal path that reaches the end point at time $T = 0.26$.

Parameter	Using NonLinear Optimization	Using new stochastic DO level-set optimization
θ_1	$23.5°$	$22.4°$
θ_2	$23.5°$	$20.7°$
β	$65.8°$	$65.9°$
F_1	2.9	2.8
F_d	2.6	2.5
F_2	2.9	3.0

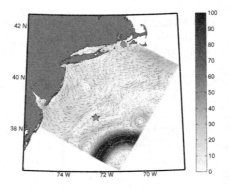

Fig. 2. The start point is marked as a circle and the end point is marked as a star. The initial flow on Aug 28, 00 UTC is shown on the color axis in cm/s.

adequate stochastic class of $F(t; \omega)$. First, we remark that all vehicles will reach faster than a vehicle which travels throughout the distance at $F_{\min}$. Hence, the total time required will at most be the time required by this slowest vehicle. Let this be denoted as $T_{\max}$. The number of $F(t; \omega)$ samples (i.e. $F_{DO}(t; r)$, see Sect. 3) required grows with the resolution in time axis in an exponential manner, i.e., even if only two engine speed choices are allowed, and if the time axis that ranges from 0 to $T_{\max}$ is divided into n intervals, a total of 2^n $F_{DO}(t; r)$ samples are required for an exhaustive search (in the bang–bang control sense). With the available computing resources and reasonable run–time, we choose to resolve the time axis into $n = 26$ intervals. The energy optimal path planning is then performed using our new stochastic DO level set equations with this choice of $F_{DO}(t; r)$, i.e. an exhaustive sample space but only for those two speeds and 26 time–intervals (25 speed switches). The result of this stochastic DO level–set optimization with the same parameters as above is presented in Tabel 1. Critically, we note that our stochastic solution provides answers for a wide range of arrival times (instead of the single fixed time T).

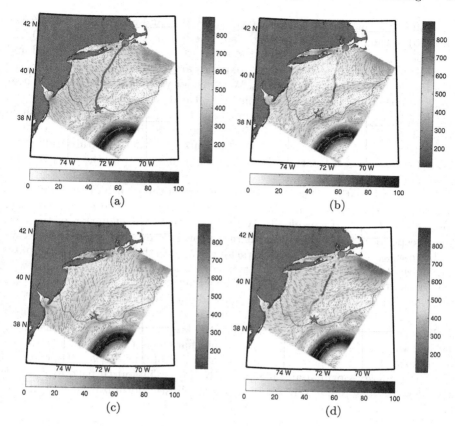

Fig. 3. (a) Path that reaches in the shortest time, 12.96 days, but consumes the highest energy. (b) Path that takes 6 more days to reach the end point (18.78 days), but utilizes 40 % less energy. (c) Path that reaches in 16 days using a constant speed. (d) Path that also takes 16 days but is energy optimal: it utilizes about 10 % less energy than the path at constant speed. The energy utilized by the vehicle along the path is plotted in color. Flow field at arrival time is shown in blue. All paths are time optimal for the $F(t)$ utilized (Color figure online).

4.2   Realistic Dynamic Data–Driven Ocean Simulation

In this section we explore the application of our approach in realistic dynamic data–driven ocean simulations. The mission is to start just offshore of Buzzard's Bay near WHOI and reach a target in the AWACS region, as shown in Fig. 2. A glider that can travel at relative horizontal velocities between $F = 10$ cm/s and 30 cm/s is assumed to be released on Aug 28, 2006 at 00 UTC. The flow data is obtained from the MSEAS free–surface primitive–equation model utilized in an implicit two–way nested computational domain set–up [11], with both tidal and atmospheric forcings. These simulated ocean flows assimilate real ocean data and correspond to a reanalysis of the real–time AWACS and SW06 exercises (Aug.-Sep. 2006) in the Middle Atlantic Bight and shelfbreak front region [7,18,20,33].

All gliders are assumed to follow the same yo–yo pattern in the vertical and the effects of the small vertical ocean velocities are assumed to be accounted for in the forward motions of the vehicles. We consider yo–yo patterns from the near surface to either the local near bottom or 400 m depth, whichever is shallower (for the mission considered, a large portion of the paths occurs on the shelf, within about 20 to 100 m). The horizontal currents that a glider encounters during its yo–yo motion are then the horizontal currents integrated along its path. Of course, it is the path to–be–determined that specifies the currents that are actually encountered.

The new stochastic DO level–set based energy optimal path planning method is employed to determine the time–optimal level sets for the class of relative glider speeds $F_{DO}(t; r)$ considered. Within that class, the evolution of the level sets corresponding to the minimum energy is obtained by sorting and the energy–optimal paths are computed by backtracking. We note that our method computes a large set of energy optimal paths, for a range of arrival times. Only a few of such paths are shown in Fig. 3, three of which are energy–optimal.

We first show the path that reaches the end point in shortest time on Fig. 3(a), corresponding to the glider with relative horizontal speed of $F = 30$ cm/s. Based on [21], the fastest glider indeed travels at the largest relative speed considered. The second path selected on Fig. 3(b) is one that takes 18.78 days to complete, but utilizes 40 % less energy. The third path on Fig. 3(c) is a constant speed path that is not energy–optimal and reaches in 16 days. The fourth path in Fig. 3(d) also takes 16 days but is the result of our stochastic optimization and utilizes about 10 % less energy than the path at constant speed.

5   Conclusion

A novel method for energy optimal path planning based on new stochastic dynamically orthogonal level set equations was introduced. It was first used to obtain an energy optimal path among time–optimal paths for crossing a steady front. We showed that the results agreed with those of a semi–analytical path obtained by solving a dual nonlinear optimization problem that minimizes energy and time. We also applied our methodology to realistic dynamic data–driven ocean flows and obtained promising results that illustrate that open–loop energy–time optimal paths can be computed quickly. This opens up the possibility to use our methodology for dynamic data–driven re–planning. Environment uncertainty was considered in [19] and this can be utilized in the future. Future studies can investigate the methodology in greater detail, providing derivations and algorithms for handling non–polynomial nonlinearities. Capabilities will also be illustrated in a wider range of idealized and realistic scenarios.

Acknowledgements. We thank the members of our MSEAS group for useful discussions. We are grateful to the Office of Naval Research for research support under grants N00014-09-1-0676 (Science of Autonomy - A-MISSION) and N00014-14-1-0476 (Science of Autonomy - LEARNS) to the Massachusetts Institute of Technology (MIT). The MSEAS ocean re-analyses employed were made possible by research support from the Office of Naval Research under grants N00014-11-1-0701 (MURI-IODA) and the National Science Foundation under grant OCE-1061160 to MIT. Finally, we also thank all of our colleagues involved in collecting observations during SW06 and AWACS-06 that allowed the realistic simulations component of the present study.

References

1. Alvarez, A., Caiti, A., Onken, R.: Evolutionary path planning for autonomous underwater vehicles in a variable ocean. IEEE J. Oceanic. Eng. **29**(2), 418–429 (2004)
2. Athans, M., Falb, P.: Optimal Control: An Introduction to the Theory and Its Applications. Dover Books on Engineering Series. Dover Publications, New York (2007)
3. Bachmayer, R., Leonard, N.E., Graver, J., Fiorelli, E., Bhatta, P., Paley, D.: Underwater gliders: Recent developments and future applications. In: Proceedings of IEEE International Symposium on Underwater Technology (2004)
4. Bellingham, J.G., Rajan, K.: Robotics in remote and hostile environments. Science **318**(5853), 1098–1102 (2007)
5. Bryson, A.E., Ho, Y.C.: Applied Optimal Control: Optimization, Estimation and Control. CRC Press, New York (1975)
6. Carroll, K., McClaran, S., Nelson, E., Barnett, D., Friesen, D., William, G.: AUV path planning: An A* approach to path planning with consideration of variable vehicle speeds and multiple, overlapping, time-dependent exclusion zones. In: Proceedings of Symposium on AUV Tech. pp. 79–84, June 1992
7. Chapman, N.R., Lynch, J.F.: Special issue on the 2006 shallow water experiment. IEEE J. Oceanic Eng. **35**(1), 1–2 (2010)
8. Choi, M., Sapsis, T.P., Karniadakis, G.E.: On the equivalence of dynamically orthogonal and bi-orthogonal methods: Theory and numerical simulations. J. Comp. Phys. **270**, 1–20 (2014)
9. Curtin, T.B., Bellingham, J.G.: Progress toward autonomous ocean sampling networks. Deep-Sea Res. Pt. II **56**(3), 62–67 (2009)
10. Garau, B., Bonet, M., Alvarez, A., Ruiz, S., Pascual, A.: Path planning for autonomous underwater vehicles in realistic oceanic current fields: Application to gliders in the western mediterranean sea. J. Marit. Res. **6**(2), 5–22 (2009)
11. Haley Jr., P.J., Lermusiaux, P.F.J.: Multiscale two-way embedding schemes for free-surface primitive equations in the "multidisciplinary simulation, estimation and assimilation system". Ocean Dyn. **60**(6), 1497–1537 (2010)
12. Hwang, Y.K., Ahuja, N.: Gross motion planning - a survey. ACM Comput. Surv. (CSUR) **24**(3), 219–291 (1992)
13. Inanc, T., Shadden, S.C., Marsden, J.E.: Optimal trajectory generation in ocean flows. In: Proceedings. of ACC, vol. 1, pp. 674–679 (2005)
14. Jaillet, L., Cortés, J., Siméon, T.: Sampling-based path planning on configuration-space costmaps. IEEE Trans. Rob. **26**(4), 635–646 (2010)
15. Kruger, D., Stolkin, R., Blum, A., Briganti, J.: Optimal AUV path planning for extended missions in complex, fast-flowing estuarine environments. In: 2007 IEEE International Conference on Robotics and Automation, pp. 4265–4270 (2007)
16. LaValle, S.M.: Planning algorithms. Cambridge University Press, Cambridge (2006)

17. Leedekerken, J.C., Fallon, M.F., Leonard, J.J.: Mapping complex marine environments with autonomous surface craft. In: Expt. Robotics, pp. 525–539 (2014)
18. Lermusiaux, P.F.J., Haley Jr., P.J., Leslie, W.G., Logoutov, O., Robinson, A.R.: Autonomous Wide Aperture Cluster for Surveillance (AWACS): Adaptive Sampling and Search Using Predictive Models with Coupled Data Assimilation and Feedback (2006). http://mseas.mit.edu/archive/AWACS/index_AWACS.html
19. Lermusiaux, P.F.J., Lolla, T., Haley Jr., P.J., Yigit, K., Ueckermann, M.P., Sondergaard, T., Leslie, W.G.: Science of autonomy: time-optimal path planning and adaptive sampling for swarms of ocean vehicles. In: Curtin, T. (ed.) Springer Handbook of Ocean Engineering: Autonomous Ocean Vehicles, Subsystems and Control, ch. 11 (2015). (in Press)
20. Lin, Y.T., Newhall, A.E., Duda, T.F., Lermusiaux, P.F.J., Haley, P.J.: Merging multiple-partial-depth data time series using objective empirical orthogonal function fitting. IEEE J. Oceanic Eng. **35**(4), 710–721 (2010)
21. Lolla, T., Lermusiaux, P.F.J., Ueckermann, M.P., Haley Jr., P.J.: Time-optimal path planning in dynamic flows using level set equations: Theory and schemes. Ocean Dyn. **64**, 1373–1397 (2014). doi:10.1007/s10236-014-0757-y
22. Lolla, T., Ueckermann, M.P., Yigit, K., Haley, P.J., Lermusiaux, P.F.J.: Path planning in time dependent flow fields using level set methods. In: Proceedings of IEEE International Conference on Robotics and Automation, pp. 166–173 (2012)
23. Lolla, T.: Path Planning in Time Dependent Flows using Level Set Methods. Master's thesis. Department of Mechanical Engineering, Massachusetts Institute of Technology, September 2012
24. Rao, D., Williams, S.B.: Large-scale path planning for underwater gliders in ocean currents. In: Proceedings of Australasian Conference on Robotics and Automation (2009)
25. Reed, B., Hover, F.: Oceanographic pursuit: Networked control of multiple vehicles tracking dynamic ocean features. Methods Oceanogr. **10**, 21–43 (2014)
26. Rudnick, D.L., Davis, R.E., Eriksen, C.C., Fratantoni, D.M., Perry, M.J.: Underwater gliders for ocean research. Mar. Tech. Soc. J. **38**(2), 73–84 (2004)
27. Sapsis, T.P., Lermusiaux, P.F.J.: Dynamically orthogonal field equations for continuous stochastic dynamical systems. Phys. D: Nonlinear Phenom. **238**(23–24), 2347–2360 (2009). doi:10.1016/j.physd.2009.09.017
28. Schofield, O., Kohut, J., Aragon, D., Creed, L., Graver, J., Haldeman, C., Kerfoot, J., Roarty, H., Jones, C., Webb, D.: Slocum gliders: Robust and ready. J. Field Rob. **24**(6), 473–485 (2007)
29. Sherman, J., Davis, R., Owens, W., Valdes, J.: The autonomous underwater glider "spray". IEEE J. Oceanic Eng. **26**(4), 437–446 (2001)
30. Stommel, H.: The slocum mission. In: Oceanography, pp. 22–25 (1989)
31. Subramani, D.N.: Energy optimal path planning using stochastic dynamically orthogonal level set equations. Master's thesis. School of Engineering, Massachusetts Institute of Technology, September 2014
32. Warren, C.W.: A technique for autonomous underwater vehicle route planning. In: Proceedings Symposium on AUV Tech., pp. 201–205, June 1990
33. WHOI: Shallow water experiment (2006). http://acoustics.whoi.edu/sw06/
34. Witt, J., Dunbabin, M.: Go with the flow: Optimal auv path planning in coastal environments. In: Proceedings of Australasian Conference on Robotics and Automation (2008)
35. Zhang, W., Inanc, T., Ober-Blobaum, S., Marsden, J.E.: Optimal trajectory generation for a glider in time-varying 2D ocean flows B-spline model. In: Proceedings of ICRA, pp. 1083–1088, May 2008

Author Index

Ait-El-Fquih, Boujemaa   207
Aminzadeh, Fred   157
Apte, Amit   263
Attia, Ahmed   215

Bauer, Jennifer   157
Belden, Jesse   28
Blackwell, W.   3
Brun, Carlos   54
Bursik, Marcus   41

Cahoy, K.   3
Chen, Jie   167
Choi, Han-Lim   182
Cortés, Ana   54
Cousins, Will   134

de Andrade Soares, Tainara Mendes   89
Diaz, Jorge Andres   16
Disenhof, Corinne   157
Douglas, Craig C.   89

Elkins, James W.   10
Elo, Matias   100
Euler, Juliane   322

Fang, Nick   68
Flikkema, Paul G.   100
Frost, Gregory J.   10

Gao, Jean   68
Gao, Ru-Shan   10
Ghanem, Roger   157
Gharamti, Mohamad E.   207, 301
Godinez, Humberto C.   274

Haley Jr., Patrick J.   347
Haller, George   115
Higdon, David   274
Hoang, Trong Nghia   167
Hoteit, Ibrahim   207, 301
Huan, Xun   301

Jabbari, Nima   157
Jafek, Alexander   28
Jaillet, Patrick   167

Kerkez, Branko   68
Khodabakhshnejad, Arman   157
Klimenko, Alexei   274
Knapp, JD   100
Koller, Josef   274
Kritz, Mauricío Vieira   89

Lagor, Francis D.   334
Lawrence, Earl   274
Lee, Su-Jin   182
Lermusiaux, Pierre F.J.   347
Lolla, Tapovan   347
Low, Kian Hsiang   167

Madankan, Reza   310
Margalef, Tomàs   54
Marzouk, Youssef M.   301
McComiskey, Allison C.   10
Mittal, Rashmi   284
Mohamad, Mustafa A.   144
Mohanty, Sachiko   79
Mohseni, Kamran   195
Moore, Fred L.   10
Murphy, Daniel M.   10

Nino, Elias D.   239

Ogren, John A.   10

Paley, Derek A.   334
Patra, Abani   41
Pendlebury, Jonathon   28
Peng, Liqian   195
Petropavlovskikh, Irina   10
Pieri, David   16
Pitman, E. Bruce   41
Poulose, Jismy   79

Rao, A.D.   79
Rao, Vishwas   215
Ravela, Sai   121, 227
Ridley, Aaron   274
Ritter, Tobias   322
Rose, Kelly   157
Rosenlof, Karen H.   10

Sandu, Adrian   215, 239
Sapsis, Themistoklis P.   134, 144
Seo, Dong-Jun   68
Seok, Joon-Hong   182
Seybold, Hansjörg   227
Shaeffer, James   100
Singh, Tarkeshwar   284
Singh, Tarunraj   41, 310
Singla, Puneet   41, 310
Sledge, Isaac J.   195
Slivinski, Laura   263
Spiller, Elaine   263

Stefanescu, E. Ramona   41
Subramani, Deepak N.   347

Tagade, Piyush   227
Thimmisetty, Charanraj   157
Truscott, Tadd   28

Ulbrich, Stefan   322
Upadhyay, Puja   79
Upadhyaya, H.C.   284

van Leeuwen, Peter Jan   251
von Stryk, Oskar   322

Xu, Nuo   167

Yu, Xinbao   68

Zink, Michael   68

Printed in the United States
By Bookmasters